GLOBAL & N.   SECURITY LAW:
Assessing the War on Terror
Materials, Cases, Comments

Eighth Edition

Jeffrey F. Addicott, BA, JD, LLM, SJD

Distinguished Professor of Law & Director,
Warrior Defense Project
St. Mary's University School of Law

**Lawyers & Judges
Publishing Company, Inc.**
Tucson, Arizona

This publication is designed to provide accurate and authoritative information in regard to the subject matter covered. It is sold with the understanding that the publisher is not engaged in rendering legal, accounting, or other professional service. If legal advice or other expert assistance is required, the services of a competent professional person should be sought.

—From a Declaration of Principles jointly adopted by
a Committee of the American Bar Association
and a Committee of Publishers and Associations.

The publisher, editors and authors must disclaim any liability, in whole or in part, arising from the information in this volume. The reader is urged to verify the reference material prior to any detrimental reliance thereupon. Since this material deals with legal, medical and engineering information, the reader is urged to consult with an appropriate licensed professional prior to taking any action that might involve any interpretation or application of information within the realm of a licensed professional practice.

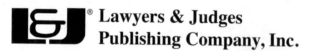
**Lawyers & Judges
Publishing Company, Inc.**

P.O. Box 30040 • Tucson, AZ 85751-0040
(520) 323-1500 • FAX (520) 323-0055
e-mail: sales@lawyersandjudges.com
www.lawyersandjudges.com

Library of Congress Cataloging-in-Publication Data

Addicott, Jeffrey F., author.
 Global and national security law : Assessing the War on Terror : materials, cases, comments / Jeffrey F Addicott, BA, JD, LLM, SJD, Distinguished Professor of Law & Director, Warrior Defense Project, St. Mary's University School of Law. —Eighth edition. | Tucson : Lawyers & Judges Publishing Company, Inc., 2021. | Series: Terrorism law : materials, cases, comments, 2051-9966 | Includes bibliographical references and index
 ISBN 978-1-936360-8-33 (paperback)
 1. Terrorism (International law) 2. Terrorism—Prevention—Law and legislation. 3. Security, International. 4. Security, National—Law and legislation.
 KZ7220 .A94 2021
 345/.02—dc23

2020048910

Printed in the United States of America
10 9 8 7 6 5 4 3 2 1

ST. MARY'S
UNIVERSITY
SCHOOL *of* LAW
WARRIOR DEFENSE PROJECT

R.B. Thieme, Jr. (1918-2009)—

pivot of the nation, theologian, soldier, educator, patriot

Contents

Table of Cases

Acknowledgments

The author wishes to acknowledge with appreciation: Lawyers & Judges Publishing Company; Albany Government Law Review; Georgetown Journal of International Affairs; University of Dayton Law Review; Case Western Reserve Journal of International Law; St. Mary's University Law Journal; University of Massachusetts Roundtable Symposium Law Journal; Pace Law Review; University of Kentucky Law Journal; Barry Law Review; University of Richmond Law Review; University of Florida Journal of International Law; Houston Journal of International Law; Military Law Review; Israeli Defense Forces Law Review; The Scholar: St. Mary's Law Review on Minority Issues; Texas Review of Law and Politics; The Review of Litigation; for permission granted to reprint segments of materials previously published.

Introduction

In any civilized society the most important task is achieving a proper balance between freedom and order. In wartime, reason and history both suggest that this balance shifts to some degree in favor of order—in favor of the government's ability to deal with conditions that threaten the national well-being.

—William H. Rehnquist

Be it the Middle Ages or the Renaissance, the Great War or the Cold War, the trends of human history have always been characterized by epochs or eras. While it is sometimes difficult to find the exact chronological line separating one era from the next, some eras are born from a single dramatic event of such enormity that the very date overshadows the general theme of the times. As December 7, 1941, was to the World War II generation, so too was September 11, 2001, to a new era that many believe characterized the next twenty years of history. This post-Cold War period was called the "War on Terror" or alternatively the "Global War on Terrorism." Although terrorism is not new, the intensity and frequency of militant Islamic terrorism seen in such groups as Qa'eda and ISIS engulfed the entire civilized world for two decades and gave rise to novel methodologies for combating the threat. Now, with the withdrawal of U.S. combat forces from both Iraq and Afghanistan, the War on Terror is over, *de facto* if not *de jure*. Thus, one of the purposes of this book is to review the long established traditional legal and policy themes associated with Global/National security law and to see how those norms were applied to the War on Terror. Since national security law rests upon a global rule of law regulating the lawful use of force, the term Global/National security law deals with all those customary and legal norms and standards associated with maintaining peace and responding to aggression.

It is reasonable to observe that while some adjustments were made in fighting the War on Terror the core principles of Global and National security law remained fundamentally sound throughout. Indeed, with the destruction of the al-Qa'eda terror bases in Afghanistan; the removal of the brutal Taliban regime in Afghanistan (2001); the removal of Saddam Hussein in Iraq (2003); and the geographic destruction of ISIS in Syria and Iraq (2018); the United States and the civilized world faced a plethora of legal and policy challenges that strained but never broke the traditional constructs associated with the law of armed conflict.

A second purpose of this book is to look at American domestic legal and policy responses to the War on Terror. While it is certainly true that the War on Terror saw the United States craft a variety of robust antiterrorism responses designed to disrupt the terrorist networks and prevent future terrorist attacks from occurring, all of these actions were well within acceptable legal constructs — both under domestic and international law. Some of these actions included the passage of the Uniting and Strengthening America by Providing Appropriate Tools Required to Intercept and Obstruct Terrorism Act (USA

PATRIOT Act); the creation of the Cabinet level post of Homeland Security; the establishment of United States Northern Command, in Colorado; the preemptive use of military force against the Iraqi regime of Saddam Hussein; and the indefinite detention of certain unlawful enemy combatants.

Due to the universalist designs of militant Islam, the combination of traditional law enforcement with the more muscular use of military force under approved law of war norms was essential. In other words, the one-dimensional use of the criminal justice system, used so ineffectively in the 1990's against various radical Islamists, could not confront an ideology of hate able to seize sizable swaths of territory (Iraq and Syria), recruit tens of thousands of followers, and field terrorist cells throughout the world. Accordingly, in tandem with the use of domestic federal criminal law tools, the United States utilized the legal rules associated with the law of war.

Without question, shifting the tactical focus from punishing those individuals, organizations, or nations who commit terrorist crimes or engage in aggression to broad new methodologies designed to thwart such murderous acts in the first place caused some to challenge these governmental measures as illegal or at least as inconsistent with American values. Considering, for instance, that a nuclear truck bomb could obliterate an entire American city and cause a "panicky stampede into truly oppressive police statism, in which measures now unthinkable could suddenly become unstoppable," a 2003 Brookings Institute report aptly argued that "[s]tubborn adherence to the civil liberties status quo would probably damage our most fundamental freedoms far more in the long run than would judicious modifications of rules that are less fundamental." Indeed, should a major weapon of mass destruction event occur in America, a Pandora's box filled with draconian security measures would truly be opened; we might eventually close it again but we could never get everything back in.

Nevertheless, a fundamental obligation of any State is to protect its citizens from external as well as internal threats to person and property. Nowhere is this obligation more difficult to perform than in the realm of militant Islamic terrorism, particularly when one considers the apocalyptic horrors that might be unleashed through the terrorist use of weapons of mass destruction. In the War on Terror, the United States was concerned not only with those renegade States which might commit or sponsor terror attacks using weapons of mass destruction, but also there was deep consternation about how to best deal with international or domestic terrorist groups, and even individuals.

For those who follow the studies and trends, the lethality of terrorism continues to grow. The number of serious international terror incidents more than tripled since 2004. According to the State Department there were 655 significant terror attacks in 2004, up from 175 in 2003. The increase in 2004 reflected the rise of terrorism in Iraq, but included large scale events in Spain and Russia as well. The National Counterterrorism Center recorded approximately 14,000 terrorist attacks across the globe for 2007, resulting in over 22,000 deaths. Of the 355 casualty attacks that killed 10 or more people in the 2007 report, 87 percent occurred in the Near East and South Asia. In 2008 there were 11,770 attacks resulting in 15,765 deaths. With the rise of ISIS, however, the numbers of victims dramatically spiked. The State Department's Country Report on Terrorism for 2016 reported 11,072 global terror attacks resulting in 25,082 deaths. In 2018 there were 32,836 deaths, but in 2019 (with ISIS knocked out of action) the number dropped back to 25,082. The figures for 2021 will likewise decrease even further given the waning influence of ISIS and the end of the War on Terror.

Of course, such studies are rather inconsequential when one considers the aftermath of a terrorist directed nuclear, biological, chemical, radiological, or cyber attack in an urban area of the United States. The attacks of September 11, 2001, could very well pale in comparison. Furthermore, to the mass casualties and devastating economic disruption, one must add the troubling impact such an event might have on future civil liberties and freedoms that Americans now enjoy. Considering that al-Qa'eda-styled terrorists have targeted the United States more often than any other country in the world, save Israel, the specter of the use of weapons of mass destruction still demands top priority in thinking and planning in the post-War on Terror era. Indeed, the damage done on society by the COVID-19 virus has alerted the public to the need for national preparedness for other potential hazards that might involve biological attacks or cyber attacks.

Karl von Clausewitz observed "[e]very age has its own kind of war, its own limiting conditions and its own peculiar preconceptions." One characteristic of the War on Terror was undeniable: the United States stood as the world's bastion of stability and sphere of power and influence. Under American leadership over the span of three administrations—George W. Bush, Barack H. Obama, and Donald J. Trump—the United States employed the rule of law to combat militant Islamic global terrorism—domestic and international—to better bring the battle to the terrorists and to the nations that harbored them. Finally, in the context of the new Afghani and Iraqi governments, America did what it could to drain the totalitarian swamps in which all mega terrorist groups breed. After twenty years of effort American troops are now departed.

At the end of the day, terrorism, like crime and war, can never be eradicated by mankind. In this context, even if one is cynical enough to believe that the world politic is ruled primarily by the application or threat of force, it is nevertheless of critical importance from both a national and international perspective that America rubricate its leadership role by thoughtful concerns for the positive advancement of the rule of law and the protection of cherished civil liberties.

While a new body of law called *terrorism law* has emerged to deal with myriad legal issues associated with terrorism, the bedrock of Global/National security law remains firm. It is vital that lawyers skilled in both legal disciplines become involved in the national effort to protect the homeland and civil liberties.

Selected Bibliography

Brookings Review, *Rights Liberties and Security*, Vol. 21, Issue 1, 2003 WL 11169678, Jan. 1, 2003.

Rehnquist, William H. ALL THE LAWS BUT ONE 222, 1998.

Uniting and Strengthening America by Providing Appropriate Tools Required to Intercept and Obstruct Terrorism Act (USA PATRIOT Act) of 2001, Pub. L. No. 107-56, 115 Stat. 272. Oct. 26, 2001.

U.S. Department of State. *Country Reports on Terrorism 2009*. August 2010.

U.S. Department of State. *Country Reports on Terrorism 2016*. July 2017.

U.S. Department of State. *Country Reports on Terrorism 2019*. July 2020.

Chapter 1

What is Terrorism?

The goal of the terrorist is to kill one and frighten 10,000.

—Chinese proverb

Things must be properly defined before they can be intelligently discussed. Although many trace the etymology of the word *terror* to France's "reign of terror" under Robespierre and the Jacobin Committee of Public Safety (*regime de la terreur*), the employment of terror is a phenomenon that has been around for a very long time in human history. Notwithstanding the fact that terrorism is the antithesis of the rule of law, there exists no consensus on a precise definition of terrorism either in the international community or in the United States. This is due in part to the tensions of the Cold War era when West and East could agree on precious little, but also continues today under the postmodernist cliché, "one man's terrorist is another man's freedom fighter." For instance, a Palestinian suicide bomber in Israel who intentionally kills innocent Jewish civilians may be considered a "hero" by certain segments of the Palestinian population.

1.1 Defining Terrorism

The concept of terrorism is now firmly embedded in the daily lexicon. Yet there is still no specific international definition. Recognizing the politics associated with reaching an acceptable global definition for terrorism, the United Nations has very often elected to avoid the term terrorism altogether, use it in a general sense only, or to carefully carve out very specific acts in selected international treaties to characterize as "terrorism." Not only do debates turn on whether a State or just individuals can engage in terrorism, but the issue of using violence in so-called wars of "national liberation" remains a perennial stumbling block. In fact, definitional agreement seems always hindered by whether or not terrorist events are viewed as working for or against one's own national, political, or religious interests. Five examples serve to illustrate this delinquency among the 193 member States of the United Nations.

First, the International Law Commission's 1954 *Draft Code of Offenses Against the Peace and*

1

Security of Mankind contained the following proposed language in Article 25 to define terrorism: "[T]he undertaking or encouragement by the authorities of a State of terrorist activity in another State, or the toleration by the authorities of a State of organized activities calculated to carry out terrorist acts in another State." Even though the proposed sentence failed to define the term, no agreement could be reached. As of this writing, over fifty years later, the United Nations General Assembly has still not been able to reach agreement on a final version of the document.

Second, the latest attempt by the United Nations Sub-Commission on Human Rights to come up with a definition of terrorism has met similar troubles. The first draft report of February 2001 listed three essential elements of terrorism. A terrorist act: (1) must be illegal, violating national or international law; (2) must be intended to harm the State for political reasons; and (3) must be capable of generating a state of fear in the general population. However, in order to reach consensus amongst the committee members on its first progress report, the special rapporteur had to delete the entire definition relating to terrorism.

Third, perhaps the greatest missed opportunity for the United Nations to establish a firm international definition of terrorism as it relates to States that sponsor or support terrorists occurred in its failure to employ the word "terrorism" in the context of the key 1957 United Nations General Assembly resolution defining aggression as it relates to when a nation may engage in armed self-defense under Article 51 of the United Nations Charter. The United Nations chose to classify the activities of States that send, organize, or support "armed bands, groups, irregulars, or mercenaries, which carry out acts of armed force against a State," as simply engaging in unlawful aggression in direct violation of the U.N. Charter. It failed to refer to any of these activities as engaging in terrorism. Terrorism, of course, could have certainly fit into this expression of unlawful aggression, but it was not used.

Currently, there are at least twelve international conventions related to terrorism and ten criminal acts identified as terrorism in various United Nations conventions and protocols. The identified acts are: hijacking, aviation sabotage, acts of violence at airports, acts of violence regarding maritime navigation, acts of violence against fixed platforms, crimes against internationally protected persons, unlawful taking and use of nuclear material, hostage taking, terrorist bombings, and supporting front organizations serving as financial conduits for terrorists groups. Obviously these ten do not cover terrorism in all its manifestations, but until the international community can provide a universal definition, one can certainly reference these documents regarding specific acts of terrorism.

Fourth, in the wake of the September 11, 2001, terror attacks on the United States, the Ad Hoc Committee on Terrorism proposed a definition of terrorism for the General Assembly. Unfortunately, the General Assembly was unable to reach consensus due in large part to strong opposition from the 56-member Organization of Islamic Cooperation (all Muslim nations) who insisted that any international definition of terrorism contain a certain caveat. In short, the Organization of Islamic Cooperation demanded that the definition exempt all so-called wars of national liberation against foreign occupation, i.e., if the violence utilized is to further a "just cause," such as the ambiguous concept of "national liberation," then acts of terror may be tolerated as legitimate expressions of resistance. To put it bluntly, the slaughter of innocent civilians is justified if the cause is just. Those familiar with the Organization of Islamic Cooperation already know that they define "terrorism" internally to exclude Israelis as victims of terrorism while excluded the terror groups of Hamas and Hezbollah as terrorists.

Fifth, on September 28, 2001, the Security Council adopted Resolution 1373. The resolution's legal requirements are meant to create a common legal basis for all States to take effective action against terrorists by criminalizing terrorist fundraising and blocking terrorist assets. Quite impressive on paper, Resolution 1373 requires all member States to "[r]efrain from providing any form of support, active or passive, to entities or persons involved in terrorist acts;" "take the necessary steps to prevent the commission of terrorist acts;" "deny safe haven to those who finance, plan, support, or commit terrorist acts;" and "prevent those who finance, plan, facilitate, or commit terrorist acts from using their respective territories for those purposes against other States or their citizens...." To implement these obligations, a Counter-Terrorism Committee (CTC) was created to receive hundreds of State reports on progress in each of the mentioned areas. Amazingly, the CTC has not yet managed to name a single terrorist organization, individual, or State sponsor of terrorism.

Since the victims of terrorism are invariably innocent civilians, it appears fundamentally logical that a definitional approach should concentrate on the act and not the political, religious, or social causes which motivate the act. Under this regimen, the use of violence on a civilian target with intent to cause fear in a given civilian population for ideological purposes is easily classified as a terrorist act. In other words, to the common understanding of the general public, terrorism is immediately associated with violence that is directed at the indiscriminate killing of innocent civilians in order to create a climate of fear. Thus, in the 1980s, acts of bombings and the public murder of civilians (by burning them in tires) by the "Spear of the Nation," the armed wing of the African National Congress, were acts of terrorism. The ends—getting rid of apartheid—can never justify the means.

In this light, bombings of public places, the sending of letter bombs or poisons through the mail, hijackings of aircraft, hostage taking, and so on, are all acts of terrorism regardless of the underlying cause said to justify the attack, or whether the attack occurs in peacetime or during war. In a sense, terrorism can simply be described as making "war" on civilians. Former United States Senator George Mitchell defined terrorism in February 2002 as follows: "Terrorism involves the deliberate killing of randomly selected noncombatants for political ends. It seeks to promote a political outcome by spreading terror and demoralization throughout a population."

In summary, if a universal definition is not practicable, one can at least list four key characteristics of terrorism that better reflect the activity:

1. The illegal use of violence directed at civilians to produce fear in a target group.
2. The continuing threat of additional future acts of violence.
3. A predominately political or ideological character of the act.
4. The desire to mobilize or immobilize a given target group.

Although never adopted by the United Nations General Assembly, the Secretary General of the United Nations, Kofi Annan, offered this wonderfully succinct 2005 definition:

[A]ny action constitutes terrorism if it is intended to cause death or serious bodily harm to civilians or non-combatants, with the purpose of intimidating a population or compelling a Government or an international organization to do or abstain from doing any act.

In the United States, the difficulties in definition are not related to a reluctance to use the term terrorism, but rather they rest in the sheer number of different government instrumentalities and federal statutes that have offered independent interpretations of terrorism which, while similar, are not identical. One of the latest American efforts to define terrorism is found in Section 411 of the USA PATRIOT Act, which was signed into law with overwhelming bipartisan support in November of 2001.

Actually, the USA PATRIOT Act provides similar definitions for "terrorist organization," "domestic terrorism," and "international terrorism." A terrorist organization is defined as one that is:

(1) designated by the Secretary of State as a terrorist organization under the process established under current law; (2) designated by the Secretary of State as a terrorist organization for immigration purposes; or (3) a group of two or more individuals that commits terrorist activities or plans or prepares to commit (including locating targets for) terrorist activities.

Domestic terrorism is defined in the USA PATRIOT Act with a slightly different emphasis. Domestic terrorism is the "unlawful use, or threatened use, of force or violence by a group or individuals based [in the United States]…committed against persons or property to intimidate or coerce a government, [or] the civilian population…in furtherance of political or social objectives."
International terrorism is set out in the USA PATRIOT Act as follows:

International terrorism involves violent acts or acts dangerous to human life that violate the criminal laws of the United States or any state, or that would be a criminal violation if committed within the jurisdiction of the United States or any state. These acts appear intended to intimidate or coerce a civilian population, influence the policy of a government by intimidation or coercion, or affect the conduct of a government by assassination or kidnapping. International terrorist acts occur outside the United States or transcend national boundaries in terms of how terrorists accomplish them, the persons they appear intended to coerce or intimidate, or the place in which the perpetrators operate.

1.2 The Goal of Terrorism

Despite the lack of a fixed universal agreement defining terrorism, the essential goal of terrorism is readily identifiable. As the root word implies, the goal of terrorism is to instill fear in a given civilian population by means of violence. In the oft-repeated Chinese proverb, the objective of the terrorist is to kill one and frighten 10,000. While specific acts of terrorism may appear to be mindless and irrational, terrorism is the exact opposite of confused behavior. Terrorism is a goal-directed, calculated, premeditated use of force. Unfortunately, all too often, terrorist tactics prove effective when those who are targeted respond in a way that reinforces the demands of the terrorists. The March 11, 2004, series of coordinated train bombings in Spain by al-Qa'eda-linked terrorists not only killed just over 200 people, but the attacks caused the newly installed Spanish government to withdraw its military forces from the American-led coalition in Iraq, a coalition that was combating some of the very same forces of terror that attacked Spain. On the other hand, sometimes the use of terror tactics can result in unintended consequences for the terrorist network. The al-Qa'eda terror group certainly did not seek the destruction of its primary base of operations in Afghanistan when it attacked the United States on September 11, 2001. At most, al-Qa'eda hoped to spark a massive social and political revolution in the Middle East that would bring to power al-Qa'eda-related governments. In turn, the Islamic terror organization known to the world as ISIS had a far more ambitious goal — creating a geographic Caliphate and ultimately conquering the entire world.

1.3 Terrorism and Weapons of Mass Destruction

Apart from the traditional weapons used by terrorists, one must now add weapons of mass destruction as a special definitional subset. Although current federal statutes take an extremely broad view of what constitutes a weapon of mass destruction (to include a car bomb), an early and still relevant definition comes from Section 1403 of the National Defense Authorization Act for fiscal year 1997. Weapons of mass destruction are defined there as "any weapon or device that is intended, or has the capability, to cause death or serious bodily injury to a significant number of people through the release of toxic or poisonous chemicals or their precursors, a disease organism, or radiation or radioactivity." Thus, in its broadest sense, weapons of mass destruction include not only nuclear material, but the full range of biological, chemical, and radioactive agents. Most certainly, the COVID 19 pandemic which originated in late 2018 from China and infected the globe brought a renewed awareness to the potential massive devastation that an intentional use of a weapon of mass destruction could cause.

The December 2008 Congressionally mandated report by the Commission on the Prevention of Weapons of Mass Destruction Proliferation and Terrorism predicted that it was likely that a weapon of mass destruction would be used in a terror attack before 2013. Thankfully they were wrong on the date but their bottom line assessment on the matter still rings true. It is only a matter of when, not if.

> Terrorists are determined to attack us again with weapons of mass destruction if they can. Osama bin Laden has said that obtaining these weapons Is a "religious duty" and is reported to have sought to perpetrate another "Hiroshima." The Commission believes that unless the world community acts decisively and with great urgency, it is more likely than not that a weapon of mass destruction will be used in a terrorist attack somewhere in the world by 2013.

As is true for any terrorist event, there are three general sources from which a weapon of mass destruction terrorist attack can emanate—States, sub-State groups, or individuals. Tragically, in the so-called information age, all three categories have demonstrated a willingness to use weapons of mass murder in the physical world and there can be no doubt that this thirst for violence will soon spill over into the cyber world as well. States that engage in terrorism and have the potential of using weapons of mass destruction are further divided as either State-sponsors or State-supporters of terrorism.

1.4 State-Sponsored and State-Supported Terrorism

Perhaps the most easily identifiable category of terrorism is the State-sponsored terrorist attack. In recent times, the international community has been shocked to learn that certain renegade States, such as Saddam Hussein's Iraq, have shown an unabashed willingness to use deadly nerve gas to kill thousands of men, women, and children (the Kurds). Indeed, it can be argued that all totalitarian States pose an ever-present threat for the use of weapons of mass destruction at any given time—both against their own people and against other nations. Each year, the U.S. State Department designates certain countries as State sponsors of terrorism. This list generally includes a small handful of States such as: Cuba, Iran, and Syria. In fact, regarding weapons of mass destruction, the number is always larger. For instance, in 1999 John A. Lauder, Director of the Central Intelligence Agency's Nonproliferation Center, testified before Congress that a dozen countries "now either possess or are actively pursuing offensive biological weapons capabilities for use against their perceived enemies, whether internal or external." Lauder's statement is still true today.

In the context of a State's use of weapons of mass destruction in a terrorist attack, several commentators seek to distinguish a State-sponsored terrorist act from a State-supported terrorist act. State-sponsored terrorism exists when a State directly but secretly uses its own resources to sponsor acts of terrorism against another country. Since accountability for such acts are denied, the aggressor-State seeks to avoid responsibility. On the other hand, State-supported terrorism refers to the practice of a State providing resources or finances to a terrorist group for training and logistics, as occurred in Afghanistan, where the terrorist group headed by Osama bin Laden once took open refuge. In contrast to the State-sponsored scenario, the State-supported terrorist group generally operates in a more independent fashion from the host State.

A classic case of a State-sponsored act of terrorism occurred in 1986 when Libyan government agents bombed an American frequented discotheque in then West Berlin, Germany. This secretive act of terror was followed by a second State-sponsored act of terror in 1988, when Libyan government operatives bombed Pan Am Flight 103 over Lockerbie, Scotland, killing 278 people.

In the final analysis, it is difficult to make a practical distinction between State-sponsored and State-supported terrorism. The terms really speak only to the degree of culpability. Nevertheless, if the rule of law has any force, States that allow terrorist groups to operate with impunity on their soil should never be able to escape the attendant lawful consequences. While it is subject to legal debate whether a particular terrorist act committed apart from the support or sponsorship of a State would be considered an "act of war" under international law, a terrorist attack with the support or sponsorship of a State could very well be deemed an "act of war."

The early days of concern regarding terrorism and the use of weapons of mass destruction saw most of the emphasis focused primarily on the actions of the totalitarian State. Because many believed that ready access to weapons of mass destruction material was limited, sub-State terrorist groups and individual terrorists were generally given less attention. For these later categories of terrorism, the international community generally concentrated on making specific overt acts international crimes, e.g., airline hijacking or hostage taking. In regard to renegade States, however, the major issue turned on the proper application of appropriate sanctions against the State that sponsored or supported the terrorist incident.

1.5 Sub-State Terrorism

Sub-State terrorist groups can either be domestic or international terrorist organizations and are generally categorized by either religious or political ideologies. In 1995, for example, a RAND study found that "25 of 58, or 42 percent of known, active, international terrorist groups had a predominately religious component or motivation." In addition, from a rule of law perspective, sub-State terrorist organizations do not operate with the approval or sponsorship of the host nation.

The first significant use of a weapon of mass destruction by a sub-State group occurred on March 20, 1995, when members of the Aum Shinrikyo religious cult (now called Aleph) in Japan released a lethal nerve agent, sarin, in a Tokyo underground subway. This weapon of mass destruction attack killed twelve people and injured 3,000 others, clearly demonstrating that the scenario of terrorists using a weapon of mass destruction was not the stuff of fiction.

While attacks by sub-State groups against United States interests have yet to use weapons of mass destruction (as of this writing), many groups have shown a viciousness and disregard for human life that clearly points to a willingness to use such weapons in the future. For instance, an Islamic radical group with ties to al-Qa'eda and headed by Ramzi Ahmad Yousef conducted the 1993 bombing of New York City's World Trade Center in an attempt to topple one of the twin towers onto the other to kill thousands, an act clearly in the spirit of a weapons of mass destruction event. In fact, it has been reported that those behind the 1993 World Trade Center bombing were also gathering the ingredients for a chemical weapon that could have brought the death toll into the tens of thousands. Some early reports indicated that the bombs used in the attack might have been laced with cyanide, but the poison burned up in the detonation.

In early 2000, United States and Israeli intelligence sources reported that Hamas, the militant Palestinian terrorist group, was experimenting with chemical weapons in their rocket attacks against Israeli targets. Although no radical Islamic group has yet to use chemical or biological agents in their terror attacks on Israel, the potential for such an event certainly exists. With the increasing availability of high-tech weapons and nuclear materials from former communist countries and the ease with which some chemical and biological agents can now be manufactured, there is growing concern that sub-State groups will now actively cross over into the weapons of mass destruction domain. Further, the fear also exists that one of the world's dictators might simply give weapons of mass destruction to a sub-State terrorist group. This was certainly a major consideration for the United States-led preemptive attack on Saddam Hussein's regime in 2003 and continues to be an issue in the quest to stop the radicalized Iranian regime from developing nuclear weapons.

1.6 Individual Terrorism

The most troubling aspect of weapons of mass destruction terrorism is one not often discussed. It is the prospect of an individual not directly affiliated with any terror organization setting off a weapon of mass destruction in a major urban area. Because they operate on their own, without affiliation to any known group or State, individuals who engage in "lone-wolf" terrorism are far harder to predict, track, or deter.

To demonstrate the seriousness of individual terrorism, on March 3, 1999, William C. Patrick, III, a leading American expert on biological warfare, walked through the security check system at the Rayburn House Office Building in downtown Washington D.C., carrying 7.5 grams of powdered anthrax, enough to kill everyone in the building, in a small plastic bottle. Not only was he rubricating the ease with which a single determined terrorist could breach security systems and target, in this case, a major federal government installation, Patrick's action certainly should have provided the needed wake up call to United States government officials and the public at large. Unfortunately, it did not.

Patrick told a Congressional committee that he was trying to show how a hostile or aggressor State could smuggle powdered anthrax in to the United States in a secure diplomatic pouch. What Patrick was really demonstrating, however, was the ease with which any individual terrorist—domestic or international—could unleash untold bioterrorism horror, almost at will. In his testimony, Patrick related that he had also carried other similar deadly materials and, "like Sherman went through Georgia," had "been through all the major airports, and the security systems of the State Department, the Pentagon, and even the CIA, and nobody stopped me."

The most notorious example of an individual terrorist attack in the United States occurred in April 1995 with the bombing of the Murrah Federal Building in Oklahoma City by right-wing extremist Timothy McVeigh. The bomb killed 167 people, including women and children. Although McVeigh did not employ a weapon of mass destruction in his attack, his actions clearly raised the issue of individual domestic terrorism in the context of weapons of mass destruction. While one can ponder the bizarre "anti-government" sentiments that motivated McVeigh, the greater issue really revolves around individual access to material which can cause widespread destruction of life and property.

Furthermore, not all individual terrorism can be associated with fanatical political or religious ideologues. Individual terrorism can be committed by persons seeking personal rather than political gain, or by individuals who are mentally ill. The 2001 anthrax-tainted letter attacks that killed five people and traumatized the nation was said to have been carried out by an anthrax researcher at the U.S. Army's biodefense laboratory in Maryland (the suspect, Bruce Ivins, committed suicide in July 2008). Considering the number of "Timothy McVeighs" in any given society, the prospect of individuals obtaining access to weapons of mass destruction is chilling and will unfortunately continue to grow with time.

1.7 Al-Qa'eda-Styled Terrorism and Militant Islam

During the two-terms of the Obama Administration, many were frustrated by a lack of clarity and leadership when it came to addressing the threat of radical Islam. For instance, instead of calling the April 2013 terrorist attack at the Boston marathon an act of radical Islamic terror, the bombings were labeled as terrorist attacks and the murders as "terrorists." While it is true that the twin bombings at the Boston marathon by the Tsarmaev brothers were designed to instill fear, it is imperative that the motivation for such attacks should always serve as the key descriptive component. Again, terrorism is a tactic. Furthermore, while the Tsarmaev's may have acted alone and without specific guidance, they were not simply lone-wolf terrorists. The brothers were motivated by a global alliance of individuals that pledge allegiance to the vision of radical Islam.

Al-Qa'eda (the Base) is an umbrella organization founded in 1989 by a Saudi Arabian named Osama (or Usama) bin Laden. Osama bin Laden formed the group out of elements of the Maktab al-Khidamat, an organization founded by Osama bin Laden and Abdallah Azzam (a member of a group called the Palestinian Moslem Brotherhood) in the early 1980s to provide money, equipment, and manpower to the Afghan resistance against the Soviet Union's occupation of Afghanistan. With the withdrawal of the Soviets in 1989, bin Laden started al-Qa'eda in order to redirect his efforts to "attack the enemies of Islam all over the world." The religious view embraced by militant Islam is a fixed, comprehensive ideology that targets for death anyone that disagrees with its very narrow set of mandates. In 2004, Jordanian Abu Musab al-Zarqawi proclaimed his allegiance to Osama bin Laden and headed al-Qa'eda in Iraq. He specifically targeted Muslims and their houses of worship, killing them by the hundreds.

From the early 1990s until the end of 2001, the al-Qa'eda operated openly in the country of Afghanistan with the complete support of the Pashtun-dominated Taliban government. During the tenure of the Taliban regime, the relationship between the Taliban and the al-Qa'eda terrorist organization provided a seminal example of State-supported terrorism. In fact, under the Taliban, Afghanistan became a terror training ground for tens of thousands of Arab and non-Arab al-Qa'eda militants including Saudis, Kashmirs, Chechens, Uzbeks, Uighurs, and others (including a number of Americans). These training camps sent cells of well-trained terrorists into numerous countries where they were encouraged to recruit additional members and carry out terrorist attacks on command. While al-Qa'eda has tens of thousands of supporters and low-level operatives worldwide, only carefully selected Muslim males are offered full membership. Interestingly, the al-Qa'eda leadership does not allow volunteers to join the group. Instead, al-Qa'eda seeks out candidates for full membership. These recruits must sign an oath of allegiance called a *bayat*, swearing to carry out the dictates of al-Qa'eda leaders on penalty of death. They are then indoctrinated and trained extensively in assassination, kidnapping, explosives, small arms, hijacking, and torture.

The War on Terror began predominantly focused on defeating the al-Qa'eda terrorist network, although a second front was opened with the fall of Saddam Hussein and the rise of ISIS in Iraq and Syria. Since the release of the Department of Defense's 2005 *National Military Strategic Plan for the*

War on Terrorism, America has recognized that the number one terrorist threat to the United States is Islamic extremism. Up until 2015 when a new group called Ad-Dawlah al-Islāmiyah fīl-ʿIrāq al-Shām (known in the English-speaking world as Islamic State of Iraq and al-Sham (ISIS) overshadowed all other Islamic terror groups, the "poster-child" for militant Islam was the al-Qa'eda organization which was a new type of terrorism that combined all of the forms of terror identified in this chapter. For instance, they were at one time, State-sponsored by the Taliban government of Afghanistan and continue to be State-supported by any number of radical regimes including Iran, the Palestinian territories, Libya and so on. They also qualify as a sub-State terrorist organization because they secretly infiltrated and established "sleeper" terrorist cells in various nations throughout the world to include the United States, Canada, Britain, France, Spain, Italy, Australia, and Germany.

Until recently, the Sunni-based terror group ISIS was the primary spearhead across the globe for radical Islam. "Following *takfiri* doctrine [proclaiming people to be apostates because of their sins] the Islamic State is committed to purifying the world by killing vast numbers of people." Capitalizing on the Syrian civil war and a fractured Iraqi society, ISIS sought to create a utopian State which would eventually conquer the world. In pursuit of this self-styled Muslim Caliphate, they proudly and openly committed acts of violence and horror from 2015-2017 while unabashedly proclaiming that such was commanded and condoned by their interpretation of the Muslim religion. While it has always been obvious that the vast majority of modern Muslims around the world strongly reject this reading of the Muslim religion, for ISIS and the many followers of radical Islam the means will always justify the ends, resulting in the deaths of far more Muslims than Christians or Jews.

Furthermore, the virus of radical Islamic ideology also influences individual or lone-wolf terrorism. Both al-Qa'eda and ISIS were extremely effective at motivating terror attacks in dozens of nations. Their ideology of hate and intolerance reached the minds of individuals who, although not directly tied to the organization, choose to commit terrorist acts because they adopted the general theme and goal of radical Islam. Illustrations of this fact are many, but one of the most shocking cases occurred in the shooting murder of 13 soldiers at Fort Hood, Texas, in November 2009 by an Army medical officer named Nidal Malik Hasan. Although there can be no doubt that Hasan was motivated by radical Islamic ideology when he shouted "Allahuy Akhbar" as he opened fire on his unarmed victims, government officials and subsequent high-level military investigative reports downplayed the impact that radical Islam had as the motive for the attack, even going so far as to label the murders as "workplace violence." In reality, the slaughter committed by Hasan represented the first major terror attack inspired by radical Islam in the United States since 9/11 (an Army recruiter was murdered by a radical Muslim in Little Rock, Arkansas prior to this attack). In 2013, at the start of his trial, Hasan proudly announced that he was "defending other Muslims" and that the killings were justified in the name of "Allah."

Some have described the al-Qa'eda and ISIS terrorist groups as an entirely new type of entity in the world—not just terrorist groups but "virtual-States" that normal criminal law processes simply cannot curtail. The virtual-State description is fundamentally valid for both al-Qa'eda and ISIS. For instance, until their geographic military defeat under President Trump's leadership in 2018, the virtual-State of ISIS exhibited many of the characteristics of the classic nation-State. For instance, the ISIS virtual-State certainly had a political arm and media section that directed its policy, a military composed of tens of thousands of devoted killers, a treasury that raised funds across the globe, a large number of supporters and adherents, direct and indirect links to the leaders of other nation-states, etc. Indeed, for this reason, the United States has been obliged to reach beyond the tools of normal domestic law enforcement and to utilize its military power to make war with this virtual-State.

Certainly, the War on Terror demanded that the United States come to grips with the *modis vivendi* of the al-Qa'eda as well as all sister Islamic militant groups that seek to wage war by conducting large scale terrorist attacks on America and her allies. Again, America must know the enemy. In this context, there are three basic characteristics that define radical Islam.

First, threatened by the normative values of democracy, freedom, and human rights, the al-Qa'eda and like-minded militant Islamic terror groups are dedicated to the destruction of the West and all those who adopt Western ideals, including those moderate Muslim and Arab governments that refute their interpretation of the Islamic religion. The religious based fanaticism runs so deep that they are eagerly willing to commit suicide in the furtherance of their cause. Unlike previous terrorist groups, al-Qa'eda and ISIS suicide bombers have no "exit" strategy to save themselves, making it almost impossible for law enforcement to stop them. (The failed al-Qa'eda-styled plot to detonate liquid explosives on as many as ten U.S. bound airplanes coming from London in August 2006 provided an intelligence bonanza for British and American law enforcement.) The predominantly young male suicide bombers are lured into death (euphemistically called martyrdom) by the religious promise of automatically securing a place in Paradise for themselves where they will receive "fleshly delights [virgins] and the expectation that they will be allowed to choose seventy friends and family members to join them in heaven." The radical clerics base this belief on Qur'anic passages such as Qur'an 9:111, which promises Paradise to those who "slay and are slain" for Allah.

In this context, democracies offer a plethora of targets that can easily be attacked, particularly if one is not concerned with surviving the assault. There are, for example, over 1,000 nuclear reactors, and 15,000 chemical plants, refineries and hazardous material sites in the United States. With almost 1,000 of these sites located near large population centers, the death toll from a terror attack could easily total in the tens of thousands. Thus, employing suicide as the method of choice to inflict terror, a dedicated terrorist can target almost any public place; in New York City there are 468 subway stations, and in Chicago there are over 2,000 bus stops. Tragically, these new terrorists can successfully use the openness of the democratic society to attack from within, placing great strains on civil liberties. The November 2015 ISIS attack at a concert in Paris carried out by seven perpetrators murdered 130 people.

Second, militant Islamists have learned to use the superhighway of modern technology to establish ties across the globe and provide logistical support for terror cells in practically every country in the world. In fact, the next generation of fanatics will be far more adept at using the Internet and will no doubt engage in cyberterrorist attacks to disrupt, for instance, power plants, airports, banking institutions, and even nuclear power plants. Even now, militant Islamic terrorists use the Internet to assist in recruiting and organizing. Moreover, cyberterrorism is unique because it makes normal physical security measures totally irrelevant. There are no borders to sneak across, no security cameras to avoid and no bombs to manufacture. Terrorists can use a medium of attack that is virtually risk free.

Third, the al-Qa'eda and their like have shown an intense desire to obtain any and all forms of weapons which can inflict mass casualties on civilians, including weapons of mass destruction. Their appetite for killing knows no limits. Again, the greatest fear is that a terrorist will obtain a nuclear weapon and smuggle it into an American port of entry. In fact, such a weapon can be smuggled into the United States with very little risk of failure. With 5,525 miles of border with Canada, 1,989 miles of border with Mexico, and a maritime border of 95,000 miles of shoreline, only a tiny fraction of the millions of people (400+ million), cars (130+ million), trucks (12+ million), rail freight cars (2+ million), and maritime containers (8+ million) entering the U.S. at over 3,700 terminals and 301 ports of entry are ever subjected to inspection of any kind.

1.8 Why They Hate

Some have tried to depict the War on Terror as a war against Islam. Obviously, this was never true. The War on Terror was against those militant Islamic groups that had declared "war" on the United States, such as al-Qa'eda, ISIS, the Taliban, and associated forces. The ideological motivations of these militant Islamic terror organizations are focused on the advancement of cult-like "religious" objectives rather than the more typical aspirations of traditional old-styled terrorist groups that are primarily concerned with the achievement of political or territorial goals. Driven by extremist pseudo-Islamic radicalism, the new breed of terrorists are bent on destroying through violence those individuals and things which are deemed to be outside of a very narrow *weltanschauung* (world view). Indeed, Abu Musab al-Zarqawi, the former leader of al-Qa'eda in Iraq (he was killed by U.S. firepower in June 2006), believed that "slaughtering fellow Arabs who followed different forms of Islam was as important as killing Westerners." ISIS most definitely followed suit.

The 2004 National Commission on Terrorist Acts Upon the United States, better known as the 9/11 Commission Report, found that the United States was facing a loose confederation of people, maybe numbering in the tens of thousands, who believed in a perverted strain of Islam and were busy building the groundwork for decades of struggle. Although militant Islam is not restricted to just the al-Qa'eda-styled belief system—the current Iranian theocratic regime has its own radicalized view of Islam—the roots of al-Qa'eda and ISIS come from a narrow radicalized strain of Islam known as the Wahhabi movement. The movement arose in the eighteenth century under Mohammed Ibn Abd al-Wahab in the desert of Najd in the Arabian Peninsula. Ibn Abd al-Wahab converted a group of illiterate Bedouins under Muhammad Ibn Sa'ud and declared himself the religious leader, or *Sheik*, and Sa'ud the political leader, or *Emir*. Amazingly, one of al-Wahab's first acts was to issue a *fatwa*, a religious decree, casting all non-Wahhabi Muslims as apostates and idol worshippers. In this way, Sa'ud's men were now all cloaked in the role of fighters for *jihad* (holy war) against anyone not in the new Wahhabi movement, including other Muslims whom they killed in large numbers.

Originally funded in large part by Saudi Arabia, the Wahhabi movement has spread across much of the Islamic world. In fact, the greatest achievement of the sect has been to present Wahhabism to a large segment of the Arab world as an accepted part of Islam, even as the "true" Islam. At its heart, the most extreme segment of Wahhabism adopts the same ideology of the fascists and communists except that it cloaks itself by manipulating the Islamic religion to gain political power and social domination. Militant Islam is truly an anachronistic mind set, in complete conflict with modern concepts of plurality, human rights, and democracy. The rich tradition of religious tolerance in America is the antithesis of militant Islam. Speaking in 2003 before the Senate Subcommittee on Terrorism, Technology and Homeland Security, Alex Alexiev, Senior Fellow at the Center for Security Policy noted:

A key postulate of Wahhabi's teaching asserts that Muslims who do not believe in his doctrines are ipso facto non-believers and apostates against whom violence and Jihad were not only permissible, but obligatory. This postulate alone transgresses against two fundamental tenets of the Quran—that invoking Jihad against fellow-Muslims is prohibited and that Muslim's profession of faith should be taken at face value until God judges his/hers sincerity at judgment day. This extreme reactionary creed was then used as the religious justification for military conquest and violence against Muslim neighbors of the House of Saud. Already in 1746, just two years after Wahhabism became Saud's religion, the new Saudi-Wahhabi state proclaimed

Jihad against all neighboring Muslim tribes that refused to subscribe to it. Indeed, well into the 1920s the history of the House of Saud is replete with violent campaigns to force other Muslims to submit politically and theologically, violating yet another fundamental Quranic principle that prohibits the use of compulsion in religion.

There are numerous terrorist organizations that fit the mold of militant Islam, although not all of the militant groups are at "war" with the United States. The State Department's 2010 list of foreign terrorist organizations (FTO) contained 45 groups; at least 19 of these FTOs cloak themselves in a militant view of Islam. The State Department's 2020 list of FTO contained 69 groups with 53 directly related to radial Islam. This list includes: Abu Sayyaf Group, Al-Aqsa Martyrs Brigade, Ansar al-Islam, Gama'a al-Islamiyya, HAMAS, Harakat ul-Mujahedin, Hizballah, Islamic Jihad Group, Jaish-e-Mohammed, Jemaah Islamiya Organization, Palestinian Islamic Jihad, al-Qa'eda, and ISIS. Many of these radical Islamic groups are associated with Islamic fundamentalism spewed from radicalized *madrasas* (religious schools) which operate with impunity in such countries as Saudi Arabia, Pakistan, and Iran. In fact, in the case of many militant Islamic terrorist organizations, direct links have been established to various *Deobandi* religious schools, which are known for openly advocating the most violent forms of terrorism against Western interests. In addition, radical clerics in Western nations also preach this brand of hate to their followers. For instance, many terrorists associated with the July 7 and 21, 2005, bombings in London had direct links to the infamous Findsbury Park Mosque in London (Muslim cleric Abuy Hamza al-Masri was subsequently arrested on suspicion of terrorism links).

The number of adherents of militant Islam is large and growing, easily reaching into the hundreds of thousands if one counts the strongly messianic strain of Twelver Shiism in Iran (belief that the twelfth legitimate successor of the prophet Muhammad who is said to have disappeared in the tenth century will return to reign over a world where Islam is universal). Pakistan and other Middle Eastern nations teem with al-Qa'eda sympathizers. The most chilling hallmark associated with the spread of militant Islam is not the operation of terror training camps for the terror jihadists, but rather the established methodology of inculcating an ideology of hatred into the minds of innocent children from the moment of birth. In the homes, communities, and the *madrasas*, countless numbers of innocent children are brainwashed each and every day of their lives with no opportunity to escape. The radical *madrasas* are like conveyor belts of death where an unlimited number of suicide bombers emerge convinced that their religion demands the murder of Westerners, Jews, or anyone holding a contrary worldview. Up to 20 percent of all *madrasas* may be actively spreading radical ideologies.

Simply stated, the goal of radical Islam is to conquer the world. In 2006 alone, Ayman al-Zawahiri and Osama bin Laden made almost 20 videotaped pronouncements on the global war. In August 2006, Zawahiri told his followers: "All the world is a battlefield open in front of us." This idea of global *jihad* is one of the defining threads that bring together suicide murders from Baghdad to Bali. In this light, al-Qa'eda is both a cohesive terror organization and a source of inspiration for all like-minded fanatics. In an April 24, 2006 tape, Osama bin Laden declared: "It is the duty for the Umma [nation] with all its categories of men, women and youths, to give away themselves, their money, experiences and all types of material support....Jihad today is an imperative for every Muslim. The Umma will commit sin if it did not provide adequate material support for jihad." Just before his death in 2019, the onetime leader of ISIS, Abu Bakr al-Baghdadi, was still spewing out hate even as his Caliphate had collapsed: "Oh soldiers of Islam in every location, increase blow after blow, and make the media centers of the infidels, from where they wage their intellectual wars, among the targets."

The never-ending struggle is encompassed in their view of the seventh-century jihad—the spread of Islam by force of arms. President Trump correctly understood that in the short term the use of military force was necessary to defeat them on the ground. But the question by President Bush's Secretary of Defense Donald Rumsfeld in an October 2003 memorandum he sent to General Richard Myers, Chairman of the Joint Chiefs of Staff, entitled: Global War on Terrorism is still pertinent. In the memorandum, Rumsfeld asked, "Are we capturing, killing or deterring and dissuading more terrorists every day than the madrassas [sic] and the radical clerics are recruiting, training, and deploying against us?"

Ultimately, of course, this means that only Muslims can provide the long-term cure to militant Islam. In the aftermath of the July 7, 2005, bombing in London that killed 52 people, this theme was echoed by both the British and some Muslim leaders in England. The key to winning the conflict is addressing the ideological aspect regarding how Muslim terrorists recruit and indoctrinate new followers. Interestingly, this is not an easy task as the suicide foot-soldiers defy simplistic political, sociological, or psychological profiling. They come from extremely diverse educational, economic, and social backgrounds. The only common red thread that binds them together is an unrelenting devotion to their radicalized Islamic belief system. *United States v. Koubriti*, 199 F. Supp. 2d 656 (E.D.Mich. S.D. 2002):

> Wahhabis, Takfiris, and Salafists…These groups regard the Islam that most Muslims practice today as unpure and polluted by idolatry and Western influence….These radical fundamentalist-Islamic groups see the world divided in two spheres; that is, Dar-al-Islam (House of Islam or Islamic Zone), where peace reigns (Sallam), and the Dar-al-Harb (House of War or War Zone), which prevents a true Islamic state. The latter is viewed by these radical fundamentalist-Islamic groups to include all infidel areas that must ultimately be conquered. Global jihad is the constant effort to achieve this goal.

Perhaps one of the most chilling revelations of the vicious mindset of militant Islam is found in the "bin Laden videotape," released to the public on December 13, 2001. The tape clearly illustrates the twisted religious machinations of the al-Qa'eda terrorists and their like who pervert religion to justify the mass murder of innocent civilians. In the conversation between bin Laden and Sheik Khaled al-Harbi (who surrendered to Saudi officials in 2004) regarding the attacks of September 11, 2001, numerous references are made to "Allah," "Muhammad," the "*fiqu* [holy war] of Muhammad," and so on. At one point, bin Laden boasts that the attacks were beneficial to a "true" understanding of Islam. "The attacks made people think (about true Islam), which benefited them greatly." The video closes with the guest praising bin Laden in the name of Allah, "By Allah my Shaykh [bin Laden]. We congratulate you for the great work. Thank Allah."

The followers of al-Qa'eda and ISIS are not simply members of another isolated sub-State religious terror cult like Japan's Aum Shinrikyo. According to a thought-provoking special report from 2001 *Newsweek* entitled, "Why Do They Hate Us," these terrorists "come out of a culture that reinforces their hostility, distrust and hatred of the West—and of America in particular."

Similarly, these Islamic zealots are far different from mere criminals. Unlike criminals, they are not in it for monetary gain. They do not wish to circumvent the system, rather they desire to destroy the system. Their fantastic goal is to create an Islamic Caliphate that controls the world. Still, radical Islam has cited numerous grievances against the United States to justify their use of terror including American support of "puppet" Arab governments, importation of oil, support for Israel, support for the new Iraq and Afghanistan, Westerners living in Arab lands, morally corrupt Western culture, and so on. These complaints are hollow. Like all enemies of freedom and pluralism, be it the German Nazis or the Stalinist Communists, the radical Islamic terrorist attacks the West for what it is, not for what it has done. In a nutshell, whether the anti-Americanism is motivated by religious enmity, radical idiosyncrasies, or just blind hatred, militant Islamic terrorist groups have no regard or respect for human life let alone the human rights and fundamental freedoms of others. In this light, the overall problem is not the acts of terror but the mindset of those behind the terror attacks. To be sure, the U.N. Charter's rule of law and expression of human rights are viewed as hateful concepts of Western domination and not self-evident truths pointing the way to the betterment of mankind.

Related to the inherent dangerousness of al-Qa'eda-styled terrorist groups, is the fact that States who have provided support to these people suffer from the scourge of totalitarianism and open hostility to America and the West. This is an important phenomenon because terror groups could probably not flourish into sophisticated networks without the overt support of a State.

1.9 Questions for Discussion

1. *One man's terrorist is another man's freedom fighter.* "The causes of terrorism or the political motivation of the individual terrorists are relevant to the problem of definition." Under this proposition, many have argued that acts of violence against "colonialism" or in wars of "national liberation" fall outside of the definition of terrorism. Hence, the dilemma of "[o]ne man's terrorism is another man's heroism." See John Norton Moore & Robert F. Turner, National Security Law SECOND edition, (2006).

2. *International definitions.* U.N. Sec. Coun. Res. 1368 (Sept. 12, 2001). The Security Council resolution uses the word terror or terrorism six times in the short one-page document. Like all other United Nations efforts in this area, SC 1368 uses the term terrorism but offers no definition of terrorism other than to affirm that the September 11, 2001, attacks on the United States was a "horrifying terrorist attack." Is it possible for the international community to reach an agreement on the definition of terrorism? What benefit would a totalitarian regime have for agreeing to an international definition for terrorism?

3. *Congressional definitions of terrorism.* The provision of the United States Code referenced in the USA PATRIOT Act, defines international terrorism as "terrorism involving citizens or the territory of more than one country." 22 U.S.C. § 2656f (d)(1). Furthermore, "terrorism" is defined as "premeditated, politically motivated violence perpetrated against noncombatant targets by sub-national groups or clandestine agents." 22 U.S.C. § 2656f(d)(2). Section 411 of the USA PATRIOT Act defines "terrorist activity" at length, as well as what it means to "engage in terrorist activity." 8 U.S.C. § 1182(b)(3)(B). Does the language in the different provisions of the United States Code listed above leave gaps in interpretation? In what way might the provisions be inadequate?

4. *Who is the enemy?* Following the failed August 2006 plot by British radical Muslims to blow up more than ten jetliners bound for the United States, President Bush said that the foiled plot was a "stark reminder" that "the nation is at war with Islamic fascists." Following the failed bombing of

an American aircraft on December 25, 2009, President Obama declared: "We are at war against al-Qa'eda." Following the 2019 killing of ISIS leader in al-Baghdadi by American Special Forces, President Trump said: "He will never again harm another innocent man, woman, or child. He died like a dog. He died like a coward. The world is now a much safer place. God bless America." Are these appropriate characterizations of the enemy in the War on Terror?

5. *Hatred in the classroom*. Learning why some come to hate the United States and its allies can be gleaned from what is taught in some Pakistani religious schools. In *PREACHERS OF HATE: ISLAM AND THE WAR ON AMERICA*, Kenneth R. Timmerman writes:

> In third grade, children learn hate through vocabulary. "The Zionist enemy—attacked—civilians with its aircraft." (*Our Arabic Language for Third Grade*) In sixth grade, hate became a drill. "Who is the thief who has torn our homeland?" (*Our Arabic Language for Sixth Grade*) By seventh grade, students are expected to have internalized anti-Semitism so they can recite it on their own. "Why do the Jews hate Muslim unity and want to cause division among them?" "Give an example of the evil attempts of the Jews, from events happening today." (*Islamic Education for Seventh Grade*) In ninth grade students are told, "One must beware of Jews, for they are treacherous and disloyal." (*Islamic Education for Ninth Grade*).

What is the best way to combat this dissemination of information? Is it right to do so?

Selected Bibliography

1954 Draft Code of Offenses Against the Peace and Security of Mankind, 9 U.N. GAOR Supp. (no. 9) at 11-12, U.N. Doc. A/2693. 1954.

Addicott, Jeffrey, Radical Islam Why?, 2016.

Albright, Madeleine. THE MIGHTY AND THE ALMIGHTY, 2006.

Bergen, Peter L. THE OSAMA BIN LADEN I KNOW, 2006.

Carr, Caleb. THE LESSONS OF TERROR: A HISTORY OF WARFARE AGAINST CIVILIANS, WHY IT HAS ALWAYS FAILED AND WHY IT WILL FAIL AGAIN, 2002.

Chasey, William C. THE LOCKERBIE COVERUP, 1995.

Cohen, William S. *Preparing for a Grave New World*, WASH. POST, July 26, 1999, at A19.

Combating Terrorism: Threat and Risk Assessments Can Help Prioritize and Target Program Investments, U.S. GAO Report to Congressional Requesters, Apr. 1998.

Ganor, Boaz. THE COUNTER-TERRORISM PUZZLE, 2005.

Gerges, Fawaz A. JOURNEY OF THE JIHADIST, 2006.

Gold, Dore. The RISE OF NUCLEAR IRAN, 2009.

Guiora, Amos N. GLOBAL PERSPECTIVES ON COUNTERTERRORISM, 2007.

Graham, Bob, et. al., WORLD AT RISK, THE REPORT OF THE COMMISSION ON THE PREVENTION OF WMD PROLIFERATION AND TERRORISM, 2008.

Hartigan, Richard Shelly. LIEBER'S CODE AND THE LAW OF WAR, 1983.

Heather Saul, ISIS Leader Abu Bakr al-Baghdadi resurfaces in audio urging supporters to join terror group, INDEPENDENT (Friday 15 May 2015) https://www.independent.co.uk/news/world/middle-east/ isis-leader-abu-bakr-al-baghdadi-resurfaces-audio-urging-supporters-join-terror-group-10251955. html.

Lesser, Ian O., Bruce Hoffman, John Arquilla, David Ronfeldt and Michele Zanini. COUNTERING THE NEW TERRORISM. Santa Monica, CA: Rand, 1999, at 17.

Lifton, Robert Jay. DESTROYING THE WORLD TO SAVE IT: AUM SHINRIKYO, APOCALYPTIC VIOLENCE, AND THE NEW GLOBAL TERRORISM, 2000.

Loeb, Vernon. *Anthrax Vial Smuggled In To Make A Point At A Hill Hearing*, WASH. POST, Mar. 4, 1999, at A1.

Michel, Lou, and Dan Herbeck. AMERICAN TERRORIST: TIMOTHY MCVEIGH AND THE TRAGEDY AT OKLAHOMA CITY, 2001.

Moore, John Norton, and Robert F. Turner. NATIONAL SECURITY LAW, SECOND EDITION, 2006.

Rollins, John, Al Qaeda and Affiliates: Historical Perspective, Global Presence, and Implications for U.S. Policy, Congressional Research Service, R41070, Feb. 5, 2010.

Sun-tzu, THE ART OF WAR, Ralph D. Sawyer trans., 1994.

THE COMPLETE WORKS OF FLAVIUS JOSEPHUS, William Whiston trans., 1981. The Hebrew Zealots conducted random acts of assassination against the occupying Romans in Judea prior to Jerusalem falling to the Roman legions under Titus in A. D. 70.

USA PATRIOT Act of 2001, 115 Stat. 272; Pub. Law 107-56 § 411. Oct. 26, 2001.

Chapter 2

The Use of Force Under International Law

The views of men can only be known, or guessed at, by their words or actions.

—George Washington

If the mark of a civilized State is measured by how well it follows the rule of law it is necessary to understand what that term means, particularly in the realm of waging war. In addition, it is equally vital to understand the origin of the rule of law as it applies to that body of law known as the law of war — a system of legality by which the use of violence in warfare is both authorized and conducted.

2.1 Rule of Law

The concept called the "rule of law" was first coined by Western legal scholars in the late sixteenth century. The term was initially used to refer to the common law system of jurisprudence with particular emphasis on equality before the courts. However, the more modern and common meaning is directly associated with all of those rules and legal standards of behavior recognized and practiced between civilized States in the context of the community of nations.

In this setting, one can logically trace the origins of the rule of law back to the 1648 Peace of Westphalia, which concluded the Thirty Years War in Europe. At that time a number of Christian European States officially recognized themselves as being in a community of sovereign nation-states and guided by certain rules of international and social intercourse. The utility of the nation-state concept soon spread throughout Europe, typified by the colonial powers of Europe holding themselves out as the "self-appointed executive committee of the family of nations." With the Treaty of Paris in 1856, non-Christian nations were also admitted and periodic international conferences were held in such cosmopolitan cities as Vienna and Geneva.

In early days, this community of nations was not deemed to be anything other than a loose association bound together by only a few international agreements and the thinnest of diplomatic threads. Although the primary purpose of this association was to promote world peace and to mitigate, when necessary, "the miseries of war," independent sovereignty reigned supreme because the association lacked any legal character or corporate personality. Thus, the rule of law remained a concept with little viability behind it.

After World War I reflected the total impotence of the association to deter those nations bent on aggression, the victorious European nations created the first international organization with legal parameters, the League of Nations. Formed in large part with the direct assistance of President Woodrow Wilson (the United States never joined the League of Nations), the much-heralded League of Nations was the first truly international organization specifically directed toward the curtailment of war. As laudable as that goal might be, the League of Nations' efforts to maintain the peace were totally ineffective. In fact, they were actually counterproductive.

First, accepting the false premise that World War I had somehow been caused by a combination of misunderstandings and entangling collective security alliances, the League of Nations naively adopted a series of procedural requirements focused on third-party dispute settlement processes. The framers assumed that wars, like all disputes, could be settled through negotiation and arbitration. This approach is best reflected in Article 12 of the Covenant of the League of Nations:

> The members of the League agree that if there should arise between them any dispute likely to lead to a rupture, they will submit the matter either to arbitration or to inquiry by the council, and they agree in no case to resort to war until three months after the award by the arbitrators or the report of the Council.

Second, the League of Nations concentrated almost solely on disarmament as the best guarantee of world peace. Somehow the founders of the League of Nations believed that there existed a direct correlation between the number of weapons in existence and the probability of armed conflict. In short, they naively believed that the threat of war could be reduced or eliminated if the League of Nations implemented international agreements which called for the destruction of weapons and the reduction of military forces. In the next two decades, disarmament treaties such as the London Naval Conferences (1930) saw England, France and the United States completely emasculate their military while Germany and her allies, Japan and Italy, embarked on a massive buildup of their armies, navies, and air forces.

During this rush to disarm, other international agreements relating to armed conflict were drafted and adopted by the world community, of which the Geneva Conventions of 1929 was the most prominent. The most controversial document that came out of the post-World War I era was the Kellogg-Briand Pact. Signed by almost all of the major world powers, the Pact wishfully prohibited war as the solution to international disputes or as an instrument of national policy.

Although the Kellogg-Briand Pact was viewed by many as an idealistic proscription against war, the abolition of war did not mean that States gave up the inherent right of self-defense; all signatories strongly asserted that the defensive use of military force was absolutely legitimate under the Pact. Paradoxically, the Pact, spawned by a sincere desire to rid mankind of the scourge of war, was actually a dramatic and positive shift in the focus of the rule of law pertaining to war.

The Kellogg-Briand Pact shifted the emphasis from procedural and moral issues related to the legitimacy of war to simply prohibiting all *aggression* under "any circumstances." In effect, a red line of distinction was made between the aggressive use of force, which was always prohibited, and the defensive use of force in response to aggression, which was always lawful. Unfortunately, the Pact did not specifically spell out what it so strongly implied concerning permissive self-defense. The Kellogg-Briand Pact did not devote a single word to the traditional and inherent right of self-defense.

In summation, most of the League of Nations' activities were rooted in the sincere but naive assumption that war was intrinsically irrational and that rational Man could solve his differences simply through negotiation and reason. Incredibly, many nations thought this philosophy of negotiating, coupled with a massive disarming effort, would lead to the abolition of war.

In the first major application of this philosophy of negotiation, Neville Chamberlain, Prime Minister of England, tried to appease the Nazi dictator, Adolf Hitler, by traveling to Munich, Germany, in October of 1938. The resulting Munich Agreement prompted Chamberlain to foolishly remark, "I believe it is peace for our time…peace with honor." Of course, the fruits of appeasement produced the exact opposite. The clear signal given to the aggressor—peace at any price—prompted the Axis powers to launch the most destructive war in the history of mankind. A similar pattern has developed with how some nations have chosen to deal with the forces of Islamic terrorism. Many countries have simply decided that they will not engage in the War on Terror. Prior to the events of September 11, 2001, this attitude was also widely held in the United States.

When World War II ended in 1945, the international community once again sought to create a new methodology to reduce or to eliminate armed international conflict. Just as they had done following World War I, work quickly began on a series of international agreements and instruments designed to accomplish this ideal. Many of the efforts, ranging from the creation of the United Nations in 1945 to the 1949 Geneva Conventions, produced widespread and immediate acceptance throughout the world. In this regard, the civilized world recognized the necessity of anchoring its desire for world peace on ideas that would inhibit both the external and, to a lesser degree, the internal dimensions of State sovereignty. The unfettered power of member States to pursue activities and policies that threatened international peace and security had to be squarely addressed. In addition, great concern was voiced about the acts of States in regard to the treatment of their own citizens.

Since the sovereignty of each State would serve as the basis for the new world organization, internationally recognized legal constraints and attendant enforcement mechanisms had to be placed on those nations that threatened the peace. In leading the effort to create such an organization, the United States held out to the world community the vision of a world order based on four essential human freedoms. These four freedoms were first articulated in President Franklin Roosevelt's major speech before Congress on January 6, 1941: freedom of speech, freedom of religion, freedom from want, and freedom from fear. Echoing these ideals, the victorious powers of World War II formed the United Nations.

2.2 The United Nations Charter

With the emergence of the United Nations and the principles of international behavior firmly embodied in the Charter of the United Nations, the deficiencies in the Kellogg-Briand Pact were largely corrected. Prohibiting all forms of armed aggression, the U.N. Charter also specifically recognized a nation-state's inherent right of self-defense if attacked. Today, in the search for a workable model to address conflict management—deemed to be the most pressing issue facing humanity—the U.N. Charter is considered by many to be synonymous with the international rule of law.

As embodied in Articles 2(3) and 2(4) of the U.N. Charter, the maintenance of "international peace and security" is, in fact, the very purpose of the United Nations. Since all members of the United Nations are recognized as sovereign equals, no nation may resort to "threat or [the] use of force against the territorial integrity or political independence of any State" to settle any form of dispute. This, as well as the clear prohibition in Article 1 against any nation committing "acts of aggression or other breaches of the peace," resulted in a workable, legal framework dedicated to curtailing unlawful aggression. It established a concrete legal framework by which behavior could be gauged.

Recognizing that even the most brilliantly crafted legal framework is useless without an enforcement mechanism, the drafters of the U.N. Charter also established an extensive and flexible international framework for responding to those rogue nations which might choose to violate the provisions of the U.N. Charter and engage in unlawful aggression. Chapter VI of the U.N. Charter authorizes the Security Council to investigate any situation that might endanger the maintenance of international peace and security and to make recommendations for the peaceful resolution of such disputes. Chapter VII of the U.N. Charter authorizes the Security Council to determine the existence of a threat, a breach of peace, or act of aggression, and to take appropriate measures in response. Even though Article 43 provides for the mechanism for member nations to make troops available on the call of the Security Council, no such agreements have ever been concluded. Instead, to enforce the peace, the Security Council relies on the forces of member nations, contributed and organized on an ad hoc basis for each situation.

Finally, recognizing the utopian absurdity of outlawing war, but building upon the framework of the Kellogg-Briand Pact, the U.N. Charter does not restrict all uses of force; it only restricts the unlawful use of force: aggression. Thus, the final element in this legal structure, and the one that is of immeasurable value in the real world, rests upon the U.N. Charter's recognition of the lawful use of force to deter unlawful armed aggression.

Explicitly acknowledging the long-standing customary right of self-defense, Article 51 states that "nothing in the present Charter shall impair the inherent right of individual or collective self-defense if an armed attack occurs against a Member of the United Nations...." While there still exists lingering controversy over such matters as to what constitutes an armed attack and the utility of the term inherent, the modern rule of law specifically recognizes the fundamental distinction between unlawful aggression and lawful self-defense. In the overall picture, the rule of law has evolved from a vision of an "ideal aspiration towards universal values of law," to the reality of a world that acknowledges the existence and validity of established legal norms. If a nation operates in accordance with this rule of law, it can rightly claim the legal and moral high ground in any conflict.

2.3 The Use of Force

There are four primary provisions of the U.N. Charter under which the use of force is analyzed. The starting point, of course, requires a firm understanding that the U.N. Charter does not outlaw the use of force in self-defense; it only outlaws the use of *aggressive* force.

First, Articles 2(3) and 2(4) set out the general obligations of member States to settle disputes in a peaceful manner and to refrain from "the threat or use of force." U.N. Charter Article 2(3) requires that, "[a]ll Members shall settle their international disputes by peaceful means in such a manner that international peace and security, and justice are not endangered." U.N. Charter Article 2(4) states, "[a]ll Members shall refrain in their international relations from the threat or use of force against the territorial integrity or political independence of any State, or in any other manner inconsistent with the purposes of the United Nations."

Second, if a State engages in the use of aggressive force, Article 24 of the U.N. Charter actually gives the Security Council the "primary responsibility for the maintenance of international peace and security." Then, Article 27 requires that all permanent members of the U.N. Security Council must agree on enforcement provisions, e.g., the use of armed force. These five permanent members are listed in Article 23 of the U.N. Charter. They are China, France, Russia, Britain, and the United States. Still, even if the Security Council issues an enforcement ruling authorizing the use of military force against an aggressor nation, there is no standing U.N. military force to enforce the ruling. Historically, the United States has provided the lion's share of military muscle to back up the Security Council's authorization for use of military force.

The third element of the analytical framework rests in Article 51 of the U.N. Charter and is certainly the most powerful consideration of all. Article 51 does not create a new legal regimen, instead it merely codifies the longstanding "inherent right of self-defense." The inherent right of self-defense refers to the right of a country to unilaterally engage in acts of self-defense, regardless of what any other nation or organization, to include the United Nations, may or may not do. This is a well-known and ancient component of international law, a concept specifically recognized in U.N. Security Council Resolution 1368. Article 51 of the U.N. Charter states:

> Nothing in the present Charter shall impair the inherent right of individual or collective self-defense if an armed attack occurs against a Member of the United Nations, until the Security Council has taken measures to maintain international peace and security. Measures taken by Members in the exercise of the right of self-defense shall be immediately reported to the Security Council and shall not in any way affect the authority and responsibility of the Security Council under the present Charter to take at any time such action as it deems necessary in order to maintain or restore international peace and security.

Finally, to complete the analysis, one must determine what is meant by the term "armed attack." In order to clearly define when an unlawful use of force in violation of Articles 2(3) and (4) occurs, international law looks primarily at the non-binding, but often cited, definition of aggression as adopted by resolution of the U.N. General Assembly. A State engages in aggression in the following ways according to the U.N. Definition of Aggression, U.N. General Assembly Resolution 3314 (XXIX), Dec. 14, 1975:

Article 1
Aggression is the use of armed force by a State against the sovereignty, territorial integrity, or political independence of another State, or in any manner inconsistent with the Charter of the United Nations....
Article 2
The first use of armed force by a State in contravention of the Charter shall constitute prima facie evidence of an act of aggression....
Article 3
Any of the following acts, regardless of a declaration of war, shall...qualify as an act of aggression:
    (a) The invasion or attack by the armed forces of a State...of another State or part thereof;
    (b) Bombardment by the armed forces of a State against the territory of another State...
    (c) The blockade of the ports or coasts of a State by the armed forces of another State;
    (d) An attack by the armed forces of a State on the land, sea, or air forces, or marine and air fleets of another State;
    (e) The use of armed forces of one State...in contravention of the conditions provided for in

the agreement or any extension of their presence in such territory beyond the termination of the agreement;

(f) The action of a State in allowing its territory, which it has placed at the disposal of another State, to be used by that other State for perpetrating an act of aggression against a third State;

(g) The sending by or on behalf of a State of armed bands, groups, irregulars, or mercenaries, which carry out acts of armed force against another State of such gravity as to amount to the acts listed above, or its substantial involvement therein.

2.4 Anticipatory Self-Defense

In tandem with the customary rule of law authorizing self-defense, is the concept of anticipatory self-defense. As discussed in Chapter 4, the Bush Administration sought to justify its use of force against Saddam Hussein's Iraq under the doctrine of anticipatory self-defense. In Bush's view the challenging question for the United States and the entire civilized world was how to legally frame a rule of law that could speak to preventing future attacks by sophisticated virtual-State terrorist groups, particularly in light of their potential use of weapons of mass destruction and the existence of renegade States that support them. If the employment of a weapon of mass murder is on the near horizon, do the current international rules relating to the use of force (i.e., only used in self-defense) actually work in the post-9/11 world? In other words, must a State wait for a catastrophic State-sponsored or State-supported terrorist attack before it can respond, or does a threatened State have the right to engage in "anticipatory self-defense," or perhaps even in a controversial legal theory known as "counter proliferation self-help," against a regime or sub-State terror group it believes capable of such acts?

The concept of anticipatory self-defense is also termed alternatively as "preemption self-defense" or "preventative self-defense," and has been used more than once by the Israelis, as illustrated by Israel's preemptive air strike on Arab airfields in the 1967 War and on many occasions against individual Palestinian terrorists like HAMAS in the ongoing Palestinian conflict. President Trump also gave nod to the theory in the targeted killing by the United States of Iran's top terror chief General Qasem Soleimani in 2020, although most legal scholars justified the death under traditional self-defense arguments.

In any event, the United States has long recognized the right of anticipatory self-defense to counter threats to its national security. American scholars regularly cite the famous Caroline Doctrine, which domestically defines the circumstances permitting forcible self-help or self-defense. The Caroline Doctrine grew out of an 1837 raid by Canadian troops to burn a ship harbored in New York. Responding to the Canadian military attack on the ship (which was being used by Canadian rebels) under the concept of self-defense or, more precisely, anticipatory self-defense, the United States Secretary of State, Daniel Webster, penned the Caroline Doctrine. Under the Caroline Doctrine a nation may resort to necessary and proportional acts of self-defense if such acts arise out of an instant and overwhelming necessity, leaving no choice of means and no moment of deliberation.

The problem, of course, is that a State may claim the right of anticipatory self-defense as a pretext for aggression. To weigh the validity of the concept of anticipatory self-defense, international law views the employment of this doctrine in the context of an "imminent" armed attack and which would then tie in as an addendum to the inherent right of self-defense found in Article 51 of the U.N. Charter. Traditionally, the analysis was fairly clear cut; the concept of imminent was viewed in terms of the actual mobilization by the aggressor State of its conventional military forces in preparation for an armed attack. In the War on Terror, however, the enemy was not a nation-state and did not rely on conventional forces, although ISIS came closer to this characterization. The real fear is that al-Qa'eda-styled suicide terrorists might rely on the use of weapons of mass murder targeted at civilians which, in their hands, might very well satisfy the rule of law requirement of imminent. Regardless, the use of force in preemption must be reasonably proportionate to the specific danger that is to be averted.

During the War on Terror, former United States Deputy Secretary of Defense Paul Wolfowitz was an early and vocal proponent of anticipatory self-defense, speaking with approval for the Israeli military's use of preemptive force in regard to the killing of known Palestinian terrorists and embracing the idea as a necessary instrument of United States policy in the War on Terror. According to Wolfowitz: "Our approach has been to aim at prevention and not merely punishment. We are at war. Self-defense requires prevention and sometimes preemption." The White House's 2002 National Security Strategy of the United States spelled out America's intention to employ the concept of preemption.

The United States has long maintained the option of preemptive actions to counter a sufficient threat to our national security. The greater the threat, the greater the risk of inaction—and the more compelling the case for taking anticipatory action to defend ourselves, even if uncertainty remains as to the time and place of the enemy's attack. To forestall or prevent such hostile acts by our adversaries, the United States will, if necessary, act preemptively.

The 2002 National Security Strategy (retained in the 2006 National Security Strategy) document spelled out a three-part approach to weigh the use of preemption.

We will always proceed deliberately, weighing the consequences of our actions. To support preemptive options, we will:
- build better, more integrated intelligence capabilities to provide timely, accurate information on threats, wherever they may emerge;
- coordinate closely with allies to form a common assessment of the most dangerous threats; and
- continue to transform our military forces to ensure our ability to conduct rapid and precise operations to achieve decisive results.

The concept of counter proliferation self-help takes the matter of anticipatory self-defense to the next level, although in the 2002 National Security Strategy the distinction was essentially swallowed under preemption. Counter proliferation self-help is focused specifically on rogue totalitarian States that seek to acquire weapons of mass destruction. The concept argues that when the threat of a totalitarian State or terrorist group using a weapon of mass destruction directly threatens the national survival of another State, a new international legal regimen should allow for the threatened State to engage in, as international law expert Guy Roberts argues, "preventive or preemptive use of force to either deter acquisition plans, eliminate acquisition programs, or destroy illicit weapons of mass destruction sites at any stage in the proliferators acquisition efforts."

The 1981 Israeli air attack on Iraq's Osiraq nuclear reactor is the best illustration of this emerging and doctrine. Although the international community condemned the Israelis for violating the rule of law regarding the use of force in self-defense, both history and common sense prove their actions were entirely justified. In contrast, the 2008 Israeli air attack on an alleged Syrian proto nuclear facility was greeted by silence from the international community.

Tragically, the totalitarian Iranian regime under the direct thumb of supreme religious leader Ayatollah Ali Khamenei (a position he has held since 1989) is now approaching the same level of development for its own nuclear program. Some experts believe that Iran will have nuclear capability by 2021. Not only does Iran support and sponsor terrorist organizations like Hezbollah, but the findings of the 9/11 Commission Report amplify the danger of a nuclear Iran, recognizing that Iran provided al-Qa'eda operatives pass-through rights without border stamps. In fact, eight to ten of the 9/11 hijackers passed through Iran between October 2000 and February 2001.

Although Iran continues to act in direct defiance of the U.N. Security Council by refusing to cooperate with the International Atomic Energy Agency (IAEA) and is violating its own treaty obligations, it remains to be seen if free nations will simply do nothing or engage in preemptive force to shut down the Iranian program before Iran either uses the nuclear weapons it is developing or passes them on to terrorists for use against the United States or other free nations. The U.N. Security Council has taken some limited action, but few anticipate that the use of force will ever be authorized. In many respects, Iran represents a greater danger than Saddam Hussein. With Iran's 18 to 30 nuclear-related facilities dispersed around the country, the West may have to focus its efforts on the slim hope that Cold War deterrence strategies will keep Iran at bay. The Trump Administration increased economic sanctions on Iran to move Iran away from nuclear weapons. The Biden Administration will now be tested on how to stop Iran.

2.5 Humanitarian Intervention

Finally, a less-discussed legal basis for military intervention against a rogue nation falls under the evolving legal theory known as humanitarian intervention. For example, although conducted with the specific approval of the United Nations, the December 1992 United States military intervention in Somalia was motivated purely on humanitarian grounds to alleviate human suffering and, even without United Nations sanction, would appear on its face to be a proper exercise of the developing customary legal theory of humanitarian intervention. This theory was also advanced when President Clinton unilaterally directed a military bombing campaign against Serbia in 1999.

The theory of humanitarian intervention, recognized by many modern international scholars, holds that when the government and infrastructure of a country have disintegrated to the point that its people are being subjected to a widespread pattern of gross human rights violations over a prolonged period of time, another nation may intervene to stop the loss of life and to assist in the restoration of law and order. The caveat to the theory, of course, is that once the loss of life has stopped and law and order have been restored, the intervening force must immediately depart.

2.6 Power versus Words—the Rule of Law

The argument is sometimes made, rather cynically, that what really matters in achieving a particular goal is the possession of the necessary power to influence the desired outcome. Since the overriding goal of the War on Terror is the protection of American interests and the maintenance of global stability through prevention of terrorism and unlawful aggression, the United States should depend upon dispositions of effective power without concern for the rearrangement of authoritative words to color that power. In other words, in weighing the use of force in the War on Terror, some argue that concentration should simply rest on the use of power, downplaying the necessity or impact of words. This approach might be termed a power over words argument, a phenomenon which rests particularly well with totalitarian regimes, but is also periodically raised by members of democratic societies facing peril.

Thus, when Iraq invaded and conquered the sovereign nation of Kuwait in 1990, no amount of words, treaty obligations or diplomacy halted their exercise of total and brutal aggression against the territory, people, and environment of Kuwait. Exercising what is termed the law of the jungle, Iraq simply took what it wanted. The fact that Iraq was a member of the United Nations and bound by the principles relating to dispute settlement through means other than the use of force had no effect whatsoever on its activities. In this regard, the words and ideas contained in the U.N Charter deterred neither Iraq's open and brutal aggression of Kuwait, nor Saddam Hussein's lust for power and territory.

In fact, throughout the entire Gulf crisis, Iraq made no real attempt to conceal, let alone justify, its violations of the U.N. Charter, the Geneva Conventions, or other applicable treaties. In the end, it was only the application of power through the superior military might of the allied coalition headed in chief by the United States which succeeded in halting Iraq's aggression.

Other examples of the apparent disconnect of power *vis-à-vis* words can be found in the arena of human rights. The willingness of many States to eagerly endorse numerous human rights covenants that are never put into practice shows that this cynical model finds some basis in fact. If power is all that ultimately counts, then what use do words have in the real world of dealing with international conflict?

On the other hand, casting the use of power as the dominant factor in the use of force captures only a portion of the issue at hand. While it is true that words without corresponding force have little effect in the deterrence of unlawful activities, such a model incorrectly dismisses the positive role of words in the process. Of course, aggression can never be halted by words alone, no matter how much those words reflect accepted norms. However, the deficiency of this reasoning ultimately rests on misunderstanding the critical role which universally defined norms play in the process of deterrence. Clearly defined norms actually provide stimulus and sinew for subsequent action. Such norms are the very building blocks necessary for a democracy to generate the home front support to defeat unlawful activities by the use of force.

If words are the basis for viable action, words must impart unambiguous understanding. A basic tenet of providing instruction is simplicity, appropriately known in the vernacular of the military as KISS (keep it simple stupid). To be efficacious to a wide audience, concepts should be kept as simple as possible. Additionally, since each discipline of study has its own unique system of terminology, effective communication mandates that the more complex the body of material to be learned, the greater one must rely on shorter concepts which take the place of longer chains of thought. Hence, although the proper designation for the War on Terror should be the "War Against Taliban, al-Qa'eda, and Associated Forces," that concept is far too long to be effective.

Along with simplicity, concepts must be thoroughly inculcated to be retained. Repetition is also key to all learning; it alone can ensure comprehension and, hence, meaningful communication. Thus, the more complex the body of learning, the greater the need for repetition.

In the War on Terror against al-Qa'eda and the Taliban the Bush Administration made many mistakes, but it actually demonstrated a high level of sophistication concerning the need to couch actions in simple, yet meaningful terminology. And, more importantly, the terminology employed was largely cemented in the rule of law as it pertained to the use of force.

One of the lessons contemporary science has taught us about human behavior is that it helps in creating the conditions necessary for the achievement of a goal to have the goal sharply delineated. The clarification in detail of distinctions between lawful and unlawful coercion will not, of course, by itself establish all the necessary conditions for restraint of unlawful coercion. Nevertheless, it may perform the very necessary task of outlining the major contours of the effects sought in terms of which alternative choices in the rearrangement of effective power and in the adoption of new modalities in practice that must be appraised.

As outlined in Chapter 4, when President Bush formed the allied coalition against the Taliban, he firmly rooted the campaign in the norms of the U.N. Charter and under the domestic law of the United States. The subsequent force applied by the United States and its allies had the full backing of a universally recognized set of lawful standards contained in Article 51 of the U.N. Charter. Similarly, the primary Security Council resolution dealing with the attack on America was based upon the lawful authority of the U.N. Charter. Conversely, the Taliban regime had no legal basis in which to frame its aggression and, apart from a few non-democratic States, almost no supporters within the community of nations.

In turn, as the decade worth of U.N. Security Council resolutions over weapons inspections in Iraq also demonstrated, words issued without the necessary power to enforce them are almost as counterproductive as power applied without the framework of words. Unfortunately, the same pattern of behavior is unfolding in the context of Iran's nuclear ambitions. Still, to emphasize power in the power-versus-words analysis fails completely in the long run because words are the very basis for establishing acceptable norms of agreed behavior which, in turn, distinguish lawful actions from those that are unlawful.

Furthermore, most of the world can quickly grasp the idea of following the democratically based rule of law in halting an aggressor who has broken the law, or who threatens the employment of weapons of mass murder. In this light, America is only defending itself against rogue nations; *they* have been at war with the United States for a long time.

The rule of law has its problems, but those problems are more in the context of application rather than definition; the meaning is simply framed, the application is not. In its strict meaning, the rule of law has immediate association. The meaning of the rule of law will always refer to that body of well-recognized principles of international law accepted by democratic nations, the most critical being in the context of the use of force. It is safe to say, in terms of international behavior, that the phrase rule of law will always bring to mind the illegality of the use of aggressive force. The struggle is not so much in meaning, it is whether the rule of law will prevail as the means of justification in a given situation.

If respect for the rule of law is to survive as the measure of civilized behavior, it does not contribute to the discussion to advocate the use of force apart from legal parameters. At a minimum, the United States must abide by the international principles as they now exist. While it is certainly prudent to sternly warn States that support or sponsor terrorism that they will be held absolutely accountable for any acts of aggression, anticipatory self-defense can only be used if the United States reasonably makes the case to the nation that a significant attack by terrorists using weapons of mass murder is imminent.

Historically, the United Nations has only authorized armed force on two occasions; both instances related to stopping clearly defined acts of aggression. In a stunning show of world solidarity immediately following the Cold War era, President George H. Bush was able to obtain a clear "use of force" resolution from the U.N. Security Council prior to using lawful violence to expel the 1990 illegal Iraqi invasion and occupation of Kuwait. Resolution 678 reads in relevant part:

The Security Council...
Authorizes member States cooperating with the government of Kuwait, unless Iraq on or before January 15, 1991 fully implements...the foregoing Resolutions, to use all necessary means to uphold and implement the Security Council Resolution 660 and all subsequent relevant Resolutions and to restore international peace and security in the area....

The only parallel to the Security Council's authorization for the use of force in the 1991 Gulf War was in the Korean War. On July 7, 1950, responding to North Korea's armed aggression into South Korea, the Security Council authorized the creation of a unified command under the authority of the United States. The resolution was passed, however, only due to the temporary absence of the Soviet Union's ambassador.

Juxtaposed to pressing the international community for concrete definitions and new legal approaches on how to fight terrorism in the post-9/11 world, the United States should continue to earnestly endorse the spread of democratic values as the absolute best avenue to promote terrorism and war avoidance over the long term. Democracy is not an American value; democracy and human rights are normative world values. Unfortunately, the world community has not made assistance to the new Afghan government to build roads, schools, factories, homes, and so forth, contingent on its movement towards the adoption of democratic values; more must be done in this region of the world. When the Afghan government is able to sentence one of its citizens to death, as it did in 2007, for converting from Islam to Christianity, there is no reason to hope that the concepts of freedom will soon take hold. At the end of the day, the totalitarian ponds that foster terrorism must be drained. The goal is extremely ambitious, particularly with the reemergence of the Taliban in Afghanistan in 2021, but the cost of inaction is too great.

Finally, whatever the future may hold, the United States must continue to reinforce the basic truism that a democracy never answers terror with terror in the context of the employment of military force in self-defense. The United States is absolutely obligated under international law to follow the law of war as well as all applicable international and customary laws. By all level headed assessments, the American military has done an outstanding job in the combat activities in Afghanistan, Iraq, and Syria in abiding by the law of armed conflict, while caring for basic humanitarian needs of civilians caught up in the conflict. As the world's leading democracy, it is imperative that the United States continues to exercise the lawful use of military force in accordance with the letter and spirit of the rule of law or face the possibility that it will be battling the children of hate and terrorism in the next generation.

The twenty-first century is still young, but it does not appear that the road to promoting human rights and democracy will be an easy task. Accordingly, deterrence must always stand as the central pillar of national security. In turn, understanding that totalitarian regimes will respond to the rattle of the saber means that the United States must always maintain a saber that can be rattled, and used, if necessary. The Trump Administration understood this factor.

2.7 Questions for Discussion

1. *War or simply a metaphor*? Was the War on Terror a real war or just political rhetoric? Can "war" be made against a group? In *Montoya v. United States* 180 U.S. 261 (1901), the Court considered whether or not a band of Indians that had broken away from the Mescalero Apache Indian reservation in Arizona to commit a series of hostile and murderous acts would activate the Indians Depredation Act, holding the tribe and the United States government liable for civil damages. The Court held that the tribe could not be held liable for the terrorist acts of the group that "was carrying on a war against the Government as an independent organization." Why is determining whether the War on Terror is a real war the central premise from which all legal issues should be viewed?

2. *Does al-Qa'eda and ISIS qualify as virtual-States?* The so-called *Al Qa'eda Training Manual*, captured by British authorities in a 2000 raid on the home of Nahihal Wadih Rashie (available at www.fas.org/irp/world/para/aqmanual.pdf) is considered by some to be irrefutable evidence of al-Qa'eda's ability to wage global war.

Selected Bibliography

Grotius, Hugo. PROLEGOMENA TO THE LAW OF WAR AND PEACE, 1957.

Kellogg-Briand Pact of Aug. 27, 1928, 2 U.S.B.S. 732 (1930).

Kirkpatrick, Jeanne J. Speech at the Jonathan Institute's Conference on International Terrorism. Washington, D.C. June 25, 1984.

League of Nations Covenant, Treaty of Versailles, 2 U.S.B.S. 43.

McNeill, William H. THE PURSUIT OF POWER, 1982.

Chapter 3

Necessity and Rationale for the Law of War—Lessons from My Lai

Nothing is new under the sun.

—Ecclesiastes 1: 9-10

It is often remarked that what we learn from history is that we learn nothing from history. This truism has been attributed to the German philosopher Georg Hegel, but the principle is certainly one of ancient origins, reflecting the fact that the human race has generally exhibited a total inability to learn even the most elementary historical lessons. Of course, the tragedy is that this need not be so; mankind can learn from history. Indeed, if history teaches mankind anything about avoiding the mistakes and disasters of the past, it is that it must first understand the historical lessons—lessons often realized only after the expenditure of incredible amounts of human blood and treasure—and then inculcate those lessons in each succeeding generation.

In the War on Terror, the most critical lesson was that the application of lawful violence is a necessary ingredient in defeating those who employ, or seek to employ, violence in an unlawful manner. The concept of lawful violence, of course, refers to the requirement that the international law of war must be fully followed. Those who violate the law of war commit war crimes.

To a large degree, from Valley Forge (1778) to Afghanistan (2001) and Iraq (2003), the United States military can take full credit for a commendable record in its adherence to the law of war. This is because of its commitment to institutionalizing certain truisms which might be encapsulated in the old saw that "[a] right thing must be done in a right way or it is wrong."

Thus, defeating the enemy—a right thing—must be done under the law of war—in a right way—or the entire activity is wrong. This assessment is not only true in the day-to-day functioning of a democratic society, it is fundamentally necessary for the continuation of that democracy. On the other hand, there is no such thing as a "clean" war. In its War on Terror, America made a significant number of tactical errors in the use of its military, ranging from friendly fire incidents that killed American soldiers and the soldiers of its coalition parners, to the unintended deaths of non-combatants by coalition military fire power. While these tragedies were leveraged by some in order to criticize the legitimacy of the American led effort to employ force against its enemies on the battlefield, all such attempts to denigrate the United States pale in the wake of the prisoner abuse scandal at Abu Ghraib. The 2003 release of photographs of American soldiers abusing Iraqi detainees at the Abu Ghraib prison in Iraq created a firestorm of concern that threatened to derail several of the most fundamental policy and legal pillars on which America conducted the War on Terror. While it is now well established that the abuses were not systemic, they provided a propaganda bonanza to the terrorists.

Accordingly, it is necessary to explore the law of war and the rationale and necessity for abiding by those rules. Because these lessons are timeless, the very best lesson plan for the United States flows not from Abu Ghraib, but from a notorious war crime committed by American forces in the Vietnam War—the My Lai massacre.

The War on Terror involved the use of traditional combat techniques last seen in the 2003 war against Saddam Hussein, where two armed groups of soldiers engaged in open combat. It also involved the more troubling type of combat which Americans faced in Afghanistan and other parts of the Middle East and Africa, and encountered in larger measure in the Indo-China conflict, where the Viet Cong and their Communist allies regularly violated the law of war by refusing to wear distinctive uniforms, hiding amongst the civilian population, torturing and murdering American prisoners of war, and murdering noncombatants by the thousands. Tragically, the Vietnam War also saw several instances of abuse of the law of war by American soldiers, the most notorious being the massacre at My Lai. While American forces in Afghanistan, Iraq, and Syria generally exhibited broad compliance with the law of armed conflict and an understanding that ethical conduct and military prowess go hand in hand, it is absolutely imperative that the significance of the lessons learned at My Lai are revisited and impressed on every American soldier. Indeed, in the War on Terror the nation faced an illegal enemy combatant who engaged in the same tactics as the Viet Cong and who viewed our adherence to the rule of law as a weakness.

For many Americans, the knowledge of enemy violations of the law of war elicits a negative reaction to the United States being required to follow the law of war when the enemy does not. In other words, if the terrorists and allies of the terrorists do not abide by the rules, e.g., ISIS militants in Iraq and Syria decapitated many coalition soldiers and engaged in the wholesale slaughter of innocent civilians, why should America? For this reason it is imperative that individuals who are unfamiliar with the law of war understand both the basic rationale and the necessity for the law of war. This applies to the American people in general and, more importantly, to the fighting men who actually engage the enemy in combat.

Again, while it may seem out of place to discuss the law of war against the lessons learned at My Lai, there is no better model to serve as the perfect vehicle for learning or relearning the necessity and rationale for the rules of armed conflict. Furthermore, it is equally necessary that American forces impress upon their allies the need to comply with the law of war. In fact, reports filtered out of Afghanistan in 2002 that some of our Afghan allies had engaged in gross violations of the law of war.

One incident is said to have occurred in the case of the deaths of 200 Taliban prisoners of war that died while being transported by Afghan fighters in shipping containers from the battlefield to internment camps. Similarly, abuses by the new Iraq and Afghan security forces are becoming regular fare. Not only is America relentlessly scrutinized and judged on how it complies with the law of war, but the conduct of our allies is also factored into the assessment.

As a nation that is governed by the rule of law, it is vital that America validate—for itself and for the civilized world—the legitimacy of any conflict by the manner in which it conducts that war. Clearly, the United States cannot claim that its forces are the "good guys" unless the rules of armed conflict are meticulously observed. Enforcement of the rules of war is a demonstration to the world and the American people that America is waging a *jus in bello*. No doubt, as in the War on Terror, many times the attention of the world shifted from the murderous machinations of the al-Qa'eda and their like, to an extreme focus on how well the United States and its allies adhered to all aspects of the rule of law in battling these people. For better or worse, this phenomenon is a reality. No one shows interest regarding the fact that the "bad guys" behave in gross violation of the law of war as their very *modus vivendi*. After all, that is precisely why they are the "bad guys." On the other hand, the civilized world has an intense interest in how the "good guys" perform. If a State claims that their cause is just, they must act accordingly. Of course, this does not mean that the United States should tie the hands of its warfighters with absurd layers of supercilious rules of engagement.

3.1 The Law of War

Warfare is not a novel phenomenon: it is as old as human history itself. Even a cursory review of the practice reveals that all cultures and societies have participated in warfare, either in defense or in aggression. Prior to the adoption of the U.N. Charter, which mandates that the analysis for determining the legitimate use of force turn under the self-defense provisions of Article 51, the concept of waging a just war was known as *jus ad bellum*. *Jus ad bellum* encompassed several elements to include: (1) the nation had a just cause; (2) the nation was acting under the legitimate governing authority; (3) the nation had just intentions; (4) the nation issued a public declaration of the causes for the use of force and the intentions associated with the use of that force; (5) the nation considered the proportionality in the results; (6) the nation demonstrated that the use of force was only used as a last resort; and (7) there existed a reasonable hope of success.

As outlined in Chapter 2, international law no longer recognizes *jus ad bellum* as a viable legal tool in determining when military force is lawful. The bedrock rule of law is the U.N. Charter. Nevertheless, as a practical matter, *jus ad bellum* still has great moral weight in the context of demonstrating the validity of the use of force and ensuring the continuation of public support by a pluralistic society.

In tandem with the concept of *jus ad bellum*, the term *jus in bello* refers to just conduct in war or, simply put, abiding by the law of war. This means that a nation that goes to war engages enemy targets under the concepts of military necessity, proportionality, and unnecessary suffering. In contrast to *jus ad bellum*, *jus in bello* is still a recognized concept in international law. As a matter of fact, as long as mankind has practiced war there have been rules to lessen and regulate the attendant sufferings associated with warfare.

To the uninitiated in the study of war, it seems somewhat incongruent that one of mankind's most violent activities should be governed by rules of conduct. Some writers, such as Leo Tolstoy, have even argued that the very establishment of rules which seek to regulate warfare are per se immoral because such rules wrongfully cloak war with a form of legitimacy and are therefore counterproductive to the oft dreamed goal of eliminating the scourge of war. Tolstoy advanced the notion that the waging of war should not be regulated at all because "when it becomes too horrible, rational men will outlaw war altogether."

Fortunately, most serious thinkers reject this utopian attitude, acknowledging the necessity of rules of conduct to mitigate the various categories of sufferings that are the natural consequence of war. The law of war was never intended to be an idealistic proscription against war.

The current corpus of the law of war consists of all of those laws, by treaty and customary principles, which are applicable to warfare. Most nations have bound themselves by international agreements to follow the law of war. Those nations that have not signed these international agreements are nevertheless bound by them if the rules have reached the status of customary international law. Customary international law comes from observing past uniformities among nations of a norm or standard that has reached widespread acceptance in the international community. Evidence of customary international law may be found in judicial decisions, the writing of noted jurists, diplomatic correspondence, and other evidence concerning the practices of nations.

In general, the rules of warfare are focused both on the proper targeting of military objectives and the treatment of enemy detainees, prisoners of war, and other noncombatants. Examples of the law of war include such common sense rules as the requirement to treat prisoners and detainees humanely; they may not be abused under any circumstances. Also, the prohibition on targeting for military attack civilians or protected places, such as hospitals and religious sites, and the duty to treat all noncombatants with dignity and respect are integral components of the law of war.

The cornerstone of the law of war is a comprehensive international treaty known as the Geneva Conventions of 1949. Because it is so widely accepted every nation on the planet is absolutely obligated to abide by the Geneva Conventions of 1949, whether they have signed the Conventions or not. The 1949 Geneva Conventions come in four parts and cover four categories of concerns:

- Geneva Convention of August 12, 1949, for the Amelioration of the Condition of the Wounded and Sick in Armed Forces in the Field;
- Geneva Convention of August 12, 1949, for the Amelioration of the Condition of the Wounded, Sick, and Shipwrecked Members of Armed Forces at Sea;
- Geneva Convention of August 12, 1949, Relative to the Treatment of Prisoners of War; and
- Geneva Convention of August 12, 1949, Relative to the Protections of Civilian Persons in Time of War.

In the War on Terror, Congress never declared war under the authority granted in Article I of the Constitution. This fact makes absolutely no difference in regard to America's obligation to follow the law of war. In fact, the law of war immediately applies whenever there is an international armed conflict involving two or more States, regardless of how the parties to that conflict care to label the conflict under their own domestic law.

Mirroring the Geneva Conventions, the United States military has codified the law of war in Field Manual (FM) 6-27, The Commander's Handbook on the Law of Land Warfare. FM 6-27 affirms that the basic goal of the law of war is to limit the impact of the inevitable evils of war by:

- protecting both combatants and noncombatants from unnecessary suffering;

- safeguarding certain fundamental human rights of persons who fall into the hands of the enemy, particularly prisoners of war, the wounded and sick, and civilians; and
- facilitating the restoration of peace.

Violations of the law of war are called war crimes. In FM 6-27: "The term war crime is the technical expression for a violation of the law of war by any person or persons, military or civilian. Every violation of the law of war is a war crime." The definition in FM 6-27 would include both customary and treaty law within the parameters of the law of war.

War crimes are categorized as either grave breaches or simple breaches. The term grave breach is technically only related to those named violations set out as such in the Geneva Conventions. Grave breaches would include the following acts committed against persons or property specifically protected by the Geneva Conventions: willful killing; torture or inhuman treatment, including biological experiments; or willfully causing great suffering or serious injury to body or health.

Under the Geneva Conventions, each nation is under a strict obligation to search for all persons alleged to have committed grave breaches or war crimes. They must investigate the allegations of war crimes and if a grave breach of the law of war is discovered, the nation must either prosecute or extradite those so accused. It is the policy of the United States that all American military personnel so accused are prosecuted by military courts martial under the substantive provisions of the Uniform Code of Military Justice (UCMJ).

3.2 Voices from the Past—My Lai

Every army has its own mythology, its symbols of heroism as well as its symbols of shame. The Army of the United States is no exception. In the sphere of heroism, the American military has an incredible reservoir of noble and fantastic figures to draw from—men whose military proficiency and ethical conduct in combat have directly helped to maintain an impeccable American reputation for both battlefield excellence and strict adherence to the laws regulating warfare. More than any other army in modern history, the American army is able to proudly claim as its own some of the greatest soldiers in the history of warfare. Robert E. Lee and Douglas MacArthur certainly are two of the very best this country has ever produced and therefore the subject of much study in American military schools and academics.

Unfortunately, the United States military also has its figures of shame; soldiers who have engaged in blatant violations of the most fundamental and civilized rules regulating behavior in combat. While American misconduct is certainly an aberration and not the norm, this fact does not lessen the severity of the shame. Without question, each and every grave breach of the law of war represents a horrible scar on the credibility of the American armed forces, as well as on the civilized democracy which they are sworn by duty to protect.

The greatest emblem of American military shame in the twentieth century occurred during the Vietnam War, a war many Americans have yet to properly understand. While there were several cases of unlawful killings of unarmed civilians committed by American troops during the Indo-China War, by far the most violent, and hence the most infamous, has come to be called the My Lai massacre.

Of course, any discussion of American violations of the law of war during Vietnam in general, and at My Lai in particular, must be viewed against the background of the enemy's activities. In this context, American violations absolutely pale in comparison to the thousands upon thousands of command directed slaughters that were committed by the Communist regime of then North Vietnam and their Viet Cong allies. With respect to the American presence in Vietnam, My Lai can certainly be characterized as an aberration. Professor Rudy Rummel noted:

> The American record in Vietnam with regard to observance of the law of war is not a succession of war crimes and does not support charges of a systematic and willful violation of existing agreements for standards of human decency in time of war, as many critics of the American involvement have alleged. Such charges were based on a distorted picture of the actual battlefield situation, on ignorance of existing rules of engagement, and on a tendency to construe every mistake of judgment as a wanton breach of the law of war.

As was the case for the Taliban and al-Qa'eda in Afghanistan and the ISIS terrorists in Iraq and Syria, blatant violations of numerous provisions of the law of war, to include murder, torture, and intimidation, were standard policy for the Communists. In the estimate of Rummel, North Vietnam sponsored the slaughter of over one and a quarter million of its own people from 1945 to 1987. Included in this figure, since the fall of South Vietnam in 1975, are over 250,000 boat people and 250,000 other civilians who were either ruthlessly murdered outright or who perished in Communist death camps set up to "re-educate" all non-Communists. Sadly, these massive crimes have never been punished, much less acknowledged by numerous human rights groups who profess to care about such things. According to Rummel: "In sum, re-education was a label for revenge, punishment, and social prophylaxes. But unlike the Khmer Rouge who were too public about their mass killing, the Vietnamese regime at first cleverly hid it from the outside world."

Of course, the enemy's barbaric conduct offers little solace to the American conscience in the wake of My Lai. Misconduct by the enemy, be it the Communists of North Vietnam, the al-Qa'eda-styled terrorists, or the minions of Saddam Hussein, in no way justifies American violations of the law of war. For the Viet Cong and North Vietnamese, the strategy for a Communist victory was intentionally predicated on terror and propaganda; for the United States, the massacre at My Lai was a horrible contradiction.

3.3 Facts of My Lai

The hard facts relating to the My Lai massacre are now fairly certain, thanks to a thorough criminal investigation aimed at the perpetrators of the crime and a collateral administrative investigation ordered by the Secretary of the Army and headed by Lieutenant General W. R. Peers. Despite an initial cover-up by some of those associated with the crime, the enormity of the atrocity made it unlikely that it could long be kept secret, although for well over a year the general public knew nothing of the incident.

On March 16, 1968, an American combat task force of the 23rd Infantry Division (the Americal Division) launched an airmobile assault into the village complex of Son My in the province of Quang Ngai, South Vietnam. As was the case for all such operations, the attack was executed only after the commander of the task force, Lieutenant Colonel Frank Barker (the task force was called Task Force Barker), had assembled the key junior commanders for a final review of the details of the combat operation. This briefing, which took place on March 15, 1968, involved discussions on the positioning of helicopters, artillery preparation, and the specific assignments of the three companies that comprised the task force. While the other two companies provided blocking and support functions, Charlie Company, commanded by Captain Ernest Medina, would take the primary responsibility for battling any enemy resistance encountered in the village.

At the briefing, the commanders were reminded that intelligence reports had indicated that the village complex was a staging area for the 48th Viet Cong local force battalion and that the Americans could expect an enemy force of up to two hundred and fifty soldiers. In short, the United States soldiers anticipated that they would be outnumbered by the enemy. Still, having yet to engage any enemy forces in direct combat, the Barker Task Force saw the operation as an opportunity to finally fight the ever-elusive Viet Cong in the open.

The intelligence regarding a large enemy force proved to be incorrect. When the American combat forces landed they soon found that the village was occupied almost totally by noncombatants. Although the civilians offered no resistance whatsoever, some of the members of Charlie Company went on a command directed killing spree. Under the direct supervision of several company grade officers, First Lieutenant William L. Calley, Jr., being the most notorious, American troops murdered well over 200 unarmed South Vietnamese civilians.

Since the largest killing of civilians occurred in the hamlet of My Lai, known to the Americans by the nickname of "Pinkville," a part of the Son My complex, the entire massacre came to be known as the My Lai massacre. The murdered consisted primarily of women, children and old men; some shot in groups, others as they fled. At My Lai proper most of the civilians had been methodically herded into large groups and then gunned down, primarily under the direct supervision of Lieutenant William Calley.

In addition to the unlawful killing of civilians, the soldiers engaged in the destruction of most of the homes and in the killing of the domestic animals in the village. Several cases of rape were also reported to have taken place during the killing spree. When it was over, the statistics told the story: one American soldier in Charlie Company had been wounded by friendly fire and hundreds of South Vietnamese women, children, and old men were dead.

The only positive aspect of the incident was the fact that some of the American soldiers had either refused to participate or had openly attempted to halt the killings. Chief Warrant Officer Two (CW2) Hugh C. Thompson, Jr., was one of those who took specific actions to halt the murders. Tasked with piloting one of the helicopters during the operation, CW2 Thompson testified that he noticed large numbers of "wounded and dead civilians everywhere." Assuming that the Americans on the ground would assist those who were wounded—as was the standard procedure—CW2 Thompson began to mark the location of the wounded Vietnamese civilians with smoke canisters as he flew overhead. To his horror, he witnessed the exact opposite. Drawn to the smoke, American soldiers were shooting the wounded that CW2 Thompson had so accurately marked. Still only partially realizing the full impact of what was happening on the ground, CW2 Thompson landed his helicopter in My Lai, near a large drainage ditch filled with dead and dying civilians. As he began to assist those Vietnamese who were still alive to leave the area, Lieutenant Calley and a handful of troops approached.

When CW2 Thompson asked for assistance in caring for the civilians, Lieutenant Calley made it clear that he intended to kill the remaining noncombatants. CW2 Thompson recalled that Lieutenant Calley said: "The only way you'll get them [the civilians] out is with a hand grenade." However, instead of backing down from the designs of his superior officer, CW2 Thompson quickly ordered his M60 machine gunner, Private First Class Lawrence Colburn, to open fire on the American soldiers if they came any closer to the remaining civilians. CW2 Thompson then placed all the civilians he could on his helicopter and ferried them to safety.

3.4 My Lai Comes to Light

The initial attempts to cover up the crime could not quell the nightmares of those who had witnessed the slaughter. Rumors of the massacre persisted, coming to a boiling point when an ex-serviceman named Ron Ridenhour sent a secondhand account of the massacre to President Richard Nixon, "twenty three members of Congress, the Secretaries of State and Defense, the Secretary of the Army, and the chairman of the Joint Chiefs of Staff." Ridenhour had written a four-page letter that chronicled detailed information from several of the soldiers who had either taken part in the bloody killings or had witnessed it firsthand.

Ron Ridenhour's letter received prompt attention both in the media and in the legislative and executive branches of government. Needless to say, the initial military reaction was one of disbelief; no one believed that a massacre of that magnitude could have been committed by American soldiers or that the massacre "could have remained hidden for so long."

As the horrible truth of the crime became known, the army quickly launched the comprehensive Peers Commission investigation, popularly known as the Peers Report. At the same time the general public tasted the horror of the My Lai massacre through a series of gruesome photographs of the dead which had been taken by a former army photographer named Ronald Haeberle. The color photographs appeared in the December 1969 issue of *Life* magazine.

3.5 Impact of My Lai

In the subsequent UCMJ judicial actions associated with the murders at My Lai, criminal charges were brought against four officers and nine enlisted men. Twelve other officers were charged with military type offenses associated with the cover-up. Of these, only Lieutenant William Calley was convicted. The other officers and enlisted men either had the charges against them dismissed or were found not guilty at their courts martial.

Tried before a military panel composed of six officers, Lieutenant Calley was found guilty of the premeditated murder of twenty-two noncombatants and of assault with intent to murder a two-year-old child. Although Calley was sentenced to a dismissal and confinement at hard labor for life, the convening authority reduced this to a dismissal and twenty years at hard labor, and the Secretary of the Army further reduced the sentence to a dismissal and ten years at hard labor.

Aside from the issue of individual culpability for those involved in the massacre, My Lai had a devastating impact on the outcome of the Vietnam War. Given the total lack of any semblance of a grand strategy on the part of the United States to win the war, it can be argued that this atrocity did as much to harm the survival of an independent South Vietnam as any other single event in the Indo-China War. The public revelation of this massacre not only solidified the anti-war movement in the United States, but it cast a pall of confusion and disgust over the nation at large that significantly contributed to the eventual abandonment of South Vietnam to the Communist forces in the North following the Paris Peace Accords. Beginning in 1969, a vocal and radical minority of war protestors incorporated opposition to the American ground soldier to their general opposition to the War. For these people, the enemy was now the American soldier, not the Communists. Indeed, there is no question that the revelation of what happened at My Lai dealt a blow to the *esprit de corps* and professionalism of the United States Army that can still be felt to this very day.

3.6 Why Did My Lai Happen?

Taken out of the context of the social and political climates that were brewing in the United States in the late 1960s and early 1970s and viewed from a purely objective perspective, the immediate focus in the aftermath of the crime was summed up in a single word: "Why?" Why did it happen? How could so many American young men have become involved in such a heinous war crime? And, more importantly, how could the officers in command of the operation have ordered such atrocities or participated in the attempt to cover them up? To realize that some civilians were killed as a collateral matter through military action against legitimate military targets was one thing, to have ground forces intentionally shoot innocent noncombatants in cold blood was incomprehensible.

The Peers Report did not cite any one factor as the cause for the massacre at My Lai. While the panel observed that "what may have influenced one man to commit atrocities had had no effect on another," General Peers was determined that the final report should reflect some explanation as to why the massacre had occurred. Recognizing the inherent difficulty in finger pointing, the panel nonetheless identified several factors that seemed to be conducive to an environment which might have led to the grave breaches of the law of war. In fact, the so-called "Peers factors" are a witches' brew that would similarly apply to any war, particularly a conflict like Iraq and Afghanistan in which the enemy has no regard for the rule of law.

The lack of proper training in the law of war was a common theme in the interviews of the witnesses and subjects involved in My Lai. Perhaps the most graphic illustration of this factor was reflected at the trial of Lieutenant Calley when he testified that the classes on the Geneva Conventions conducted during Officer Candidate School were inadequate. In any event, the Peers Report entered specific findings that the soldiers that made up Task Force Barker had not received sufficient training in the "Law of War (Hague and Geneva Conventions), the safeguarding of noncombatants, or the Rules of Engagement." Although the requirements set out in United States Army Republic of Vietnam (USARV) Regulation 350-1, dated November 10, 1967, made it clear that, at a minimum, all soldiers were required to have annual refresher training on the Geneva Conventions, in many cases there was no command emphasis on this requirement. Hence, to that degree, the individual soldier did not know what was required of him.

Pocket-sized guidance cards, which were a mandatory issue item to all soldiers to assist in learning and abiding by the law of war, were usually never read and seldom lasted past the first monsoon rains. In addition, Military Assistance Command Vietnam (MACV) Directive 20-4, which required the immediate reporting of all violations of the law of war, was seldom stressed by the command structure.

Regardless of the deficiencies in providing training in the law of war, the Peers Report did not find this to be a significant reason for the grave breaches of multiple murders which occurred at My Lai. Such deficiencies in training might excuse minor or technical breaches of the law of war, but not the grave *malum in se* breaches. The members of the Commission correctly noted that "there were some things a soldier did not have to be told were wrong—such as rounding up women and children and then mowing them down, shooting babies out of mother's arms, and raping." It was patently obvious to the Commission that some of the members of the company were simply cold-blooded criminals dressed in military uniforms, both enlisted and officers. Clearly these individuals found themselves in an environment where there was little, if any, deterrence to the overt expression of their criminal propensities.

A tendency by some of the members of Charlie Company to view the Vietnamese people as almost subhuman was thought to be another factor which may have contributed to the massacre. Of course, the use of derogatory terms to describe the Vietnamese as nothing but "gooks," "dinks," or "slopes" was not uncommon during the Vietnam War. In fact, soldiers in all wars have developed derogatory phrases to describe their enemies; it is easier to dispatch an enemy who can be disparaged. In the My Lai case, however, the Peers Report concluded that some of the members of Charlie Company had carried this tendency to dehumanize the enemy to an unreasonable extreme, viewing the "Vietnamese [people] with contempt, considering them subhuman, on the level of dogs."

To discover the reason for this degree of hatred, the Peers Report had a detailed background analysis done on each individual in Company C. The results showed nothing unusual. The company was an average unit with 70 percent of the troops having high school diplomas and nineteen having some college credits. The reason for the hatred was a result of a combination of several factors, the greatest of these merely a reflection of the locked-in arrogance inherent in the human soul, and the least, but more common, related to the frustration of having to fight an enemy who refused to abide by the law of war.

One of the most telling factors listed in the Peers Report dealt with examining the nature of the enemy that infested South Vietnam, with the implicit criticism that the United States military was never allowed to take the war to the real enemy—North Vietnam. In the South, the United States military was asked to carry out primarily defensive operations against a well-trained and well-equipped guerilla force that could not be distinguished from the local population and that refused to abide by the established principles of the law of war. The Peers Report stated:

> They would set up their bunkers in villages and attack from the midst of helpless civilians. Thus, surrounding themselves with and using innocent civilians to protect themselves is in itself a war crime and makes them criminally responsible for the resulting civilian dead....[T]hey would also directly attack villages and hamlets, kill the inhabitants, including children, in order to panic the civilians in the area and cause social chaos that the communist then could exploit.

Like the al-Qa'eda and the sectarian murderers of ISIS, the Viet Cong and regular North Vietnamese Army soldiers knew their environment; they knew every path, trail, and hut in their area of operation. In addition, whether by brute force, which included public torture and execution, or by psychological intimidation, the Viet Cong could count on the local support of the civilian population for shelter, food, and intelligence. As such, it was not uncommon for women and children to actively participate in military operations against American forces. With women and children participating in combat activities, by laying booby traps, serving as scouts or actually bearing arms, the American soldier had to disregard the traditional indicators such as sex and age as criteria for categorizing the noncombatant and concentrate instead on the extremely difficult issue of hostile intent. The Peers Report recognized this dilemma:

> The communist forces in South Vietnam had long recognized our general reluctance to do battle with them among the civilian populace and had used that knowledge to our tactical and strategic disadvantage throughout the history of the war in Vietnam. Exploitation of that reluctance by... [the enemy] forces caused a distortion of the classic distinction between combatants and noncombatants.

The difficulty of determining friend from foe was also woefully apparent in regards to the military-aged male Vietnamese. Having developed an incredible system of underground tunnels and caves, members of the Viet Cong and North Vietnamese Army were able to appear and disappear at will. Also, when under pressure, it took only seconds to remove all military insignia or equipment and to blend in with the local population.

Without question, the use of guerilla tactics, characterized by a heavy reliance on booby traps and hit-and-run missions, had a tremendous adverse psychological impact on the American commanders and their troops. In numerous interviews, the Peers Report noted that the general attitude of the soldier was one of extreme tension at engaging this unseen enemy, an enemy who hid behind women and children and would not come out in the open to do battle.

Consequently, every civilian was viewed as a potential threat, every inch of ground as hiding a potential booby trap or mine. Descriptive terms such as "keyed up" were frequently used to describe the apprehension and frustration associated with going out on patrol or, in many cases, just being in friendly villages. It was not uncommon for a friendly village to be visited by the Communists on any given night, setting landmines that would kill Americans the next day. Consequently, some of those who testified before the Peers Commission naturally assumed that the "effects of mines and booby traps were the main reason for the atrocities committed by the task force." This view is incorrect. While such factors undoubtedly contributed to the extraordinary level of tension in the Barker task force, it would be far too simplistic to rely on the illegal warfighting tactics of the enemy as the primary reason for the atrocity. If this factor was the main cause for My Lai, one would have expected many massacres similar to My Lai to have taken place throughout Vietnam.

Taking strong note of the overall organizational problems throughout the Army structure in Vietnam, the Peers Report actually believed that certain specific organizational problems in Task Force Barker "played the most prominent part in the My Lai incident." In focusing on Task Force Barker, it was apparent that the lack of staff personnel was a serious impediment to effective command and control. The task force "could hardly function properly, particularly in such matters as development of intelligence, planning and supervision of operations, and even routine administration."

One of the dominant characteristics of the Vietnam War was the lack of effective organization in the United States Army's force structure. From brigades to platoons, shortages of personnel and frequent rotations resulted in ad hoc arrangements regarding the composition of military units. Adding to the organizational deficiencies was the influx of poorly trained or ill-disciplined troops who were on "short" tours of a year. The short tour ensured problems in command and control; by the time the soldier had gained the necessary experience to be an effective member of the unit, he was eligible for transfer back to the "States." In the realm of directing combat operations, the lack of effective command and control can be disastrous. Indeed, the majority of abuses of detainees in the War on Terror have occurred at the hands of ill-trained and ill-disciplined National Guard and Reserve units.

Along with the general organizational problems in the task force, there was the lack of clear plans and orders concerning the operation into Son My. Because the entire operation was based on intelligence that anticipated a large enemy force in the area, the American soldiers initially expected that they were going to be outnumbered by at least two to one. In addition, the task force leaders regularly employed the term "search and destroy" without providing an adequate definition to the troops. The phrase search and destroy was never meant to provide license to kill whatever was encountered on an operation, despite the connotation of the term. In this regard, the Peers Report found that no instructions were ever given as to how to handle the civilians that might be encountered during the Son My operation.

In the final analysis, the organizational problems outlined above contributed to an overall atmosphere that made the events at My Lai possible. But the real pin in the grenade was the most fundamental aspect of the command and control problem—lack of leadership at the ground level of the operation.

3.7 Leadership

The constant mental and emotional strain associated with combat conditions is certainly exacerbated by having to face enemies the likes of al-Qa'eda and ISIS who engage in violations of the law of war, but the factor that weighed the heaviest in explaining the massacre at My Lai was none of the four discussed above. Rather, it was the lack of responsible leadership at the very level where it was most critical—at the junior officer level. Although the Peers Report faulted all levels of command—"[i]t appears...that at all levels, from division down to platoon, leadership or the lack of it was perhaps the principal causative factor in the tragic events before, during, and after the My Lai operation"— the direct underlying deficiency most certainly rested at the company and platoon level. One of the participants of the massacre, Private Paul Meadlo recalled the orders of his officer:

> You know what to do with them, [Lieutenant] Calley said, and walked off. Ten minutes later he returned and asked, "Haven't you got rid of them yet? I want them dead. Waste them."...We stood about ten to fifteen feet away from them [a group of 80 men, women and children herded together] and then he [Lieutenant Calley] started shooting them. I used more than a whole clip—used four or five clips.

By virtue of the chain of command structure of the military, the primary responsibility for ensuring adherence to the law of war rests on the officer corps, with particular professionalism demanded of those junior officers at the platoon and company level, where soldiers are most apt to encounter the vast majority of issues associated with the law of war. Simply put, soldiers are expected to obey the law of war and their officers are expected to see that they do.

In their 300-page report on the Abu Ghraib abuse cases from the Iraq War, the Department of the Army Inspector General mirrored the Peers Commission finding that "in some cases, abuse was accompanied by leadership failure at the tactical level." Another 2003 report, entitled the Taguba Report, issued by Major General Antonio Taguba, found that leadership failure was a critical problem within the chain of command at the Abu Ghraib prison. Interestingly, although several of the soldiers who were charged with abuse contended that they were ordered to commit the abuses, both reports concluded that the abuses at Abu Ghraib were not the result of soldiers following orders from superiors.

Of course, the difficult issue is not how to deal with those soldiers or officers who in their individual capacities violate the law of war—they are punished by military courts martial. Rather, the real difficulty is presented by the officer who orders his soldiers to commit war crimes, or who knowingly fails to control those under his command who violate the law of war. Clearly, the difficulty at My Lai was a result of command-directed breaches of the law of war in the context of lawful versus unlawful orders. Beginning with the premise that all soldiers are expected to obey lawful orders and are subject to courts martial if they do not, how should one expect the soldier to react to an unlawful order, assuming, of course, that the soldier can even recognize the order as unlawful?

In considering the question of whether a superior order constitutes a valid defense, military courts must take into consideration the fact that obedience to lawful military orders is the duty of every member of the armed forces; that the latter cannot be expected, in conditions of war discipline, to weigh scrupulously the legal merits of the orders received; that certain rules of warfare may be controversial; or that an act otherwise amounting to a war crime may be done in obedience to orders conceived as a measure of reprisal. At the same time, it must be borne in mind that members of the armed forces are bound to obey only lawful orders.

Furthermore, soldiers may not normally rely on the defense of superior orders should they obey an unlawful order; they are responsible for their own acts or omissions. When the defense of superior orders is raised, however, a two-tier test is applied. The first tier is a subjective one concentrating on whether or not the accused knew that the order was illegal. If the accused did not know that the order was illegal then the inquiry shifts to what the accused could reasonably have been expected to know regarding the legality of the order. "The fact that the law of war has been violated pursuant to an order of a superior authority…does not constitute a defense…unless [the accused] did not know and could not reasonably have been expected to know that the act ordered was unlawful." Although the objective tier of the two-part test draws upon the reasonable man standard, it is really a reasonable man under the stresses present in that particular combat environment.

Moreover, the job of distinguishing the legitimacy of the orders of a superior must be viewed against the backdrop of the entire concept of enforced discipline, extending from boot camp until discharge. The requirement for enforced discipline is absolutely essential to ensure that in the unnatural conditions of the combat environment soldiers will be able to function properly. No army could ever survive without a system promoting genuine and enforced discipline, which is firmly rooted in the requirement to obey the directions of superiors. It follows then, that if soldiers are expected to obey all lawful orders, they cannot be expected to scrupulously weigh the legal merits of orders received under the stresses of combat.

Accordingly, this means that the officer corps of any army must be filled with only the finest available men and women. Nowhere is this requirement more essential than in the selection and placement of the men who serve as officers in combat units. Only men of the highest moral caliber and military skill should be assigned the responsibility of combat command. In commenting on leadership skills for officers, General George S. Patton, Jr., correctly stated, "If you do not enforce and maintain discipline, you [officers] are potential murderers."

Under the concept of command responsibility or indirect responsibility, commanders can be charged with violations of the law of war committed by their subordinates if they ordered the crimes committed or knew that a crime was about to be committed, had the power to prevent it, and failed to exercise that power. In the United States, this standard has come to be called the Medina standard, so named for Captain Ernest Medina.

A second standard for indirect responsibility for commanders that has been the object of much debate and is recognized only in the United States is the Yamashita standard. The Yamashita standard is named for the World War II Japanese general, Tomoyuki Yamashita, who was tried before a military commission for war crimes committed by soldiers under his command. The primary charge against Yamashita revolved around the 20,000 Japanese sailors who went on a murder and rape rampage in Manila near the end of the war. Although the prosecution was unable to prove that Yamashita ordered the crimes or even knew about them, he was convicted under a "should-have-known" standard. This should-have-known theory held that if, through normal events, the military commander should have known of the war crimes and did nothing to stop them, he is guilty of the actions of his soldiers. This should have known standard applies only when the war crimes are associated with a widespread pattern of abuse over a prolonged period of time. In such a scenario, the commander is presumed to have knowledge of the crime or to have abandoned his command.

Herein is the underlying tragedy at My Lai and the essential lesson for battling terrorists, be it in Iraq or Afghanistan: several of the junior officers on the scene were totally inadequate, not only in moral character and integrity, but also in basic military skills. As exhibited by their gross behavior, these officers were completely unworthy of the responsibility of command.

When one details the background of William Calley, the centerpiece of the command-directed killings, it is not surprising to discover that he was not the type of individual who should have been charged with leadership responsibilities of any nature. Having flunked out of a junior college in Miami, Florida, Calley moved west before enlisting in the army in 1966. Once in the army, Calley was somehow selected to attend Officers Candidate School, where he graduated despite poor academic marks. Assigned to the field as a platoon leader in a combat unit, the soldiers under his command quickly discovered that Lieutenant Calley did not even understand basic military combat skills. As one rifleman in the platoon put it, "I wonder how he ever got through Officer Candidate School. He [Calley] couldn't read no darn [sic] map and a compass would confuse his ass."

In summation, the factor that most directly resulted in the crimes at My Lai clearly rests on the shoulders of a few junior officers on the ground, Lieutenant William Calley being one of the worst. All the evidence suggests that it was Lieutenant Calley who initiated much of the murdering, acting both in his individual capacity and, far more shamefully, in his capacity as an officer in charge of subordinates. Abusing the authority of his position, Lieutenant Calley directly ordered the soldiers under his command to commit murder; some of the men obeyed while a few did not. While no one can pardon the behavior of those who carried out the illegal orders, the real tragedy of My Lai was the absence of competent and virtuous leadership.

Instead of setting the standard for moral conduct, Calley performed in the exact opposite fashion. He represented the antithesis of what a commander should be. As Sun Tzu laid out almost 500 years before Christ, "[t]he commander stands for the virtues of wisdom, sincerity, benevolence, courage, and strictness."

3.8 Lack of a Grand Strategy

A final factor that must be explored in any war and one that few commentators on Vietnam have properly gauged is the full impact that the lack of a grand strategy by the United States had on the outcome of the Indo-China conflict. In this regard, My Lai was possible due to the total and complete absence of a strategy to deal with the Communist-sponsored aggression against South Vietnam. At the beginning of the War on Terror President Bush established clear objectives and achieved those objectives quickly. His unequivocal vision for the total defeat of the Taliban government of Afghanistan in 2001 and the regime of Iraq's Saddam Hussein in 2003 could not have been clearer. The American military understood that vision and carried it out in a magnificent manner. Things became grossly confused when the Bush Administration decided to embark on nation building with an open ended date for keeping military troops on the ground. It would not be until President Trump took office in 2017 that a second grand strategy would spell a clear beginning of combat operations and an end—particularly in dealing with ISIS.

If the concept of a grand strategy is defined as the use of a nation's full national power to achieve a particular objective, it is clear that at no time did the United States have a grand strategy in Vietnam for dealing with the Communist aggression. On the other hand, it is just as obvious that the Communists had from the very beginning a complete and dedicated grand strategy for conquering all of Indo-China through the use of revolutionary warfare. Similarly, the al-Qa'eda attack on September 11, 2001, was certainly motivated by a grand strategy to incite the whole of the Arab world in a crusade against the West and against "moderate" Arab rulers.

The basic mechanics of a sound grand strategy takes advantage of one's strengths and the enemy's vulnerabilities, while neutralizing the enemy's strengths and one's own vulnerabilities. In practically every category of factors associated with the art of waging war, the Communists in Vietnam were able to fulfill this formula; the United States was not. Thus, while the Communists mobilized all of the people under their control in a unity of effort—from the military to the political—the United States consistently sought to disassociate the American people from the war.

In the sphere of combat operations in Vietnam, the Communists were particularly effective in drawing on their strengths. Conversely, the Americans typically refused to rely on their strengths. Aware that they were no match for the far superior power of American combat forces, the Communists primarily employed small hit and run tactics against selected targets; like the Saddam loyalists, they quickly discovered that engaging the United States military in conventional warfare was pure folly. Coupled with guerilla tactics deliberately focused on becoming the unseen enemy, the Communists illegally took advantage of the American respect for the law of war. By hiding themselves in civilian populations, the Communists intentionally sought to blur the distinction between the combatant and the noncombatant. In the words of commentator and author Thomas Begines, they were "hoping either for immunity from attack or to provoke…indiscriminate attack."

Establishing well-stocked sanctuaries in neighboring Cambodia and Laos, they were immune from defeat as long as the United States refused to seriously attack those bases. In short, the United States never effectually used the overwhelming strength of its military to subdue and defeat North Vietnam. Instead, American measures were confined to patrolling efforts in reaction to Communist attacks in the territory of South Vietnam.

Finally, in tandem with their guerilla tactics, the Communists relied heavily on all forms of propaganda, placing special emphasis on the ambiguity of words to erode the will of the United States to continue the war. For example, they falsely portrayed the conflict as a protracted war waged by agrarian reformers with no end in sight, while simultaneously promising a negotiated settlement at any moment.

In summation, the ultimate success of the Communist strategy in Vietnam rested primarily in the fact that the United States never developed a coherent overall strategy of its own. Necessarily, this mandated that the Communist's grand strategy would eventually prevail. What is surprising is that it was not until 1968 that the impact of not having a viable grand strategy became apparent to the American soldier. When it did, however, the painful beginning of the demoralization of the United States military quickly followed. As the attendant anti-war protests at home increased, many soldiers questioned the efficacy of their sacrifices in Vietnam. More importantly, the soldiers realized that the emphasis of the American leadership was not on achieving peace through a military victory, but on peace through negotiations—negotiations which constantly promised an end to the war at any time. As a consequence, no one wanted to be the last casualty in a war that was not supported at home and which the United States government refused to let the military win.

3.9 Rules of Engagement

The command by an American officer at the battle of Bunker Hill in 1775: "Don't shoot until you see the whites of their eyes." Since the start of the War on Terror in 2001, the United States has engaged in two major military actions—Iraq/Syria and Afghanistan. In those conflicts, the United States has lost more than 6,000 American lives, mostly in combat operations. While the war in Iraq is now completely at an end and ISIS has been geographically crushed, the war in Afghanistan ended without a final battlefield victory. As Afghan forces take responsibility for their own national security in 2021, insurgent groups have stepped up attacks across the region in order to regain lost ground and consolidate power in areas they control. Undoubtedly, Afghanistan will quickly revert back to its pre-9/11 configuration of competing tribal rivalries, criminal syndicates, and as a safe-haven for any number of radical Islamic terrorist groups, the chief being the Taliban.

In conjunction with the lack of a grand strategy in Vietnam, another factor that directly contributed to the failure were self-imposed so-called Rules of Engagement (ROE), many of them totally unreasonably crafted and imposed. Overly restricted ROE also plagued American fighters during much of the War on Terror.

In tandem with the strict mandates associated with the law of war, all Western democracies, to include the United States, self-impose ROE as restrictive additions to the law of war. These ROE are designed to further limit the application of the use of force in combat apart from the law of war. In both Iraq and Afghanistan the United States promulgated numerous ROE to further limit the use of force associated with combat operations. Furthermore, ROE have been changed many times over the years as dictated by political considerations. Indeed, as the fighting in Afghanistan continues, ROE are still subject to constant revision. While the efficacy of ROE can be argued as a matter of premise, it appears certain that some of the ROE promulgated are simply supercilious in nature and their overboard restrictions on the use of force have directly contributed to large numbers of American causalities. For the sake of distinction, this paper will refer to this category of ROE as "overly restrictive."

Unlike the law of war, which is static in nature until revised by international treaty or customary practice, ROE can be changed at any time based on political or policy objectives. While the rule of law provisions related to the law of war reflect fundamental concepts of human behavior that comport with universal moral values recognized across cultural lines—don't kill civilians, don't kill enemies that surrender, don't destroy civilian property, etc.—ROE address restrictions on behavior that are not intrinsic in nature. In many instances, the prohibited behavior set out in a ROE is extremely subtle and invariably produces random outcomes. Micromanaging the otherwise lawful use of force under the law of war, as ROE require, can result in confusion on the one hand, and inaction on the other. As a consequence, service members are often unsure what the ROE requires and may simply choose to do nothing for fear of violating the ROE.

Tragically, as a consequence of the proliferation of overly restrictive ROE during the War on Terror many service members were wrongfully accused of violating various applicable provisions. In some instances, the soldiers were unaware of the violation, but in others it was evident that even the highest levels of the chain of command itself were equally unclear about the application and function of a given ROE. Furthermore, in some instances similar violations of ROE by different actors were not punished equally. Not only were some service members disciplined by criminal action while others are disciplined by administrative action, in many cases service members received absolutely no punishment whatsoever for violations of ROE.

Additionally, some American administrations used overly restrictive ROE in an effort to create and manage a desired reputation in the national media and as well as in the international community. This was not a new phenomenon as a similar pattern of shifting ROE based on political objectives occurred during the Vietnam War. It is widely acknowledged that the ROE during the Vietnam War were equated to "micromanagement taken to the highest level." This level of micromanagement created by politicians defining the ROE rather than military experts created rules that were so restrictive and confusing that they ultimately ran counter to the military mission on the ground.

Like Vietnam, the insurgent tactics in Afghanistan and other locations (Iraq and Syria) made it nearly impossible for soldiers to distinguish between combatants and noncombatants. In this context, the War on Terror was also a fight against non-State actors and terrorist groups that observed no territorial boundaries and preferred targeting civilians. Enemy combatants hid amongst the general population and did not wear uniforms in an effort to challenge the ROE and make it difficult if not impossible for U.S. forces to discern civilians from combatants.

The basic conundrum is that one party fights by the ROE while the other does not—terrorists don't even follow the law of war. Predictably, the strategy of the enemy combatant is to use overly restrictive ROE to their own advantage. There is no argument that U.S. forces should uphold the law of war, however, much of the War on Terror's self-imposed ROE left soldiers with rules that simply could not be applied in a practical manner to defeat the enemy.

It is just as obvious today as it was over fifty years ago, when the term ROE was first coined, that by limiting the way in which our military engages and kills the enemy in combat the United States would suffer a greater loss of American lives at the tactical level of war. This loss of lives is only one byproduct. ROE can directly contribute to a loss of morale and fighting spirit that can directly contribute to defeat at the strategic level of war.

To the uninformed, the origin and function of ROE is certainly news. The assumption of the uninformed is that ROE and law of war are synonymous concepts. To the informed, however, it is a continuing reminder that the logical outcome to the employment of overly restrictive ROE spells extreme hazard or disaster to many troops in combat environments and in many cases can actually directly contribute to tactical and even strategic defeat. Tragically, the general ignorance associated with ROE is fueled by the a "sophisticated approach" to warfare which demands the use of overbearing ROE on our American forces under the naïve notion that the enemy will respond to our restrictive use of force with similar acts of kindness. In essence, our armed forces are ordered to fight the enemy with one hand tied behind their back. Ironically, the delusion of the sophisticated approach to warfare is so disoriented to reality that no one with any common sense can understand it.

Not surprisingly, during President Obama's tenure, the Bush-era ROE were tightened even further restricting the use of force. Amazingly, after years of having ROE imposed on the military planners by the political elites of the Executive Branch there was little serious critical thinking or analysis that addressed the basic premise regarding their necessity. At the end of the day, many critics argued that much of the ROE that were imposed on the American military were really byproducts of crusader arrogance by a government bent on using the military to promote political and social objectives that had nothing to do with winning an actual war.

ROE apply to both combat operations on the battlefield in time of war and contingency operations, also called military operations other than war (MOOTW). The term ROE is also employed in other arenas as well to include, for instance, maritime security. The how and when the military can employ force are set out in a standardized definition of ROE found in the *Department of Defense Dictionary of Military and Associated Terms*: "[D]irectives issued by competent military authority that delineate the circumstances and limitations under which U.S. [naval, ground, and air] forces will initiate and/or continue combat engagement with other forces encountered."

The actual term "rules of engagement" was coined during the Korean War and described the practice of restricting where American aircraft could fly and what they could target. The term was formally adopted in 1958 by the Joint Chiefs of Staff to pertain to restrictions on how American fighter pilots would respond in confrontations with Soviet aircraft during the Cold War. Then, with the decade-long war in Vietnam, myriad ROE were produced at all levels of command that applied to ground, sea, and air forces.

While it is true that all ROE are internally-imposed restrictions, there are many levels and types of ROE with which the military must comply. Today, the starting point for reviewing ROE begins with what is known as the Standard Rules of Engagement (SROE), which are written and promulgated by the Chairman of the Joint Chiefs of Staff. The SROE establish the basic policies and procedures governing the actions that ground commanders can take during all forms of military operations—ranging from terrorist attacks to prolonged conflict outside of the borders of the United States. The SROE represents the first indication that the leadership is making illegal or improper what the law of war would otherwise allow. Although all ROE recognize the inherent right of self-defense if attacked by an enemy, all ROE center on the concept of employing minimum force to complete any given activity, even at the expense of increased levels of harm to friendly forces.

As expected, the ROE below the SROE are generally classified documents and unavailable for public view. Nevertheless, ROE stem from two general arenas: (1) ROE that require the approval of the Secretary of Defense; and (2) ROE that allow the subordinate commanders to restrict the use of force regarding particular missions. In turn, ROE may also be distinguished by whether they are conduct-based ROE or status-based ROE. The first category of conduct-based ROE deal with self-defense matters, and the latter deals with the ability to use deadly force against a particular individual based on their identification as a hostile threat, e.g. an enemy combatant.

To better visualize the relationship of ROE to the use of force, it is helpful to understand that there are three basic areas of concern that directly impact the formulation of ROE: (1) national political objectives or national policy; (2) the operational requirements of the field commanders; and (3) the legal restrictions associated with the law of war. Obviously, national policy is the dominant ingredient in ROE. More than any other factor it shapes how the use of force will be applied and under what conditions. When political leadership is confused or disoriented regarding their goals and objectives, it is certain that disaster will quickly follow suit. For instance, when President Obama was asked by a CNN reporter in 2009 about how he would achieve victory in Afghanistan, he replied that he was "not comfortable with that word [victory]." If the Commander in Chief could not define victory, it was certain that disaster was waiting for the American military on the ground as President Obama launched his ill-fated 2009 "surge" which cost 1,000 American casualties and left the Taliban stronger than before the surge (see Chapter 4).

The final element of the rule of law simply means that the use of force comports with the law of war. This is perhaps the simplest factor, as ROE cannot exceed the restrictions of the law of war.

For better or worse, ROE serve as a dominant factor in military operations. Accordingly, they must be clear, concise, and comprehensive. In addition, all military personnel must receive them in a timely fashion to facilitate appropriate training prior to engaging in military operations, to include combat. Indeed, ROE must navigate the line between being too narrow and too overbroad. In many instances in the War on Terror, this requires distinction between combatants (armed forces) and non-combatants (civilians) during armed conflicts. This is critical, as American military forces are generally trained to employ the full use of force allowed under the law of war against enemy targets. In short, the nuances related to ROE that stress interaction with civilians and enemy forces hiding amongst civilians requires extensive and intensive training prior to actual combat. Obviously, specialized training in such ROE is a serious obligation for the commander to consider.

Of course, in the conflicts associated with the War on Terror where enemy forces did not wear uniforms and hid amongst the civilian population, the challenges were extremely difficult. While some may argue that without overly restrictive ROE non-combatants are unnecessarily endangered, the other side of the coin is that American forces are unnecessarily endangered by the imposition of overly restrictive ROE in such environments. In short, the national command authority should concentrate on outlined successful mission objectives that take into account the strategic goals of victory and not mire American forces in tactical combat actions that achieve nothing but American casualties. For example, in 1995 the author was the Staff Judge Advocate for the U.S. Army Special Forces, Fort Bragg, North Carolina, and was involved in providing input to the negotiating process for the ROE which were being proposed for the United Nations mission in Haiti. Since some of the very first forces on the ground would be "Green Berets," the author was extremely concerned about weapons and the restrictions on the use of force. Initial drafts of the ROE restricted American forces (as well as other UN forces) to the use of side-arms only under the bizarre notion that the Haitian people would therefore consider the multinational force as "peaceful" and not feel threatened. As the Staff Judge Advocate for all Army Special Forces, the author along with other American military commanders and their lawyers strongly objected to this inane ROE. The final ROE were subsequently revised to allow entering forces to carry a variety of light and heavy weapons in keeping with potential combat operations. Clearly, those responsible for drafting ROE must ensure that legitimate concerns are voiced at an early stage in ROE development, as limitations and constrictions result in loss of American lives in the field of battle.

On the positive side, ROE can serve a useful purpose by providing the solider with specific guidance on when, where, and how to use violence. As a practical matter a viable ROE must be written at the level where the seventeen to twenty-year-old can understand them. Accordingly, the ROE have to be simple. In turn, because the lower-commissioned officers and the non-commissioned officers enforce the ROE, it is imperative that this level of leadership completely understand their responsibility.

While violations of the ROE are not necessarily violations of the law of war, most ROE are set out as general orders and are thus punishable under the UCMJ if violated. For those who violate the ROE, the military command would generally charge the service member with a formal crime such as disobeying a lawful order. In many instances, however, the military does not charge the service member with a crime under the UCMJ but instead uses adverse administrative measures to punish. As stated, this tactic of punishment would also apply to a violation of the so-called tactical directive. While a service member has numerous due process rights when charged with a crime, due process rights associated with adverse administrative actions are far more limited in nature. Without some level of additional impartial review, the service member has few due process rights to defend himself from the all too common occurrence of abuse of power.

3.10 Lessons of My Lai

One of the most troubling issues for American soldiers is the realization that in many of the wars the United States has fought, the enemy has openly and repeatedly violated numerous provisions of the law of war. In the Vietnam War, the Communist forces regularly engaged in command-directed atrocities on a massive scale. Just in relation to the treatment of prisoners, for example, every single American prisoner of war was subjected to torture and maltreatment in flagrant violation of the Geneva Conventions.

For many American soldiers, knowledge of enemy violations presents an immediate negative response to the law of war. The realization that the enemy may often refuse to abide by the law of war prompts an immediate gut response: Why should I care about the rules if the enemy doesn't? Faced with such questions, it is not enough to simply inform the soldier that he will be punished for violations, it is imperative that the soldier understand the rationale for abiding by the law of war. Thus, it is critical that the soldier's question be answered so that he possesses a basic understanding of the entire concept of the development of rules regulating combat. There are three answers.

3.11 Lesson One—Rationale for the Law of War

Many people have some vague notion that rules regulating warfare came out of the aftermath of World War II or, at the most, World War I. Nothing could be further from the truth. As long as there have been wars there have been rules established to reduce the suffering to both the environment and to other humans. While some of these ancient rules would not be consistent with the modern humanitarian concepts reflected in the current law of war, it is interesting to note that many of the provisions in the modern law of war are derived directly from some of the earliest formulations of rules regulating warfare.

For example, in the book of *Deuteronomy*, the ancient Hebrews were given specific instructions on the protections that were to be afforded to the persons and property of an enemy city under siege. Generally, if the city surrendered, the inhabitants were not to be harmed. If the city refused to surrender, but was subsequently captured, no women or children were to be molested. In all cases, torture was absolutely prohibited. Similarly, protection for the environment was also codified; fruit trees located outside of a besieged city were protected from unnecessary damage; the fruit could be eaten but it was unlawful to cut down the trees.

To observe that the modern law of war rests firmly upon an ancient foundation of humanitarian concerns that are intrinsically acceptable is only one reason why the rules have enjoyed universal acceptance through time—the fact that such rules are morally valuable axioms only captures part of the truth as to their development and utility. Clearly, the historical development of rules regulating warfare also follows a general pattern of what might be termed pragmatic necessity. While many of the rules limiting suffering were undoubtedly based on humanitarian concerns, it can be argued that the basic rationales for having a law of war are rooted in several collateral principles of self-interest.

First, under the concept of reciprocity, nations would develop and adhere to laws of warfare because they were confident that the enemy would also do the same under a quid-pro-quo theory. This mutual assurance theory has long been recognized as not only a primary motivator for establishing rules regulating warfare, but as the centerpiece in almost every other function of international intercourse.

The second element in the historical development of the law of war centers on a similar vein of self interest, reflected so aptly by Alexander the Great's admonitions to his incredible army on the eve of practically every battle: "Why should we destroy those things which shall soon be ours?" Under this reasoning, particularly in the context of securing limited amounts of spoil, the destruction of anything beyond military targets to subdue the enemy's military forces would be neither beneficial nor reasonable. Under modern principles, similar violations of the law of war would not contribute to the goal of the collection of legitimate reparations, a measure often employed against the aggressor nation.

A third line of reasoning draws on the related fact that abuses seldom shorten the length of the conflict and are never beneficial in facilitating the restoration of peace. The targeting of nonmilitary property usually produces unwanted effects for those who engage in such activities. Despite the best efforts of historical revisionists to brush over the war crimes of Union General William T. Sherman, the event in American history that best illustrates this point comes from the illegal activities of General Sherman during the American Civil War. General Sherman's widespread looting and burning of Southern—black and white— civilian homes and personal property, coupled with the deliberate slaughter of all domesticated animals on his march through Georgia and the Carolinas in the last two years of the War did not significantly contribute to the collapse of the Confederacy. On the contrary, his brutal actions simply strengthened the resolve of Southerners to resist while sowing the seeds of hatred against "Yankees" for generations to come.

Clearly, the intelligent warfighter makes every effort to comply with and even exceed the requirements of the law of war, particularly in regard to the treatment of prisoners of war and noncombatants. Not only does humane treatment demonstrate the best evidence that your side is the one that is waging a *jus in bello*, but it often serves as the best avenue to counter enemy propaganda concerning law of war violations. As the pragmatic Prussian soldier and author, Karl von Clausewitz observed, "If we find that civilized nations do not…devastate towns and countries, this is because their intelligence exercises greater influence on their mode of carrying on war, and has taught them a more effectual means of applying force.…"

A fourth factor approaches the matter from a purely military perspective. Plainly put, the use of limited military resources for the destruction of civilian targets is a waste of assets and hence, detrimental to the goal of defeating the enemy's military. In short, such conduct is simply counterproductive because "it rarely gains the violator a distinct military advantage."

The final rationale, albeit of greater impact in an era characterized by the widespread dissemination of information, rests in the very nature of the modern civilized nation-state. States that adhere to the principles of democratic institutions and fundamental human rights will not tolerate activities that are conducted in defiance of the rule of law. As brought out so strongly by the My Lai incident, civilized societies will not provide the necessary homefront support for an army that is perceived as acting in violation of the law of war. Although in the radical totalitarian regime this factor is generally ignored, in the United States, as in all democratic societies, this element of homefront support is absolutely essential to any deployment and sustainment of military forces. The basic minimum standards of morality transcend national boundaries.

The necessity of homefront support is not always easy for the military to sustain. In part the difficulty rests in the associated phenomenon of "imputed responsibility." With reference to any military in a democratic society, the term imputed responsibility recognizes the fact that the acts of a few soldiers who engage in egregious abuses of the law of war are immediately imputed to the entire military establishment. For instance, because Lieutenant Calley and a handful of others murdered babies at My Lai, large segments of the public might tend to view all American soldiers in Vietnam as baby killers. To a large degree, the mass media feeds this phenomenon, as reflected by almost every Hollywood movie concerning the Vietnam War. In American cinema, the soldier is routinely depicted as engaging in abuses of the law of war or ingesting large quantities of illegal drugs. The fact that the vast majority of American soldiers did neither is not shown. Accordingly, the best way for the military to combat the concept of imputed responsibility is to make every effort to see that abuses do not occur and, if they do, promptly investigate and punish those proven to be guilty. Complete transparency must be the guide. Under no circumstances can a cover-up be justified—the light must be shed promptly and fully on all allegations of war crimes. The U.S. military learned this lesson from My Lai as demonstrated by the handling of the prisoner abuse cases in Iraq. Again, the military self-reported the individual acts of criminal behavior to the media and also launched its own investigation (the Taguba Report) prior to the photographs appearing in the media.

In the modern era, then, the law of war is based on a combination of rationales reflecting a mixture of pragmatism and moral concerns. The competent warfighter should understand that the factors include:

- humanitarian concerns based on moral precepts;
- the concept of reciprocity in behavior;
- the desire for reparations;
- the desire to limit the scope and duration of the conflict and to facilitate the restoration of peace;
- the effective use of military resources; and
- the necessity for securing homefront support.

3.12 Lesson Two—Soldiers Must Be Trained in the Law of War

The second lesson from My Lai needs little introduction—to be effective the law of war must be constantly taught to soldiers. To a large degree the United States military has long held an outstanding reputation for adherence to the law of war because of its commitment to training. Unfortunately, there have been periods where training has not been properly emphasized, providing fertile ground for violations of the law of war. Colonel H. Wayne Elliott, former Chief of the International Law Division at the Army's Judge Advocate General's School wrote that, the massacre at My Lai served as the "catalyst for a complete review of Army training in the law of war."

The United States Army has proponency for the law of war for all branches of the military. This means that the Army is responsible for developing and publishing the written doctrine. The current methodology for teaching the law of war attempts to tailor the training to the particular unit.

Since Special Operations Forces are a primary tool used on the ground in the War on Terror, it is efficacious to review the current level of training that these forces receive in the law of war. In short, Special Operations Forces not only receive constant classroom instruction on the law of war but also have difficult law of war questions dealing with special operations built into their training missions which are constantly practiced. The much-reported event in the 1991 Gulf War in which an Army Special Forces team had to choose between killing an Iraqi girl and being discovered by enemy forces was actually a well-rehearsed scenario resulting in a correct application of a very difficult law of war issue. The girl was spared.

A red thread that runs throughout the issue of training in the law of war is the role of the military lawyer or judge advocate. Since Vietnam, the Army has dramatically expanded its use of military attorneys to ensure that its forces comply with all aspects of the law of war. All combat forces have an operational law attorney assigned at the Division level. Likewise, all Army Special Forces Groups have a specialized military attorney assigned. The function of this judge advocate is not only to ensure compliance with and adherence to the law of war, but to examine the full range of international and domestic laws that affect specifically legal issues associated with the planning for and deployment of United States forces overseas in both peacetime and combat environments. This is a major change from the role of the judge advocate in Vietnam—a role primarily delegated to the administration of criminal law, well behind the front lines of combat.

Currently, the function of the judge advocate in the field can be divided into two elements—he has both preventive and active roles. In the preventive role, the judge advocate advises commanders on potential issues dealing with rules of engagement, targeting enemy military objectives, and all other relevant aspects of the law of war. In addition, the judge advocate is deeply involved in providing instruction and training to soldiers within his particular command.

In the active role, the judge advocate is involved in the investigation of allegations of war crimes. The requirement to investigate is either carried out directly by the legal officer or is closely monitored by the judge advocate. Finally, judge advocates will be called upon to either prosecute or defend those charged with violations.

3.13 Lesson Three—Preventing Violations of the Law of War in the War on Terror

As noted, the importance of professional conduct on the battlefield extends to the strategic, political, and social realms. In turn, the primary responsibility for inculcating professional conduct falls directly on the officer corps. Nowhere is the need for training in the law of war more critical than in the proper development of the military's officer corps. Thus, no officer should be given the responsibility of leadership without two essential factors: (1) technical proficiency in the profession of arms; and (2) the highest ethical and moral courage. Under the ancient Roman adage that no man can control others until he can first control himself, officers must be thoroughly prepared in both of these areas. Combat command should only be offered to officers who have been thoroughly scrutinized and put through extensive field training exercises designed to test their reaction under combat pressures.

There can be no question that the primary cause of My Lai was the lack of disciplined control, i.e., the lack of any real leadership. Such leadership is absolutely essential in preventing war crimes. The associated tensions set out by the Peers Report were not the real problem at My Lai—tensions of combat will always be present in one form or another. The real problem was in the effective control of those tensions. Control of warfighting pressures rest not only with the individual soldier but directly with his commanding officer. Sadly, many of the officers in Charlie Company not only allowed the illegal manifestations of battlefield stress to be exhibited by their troops, but through their orders and example they initiated and actively participated in the atrocities. There can be little doubt that proper officer leadership could have prevented the murders at My Lai. Consequently, the primary responsibility for these crimes is on their heads. The function of leadership is to hold up the professional torch at all times, at all costs.

Great armies are neither created, nor sustained, by accident. To a large degree, great armies are maintained by officers who understand, and then are able to apply, the lessons of military history. In this respect, no officer can truly be called a professional without a firm commitment to the moral and ethical rules regulating combat. Quite naturally, this objective requires constant training, as well as a comprehensive understanding of one's moral roots. Consequently, the military of the United States must constantly reaffirm its commitment to the positive values of military proficiency and ethical integrity.

Currently, U.S. Army training doctrine places a great deal of emphasis on the concept of duty and still uses General Robert E. Lee as its illustration to all soldiers. For instruction, inspiration and inculcation, American officers can find no better role model than General Lee. While some may forget, ignore, or purposefully deny the role that Lee has had in shaping our modern military, to those who are objective students of history his impact on American tactics and humanitarian concerns can never be obscured.

Lee's tactics and civility have become ingrained into the character of the United States military establishment. Although these qualities certainly existed before the emergence of Lee the general, his genius and humanity have epitomized and translated them into the very fabric of subsequent American military doctrines. For this reason, any analysis of the United States military, either in terms of tactics or comportment with the law of war, that ignores the tremendous contributions of Lee can never be more than a fraction of the truth.

For example, although some Southerners criticized Lee for not authorizing lawful reprisals to deter widespread Union violations of the law of war, General Lee firmly believed that reprisals were not the answer. Responding to a letter from the Confederate Secretary of War regarding possible Confederate responses to widespread Union atrocities committed by Union forces under Sherman, Lee reiterated his position in the summer of 1864:

> As I have said before, if the guilty parties could be taken, either the officer who commands, or the soldier who executes such atrocities, I should not hesitate to advise the infliction of the extreme punishment they deserve, but I cannot think it right or politic, to make the innocent… suffer for the guilty.

With Americans fighting Americans, Lee knew that the long-term effects of engaging in reprisals would not be profitable for the nation or the South. He was undoubtedly correct; Lee's strict adherence to the rules regulating warfare, coupled with his firm policy prohibiting reprisals, contributed greatly to the healing process after the Civil War.

One of the driving forces that created the legend of Lee, the ultimate gentleman, was his unmatched sense of humanity. In a 1902 article, the *Southern Historical Society Papers* called Lee "the soldier-gentleman of tradition, generous, forgiving, silent in the face of failure…a hero of mythology." No matter how great the temptation for legitimate reprisals, a concept well-recognized in international law, R. E. Lee would not stoop to the level of his enemies. This is one of the reasons he has been called the "Christian General," as reflected in his address to the troops as they marched into Pennsylvania during the Gettysburg campaign of 1863: "It must be remembered that we make war only on armed men, and that we cannot take vengeance for the wrongs our people have suffered without lowering ourselves in the eyes of…Him to whom vengeance belongeth." Instructing his officers to arrest and punish all soldiers who committed any offense on the person or private property of Northern civilians, he reminded them that "the duties exacted of us by civilization and Christianity are not less obligatory in the country of the enemy than in our own."

Perhaps the most telling tribute to Lee came from his former enemies. When General Lee died in 1870, newspapers throughout the North universally praised his military genius and morality. The *New York Herald* said, "In him the military genius of America was developed to a greater extent than ever before. In him all that was pure and lofty in mind and purpose found lodgment. He came nearer the ideal of a soldier and Christian general than any man we can think of."

Unfortunately, despite America's rich tradition in fairness in combat operations, even the best lessons of history quickly fade unless they are inculcated. Future My Lai's cannot be prevented unless the answers to the "why" of My Lai are repeated over and over until they are ingrained into every warfighter in uniform. Just as Americans must never forget their rallying cries of honor and nobility—"Remember the Alamo"—they must be forced to deal with their nightmares—"My Lai." On the other hand, it is precisely because of its horror and repulsiveness that My Lai is uniquely suited to serve as the primary vehicle to address the entire issue of adherence to the law of war as well as the necessity for effective leadership in the extremely trying War on Terror.

3.14 Questions for Discussion

1. *Responding to war crime allegations.* Considering the lessons of My Lai, what is the best course of action for the military command to take when it receives allegations of war crimes committed by American forces?

2. *Role of propaganda in the War on Terror.* How did the al-Qa'eda and ISIS terror networks employ the media as a tool of warfare? Is it effective?

3. *Grand strategy.* What impact does a grand strategy have on victory in war? In the War on Terror, compare Obama's strategy to Trump's. Who had the correct strategy in dealing with ISIS and the Taliban in Afghanistan?

4. *Why follow the law of war if the enemy does not?* The Roman practice of offering Roman citizenship to tribes who agreed to serve in the Roman army as auxiliary troops greatly benefited the expansion of the empire. For example, the *Honariani Atecotti Seniores* were formed from captured pirates from the Scottish Atecotti tribe circa A.D. 300 and served in the *Auxilium Palatinum*. On the other hand, the later Roman practice of slaughtering civilians only stiffened resistance amongst the German tribes who eventually conquered Rome.

5. *Did the Calley trial follow the rules of war that were set in the aftermath of World War II at the Tokyo and Nuremberg War Crimes Tribunals?* The Tribunals had set the precedent that no soldier could rely on the excuse that he was following orders from a superior in order to excuse his war crimes. Then Secretary of the Army Howard H. Callaway stated to the *New York Times* that Lt. William Calley believed he was following orders, and thus his sentence was reduced. This contradicted the standards set in Tokyo and Nuremberg, where some Japanese and German soldiers were executed for their purported war crimes despite the fact that they raised the defense of superior orders. In light of these facts did the United States set a precedent that it did not have to abide by international law? Could a subordinate in a terrorist organization such as ISIS rely on the same defense Lt. Calley used if he were charged with a war crime?

Selected Bibliography

Addicott, Jeffrey F. *Operation Desert Storm: R. E. Lee or W. T. Sherman?* 136 MILITARY LAW REVIEW 115 (1992).

Elliott, H. Wayne. *Theory and Practice: Some Suggestions for the Law of War Trainer*, THE ARMY LAWYER, July 1983, at 1.

Graham, David E. *Operational Law (OPLAW)—A Concept Comes of Age*, THE ARMY LAWYER, July 1987, at 9.

Henkin, Louis, et al. MIGHT V. RIGHT, 1991.

Jones, J. William. LIFE AND LETTERS OF GENERAL ROBERT EDWARD LEE, 1906.

Moore, John Norton. LAW AND THE INDO-CHINA WAR, 1972.

Nagel, Paul C. THE LEES OF VIRGINIA, 1990. Lee's view on Christian salvation was devoid of any form of human merit or morality although by the measure of any society, his own moral standards were impeccable. Grace oriented to Biblical Christianity, he wrote, "I can only say that I am a poor sinner, trusting in Christ alone for salvation."

O'Brien, William V. THE CONDUCT OF JUST AND LIMITED WAR, 1981.

Peers, Lt. Gen. W.R. THE MY LAI INQUIRY, 1979.

Samenow, Stanton E., Jr. INSIDE THE CRIMINAL MIND, 1984.

Schindler, Dietrich, ed., and Jiri Toman. THE LAWS OF ARMED CONFLICTS, 1988.

Taylor, Lawrence. A TRIAL OF GENERALS, 1981.

von Clausewitz, Karl. ON WAR. J. Graham trans, 1918.

Walsh, Gary L. *Role of the Judge Advocate in Special Operations*, THE ARMY LAWYER, Aug. 1989, at 6-8.

Weigley, Russel F. HISTORY OF THE UNITED STATES ARMY, 1984

Chapter 4

The War on Terror

We are at war. We are at war against Al-Qa'eda.

—Barack H. Obama

The War on Terror began for the United States on September 11, 2001, with coordinated suicide attacks using hijacked domestic airplanes by 19 members of a sophisticated international terrorist network known as al-Qa'eda. The simultaneous attacks occurred in New York, Washington, D.C., and Pennsylvania, incinerating 3,000 people and destroying billions of dollars in property. Prior to this attack, America responded to al-Qa'eda and al-Qa'eda-styled terrorism with traditional domestic criminal law tools rooted in the American Constitution. After 9/11 America determined that it would have to resort to the tools associated with the regulation of international armed conflict or law of war. In short, the rule of law shifted from domestic criminal law to the law of war.

The question of how to best neutralize members of the al-Qa'eda terror network and associated forces was the central focus of the War on Terror. Prior to 9/11 the United States dealt with al-Qa'eda members in the same fashion as other radical Islamic terrorists—when individuals were taken into custody the United States used domestic criminal law to punish them for various terror related crimes. After 9/11, the United States added the more robust rule of law associated with the law of war to address al-Qa'eda enemy combatants. Consequently, it was the application of the provisions of the law of war to al-Qa'eda enemy combatants that was most often challenged as "illegal" by critics.

In essence, the central issue in the War on Terror pivoted around the question of whether or not the War on Terror was a real war which would fall under the parameters of the law of war or simply a metaphor, like the "war on drugs" or the "war on poverty." Simply put, if the War on Terror was a real war, or international armed conflict, then the United States was perfectly at liberty to apply the law of war to kill, capture, or detain enemy combatants (belligerents). For instance, under the law of war the United States had a wide variety of powerful legal tools at its disposal that would otherwise be unavailable. In accordance with the law of war the United States had the right to: (1) kill al-Qa'eda,

Taliban, and associated enemy belligerent forces in armed conflict wherever they are found; (2) detain said enemy belligerents indefinitely until the war is over; and (3) try by military commissions certain enemy belligerents that violated the law of war. On the other hand, if the War on Terror against al-Qa'eda was not a real war, then by taking such actions the United States was most certainly engaging in gross violations of both international and domestic law.

While various ideologues were quick to condemn the actions of the United States in the War on Terror at almost every turn, representative democracy mandates that the answer to the question of illegality can only be found in the official pronouncements emanating from the three branches of America's Constitutional government. Of course, the primary dilemma for the United States was set in the fact that the law of war was written to address an armed conflict between nation-states, not an armed conflict between a nation-state and a non-state actor such as al-Qa'eda or, later, ISIS.

As this chapter will demonstrate, all three branches of the United States government strongly signaled that the United States was acting lawfully in applying the law of war to the conflict with al-Qa'eda and associated forces to include ISIS. From September 11, 2001, when al-Qa'eda foot soldiers killed 3,000 people, President Bush (2001-2008) remained unequivocal in his contention that, acting under his authority as the Commander in Chief, the law of war applied. Although not as pronounced as President Bush in his public declarations that the nation was engaged in a real war with al-Qa'eda, his successor President Obama (2009-2016), adopted the policies of the Bush Administration by continuing to label enemy combatants, kill them, detain them, and prosecute them by military commissions. In a speech on January 7, 2010, Obama reminded the nation: "We are at war. We are at war against al-Qa'eda, a far-reaching network of violence and hatred that attacked us on 9/11, that killed nearly 3,000 innocent people, and that is plotting to strike us again. And we will do whatever it takes to defeat them." On the other hand, President Trump (2017-2020) was extremely forceful in his unabashed desire to not only adopt the full provisions of the law of war and use the military to achieve victory over ISIS, but to end the War on Terror by closing down the ground wars in Iraq (against ISIS) and Afghanistan (against the Taliban).

In tandem, the Congress of the United States never formally "declared war" under Article I of the Constitution against al-Qa'eda, but there can be no doubt that it most certainly fully endorsed and "authorized" the War on Terror. Among the indicators of this fact are the 2001 Congressional Authorization for the Use of Military Force and the striking "war" language first set out in the 2006 Military Commissions Act and subsequently followed by the 2009 Military Commissions Act.

Finally, the Supreme Court generally followed suit and allowed both the Congress and the President to conduct this conflict under the provisions of the law of war with some restrictions. In a nutshell, the Court clearly signaled that the United States had the legal power to designate enemy combatants and detain them subject to additional safeguards, e.g., habeas rights (if detained at Guantanamo Bay, Cuba), due to the nature of the non-State actor enemy. What makes the Supreme Court cases a source of contention is the fact that they are slowly, and quite painfully, unilaterally developing addendums to the law of war that might one day bridge the gap between traditional law of war concepts and domestic criminal law concepts. Given the new threat of al-Qa'eda-styled mega terrorism, it is perfectly understandable that such additions to the law will come in bits and pieces and that the Court itself will exhibit confusion along the way with opinions that are bitterly divided, and broadly presented. Nevertheless, the judicial phrase that best exemplifies the evolving legal theme was rendered in 2004 in *Hamdi v. Rumsfeld*, where Justice O'Connor "made it clear that a *state of war* is not a blank check for the president [emphasis added]...."

Another problem which confronted the United States in its characterization of the War on Terror as an international armed conflict came from the international community. Out of the 193 member nations of the United Nations, the United States was the only nation that openly proclaimed that it would use the law of war against al-Qa'eda. Other nations plagued by radical Islamic terrorism elected to amend their domestic criminal laws to, for example, detain suspected terrorists for extended periods of time, e.g., at one time, 28 days in the United Kingdom, without charging the terror suspect with a crime.

In short, the legal and policy frustrations stemmed from the fact that the United States looked at a square block called the law of war and tried to fit it into a round peg called the al-Qa'eda virtual State. Obviously, it would be helpful if the international community would come together to develop a new set of rules to deal with the new phenomenon of al-Qa'eda-styled terrorism. However, such is not likely, given the fact that the United Nations can't even agree on a definition of the term "terrorism."

4.1 September 11, 2001

Just as the term "World War II" did not describe who the United States was at war with in 1941-1945, the term War on Terror was a poor description of the enemy forces. Of course, the word "terror" is not an "enemy," it is simply a tactic employed by an enemy—a method that intentionally targets innocent civilians. In turn, the War on Terror was not a war against a tactic, but a war against an identifiable enemy—primarily al-Qa'eda and ISIS terrorists who murder in the name of militant Islamic rhetoric. To be sure, the War on Terror was not against all militant Islamic groups in the world, but only against those militant Islamic groups that targeted the United States with open-ended physical violence. Again, this would include al-Qa'eda, ISIS, and all associated forces who adopt their goal of making "war" on the United States. While President Obama's January 2010 description of the conflict as a "War Against Al-Qa'eda" was far superior in terms of clarity, the term War on Terror remained as the most popular for the conflict.

In 1996, Osama bin Laden issued his first declaration that he was at war with the United States. After listing a rambling series of so-called grievances against the "Zionist-Crusaders," he stated:

> The walls of oppression and humiliation cannot be demolished except in a rain of bullets. The freeman does not surrender leadership to infidels and sinners. My Muslim Brothers of the World: Your brothers in Palestine and in the land of the two Holy Places are calling upon your help and asking you to take part in fighting against the enemy—your enemy and their enemy— the Americans and the Israelis.

On May 10, 1997, CNN aired a March 22, 1997, interview with Osama bin Laden by Peter Arnett. Bin Laden stated, "We declared jihad against the U.S. government, because the U.S. government is unjust, criminal and tyrannical." On February 22, 1998, Osama bin Laden and his so-called "World Islamic Front" again declared a religious *fatwa* (a formal statement backed by a religious declaration) urging in the strongest terms that all Muslims should engage in violence against "Jews and Crusaders." Rooting his hatred in his interpretation of Islam, he proclaimed:

> All these crimes and sins committed by the Americans are a clear declaration of war on Allah, his messenger, and Muslims. And *ulema* (clerics) have throughout Islamic history unanimously agreed that the jihad is an individual duty if the enemy destroys Muslim countries. On that basis, and in compliance with Allah's order, we issue the following fatwa to all Muslims: The

ruling to kill the Americans and their allies—civilians and military—is an individual duty for every Muslim who can do it in any country in which it is possible to do it, in order to liberate the al-Aqsa Mosque [in Jerusalem] and the holy mosque [in Mecca] from their grip.

Any reasonable doubts as to the involvement of Osama bin Laden's terrorist network in the attacks of September 11, 2001, were dispelled by the December 13, 2001, public release of the so-called "bin Laden videotape." The tape established that bin Laden: (1) knew when the hijackers would strike; (2) knew that the hijackers understood that they were on a "martyrdom operation," but had no details until shortly before the attacks; (3) was pleasantly surprised by the total collapse of the two towers of the World Trade Center in New York; (4) listened with anticipation to radio broadcasts to confirm the terror attacks; and (5) expressed joy and amusement as he detailed the story of the attacks. The most damning segment of the thirty-nine-minute tape occurred when bin Laden stated:

We calculated in advance the number of casualties from the enemy who would be killed based on the position of the tower. We calculated that the floors that would be hit would be three or four floors. I was the most optimistic of them all. Due to my experience in this field, I was thinking that the fire from the gas in the plane would melt the iron structure of the building and collapse the area where the plane hit and all the floors above it only. This is all that we had hoped for.

Almost a year to the day after the attack of September 11, 2001, the al-Qa'eda terrorist organization released another videotape claiming full credit for the attacks. The video specifically mentioned the World Trade Center attack, the Pentagon attack, and the attempted attack on the United States Capitol.

4.2 An Act of War

"America is at war." So stated President Bush's letter of introduction to the March 2006, National Security Strategy of the United States of America. The phrase "War on Terror" was first used by President Bush on September 11, 2001, aboard Air Force One and his first major public address the next day also declared the terrorist attacks as "acts of war." In fact, the Bush Administration never departed from the position that the fight against al-Qa'eda and the Taliban constituted a global war. Although the term War on Terror is not descriptive, all three Presidents who presided over the conflict rejected the idea that the War on Terror was a metaphor similar to the "war on poverty" or the "war on drugs." With the passage of the first Military Commissions Act of 2006, followed by the Military Commissions Act of 2009, there can be no question that both the executive and the legislative branches of the United States clearly viewed the War on Terror as real war or, in the vernacular of modern usage, a real international armed conflict between the United States and the Taliban, al-Qa'eda, and associated forces (ISIS).

In a speech delivered in 1984, Ambassador Jeanne J. Kirkpatrick prophetically spoke of a coming "terrorist war [against the United States], [that] is part of a total war which sees the whole society as an enemy, and all members of a society as appropriate objects for violent actions." Her words became reality on September 11, 2001, and the United States came to understand that viewing al-Qa'eda-styled terrorism as an act of war was a new manifestation of the changing nature of armed conflict. As such, it posed a new challenge for the historically fixed international rules relating to international armed conflict.

Apart from the enormity of the al-Qa'eda attack, what made the events of September 11, 2001, so vastly different from all previous incidents of terror was that the United States and the North Atlantic Treaty Organization (NATO) both specifically characterized the attack as an "armed attack" on the United States. The unprecedented armed attack determination was significant because it, in turn, immediately signaled that the United States intended to frame the terror attack as an event equivalent to an "act of war" under international law, and not simply a criminal affair to be dealt with by means of traditional law enforcement tools.

Under the law of war, the use of the terms "war" or "act of war" refer to the use of aggressive force against a sovereign State by another State in violation of the United Nations Charter and customary international law. Historically, such illegal acts most often occur without a formal declaration of war; the aggressive act itself triggers the ensuing international armed conflict. Similarly, the term "self-defense" refers to the right of a State to respond with proportionate force to the initial armed attack.

Following September 11, 2001, the United States, NATO, and the U.N. Security Council elected to expand the legal framework concerning the use of force in self-defense to encompass not only any State that had actively participated in the attacks, but any organization or person that was responsible. Accordingly, an authorization for the "use of force" was passed by the United States Congress; the President labeled the attack "an act of war;" NATO invoked its collective self-defense clause, should a NATO member suffer an armed attack; and the U.N. Security Council passed a resolution that employed self-defense terminology associated with those responsible for the attacks. Thus, from its inception, the War on Terror was legally couched by the United States in terms of traditional international law of war terminology, even though the actual attack was carried out, strictly speaking, by a non-State actor.

4.3 Use of Force

Understanding the need for international approval for prosecuting the War on Terror under the rule of law, the United States turned to the U.N. Security Council on the day after the attack in hopes of obtaining a strong use of force resolution to address the attacks. The United States received something very close to that in U.N. Security Council Resolution 1368:

> The Security Council,
> Reaffirming the principles and purposes of the Charter of Nations,
> Determined to combat by all means threats to international peace and security caused by terrorist acts,
> *Recognizing the inherent right of the individual or collective self-defense in accordance with the Charter* [emphasis added],
> 1. Unequivocally condemns in the strongest terms the horrifying terrorist attacks which took place on 11 September 2001 in New York, Washington, D.C. and Pennsylvania and regards such acts, like any act of international terrorism, as a threat to international peace and security;...
> 3. Calls on all States to work together urgently to bring to justice the perpetrators, organizers and sponsors of these terrorist attacks and stresses that those responsible for aiding, supporting or harboring the perpetrators, organizers and sponsors of these acts will be held accountable;

4. Calls also on the international community to redouble their efforts to prevent and suppress terrorist acts by increased cooperation and full implementation of the relevant international anti-terrorist conventions and Security Council resolutions, in particular resolution 1269 (1999) of 19 October 1999;

5. Expresses its readiness to take all necessary steps to respond to the terrorist attacks of 11 September 2001, and to combat all forms of terrorism, in accordance with its responsibilities under the Charter of Nations;....

Because of the structured magnitude of the terrorist attack, Resolution 1368 specifically recognized America's "inherent right of individual and collective self-defense in accordance with the Charter" and specifically called on "all States to work together urgently to bring to justice the perpetrators, organizers and sponsors of these terrorist attacks." Resolution 1368 further addressed the issue of responsibility for those States who supported or sponsored the terrorist attacks by "stressing that those responsible for aiding, supporting or harboring the perpetrators, organizers and sponsors of these acts will be held accountable." Taken as a whole, it can be argued that Resolution 1368 provided the United States and its allies with the international legal authority necessary to respond to the terrorist attacks through the use of military force in self-defense not only against a State who supported, sponsored, or harbored the terrorists, but also against individual terrorists themselves. The rule of law would be the law of war.

4.4 NATO

NATO, of which the United States is a full member, also viewed the attacks of September 11, 2001, as an "armed attack" under international law. In fact, for the first time in its history, NATO invoked its collective self-defense clause under Article 5 of the NATO Charter where "an armed attack on one or more of [its members] shall be considered an attack on all," and that the members may exercise the right of self-defense which includes the "use of armed force, to restore and maintain the security of the North Atlantic area." The real significance of invoking Article 5, of course, rested more in the European recognition that the terrorist attacks were, in fact, tantamount to an armed attack or act of war against the United States, and not just criminal acts of terrorism by a non-State actor.

4.5 Congressional War-Making Power

Congress was also quick to address the attacks in a manner that clearly established the premise that America was engaged in a real "war." Although Congress elected not to exercise its power to "declare war" under Article I, Section 8, of the Constitution (it has enacted eleven formal declarations of war relating to only five different conflicts of the 200+ times that the United States has introduced military forces into hostilities), it did provide the President with an expansive grant of power to conduct war against al-Qa'eda. On September 18, 2001, Congress clearly authorized the Executive to conduct war. From its very title to its content, the Authorization for the Use of Military Force demonstrated the Congressional desire to frame the use of force as a military action. Specifically, Congress authorized the President to use military force, if necessary, to respond to the attacks with "all necessary and appropriate force against those nations, *organizations*, or *persons* he determines [emphasis added]" were associated with the terror attacks of September 11, 2001. In addition, the resolution also authorized the executive to take action to "prevent any future acts of international terrorism against the United States." Since the War on Terror is a global conflict, Congress placed no limit on where the President could use military force or for how long. In fact, nothing prohibits the President from applying the law of war within the continental United States. Finally, by inserting language regarding the satisfaction of the War Powers Resolution, Congress further provided the President with solid authority to introduce America's armed forces into hostilities as he saw fit. Passed only three days after 9/11 in an unprecedented show of unity, this resolution was passed by the Senate (98-0) and the House of Representatives (420-1) by an overwhelming majority, save one member from California.

AUTHORIZATION FOR THE USE OF MILITARY FORCE
Public Law 107-40, 107th Congress
Joint Resolution

To authorize the use of United States Armed Forces against those responsible for the recent attacks launched against the United States. NOTE: Sept. 18, 2001—[S.J. Res. 23]

Whereas, on September 11, 2001, acts of treacherous violence were committed against the United States and its citizens; and

Whereas, such acts render it both necessary and appropriate that the United States exercise its rights to self-defense and to protect United States citizens both at home and abroad; and

Whereas, in light of the threat to the national security and foreign policy of the United States posed by these grave acts of violence; and

Whereas, such acts continue to pose an unusual and extraordinary threat to the national security and foreign policy of the United States; and

Whereas, the President has authority under the Constitution to take action to deter and prevent acts of international terrorism against the United States: Now, therefore, be it Resolved by the Senate and House of Representatives of the United States of America in Congress assembled, NOTE: Authorization for Use of Military Force.

SECTION 1. SHORT TITLE.
This joint resolution may be cited as the "Authorization for Use of Military Force."

SEC. 2. AUTHORIZATION FOR USE OF UNITED STATES ARMED FORCES.
(a) In General.—That the President is authorized to use all necessary and appropriate force against those nations, organizations, or persons he determines planned, authorized, committed, or aided the terrorist attacks that occurred on September 11, 2001, or harbored such organizations or persons, in order to prevent any future acts of international terrorism against the United States by such nations, organizations or persons.

(b) War Powers Resolution Requirements—

(1) Specific statutory authorization—Consistent with section 8(a)(1) of the War Powers Resolution, the Congress declares that this section is intended to constitute specific statutory authorization within the meaning of section 5(b) of the War Powers Resolution.

(2) Applicability of other requirements—Nothing in this resolution supercedes any requirement of the War Powers Resolution.

Approved September 18, 2001.

Perhaps the most vivid recognition by Congress that the United States was using the law of war in a real global war came by way of the Military Commissions Act of 2006, where Congress specifically authorized the establishment of military commissions to try those illegal enemy combatants for war crimes. Understanding that military commissions can only be used in the wake of a lawful war, Congress most certainly understood this war to be a real war. Indeed, Congress spelled out exactly who the enemy combatants were in the 2006 Act:

(i) a person who has engaged in hostilities or who has purposefully and materially supported hostilities against the United States or its co-belligerents who is not a lawful enemy combatant (including a person who is part of the *Taliban, al Qaeda, or associated forces*); or
(ii) a person who, before, on, or after the date of the enactment of the Military Commissions Act of 2006, has been determined to be an unlawful enemy combatant by a Combatant Status Review Tribunal or another competent tribunal established under the authority of the President or the Secretary of Defense [emphasis added].

In 2009, a Democrat-controlled Congress passed the Military Commissions Act of 2009. In that legislation, Congress changed the term "unlawful enemy combatant" to "unprivileged enemy belligerent," but still specifically identified anyone who was a part of al-Qa'eda as the enemy. The 2009 Act states:

The term 'unprivileged enemy belligerent' means an individual (other than a privileged belligerent) who:
(A) has engaged in hostilities against the United States or its coalition partners;
(B) has purposefully and materially supported hostilities against the United States or its coalition partners; or
(C) was a part of al Qaeda at the time of the alleged offense under this chapter.

While Congress continues to pass legislation consistent with the idea that the War on Terror is a real armed conflict against al-Qa'eda, one power that Congress clearly has in war-making is over "the purse." Ultimately, Congress has the power to cut off funding to any protracted use of military forces. As a practical matter, the ongoing military operations in Iraq or Afghanistan could not continue without Congressional approval.

4.6 Presidential War-Making Power

Armed with the Congressional Joint Resolution, U.N. Resolution 1368, and the NATO Resolution, President George W. Bush exercised his authority as the Commander in Chief, under Article II, Section 3, of the Constitution, and quickly set about gathering the necessary evidence to find those who committed the attacks and to establish linkage to the State or States that may have provided material support to the terrorists. President Bush consistently held that the United States was in a state of armed conflict with al-Qa'eda. President Obama agreed, but not as loudly or consistently. President Trump forcefully agreed and took direct action to finish the conflict.

Even without a Congressional resolution authorizing the use of military force, the President is the Commander in Chief and has independent Constitutional authority to order the military into action. In fact, there is a long history of American presidents utilizing military forces abroad in situations of armed conflict or potential armed conflict to protect United States citizens or promote United States interests. The number of instances where the executive has used military forces abroad without, for example, a Congressional declaration of War, well exceeds 200 in number. Selected instances include: 1798–1800, undeclared naval war with France; 1801–1805, the First Barbary War (Tripoli declared war but not the United States); 1806, Mexico Incursion; 1806–1810, Gulf of Mexico Incursion; 1810, West Florida Incursion; 1812, Amelia Island in Florida; 1813, West Florida; 1813–1814, Marquesas Islands; 1814–1825, Caribbean (engagements between pirates and American war ships in response to over 3,000 pirate attacks on merchantmen between 1815–1823); 1815, Second Barbary War; 1950–1953, Korean War; 1958, Lebanon; 1962, Cuba; 1962, Thailand; 1964, Congo; 1964–1973, Vietnam War; 1965, Dominican Republic; 1980, Iran; 1981, El Salvador; 1982, Lebanon; 1983, Honduras; 1983, Chad; 1983, Grenada; 1986, Libya; 1989, Panama; 1989, Andean Region; 1991, Persian Gulf War; 1993, Bosnia; 1993–1995, Somalia; 1993–1995, Haiti; 1997, Serbia; 2001, Afghanistan; 2003, Iraq; Libya 2011; Syria, 2018; ISIS 2017-2018. In fact, the last time Congress "declared" war under Article I, Section 8, Clause 11 of the U.S. Constitution was in December 1941. In the vast majority of cases of armed conflict, Congress simply authorizes the President to engage in war-making.

Nevertheless, the President's authority to use the armed forces and the authority of Congress to declare war or to otherwise share in the process of war-making has been the source of much debate over the life of the Republic. Clearly the Framers gave each branch of government war-making powers in furtherance of their vision of a limited government of "checks and balances." Without question, this system of checks also ensured a built-in source of friction between the two branches.

The most well known source of contention between Congress and the executive branch is the 1973 War Powers Resolution, enacted over President Richard Nixon's veto. The War Powers Resolution seeks to curtail or limit the power of the executive in the employment of American forces abroad. It requires the President to consult with Congress if American forces are introduced into hostilities or into situations where hostilities are imminent and, after a time set at a maximum of ninety days, either obtain Congressional approval of any continued military action or withdraw. Needless to say, the War Powers Resolution raises serious separation of powers issues under the Constitution which, to date, the United States Supreme Court has not squarely addressed. In any event, no American president from either political party has directly "complied" with the War Powers Resolution. At most, when presidents have employed United States armed forces in hostile situations or in places where conflict was imminent, Congress has simply been notified in writing of the actions with the accompanying phrase: "consistent with the War Powers Resolution."

Finally, although the Bush Administration was steadfast in its view that it had the right to use the law of war against al-Qa'eda forces, it sometimes failed to apply this contention across the board. For example, while proclaiming that the law of war allowed the government to try by military commissions those al-Qa'eda members who committed serious crimes in violation of the law of war, the Bush Administration elected to prosecute at least two high-profile al-Qa'eda members in federal district court—Zacarias Moussaoui (the so-called twentieth terror plot member of 9/11) and Richard Reid (the al-Qa'eda shoe bomber). At the very least, these actions sent out some very confusing signals— some al-Qa'eda members went to federal court for trial where they enjoyed the full due process rights associated with criminal defendants while others went to military commissions for trial under less rigid due process protections. Many argued that if the United States was in a state of war then by deed and action the law of war tools must be applied to all al-Qa'eda members. Even though supporters of the Bush Administration pointed out that these two al-Qa'eda members were never labeled as "enemy combatants" by the President and thus not qualified to go to a military commissions process, the fact that the Bush Administration desired to demonstrate in the short term a "win" by prosecuting Moussaoui and Reid actually did great harm in the long term. In other words, if the government was serious about categorizing the War on Terror as a real war, then domestic politics should not have played a part in the process. Unfortunately, President Obama likewise sent extremely confusing signals in terms of dealing with issues of indentification, detention, and prosecution of enemy combatants and domestic jihadists.

In summary, like all international wars the battlefield in the War on Terror was the entire globe and the President's inherent Constitutional authority, coupled with the Authorization for Use of Military Force, allowed him to make war anywhere, even within the borders of the United States. As discussed further, however, the Bush, Obama, and Trump Administrations all agreed to self-restrict the provisions of the law of war in terms of killing enemy combatants who were found within the territory of the United States.

4.7 Article III Courts

The War on Terror created much tension in American society concerning civil liberties. Recognizing that the struggle between civil liberties and increased security faces every democracy in time of conflict, courts have traditionally avoided involvement in national security concerns, leaving the matter to the legislature and executive, which are accountable to the people. Courts realize that bad decisions will become entrenched in the case law of the nation and can serve as a magnet for the development of even more problematic decisions in the future. Nevertheless, because the enemy in the War on Terror fell outside of the traditional definitions associated with armed conflict, not the least being that they are non-State actors, the federal courts issued a variety of conflicting rulings in the years since 2001, the most important ones, of course, coming in 2004, 2006, and 2008 from the United States Supreme Court (all discussed in greater detail in Chapter 6).

In 2004, both critics and supporters of the United States government waited with great anticipation to see whether or not the Supreme Court would even insert itself in the conflict. On June 28, 2004, a fractured Supreme Court issued three decisions—*Hamdi v. Rumsfeld*, *Rumsfeld v. Padilla*, and *Rasul v. Bush*. A fair reading of these cases indicate that the Court did not assert a co-equal role in the War on Terror, but rather reminded the other two branches that some due process concerns for detainees needed to be better addressed. More importantly, the Court recognized that, as a matter of law, the nation was in fact involved in an armed conflict, or war, with al-Qa'eda and its affiliates.

In *Hamdi*, a plurality opinion (8–1) by Justice O'Connor, the Court acquiesced to the notion that a state of "war" existed and could extend even to U.S. citizens as enemy combatants. In fact, the Court noted that "there is no bar to this Nation's holding one of its own citizens as an enemy combatant." However, the Court remanded the case to give United States citizen Hamdi a "fair opportunity to rebut the Government's factual assertions [that he was an enemy combatant] before a neutral and detached decision maker." In October 2004, without charging him with any crimes, the United States released Hamdi from military detention and sent him back to Saudi Arabia (he denounced his U.S. citizenship). In *Padilla* (5–4), dealing with another U.S. citizen enemy combatant, the Court sidestepped the legal issues and dismissed Padilla's habeas petition without prejudice since, they concluded, he had filed in the wrong federal district court. In *Rasul*, the Court reversed the D.C. Circuit Court in *Al Odah v. United States*, and ruled (6–3) that U.S. courts possessed jurisdiction to consider habeas challenges of suspected al-Qa'eda and Taliban enemy combatants held at Guantanamo Bay, Cuba. The Court found that "aliens held at the base [Guantanamo Bay], no less than American citizens, are entitled to invoke the federal court's authority … to determine the legality of the Executive's potentially indefinite detention of individuals who claim to be innocent of wrongdoing."

In the controversial 2006 decision of *Hamdan v. Rumsfeld*, a deeply divided Court again provided much needed guidance when it ruled that military commissions to try illegal enemy combatants had to be created by Congress, not the President. Seemingly concerned that Congress was not fully addressing the matter of military commissions, *Hamdan* struck down the President's ability to authorize military commissions under his Article II powers. In so doing, the Court also held that Common Article 3 of the Geneva Conventions applied to the detainees because the U.S. was in an "armed conflict." The Court acknowledged that the United States was at war and "that the AUMF [the 2001 Authorization for Use of Military Force] activated the President's war powers…." As covered in Chapter 5, in quick step the United States Congress responded to the *Hamdan* decision by passing the Military Commissions Act of 2006 where it specifically authorized the creation of military commissions to try unlawful enemy combatants with a variety of criminal offenses to include war crimes.

The bitterly divided (5-4 decision with the Chief Justice Roberts joining the minority) 2008 Supreme Court ruling in *Boumediene v. Bush* represented the third decision that the Supreme Court rendered regarding various issues associated with the War on Terror. In simple terms, *Boumediene* ruled that the detainees held as enemy combatants under the law of war at Guantanamo Bay had the right to contest their status by means of filing a habeas corpus petition to a federal judge. The ruling had nothing to do with the constitutionality of the Congressionally mandated military commissions process then underway for those charged with various "war crimes," nor did it strike down the use of the law of war to kill or detain al-Qa'eda.

In summary, a fair understanding of the cases rendered to date by the Supreme Court support the view that the War on Terror was a real war and not a metaphor. Nevertheless, the Court exhibited that it too was struggling to find the line where traditional criminal law jurisprudence ends and law of war jurisprudence begins. As evidenced in *Boumediene*, this analytical process was further aggravated by ideological differences. The liberal wing of the Court tended to employ concepts more associated with criminal law jurisprudence while the conservative wing employed traditional law of war factors. Again, in *Hamdi*, Justice O'Connor "made it clear that a *state of war* is not a blank check for the president [emphasis added]." Still, the decisions to date certainly uphold the right of the government to do what it has traditionally done in previous wars—detain indefinitely without criminal charge, enemy combatants outside the regular parameters of the domestic judicial system.

4.8 The Employment of Lawful Violence

In the days immediately following the attacks of September 11, 2001, a conclusive body of evidence pointed directly to the al-Qa'eda terrorist organization as the perpetrators of the attacks, and to Afghanistan's Taliban as the State-supporter of the terrorist al-Qa'eda organization. Determined to respond if necessary under the inherent right of self-defense, the Bush Administration offered the Taliban government a time certain ultimatum to turn over the al-Qa'eda leaders and to shut down all terrorist camps in Afghanistan. President Bush issued the ultimatum in a solemn speech given to a joint session of Congress on September 20, 2001. The pertinent part reads:

And tonight, the United States of America makes the following demands on the Taliban: Deliver to the United States authorities all the leaders of al-Qa'eda who hide in your land…[c]

lose immediately and permanently every terrorist training camp in Afghanistan, and hand over every terrorist, and every person in their support structure, to appropriate authorities. Give the United States full access to terrorist training camps, so we can make sure they are no longer operating. These demands are not open to negotiation or discussion. The Taliban must act, and act immediately. They will hand over the terrorist, or they will suffer their fate.

When the Taliban leadership refused to comply with any aspect of the demand, the United States exercised, in conjunction with NATO and its other allies, the lawful use of military force to accomplish those aims. Numerous nations contributed assistance to the American led effort including Pakistan, Saudi Arabia, Britain, Russia, Germany, Australia, France, Canada, Japan, and so on. In addition, much of the actual ground combat was borne by indigenous Afghan tribal fighters, primarily the so-called Northern Alliance, under the guidance and support of United States Army Special Forces and other United States Special Operations Forces conducting direct action and unconventional warfare missions. The military campaign to dislodge the Taliban and al-Qa'eda took approximately three months, from October 7 to December 23, 2001. Approximately 6,500 air combat missions were flown which attacked over 120 fixed targets. Four hundred vehicles were destroyed and an undetermined number of combatants were killed (some have put the figure as high as 10,000).

In tandem with the removal of the Taliban regime from power, the United States and its allies were able to destroy the al-Qa'eda camps and dismantle much of the infrastructure of the terrorist group in Afghanistan by the end of December 2001. By any account, the Bush strategy of using American air power, American Special Operations Forces, and the ground forces of various Afghan resistance groups worked brilliantly in terms of mitigating the loss of life to American forces and reducing civilian suffering. Early critics of the Bush approach incorrectly predicted that the United States could not achieve success without the use of massive American ground forces and an attendant heavy loss of life. This same pessimism was seen in exaggerated predictions of American lives that would be lost in the 1991 Gulf War should the United States attempt to expel Iraq from Kuwait in accordance with U.N. Resolution 678.

Since the fall of the Taliban government, al-Qa'eda no longer operates with the open support of a State, but has been forced to revert to clandestine operations primarily as a sub-State terror group. In large part, however, they have reconstituted in the tribal regions and emerged as a major power broker in dictating the future of Afghanistan. As of early 2020, States throughout the world have arrested or detained well over 15,000 members of the al-Qa'eda network on a variety of terror related charges. The number of Islamic terrorists that have been killed is unknown, to include drone strikes in Yemen, Somalia, Afghanistan, Pakistan, Libya, Sudan, and other undisclosed locations. American drone attacks alone in the Obama Administration killed over 1,000 according to the CIA. Of the top 37 al-Qa'eda leaders identified after 9/11, over half have been captured or killed to include Mohammad Atef (killed in Afghanistan), Khalid Shaikh Mohammed (in custody), Abu Zubaydah (in custody), and Ramzi bin al-Shibh (in custody). Osama Bin Laden was killed in his hideout in Pakistan by U.S. Navy SEALS in May of 2011 and his number two confederate, Egyptian doctor Ayman al-Zawahiri, is now the leader of al-Qa'eda. Zawahiri still remains at large as of this writing.

4.9 Questions for Discussion

1. *Realistic expectations.* Is it realistic to expect nations to adhere to international law when pursuing a "war" on terrorists? Article 2(4) of the United Nations Charter states: "All Members shall refrain in their international relations from the threat or use of force against the territorial integrity or political independence of any state, or in any other manner inconsistent with the purposes of the United Nations." What roadblocks exist to international conformity on a use of force doctrine aimed specifically against terrorism?

2. *Congressional resolutions.* Following the attacks of September 11, 2001, Congress authorized the President "to use all necessary and appropriate force against those nations, organizations, or persons he determines planned, authorized, committed, or aided the terrorist attacks that occurred on September 11, 2001, or harbored such organizations or persons." *See* Authorization for Use of Military Force, P.L. 107-40 (Sept. 18, 2001). How does such a resolution conflict with the United Nations Charter, if at all? Does such a resolution violate international law?

3. *American Civil Liberties Union.* If all three branches of the government proclaimed that the War on Terror was a real war, why did the ACLU regularly criticize the United States as acting illegally?

Selected Bibliography

Cordesman, Anthony H. TRANSNATIONAL THREATS FROM THE MIDDLE EAST: CRYING WOLF OR CRYING HAVOC? 1999.

Fenwick, Charles G. INTERNATIONAL LAW, 1965.

Guiora, Amos N. FUNDAMENTALS OF COUNTERTERRORISM, 2008.

Lord Lloyd of Hampstead and M. D. A. Freeman. LLOYD'S INTRODUCTION TO JURISPRUDENCE, 1985.

Petrochilos, George. *The Relevance of the Concepts of War and Armed Conflict to the Law of Neutrality*, 31 VAND. J. TRANSNAT'L L. 575 (1998).

Chapter 5

Expanding and Ending the War on Terror

War, far as I can see.

—CIA Director Mike Morell (2015)

Following a swift battlefield victory over al-Qa'eda and the Taliban in December 2001, many urged President Bush to resist the temptation to maintain a long-term American military presence in the country, believing either that it was simply an impossible task to bring "democracy" to the region by so-called nation building, or that it was simply not the job of the U.S. military to do so. Even though Osama bin Landen, the leader of al-Qa'eda, fled into hiding where he would remain for almost ten years, Bush had achieved a significant victory with few American casualties. Not only would the War on Terror (apart from dealing with the issue of detainees) be over but the deterrence message delivered by the quick defeat of the Taliban and al-Qa'eda would resonate with other nations that might harbor terrorists groups. Bush, however, elected to establish an American military presence in the country, which ensured that in an already fractured tribal-like society that fighting would extend on into the foreseeable future

Meanwhile, with 9/11 still fresh in the collective memory, President Bush and Congress became fixated with the unpleasant specter of weapons of mass destruction (WMD) being used in a new terror strike on the homeland. Accordingly, the Bush Administration expanded the meaning of the phrase War on Terror to include those rogue nations who posed a direct threat to the United States by possessing or seeking to possess WMD. For instance, in 2002, President Bush said: "[t]he United States of America will not permit the world's most dangerous regimes to threaten us with the world's most destructive weapons." Most certainly, the 2003 war with Saddam Hussein's Iraq was waged with this maxim in mind. A US. led military coalition to topple Saddam Hussein, which lasted from March 19, 2003 to May 1, 2003, opened up a second front in the War on Terror. As it turned out American intelligence was misguided and there was no significant WMD threat to be found. Instead, the consequences of the conflict saw Iraqi society tear apart along cultural and religious fault lines between the Kurds, Shia, and Sunni. Not only was Iraq no longer a counterbalance to Iran, the number one State sponsor of terror in the world, but soon thereafter al-Qa'eda in Iraq and other insurgent groups emerged and chaos erupted throughout Iraq.

Although President Bush gained some success by a significant surge in combat troops in 2007 to stabilize Iraq, when Bush left office, Iraq and Afghanistan were still occupied by large numbers of American combat forces. America was fighting a two-front war — Afghanistan and Iraq — with no end in sight. Obama mimicked Bush many ways but was unable to end the War on Terror in his two-terms in the oval office. It was President Trump and his pragmatic leadership skills that actually brought an end to the War on Terror.

5.1 Weapons of Mass Destruction

In London in 1605, a terror plot was uncovered to use barrels of gunpowder—the weapon of mass destruction of the day—to blow up the English House of Lords and kill King James I. The terrorists were a group of Catholic radicals wishing to eliminate Protestant rule in England. Guy Fawkes, the leader of the plot was convicted and executed. Four hundred years later the United Nation's chief nuclear watchdog, El Baradei, warned that the most imminent threat facing the world is deadly nuclear material falling into the hands of extremists.

Indeed, many commentators continue to warn that the world must wake from its millenary sleep and recognize the real possibility that weapons of mass destruction will be used against large civilian population centers. Clearly, the terror attacks of September 11, 2001, demonstrated that international terrorism has now "broke us across the threshold" of creating mass casualties far in excess of anything Guy Fawkes could have imagined. The al-Qa'eda-styled terrorist is not content to kill in the tens or twenties: he aggressively seeks access to weapons of mass destruction in order to murder in the thousands and tens of thousands. Radical Islamists, for example, have openly boasted that they earnestly seek to acquire nuclear weapons. While nuclear weapons may be beyond the reach of international terrorists at this time, biological weapons, chemical weapons, and "dirty bombs" are not. Biological and chemical agents are inexpensive, easy to obtain, hard to trace, and capable of killing thousands upon thousands. Dirty bombs are devices which use conventional explosives in conjunction with nuclear, chemical, or biological byproducts. In addition, terrorists may strike "live" nuclear facilities as the arrest of the "Toronto 19" terror cell in August 2003 exemplified (reports of the alleged plot by 19 radical Muslim males included crashing a plane into the Seabrook Nuclear Reactor in Massachusetts).

Finally, as terrorists become more sophisticated in the cyber world, they will may engage in significant cyberterrorism attacks to disrupt entire networks that control vital infrastructure systems. Even now, al-Qa'eda terror cells routinely depend on the Internet for training and tactical support to, for example, provide instructions on how to make a bomb from commercial materials. According to terror expert Gabriel Weimann, the number of terror-related websites has risen from 12 in 1996, to more than 4,500 as of 2005.

Even without a renegade State to supply them with weapons of mass murder, terrorists can acquire them in the following ways. According to a *Public Agenda Special Report: Terrorism*, there are four general scenarios regarding the terrorist use of nuclear devices: (1) the terrorist makes a crude nuclear bomb using smuggled uranium or fissile material; (2) an unstable nation falls into the hands of terrorists (e.g., Pakistan is said to have dozens of nuclear weapons); (3) a conventional bomb is employed to explode radioactive materials (so-called dirty bomb); or (4) a nuclear power plant is attacked. Accordingly, in the immediate aftermath of 9/11 this doomsday scenario became a central consideration of whether or not the War on Terror should be expanded. Again, even one or two dedicated suicide bombers armed with a chemical, biological, or nuclear weapon could inflict catastrophic death and destruction in an urban environment.

If it seems obvious that third party dispute mechanisms will bear no fruit with terrorists who are filled with irrational hate, one is left with the stark truism voiced by the ancient Romans—*oderint dum metuatant* ("let them hate us as long as they respect us"). In the short term, the United States was not able to reason with the 2001 Taliban regime who had no wish to comply with the principles of peace embodied in the U.N. Charter. Fortunately, America was able to employ the proper application of force under the rule of law to, as President Bush pledged in his first major speech following the September 11, 2001, attack, "bring them to justice or bring justice to them." In addition, America was extremely fortunate that the War on Terror began prior to al-Qa'eda gaining access to a stockpile of weapons of mass murder. September 11, 2001, could have happened at any time, but thankfully 9/11 did not bring the devastation of a true weapons of mass destruction event.

The possible expansion of the War on Terror from Afghanistan to other targeted regimes was first announced by President Bush in his State of the Union Address on January 29, 2002, when the President cautioned the American people that even though Afghanistan was no longer a supporter of terrorist organizations, the War on Terror was not over. Apart from the fact that the United States would surely use its armed forces against any State that openly harbored al-Qa'eda, Bush clearly alerted the nation that he intended to embark on a policy that was certain to expand the War on Terror in a way that might include military action against other States for other emerging threats. With 9/11 still a fresh wound, the fear of a weapons of mass destruction event was considered an existential threat.

5.2 The Bush Doctrine

In a bold shift of direction, President Bush signaled that renegade regimes that either possessed or were seeking to acquire weapons of mass destruction posed "a grave and growing danger" to world peace that could no longer be ignored. President Bush specifically labeled those rogue regimes—Saddam Hussein's Iraq, Iran, and North Korea—as an "axis of evil" because of their continuing support and sponsorship of terrorist groups and their desire to acquire, or their possession of, weapons of mass destruction. Bush's key point in the message to the nation was to demonstrate his resolve that the "United States of America will not permit the world's most dangerous regimes to threaten us with the world's most destructive weapons."

In short order, President Bush's remarks led to the formulation of the so-called Bush Doctrine for the preemptive use of armed force against certain rogue nations. In September 2002, the White House issued its National Security Strategy of the United States where it spelled out both the emerging threat posed by al-Qa'eda-styled terrorism and the criteria for the preemptive use of force. The 49-page March 2006 National Security Strategy continued the preemptive theme under a section entitled, Summary of National Security Strategy of 2002:

> The security environment confronting the United States today is radically different from what we have faced before. Yet the first duty of the United States Government remains what it always has been: to protect the American people and American interests. It is an enduring American principle that this duty obligates the government to anticipate and counter threats, using all elements of national power, before the threats can do grave damage. The greater the threat, the greater is the risk of inaction—and the more compelling the case for taking anticipatory action to defend ourselves, even if uncertainty remains as to the time and place of the enemy's attack.

There are few greater threats than a terrorist attack with WMD.

To forestall or prevent such hostile acts by our adversaries, the United States will, if necessary, act preemptively in exercising our inherent right of self-defense. The United States will not resort to force in all cases to preempt emerging threats. Our preference is that nonmilitary actions succeed. And no country should ever use preemption as a pretext for aggression.

Within a year of the 2002 National Security Strategy, the application of the Bush Doctrine would see the United States and its allies topple the totalitarian regime of Saddam Hussein and cause the once terrorist State of Libya to abandon its weapons of mass destruction program and embark upon limited democratic reforms. In 2008, Libya settled with the United States all outstanding lawsuits associated with the Libya bombing of Pan Am Flight 103 over Lockerbie, Scotland. This move was certainly a byproduct of the deterrence signal related to the American combat victory over Saddam Hussein in Iraq.

The Bush Doctrine raised much debate—both as a policy matter and as a legal matter. Considering that the use of armed force can only be justified under international law when used in "self-defense," was it lawful for the United States to go beyond the rhetoric and actually carry the War on Terror to those rogue nations identified as supporters and sponsors of terrorist activities, but who had not physically engaged in a specific act of aggression against the United States? Furthermore, even if the United States had legal justification to employ its military force against, for example, Iran, practical matters would have to be carefully considered. At a minimum, the United States would have to certainly demonstrate from the particular circumstances that the use of armed force would not create an even greater danger to international peace and security. Accordingly, in the months leading up to the 2003 war in Iraq, Vice President Cheney repeatedly argued that "[d]eliverable weapons of mass destruction in the hands of a terror network or a murderous dictator, or the two working together, constitutes as grave a threat as can be imagined. The risks of inaction are far greater than the risk of action." Clearly, the two justifications for the Iraq War were the issues of weapons of mass destruction and support for terrorist networks as reflected in the Congressional authorization for the use of force against Iraq, set out herein.

107th CONGRESS
2d Session
H. J. RES. 114
To authorize the use of United States Armed Forces against Iraq.
IN THE HOUSE OF REPRESENTATIVES
October 2, 2002
JOINT RESOLUTION

To authorize the use of United States Armed Forces against Iraq.

Now, therefore, be it

Resolved by the Senate and House of Representatives of the United States of America in Congress assembled,

SECTION 1. SHORT TITLE.

This joint resolution may be cited as the 'Authorization for Use of Military Force Against Iraq Resolution of 2002.'

SEC. 2. SUPPORT FOR UNITED STATES DIPLOMATIC EFFORTS.

The Congress of the United States supports the efforts by the President to—

(1) strictly enforce through the United Nations Security Council all relevant Security Council resolutions regarding Iraq and encourages him in those efforts; and

(2) obtain prompt and decisive action by the Security Council to ensure that Iraq abandons its strategy of delay, evasion and noncompliance and promptly and strictly complies with all relevant Security Council resolutions regarding Iraq.

SEC. 3. AUTHORIZATION FOR USE OF UNITED STATES ARMED FORCES.

(a) AUTHORIZATION—The President is authorized to use the Armed Forces of the United States as he determines to be necessary and appropriate in order to—

(1) defend the national security of the United States against the continuing threat posed by Iraq; and

(2) enforce all relevant United Nations Security Council resolutions regarding Iraq.

(b) PRESIDENTIAL DETERMINATION—In connection with the exercise of the authority granted in subsection (a) to use force the President shall, prior to such exercise or as soon thereafter as may be feasible, but no later than 48 hours after exercising such authority, make available to the Speaker of the House of Representatives and the President pro tempore of the Senate his determination that—

(1) reliance by the United States on further diplomatic or other peaceful means alone either (A) will not adequately protect the national security of the United States against the continuing threat posed by Iraq or (B) is not likely to lead to enforcement of all relevant United Nations Security Council resolutions regarding Iraq; and

(2) acting pursuant to this joint resolution is consistent with the United States and other countries continuing to take the necessary actions against international terrorist and terrorist organizations, including those nations, organizations, or persons who planned, authorized, committed or aided the terrorist attacks that occurred on September 11, 2001.

(c) WAR POWERS RESOLUTION REQUIREMENTS

(1) SPECIFIC STATUTORY AUTHORIZATION—Consistent with section 8(a)(1) of the War Powers Resolution, the Congress declares that this section is intended to constitute specific statutory authorization within the meaning of section 5(b) of the War Powers Resolution.

(2) APPLICABILITY OF OTHER REQUIREMENTS—Nothing in this joint resolution supersedes any requirement of the War Powers Resolution.

...

The Iraq War, named Operation Iraqi Freedom, began on March 19, 2003, with a coordinated air attack by coalition forces against Iraqi military targets in Baghdad. Forming a "coalition of the willing" made up of like-minded democracies, President Bush acted under his Article II authority as the Commander in Chief and the Congressional use of force resolution passed by a healthy majority of both houses of Congress. Although the war occurred without specific approval for the "use of force" from the United Nations Security Council, the Security Council did pass Resolution 1441 just prior to the Iraq War. Resolution 1441 sternly warned Saddam Hussein's regime of "serious consequences" if Iraq failed to comply with full inspections by United Nations personnel regarding the regime's suspected possession of illegal biological and chemical weapons in violation of U.N. Security Council Resolution 687. Exactly what those "serious consequences" would be was left open, although the United States certainly interpreted the term to include military action.

Accompanying the 2003 military defeat of Saddam Hussein's dictatorship in Iraq was a failure to discover significant stocks of weapons of mass destruction and only some evidence of a collaborative relationship with al-Qa'eda (the 9/11 Commission Report found "extensive" and "troubling" contacts between Hussein and al-Qa'eda, but no "collaborative operational relationship"). These two revelations caused much consternation by some about whether the War on Terror should have been expanded to Iraq. Nevertheless, it seems clear that the United States—both the Executive and the Congress—acted appropriately given the basis of the information it had at the time. Indeed, considering the track record of the Hussein regime, the argument that he would acquire (if he did not still have them) and then pass on weapons of mass destruction to terrorists in the post-9/11 world remains convincing. When President Bush provided a final ultimatum to Saddam Hussein to relinquish power and avoid war, his actions were certainly colored by the realities of the post-9/11 environment in light of the following factual information:

- Saddam Hussein aggressively attacked two other nations—Iran and Kuwait—in direct violation of the principles of the Charter of the United Nations.
- Saddam Hussein launched ballistic missiles at Israel and Saudi Arabia—acts of aggressive war.
- Saddam Hussein used poison gas (a weapon of mass destruction) against Kurdish civilians in Iraq and against Iranian soldiers. In addition, Saddam Hussein's regime murdered untold tens of thousands for political purposes.
- Saddam Hussein's final declaration to the Security Council in response to Security Council Resolution 1441 was patently false.
- Saddam Hussein failed to comply with 17 United Nations Security Council resolutions regarding inspection of weapons of mass destruction. On December 16, 1998, in response to Iraq's ejection of all U.N. inspectors, the United States and Britain conducted four days of air strikes with aircraft and cruise missiles against Iraqi targets (Operation Desert Fox).
- In 1998, Congress passed a resolution that President William Clinton signed entitled the "Iraq Liberation Act," indicating that it should be the policy of the United States to support efforts to remove from power the regime of Saddam Hussein and to promote the emergence of a democratic government in Iraq.
- Saddam Hussein continued aggressive military attacks against the United States and Britain after the formal cessation of hostilities in 1991 by firing thousands of times on coalition aircraft patrolling the United Nations imposed "no fly zones" created in accordance with the cease fire of 1991. These attacks on American and British aircraft continued even after U.N. Resolution 1441 was passed and constituted an ongoing state of war under international law. This legal basis was clearly the strongest argument for the use of force by the United States.

While the end to major combat operations in Iraq was declared by President Bush in mid-2003, a new and deadly chapter in the Iraq War, now part of the War on Terror, quickly took hold—coalition forces and Iraqi civilians were targeted for murder by various groups of guerrilla fighters, common criminals, and terrorists. Even the capture of Saddam Hussein on December 13, 2003, did not significantly stem the growing volume of unconventional warfare. Only the dramatic Bush surge in combat troop strength spearheaded by General David Petraeus in 2007-2008 was able to put a halt to the cycle of violence.

The continued sectarian fighting between Shia and Sunni Muslims, as well as the al-Qa'eda terrorist attacks in Iraq, required the United States to alter its occupation strategy. Instead of reducing the number of troops on the ground in Iraq as hoped for in the occupation phase of the campaign, the United States was obliged to place about 150,000 military and 100,000 civilian personnel in Iraq (the exact number of civilian contractors was unknown but included large number of security contractors). In turn, because of the associated strain on its active duty military forces, the United States found that it had to utilize a great number of its reserve personnel to maintain the troop strength. With a death toll that exceeded 4,400 American soldiers (slightly less than 1/5 of the casualties were from non-combat related accidents), in 2009 the Bush Administration handed over a two-front conflict to President Obama.

At its heart, the Bush Doctrine was centered on a deep concern over the threat of a weapon of mass destruction passing into the hands of a terrorist group through a radical State such as Iran or Iraq, but the Bush Doctrine also embraced the concept of promoting the spread of democracy as the best long-term solution to defeating the terrorists. Bush's 2006 National Security Strategy reaffirmed that "[i]n the long run, winning the war on terror means winning the battle of ideas, for it is ideas that can turn the disenchanted into murderers willing to kill innocent victims."

5.3 The Obama Doctrine

When Senator Barack Obama ran for President of the United States in the 2008 election, his major campaign slogan was based on a cry for "change." Of course, even the novice student of political science knows that the promise of change crops up during practically every presidential campaign in American history and then quickly fades into oblivion once the winner takes office. In short, there really has been no significant changes from the Bush policies to the Obama policies. Indeed, in terms of dealing with the threat of militant Islam posed by al-Qa'eda, the Taliban, and associated forces, there can be little question that during his presidency, Obama actually retained many key Bush Administration policies. Although his efforts in the beginning to portray his ideas as somehow different played well with the mainstream media headlines of the day, Obama was largely ineffective in setting a clear departure from the policies of the Bush Administration. If anything, Obama sowed more confusion than Bush. For instance, President Obama's promises to provide a so-called "new and comprehensive strategy for Afghanistan and Pakistan" to address the threat of militant Islam took over ten months to hatch and resulted in the adoption of a Bush-styled "surge" (used in the Iraq War) to simply deploy additional troops to a level of 100,000 on the ground in Afghanistan.

President Obama's expressed desire to dismantle key elements of the Bush policies vis-à-vis al-Qa'eda, the Taliban, and associated forces began only days after taking the oath of office. Instead of creating an interagency task force to conduct a detailed study of all viable options and recommendations on how best to proceed in the War on Terror, the President issued haphazard executive orders mandating what were billed as sweeping changes in policy, and then established an interagency task force to study the consequences of his directives. In three executive orders (EO) issued on January 22, 2009, the President ordered: (1) EO 13492, the closure of Guantanamo Bay within one year; (2) EO 13492, the immediate halt of all ongoing military commissions (even though Congress had specifically authorized them); and (3) EO 13440, the suspension of the CIA's enhanced interrogation program. Ironically, within one year of the announcement, the first and second executive orders would be, for all practical purposes, functionally nullified and the third a non-event.

Strangely, while President Obama was unwilling for most of his first year in office to publicly and unequivocally call the conflict with al-Qa'eda a "war," his Administration early on vigorously argued before the federal district court in *Al Maqaleh v. Gates* that the conflict was in fact a war and that the Executive branch was entitled to detain indefinitely al-Qa'eda, Taliban, and associated enemy forces in Bagram Air Force Base, Afghanistan, under the 2001 Congressional Authorization for Use of Military Force.

Returning to his 2009 executive orders, President Obama's order to close the detention facility at Guantanamo Bay within a year never happened. In part, Obama's desire to close the facility met with a firestorm of opposition from the American people, even from his own Democrat Party. Not only did the Democrat-controlled Congress refuse to provide the Obama Administration with the $80 million it requested to close the facility, but Congress also placed numerous caveats on when, where, and how the President could transfer detainees, particularly if he wished to send them to the United States.

When President Obama took office in 2009, there were approximately 34,000 coalition troops on the ground in Afghanistan, with 30,000 from the United States. The coalition troops were under the command of NATO's ISAF (International Security Assistance Force) and drawn from approximately 30 nations. The CIA in 2010 reported that there were less than 100 al-Qa'eda fighters still in Afghanistan, but the Taliban was still very much active. Although President Obama had campaigned on a promise to get the United States out of Afghanistan, his November 2009 decision to increase American forces in a Bush-like surge saw over 140,000 troops pushed into the war-torn nation by early 2011. The Obama strategy was to convince the Taliban to come to the negotiating table so that the United States could withdraw. However, as predicted by many military experts, the Obama surge produced no lasting positive advantages against the Taliban and by 2012, just before the presidential elections in the United States, Obama announced the end of the surge and the beginning of the withdrawal of most American forces from Afghanistan. The Obama surge cost the United States military 1,000 dead and wounded and left the Taliban stronger after the surge than before the surge. Indeed, the number of American casualties passed the 2,500 mark under the Obama Administration. Critics correctly pointed out that President Obama's strategy failed because it was simply a recipe for a Viet Nam-type disaster where American soldiers were asked to take and hold ground but were never given goals for victory or allowed to take the battle to the heart of the enemy.

Still, Obama accomplished what Bush had not—Barack Obama killed the almost mythical al-Qa'eda leader Osama bin Landen. In a bold night raid on May 2, 2011, the terror leader was shot dead by American Special Forces at his heavily guarded hideout in Abbottabad, Pakistan. Unfortunately, this brilliant tactical victory which had eluded American forces for ten years was not parlayed into an overall strategic victory of withdrawing American forces and ending the conflict. In other words, instead of announcing a "mission accomplished" speech to rubricate that the ultimate goal of destroying al-Qa'eda was now complete with the death of their leader, Obama instead elected to stay the course in order to strike a deal with the Taliban. To be sure, if President Obama had ordered an immediate departure in 2011, America could have made a credible claim to victory regardless of whether or not the Taliban regained power. Indeed, it was the al-Qa'eda and not the Taliban that had attacked the United States on 9/11. When Obama left office there were about 8,400 American soldiers in Afghanistan, but no deal was ever struck.

In dealing with Iraq, President Obama took an entirely different approach. In October 2011, Obama used the disingenuous excuse that his Secretary of State was unable to secure a Status of Forces Agreement (SOFA) with the Iraqi government and precipitously ordered a rapid and complete withdrawal of all U.S. forces (about 40,000) from Iraq by the end of the year. Tragically, the Iraqi government was caught off guard by the rapid departure and the power vacuum left in Iraq was quickly filled by a terrorist group called the Islamic State of Iraq and al-Sham (ISIS) causing the War on Terror to expand exponentially across Iraq and now Syria.

At ISIS' peak of geographic power in 2016, the self-proclaimed Caliphate controlled an amazing 27,000 square miles of territory in Syria and Iraq. By then, in his final year in office, Obama came to the realization that if the War on Terror was to ever cease, the expansive radical Islamic Caliphate in Iraq and Syria had to be destroyed. He ordered an increase in drone attacks on various ISIS targets but no significant American combat forces on the ground. When Obama left office in 2017, the War on Terror was still being fought in Afghanistan and Iraq/Syria.

5.4 Trump Doctrine

On the campaign trail in 2016 then candidate Donald Trump expressed great frustration concerning the ongoing War on Terror, as well as the regional and global threat posed by ISIS in Iraq and Syria, where the War on Terror had expanded. Soon after his inauguration President Trump made it clear that it was his intention to disengage and end the conflicts. From Fort Myer, Virginia, on August 21, 2017, he stated:

> [T]he American people are weary of war without victory. Nowhere is this more evident than with the war in Afghanistan, the longest war in American history—17 years. I share the American people's frustration. I also share their frustration over a foreign policy that has spent too much time, energy, money, and most importantly lives, trying to rebuild countries in our own image, instead of pursuing our security interests above all other considerations.

Although previous visions of success by both Bush and Obama in the War on Terror were coupled to a long term commitment for the United States military to stay on the ground until a quasi-democratic government could take root in Afghanistan, President Trump early on signaled that his approach to the matter would be firmly rooted in a more achievable benchmark—some minimum level of stability on the ground coupled with an acceptable degree of security assurances from the Taliban against another 9/11-styled attack on the homeland emanating from Afghanistan. But first, Trump turned his attention to the sprawling geographic control of ISIS over large swaths of Iraq and Syria, calling his senior military and national security advisors together only days after being sworn into office to express his firm vision that the Pentagon must obliterate ISIS geographically. Trump immediately granted the military's request to lift the restrictive Obama-era Rules of Engagement and to allow combat decisions to be made at the lowest level by commanders on the ground. Under his decisive leadership, subsequent military victories against ISIS followed to include the retaking of the stronghold of Mosul in July 2017 and the destruction of the much-hardened ISIS capital of Raqqa in Syria in October 2017.

Interestingly enough, the so-called ground coalition that cut ISIS apart consisted primarily of a combined force of about 100,000 Iraqi troops and Shi'ite militia versus perhaps 20,000 heavily entrenched ISIS fighters. While the United States provided some 5,000 troops to the coalition (mostly spearheaded by America's Special Forces), it was the crucial American air power that turned the tide and provided for the spectacular victories on the ground. By early 2018, ISIS was no longer in control of any significant territory in either Syria or Iraq and untold thousands of ISIS fighters had been killed in lawful combat operations, the remnants, perhaps 3,000, escaped into the desert where they now exist like al-Qa'eda—under the ground.

Of course, the issue of what next to do in the areas vacated by ISIS demanded attention. To be sure, although ISIS was now displaced the organization was still capable of conducting limited terror attacks. In addition, large swaths of Iraq and Syria were in total ruins. In sharp contrast to previous American administrations which were fixated on notions of nation building, President Trump refused to commit American troops to either peacekeeping or nation building. Brett McGurk, the special envoy for the Global Coalition to Counter ISIS, stated that the U.S. would help stabilize areas liberated from ISIS but would not run hospitals or schools. According to McGurk, "It's not our responsibility." Instead, Trump ordered a small number of troops to remain in the region as a show of force and to conduct limited military operations when required. The most notable American military effort in this regard was the brilliant raid that killed ISIS leader al-Baghdadi in 2019.

Satisfied that his military strategy of complete battlefield victory against ISIS would work, President Trump turned his attention to Afghanistan and in late August 2017, he admitted that while his "original instinct was to pull out" of Afghanistan completely, he decided instead to order an unspecified increase in U.S. troop presence to signal to the Taliban that there were no timelines as in the Obama Administration that would dictate when the United States would leave the country. By February 2020, approximately 13,000 U.S. forces were hunkered down in Afghanistan conducting training and security missions. Of course, Trump had no intention of leaving Afghanistan without reaching a deal with the Taliban.

In contrast to Obama's blunt strategy to use the stick of increased military might in the Obama troop surge to force the Taliban to negotiate peace, the Trump strategy for negotiation was a mixture of firm resolve, persuasion, and that ever-unpredictable element of good timing. Whatever the mixture of said ingredients, Trump was able to get the Taliban and the Afghan government to sign a "condition based" peace deal on February 28, 2020. For the United States and its coalition partners, the peace plan was directly tied to a "phased withdrawal" of American forces to be completed, if all went well, within a mere 14 months—May 2021. For their part, the Taliban would cease armed attacks, pledge to shun terror groups, and coexist with the current government in Afghanistan.

Critics may ultimately be correct in predictions that the Taliban will not keep its word to shun terror and terror groups or attempt to topple the current Afghan government, although as in the case of the Paris Peace Accords which ended American involvement in Vietnam, this may not fully manifest itself until American troops have left Afghanistan far behind. What is fundamentally clear is that the United States has given much blood and treasure for the Afghan people—nearly 3,600 Americans killed in action. Most certainly, the Trump Administration believed that enough time was given to the Afghan people for them to now chart their own destiny towards a better way of life and system of rule. Twenty years was enough. The Biden Administration apparently concurs.

5.5 Ending the War on Terror

In terms of identifying a general Commander in Chief leadership theme, all three American presidents that presided over the War on Terror embraced different strategies. President Bush sought to contain by military action overseas the rising threat of radical Islam and a single nation he believed might supply weapons of mass destruction to terrorists while robustly using domestic law enforcement to keep the homeland safe from future terror attacks. President Obama sought to ignore domestic jihadi terrorism altogether and with the exception of the short-lived troop surge in Afghanistan, used the military to engage in pin point military strikes overseas in order to blunt the influence and growth of selected international Islamic terror groups. President Trump's leadership theme was distinctly different—he early on publicly recognized the domestic threat of "radical Islam" within the United States and aggressively embarked on a strategy to annihilate ISIS as a geographic entity in Syria and Iraq, the then center of gravity for radical Islam and the War on Terror. He also negotiated a peace deal with the Taliban and departed Afghanistan.

Throughout America's almost 20-year asymmetrical War on Terror many have concluded that a central problem would be the difficulty of defining "victory." To a degree, this is a valid observation, particularly given the West's penchant for nation-building and the spreading of democracy. Measured by wartime objectives by destroying the al-Qa'eda training camps in Afghanistan and expelling the Taliban from control of that country in 2001, the Bush Administration had scored a resounding battlefield victory and should have ended the war with a complete withdrawal of its forces. Nevertheless, President Bush elected to stay and rebuild (build) Afghanistan which meant that the conflict might very well continue indefinitely. Indeed, Bush vastly expanded the scope of the War on Terror with his ill-informed 2003 military campaign against Saddam Hussein and the resulting rise of a vicious terror splinter group known as al-Qa'eda in Iraq.

President Obama inherited a two-front conflict and also failed to achieve a victory in his eight years in office. Even with Obama's success in killing the elusive Osama bin Laden in 2011, he refused to parlay the brilliant tactical victory into a larger strategic victory that would have facilitated a withdrawal. Then, with the rise of ISIS in Iraq and Syria, the Obama Administration ran out of time and handed the seemingly never-ending conflict over to the new Commander-in-Chief, Donald Trump. Unlike his predecessors, President Trump was determined to end a war that cost upward of 1 trillion dollars (in Afghanistan alone) and thousands of American lives.

President Trump racked up an impressive battlefield victory over ISIS, culminating with the death of their leader and driving the remnants underground and into hiding. Unlike his two predecessors, however, President Trump grabbed this significant victory and pragmatically shunned off nation building, leaving only a handful of troops on the ground to provide assistance to the Iraqi government. To date, the region is more or less stable and the Trump policy has worked. For Trump, it was certain that stability equated to victory. In tandem with fighting ISIS, Trump also focused on Afghanistan where he slightly bumped up American troops to signal the seriousness of his intent to remain until a deal could be cut with the Taliban. While Trump had no intention of destroying the Taliban as he had done with ISIS, his desire to negotiate a settlement hinged on key guarantees from the Taliban. Amazingly, soon thereafter Trump was able to broker and sign a peace deal with the Taliban which would see the withdrawal of all U.S. forces by 2021 and the end of the Afghanistan conflict for the United States.

The twin achievements by the Trump Administration—ISIS and Taliban—certainly signaled an end to the War on Terror. To be sure, other challenges and set backs will certainly arise from both regions of concern, but the ultimate signpost for the end of the War on Terror arrived.

Finally, to those who suggest that an American departure from Afghanistan or Syria will lead to greater instability and a higher likelihood of another 9/11-styled attack on the homeland, the answer is as it has always been. In other words, if attacked or threatened with imminent attack, America will no doubt respond with overwhelming military might in self-defense as fully recognized and authorized in Article 51 of the United Nations Charter.

5.6 Questions for Discussion

1. *Roots of militant Islamic aggression.* The 9/11 Commission convened by Congress tried to explain the root of militant Islamic thought:

   They (Bin Laden and al Qaeda) say that America had attacked Islam; America is responsible for all conflicts involving Muslims. Thus Americans are blamed when Israelis fight with Palestinians, when Russians fight with Chechens, when Indians fight with Kashmiri Muslims, and when the Philippine government fights ethnic Muslims in its southern islands. America is also held responsible for the governments of Muslim countries, derided by al Qaeda as "your agents." Bin Laden has stated flatly, "Our fight against these governments is not separate from our fight against you." These charges found a ready audience among millions of Arabs and Muslims angry at the United States because of issues ranging from Iraq to Palestine to America's support for their countries' repressive rulers.

   How did the Trump approach to the War on Terror help or hinder victory?

2. *Will cold-war deterrence work against al-Qa'eda?* *See* David Rising, *Iraq Terror Boss Seeks Nuke Experts*, SAN ANTONIO EXPRESS NEWS, Sept. 29, 2006, at A1 (Before his death in 2010, Al-Qa'eda's chief in Iraq, Abu Ayyub al-Masri, called for nuclear scientists to join his group's holy war against the West).

Selected Bibliography

Lake, Anthony. Special Assistant to the President for National Security Affairs, Address to Johns Hopkins University, School of Advanced International Studies. Oct. 21, 1993.

Lesser, Ian O., et al. COUNTERING THE NEW TERRORISM, 1999.

Lillich, Richard. HUMANITARIAN INTERVENTION AND THE UNITED NATIONS, 1973.

Living with Faith and Hope After September 11, U.S. Conference of Catholic Bishops, Dec. 2001. Pub. No. 5-491 USCCB Pub. Wash. D.C.

McDougal, Myers S., and Florentino P. Feliciano. LAW AND MINIMUM WORLD PUBLIC ORDER, 1961.

McHugh, William. *Forcible Self-help in International Law*, NAVAL WAR COLLEGE REVIEW, No. 25 (1972).

National Defense Authorization Act for Fiscal Year 2010, Pug. L. No. 111-84, 12 Stat. 2190.

Quinn, Andrew. *Loss of Nuclear Material Tabulated*, SAN JOSE MERCURY NEWS, Mar. 7, 2002, at A1.

Roberts, Guy B. *The Counterproliferation Self-Help Paradigm: A Legal Regime for Enforcing the Norm Prohibiting the Proliferation of Weapons of Mass Destruction*, DENVER JOURNAL OF INTERNATIONAL LAW & POLICY 485 (Summer 1999).

Rummel, R. J. DEATH BY GOVERNMENT: GENOCIDE AND MASS MURDER IN THE TWENTIETH CENTURY, 1994.

The 9/11 Commission Report: The National Commission on Terrorist Attacks Upon the United States, 107th Cong. 51. 2004.

US-Taliban Peace Deal, Washington Post (Feb. 29, 2020), https://www.washingtonpost.com/context-t/u-s-taliban-peace-deal/7aab0f58-dd5c-430d-9557-1b6672d889c3/?itid=lk_inline_manual_3 (Contains the full text of the unclassified version of the peace deal).

Von Glahn, Gerhard. LAW AMONG NATIONS, SIXTH EDITION. 1992.

Zakaria, Fareed. *Why Do They Hate Us?* NEWSWEEK, Oct. 22, 2001, at 24.

Chapter 6

Civil Liberties and the War on Terror

The boisterous sea of liberty is never without a wave.

—Thomas Jefferson

The probability that terrorist organizations like al-Qa'eda or ISIS may employ chemical, nuclear, or biological weapons of mass destruction in suicide attacks poses not only a direct threat to the well-being of tens of thousands of innocent people, but also raises new controversies regarding the possible curtailment of long recognized civil liberties. In creating greater domestic security from future terrorist attacks, the United States government must not trample on American liberties in the name of preserving them. This concern speaks to the matter of "due process." The term due process is most commonly used to describe the rights that Americans enjoy as spelled out in the Fourteenth Amendment of the United States Constitution:

> All persons born or naturalized in the United States, and subject to the jurisdiction thereof, are citizens of the United States and of the State wherein they reside. No State shall make or enforce any law which shall abridge the privileges or immunities of citizens of the United States; nor shall any State deprive any person of life, liberty, or property, without due process of law; nor deny to any person within its jurisdiction the equal protection of the laws.

The term has also come to be associated with American values of fairness and reasonableness in the treatment of others.

By definition, the traditional approach to combating terrorism is encompassed in two terms—antiterrorism and counterterrorism. Although most associate the term *counterterrorism* to cover both concepts, strictly speaking, antiterrorism involves all those steps and actions taken by authorities to decrease the probability of a terrorist act from occurring. Antiterrorism, the proactive, preventative stage of stopping terrorism, includes techniques designed to harden potential high profile targets (e.g., government buildings or military installations), as well as actions taken to detect a planned terrorist attack before it occurs. For example, to prevent future terrorist attacks, both the Pentagon and private industry are experimenting with video surveillance, modeling techniques, and commercial technologies such as those used to identify automatic teller machine customers by scanning their faces.

One of the facets of the War on Terror in terms of domestic response was the realization that antiterrorism relies heavily on the efforts of ordinary citizens who, when observing suspicious behavior, are willing to notify law enforcement. The Department of Homeland Security regularly reminds the public that the "most effective weapon against terrorism is you." Suspicious activity is the key and can involve reporting on witnessing activity in any of the five basic elements related to conducting a terror attack: (1) target identification, (2) intelligence gathering and planning, (3) logistics and training, (4) conducting rehearsals or dry runs, and (5) the attack itself. Sometimes the suspicions prove profitable, as with the September 2002 arrest of six members of the Lackawanna radical Islamic sleeper terrorist cell in New York (based on a tip by an Arab American), the August 2006 arrest of 24 al-Qa'eda-styled radicals in the failed plot to detonate liquid bombs on ten planes bound to the United States from Britain (based also on a tip from the British Muslim community), or the failed plot by Faisal Shahzad in May 2010 to car bomb New York's Times Square. However, sometimes the suspicions prove incorrect, as in the 2003 case of three men of Middle Eastern descent who were overheard "joking" at a Georgia restaurant about a terrorist plot to be conducted in Miami, Florida (the three were subsequently stopped in Florida and, after a day-long investigation, were released). Therefore, antiterrorism is very much a bottom-up approach which must include ordinary citizens as a first line of defense.

America allows free speech in most circumstances, but never allows illegal violence. Another innovative antiterrorism program is designed to ease tensions between the government and a variety of antigovernment organizations. Following the 1995 Oklahoma terror bombing, for instance, this approach saw Federal Bureau of Investigation (FBI) agents talking directly to various so-called militia leaders. From Montana to Indiana, federal agents opened dialogues with leaders of several militia organizations to provide a forum for discussion in the hope that channels of communication would help prevent acts of violence. While this approach will bear little fruit with al-Qa'eda-styled terrorists, it is still wise to explore all avenues of prevention measures—informants can be recruited to work against the terror group.

Counterterrorism measures are those tactical actions taken by authorities in response to an actual terrorist incident. In this vein, planning and training will have a great impact on the success or failure of real world counterterrorist measures. While National Security Presidential Directive 5 and Presidential Decision Directive 39 designate the Department of Justice (DOJ), through the FBI, as the lead agency in the event of a terrorist attack on the homeland, the expected mass casualties, physical damage, and potential for civil disorder resulting from a weapon of mass destruction attack would undoubtedly see a shift to the Department of Defense (DOD) as the *de facto* lead federal agency for many counterterrorism issues. The 2013 Boston marathon bombings by Islamic extremists underscored the quick reaction by first responders, but all can agree that the time to stop a terrorist is before they strike.

In hindsight, the War on Terror touched seven main areas of concern in the context of developing durable legal and policy underpinnings. They involve: (1) the use of military commissions; (2) the power of the United States to investigate, detain, and question terrorist suspects; (3) the expansion of the use of the United States military to enforce domestic law; (4) border security/immigration; (5) the use of new information-gathering technologies; (6) the issue of targeted killing; and (7) the protection of Constitutional rights.

6.1 Past Efforts to Address Terrorism

As the world watched helplessly while hijacked planes smashed into the World Trade Center and the Pentagon, the attack exposed gaping vulnerabilities in both United States military and law enforcement strategies to guard the nation against a full-fledged terrorist assault by suicidal murderers. Although the threat of a significant terrorist attack on American soil was not an unknown topic of discussion prior to the events of September 11, 2001, very little was done by the federal government in the area of antiterrorism. In 2004, the 567 page 9/11 Commission Report, not only traced the movements of the nineteen hijackers as they circumvented various law enforcement and administrative barriers without detection, but also pointed out in detail how the entire intelligence community failed to stop the attacks.

Prior to 9/11, the actions to address the threat of organized terrorism, particularly militant Islamic groups that targeted American interests, were piecemeal and misguided. Methods were long on rhetoric but short on action. After the dual bombings of two American embassies in Africa in the summer of 1998 left more than 300 people dead, President Clinton vowed that "[n]o matter how long it takes, or where it takes us, we will pursue terrorists until the cases are solved and justice is done." Militarily, President Clinton launched seventy-five cruise missiles at some al-Qa'eda terrorist training camps in Afghanistan and a suspected VX nerve gas production facility at the Shifa Pharmaceuticals plant in Khartoum, Sudan. Nancy Soderberg, a former National Security Council senior aide in the Clinton administration later admitted: "In hindsight, it wasn't enough, and anyone involved in policy would have to admit that." In the kindest light to all administrations (including Ronald Reagan) before September 11, 2001, action by the government was ineffectual because the United States had no frame of reference in which to gauge the magnitude of the threat. The government was mired in old thinking and, as the 9/11 Commission Report related, exhibited a serious "lack of imagination" by its intelligence community.

In the international sphere, a brief survey of the American approach to global terrorism prior to September 11, 2001, reveals that America was content to enter into a handful of specific international conventions aimed at encouraging multilateral cooperation in punishing certain narrowly defined acts of terrorism such as hostage taking and hijacking of aircraft. Some examples of specific antiterrorist conventions include: The Convention on Offenses and Certain Other Acts Committed on Board Aircraft (Tokyo Convention, 1963); Convention for the Suppression of Unlawful Seizure of Aircraft (Hague Convention, 1971); Convention for the Suppression of Unlawful Acts Against the Safety of Civil Aviation (Montreal Convention, 1973); Convention on the Prevention and Punishment of Crimes Against Internationally Protected Persons, Including Diplomatic Agents (New York Convention, 1976-1977); and the International Convention Against the Taking of Hostages (Hostages Convention, 1979). As impressive as the titles sound for these ad hoc conventions, the general position of the United States was simply a mirror of the world community's ineffective approach to the emerging problem of global Islamic terrorism. Washington seemed content to react to terrorism incidents, using the criminal justice system when it could.

In the domestic arena, apart from various criminal reforms making terrorist acts abroad a crime under United States domestic law, most of the attention of the executive and legislative branches of government were focused on passing various pieces of domestic counterterrorism legislation, such as the 1996 Defense Against Weapons of Mass Destruction Act, commonly referred to as the NLD Act after its sponsors' names, Senators Nunn, Lugar, and Domenici. This legislation was limited in scope and designed primarily to assist in planning and training efforts for the use of emergency personnel responding to a major terrorist incident involving a weapon of mass destruction. Early on, these initiatives received much deserved criticism as a band-aid approach to the real world problem of a major terrorist attack.

6.2 Addressing Terrorism Since 9/11

As is often the case in addressing new threats, the exact scope of the danger posed by al-Qa'eda-styled terrorism is often very difficult to assess. Speculation concerning asymmetric tactics can run from biological terrorism to nuclear terrorism to cyberterrorism, but only probabilities serve to gauge the scenarios. Mega-terrorism is the great known unknown. We know it can happen, but we do not know when, where, or in what form it will next come. In turn, any new security measure is going to threaten, to some degree, the lifestyle and some basic rights that Americans have long enjoyed. For example, the Obama Administration's employment of almost 1,000 new body scanners at airports, following the Christmas Day 2009 attempted Detroit airplane bombing by al-Qa'eda recruit Abdulmutallab, caused a renewed debate about privacy violations. Proclaiming that any changes in the name of national security will entail a "slippery slope" that will see the nation slide into a draconian police state, some civil libertarians prefer to remain frozen in place, vehemently opposed to all changes. The proper approach, of course, is for one to identify specific notches in the slope—bright and clearly defined lines—where the new rule of law will be established for a particular security measure.

The government has taken two major steps to fulfill its obligation to protect the American people from future attacks by al-Qa'eda-styled terrorists. The first was the creation of a new cabinet-level department entitled the Office of Homeland Security and the second was the passage of an exhaustive piece of anti-terror legislation known by short title as the USA PATRIOT Act, and its many renewals for various provisions over the subsequent years. The 2001 USA PATRIOT Act passed in the Senate by a vote of 98–1. The House of Representatives passed their version by a vote of 377-56.

The Homeland Security Act (HSA) of 2002 consolidated the federal government's emergency response capabilities under the Department of Homeland Security (DHS). The Act directed the Secretary of DHS to oversee the personnel and assets of the Federal Emergency Management Agency (FEMA) and other related agencies. The DHS (through FEMA) is the lead federal agency for consequence management and support to law enforcement and has the authority to coordinate the federal government's response to both natural and man-made disasters, including terrorist attacks, on American soil. DHS houses over 170,000 employees from 22 agencies. DHS is divided into four separate entities: (1) Information and Infrastructure Protection; (2) Border and Transportation Security; (3) Science and Technology; and (4) Emergency Response. The most notable agencies under the DHS umbrella include the U.S. Coast Guard, Customs Service, Immigration and Naturalization Service (now abolished and divided into three agencies), Border Patrol, Secret Service, Transportation Security Administration and Federal Management Agency.

The HSA provides for a number of new legal standards regarding security issues. For instance, fearing that terrorists may target any number of the nation's critical infrastructures such as power plants, financial networks, airlines, etc., the HSA included rather broad exceptions to the Freedom of Information Act (FOIA) protecting private entities that voluntarily submit "critical infrastructure information" (CII) to the government. The law also provides that any government employee that willfully discloses CII information to the public shall be held criminally liable.

Another HSA provision that provides a legal liability shield to anti-terrorism technologies is the Support Anti-Terrorism by Fostering Effective Technologies Act (SAFETY Act). The Act provides that the DHS Secretary may exempt "sellers" of anti-terrorism technology from tort liability for injuries sustained by third parties resulting from a terrorist attack. Thus, sellers of "any product, equipment, service, device, or technology designed, developed, modified, or procured for the specific purpose of preventing, detecting, identifying, or deterring acts of terrorism" can apply for government certification from DHS. Once the Secretary has certified that the proposed "goods" conform to the seller's specifications, a rebuttable presumption is established that can "only be overcome by evidence showing that the seller acted fraudulently or with willful misconduct in submitting information to the Secretary during the course of the Secretary's consideration of such technology." The SAFETY Act approach departs from the government contractors defense set out in *Boyle v. United Technologies Corp*, where the private party contractor obtained immunity only if he conformed to the government's specifications.

In tandem with domestic strategies to address terrorism, the 9/11 Commission Report correctly recommended that the United States had to more sharply define a strategy that would ensure that terror groups would not find sanctuary in what it called "the least governed, most lawless places in the world." The Commission listed western Pakistan, Afghanistan, Saudi Arabia, Yemen, West Africa, and Southeast Asia as among the most troubled. Other trouble spots which bear note include places like Libya and Morocco, a known sanctuary for al-Qa'eda adherents and the home of most of the seventeen suspects jailed in the March 11, 2004, bombings which killed over 200 people in Spain.

6.3 Detainee Status

After the 2001 military campaign in Afghanistan overthrew the Taliban government, the vast majority of the Taliban fighters were processed and released in Afghanistan. Nevertheless, a large detention facility was created by the United States military at Bagram Air Force Base in Afghanistan to detain those al-Qa'eda and Taliban fighters deemed to be either too dangerous to parole or who were suspected of committing war crimes. Over the years, with the continuing war in Afghanistan, the population at Bagram grew to well over 1,000 by 2011. In 2014, the facility was finally turned completely over to the Afghan government. While the detention facility at Bagram Air Force Base never received much international attention, its sister detention facility created in 2002 at the U.S. Navy Base in Guantanamo Bay, Cuba, quickly became the epicenter of a relentless propaganda campaign by those opposed to the War on Terror. At its peak, the al-Qa'eda and Taliban enemy combatants sent to Guantanamo Bay, Cuba, numbered up to 800 detainees representing approximately 40 countries, with Saudi Arabia, Afghanistan, and Yemen the most represented. Under a "rehabilitation" policy, the Bush Administration released over 500 of those detained at Guantanamo Bay. Countries to which detainees have been released include Albania, Afghanistan, Australia, Bangladesh, Bahrain, Belgium, Britain, Denmark, Egypt, France, Germany, Iran, Iraq, Jordan, Kuwait, Libya, Maldives, Mauritania, Morocco, Pakistan, Russia, Saudi Arabia, Spain, Sweden, Sudan, Tajikistan, Turkey, Uganda, and Yemen. By early 2014, around 150 were still being held at Guantanamo Bay, to include 14 high-level al-Qa'eda operatives who had been previously kept in undisclosed locations. Although President Obama sternly vowed in January 2009 to close the Guantanamo detention facility by January 2010, as of this writing the Trump Administration still operates the facility, although the number of detainees is less than 30. Nevertheless, the legal theory employed by Bush, Obama, Trump, and Biden to detain these individuals without criminal charges is the same—they are detained under the law of war as enemy combatants and will be detained until either hostilities cease or, in the cases of many, specific charges are levied against them in a military commission or other legal forum for associated crimes.

Early on, two questions arose regarding due process concerns for these individuals. First, were they entitled to treatment as prisoners of war or as "other detainees" under the Geneva Conventions? Second, if the United States opted to try these individuals criminally, should they be tried in a United States federal district court or by means of the military commission process?

An analysis of the first question regarding the status of al-Qa'eda and Taliban fighters under international law begins with the fact that the United States has long incorporated in its laws the international law of war, both customary and codified (*Paquete Habana*, 175 U.S. 667). In a confusing 2002 determination, the Bush Administration unilaterally determined that the captured al-Qa'eda and Taliban fighters were not eligible for prisoner of war status nor were they entitled to protections contained in Common Article 3 of the 1949 Geneva Conventions, which sets out the minimum standards of treatment for all detainees in armed conflict. Acting under this line of reasoning the Bush Administration blocked the military from using the "Article 5 tribunal" provisions of the Third Geneva Convention to determine whether a particular detainee should be accorded prisoner of war (POW) status or not.

The Bush Administration reasoned that since the al-Qa'eda fighters belonged to a terrorist organization and were not recognized members of an armed force, they are unlawful belligerents under the law of war. *Army Field Manual* (FM) 27-10, The Law of Land Warfare, codifies the law of land warfare. Paragraph 60(b) of FM 27-10 indicates that "[p]ersons who are not members of the armed forces as defined in [the Geneva Conventions], who bear arms or engage in other conduct hostile to the enemy thereby deprive themselves of many of the privileges attaching to the members of the civilian population." This means that they are responsible for breaches of the law of war, but are not entitled to the status of POW - they are "illegal enemy combatants." In the view of the Bush Administration, al-Qa'eda engaged in acts of war both in the September 11, 2001, attacks and in fighting alongside the Taliban forces in the internationally recognized armed conflict which followed in Afghanistan.

As to the captured Taliban fighters, the Bush Administration determined that they were likewise not entitled to POW status under the Geneva Conventions because of their failure to comply with the Conventions' criterion which requires lawful combatants to wear distinctive military insignia, i.e., uniforms which would make them distinguishable from the civilian population at a distance. In finding that the Taliban "have not effectively distinguished themselves from the civilian population," the United States also added that the Taliban fighters had further forfeited any special status because they had "adopted and provided support to the unlawful terrorist objectives of the al-Qa'eda." While the latter finding would not necessarily indicate that the Taliban fighters would not be entitled to POW status, the former finding would. In short, POW status is conferred solely on those persons who are "[m]embers of armed forces of a Party to the conflict or members of militias and members of other volunteer corps, including those of organized resistance movements, belonging to a Party...provided that such...fulfill[s]" four specific conditions:

a) That of being commanded by a person responsible for his subordinates;
b) That of having a fixed distinctive sign recognizable at a distance;
c) That of carrying arms openly; and
d) That of conducting their operations in accordance with the laws and customs of war.

The Bush Administration also determined that the additional protections of the Geneva Conventions, i.e., Common Article 3, did not apply, although the Bush repeatedly indicated that all detainees were to be treated in accordance with the humanitarian concerns set out in the Geneva Conventions.

The Bush Administration's rejection of the long standing rules associated with detaining, classifying, and treating combatants under the law of war as codified in various Army documents to include Army Regulation 190-8, Enemy Prisoners of War, Retained Personnel, Civilian Internees and Other Detainees (Oct. 1997), was finally rejected by the June 2006 Supreme Court decision in *Hamdan v. Rumsfeld*. The Court found that even though the detainees were not entitled to the status of POW, Common Article 3 of the Geneva Conventions did apply and did in fact protect the detainees from being subjected to violence, outrages on personal dignity, torture, and cruel, humiliating, or degrading treatment. Although existing Department of Defense directives, orders, policies and doctrine already conformed with the standards of Common Article 3, the DOD quickly issued new treatment guidelines for detainees that incorporated the basic standards set out in Common Article 3.

As to the 2003 Iraq War, the Bush Administration went to war applying the Geneva Conventions in full. With the end of major combat operations against the Iraqi military in May 2003, however, the picture became far less clear. Like the Afghanistan theater of war, the Iraq War also mandated that the large number of detainees apprehended had to be categorized and housed. Accordingly, the United States grouped the Iraqi detainees into one of three categories: (1) Iraqi soldiers who qualified as POWs under the Geneva Conventions; (2) those suspected of having links to terrorist groups (to include sectarian militias such as Muatada al-Sadr's Mahdi Army and Saddam loyalists), called "security detainees;" and (3) common criminals.

Those in the first category were mostly captured during the major combat phase of the Iraq War and were quickly processed and released back into Iraqi society within a few months. While most of the prisoners were treated in accordance with the protections of the Geneva Conventions, the U.S. military self-reported several separate incidents of physical abuse by American guards, most often physical assaults during the first few hours of the detention. As POWs, this particular class of detainees was not required to give any further information upon additional questioning by American forces. To ensure that all parties to the conflict understood this rule of law, Article 17 of the Third Geneva Convention provides the following:

> No physical or mental torture, *nor any other form of coercion*, may be inflicted on prisoners of war to secure from them information of any kind whatever. Prisoners of war who refuse to answer may not be *threatened, insulted, or exposed to any unpleasant or disadvantageous treatment of any kind* [emphasis added].

Those in the second category were held for indefinite periods of time pending interrogation and then either released or transferred to the new Iraqi justice system. The number of detainees in United States custody in Iraq peaked in 2007 at 26,000. The security detainees were held in two camps, one in Baghdad and the other in southern Iraq (Abu Ghraib was closed in 2006). In 2008 the numbers fell below 20,000 and continued to dramatically decline in 2009 until all were turned over to Iraqi control by 2010. Currently, the Iraqi government now has control over all detention operations.

6.4 Case Law on Detainee Issues

This section contains the most prominent federal court cases associated with the War on Terror with the exception of the 2006 Supreme Court case of *Hamdan v. Rumsfeld*. While *Hamdan* is significant because it mandated that Common Article 3 of the Geneva Conventions applied to all detainees, its primary impact rests on the issue of military commissions and will be addressed in the next section of this chapter.

On June 28, 2004, the same day that the United States transferred power to the interim government in Iraq, the United States Supreme Court handed down a series of opinions regarding the Bush Administration's authority to designate suspected terrorists as "enemy combatants" and to hold such individuals and others without trial, without access to the courts, without charges, and incommunicado. Disregarding the Supreme Court's 1950 decision in *Johnson v. Eisentrager*, which held that the right of habeas did not attach to an "enemy alien who, at no relevant time and in no stage of his captivity, has been within the territorial jurisdiction" of the United States, the Court held in *Rasul v. Bush*, that the federal court considered Guantanamo Bay, Cuba, to be within the court's jurisdiction. In *Hamdi v. Rumsfeld*, an 8-1 plurality opinion provided that even in "a state of war" the President's decision to designate an individual, in this case a U.S. citizen, as an enemy combatant would still allow that individual a "fair opportunity to rebut the government's factual assertions before a neutral decisionmaker." Despite sensationalized news media headlines that the Bush Administration had been chastised by the Supreme Court, the Court actually upheld the major thrust of the executive's war-making power to designate an individual (even a United States citizen) as an enemy combatant and to hold that person indefinitely without criminal charges. In other words, *Hamdi* held that the President did have the authority to designate a suspected al-Qa'eda terrorist as an "enemy combatant," which means that the individual could be held without charges, but the individual so designated had the right to contest that designation before a neutral decisionmaker. Hamdi, who was apprehended in Afghanistan, was released subsequent to the 2004 Supreme Court ruling under the terms of an agreement between the government and Hamdi.

In a clear effort to get Congress to pass legislation authorizing the establishment of a judicial panel to make those determinations for all detainees held in Guantanamo Bay and for United States citizen Hamdi, the Court did not define what it meant by a neutral decisionmaker. Amazingly, leaving it up to the lower courts, Congress, or the Bush Administration to work out the exact standards, the Court did signal that the hearings might not be very extensive in nature, the burden could be shifted to the detainee, and that a reviewing judge could relax the standards for admissibility of evidence. Speaking for four members of the majority, Justice O'Connor (her husband was a former Army officer in the Army's Judge Advocate General Corps) even went so far as to observe that "[t]here remains the possibility that the standards we have articulated could be met by...[a] military tribunal."

One immediate by-product of the Supreme Court decisions was the creation of a Combatant Status Review Tribunal (CSRT) in July of 2004. The CSRT was established by the Secretary of Defense to make independent determinations about whether the detainees held at Guantanamo Bay were properly classified as enemy combatants. The term enemy combatant is "an individual who was part of or supporting the Taliban or al-Qa'eda forces, or associated forces that are engaged in hostilities against the United States or its coalition partners...." The panel, made up of three senior military officers, held an administrative hearing where each detainee had the opportunity to present reasonably available evidence and witnesses. As an administrative hearing, the CSRT was not bound by the rules of evidence that would apply in a court but was bound to assess, "to the extent practicable, whether any statement derived from or relating to such detainee was obtained as a result of coercion and the probative values, if any, of such statement." The detainee was represented by a military officer and the detainee's personal representative could view classified information. The CSRT standard for its determination was a "preponderance of the evidence," but a detainee could request a new CSRT at least once a year to present evidence that the detainee was no longer a threat and should be released. The CSRT reviewed the cases of all individual detainees in Guantanamo Bay who wished to appear. In fact, as a consequence of this process, over 500 detainees were deemed not likely to engage in future hostilities against the United States and released from Guantanamo Bay. Nevertheless, reports show that in many cases the CSRT was wrong—scores of released detainees actively rejoined hostilities and engaged in additional acts of terrorism. Some estimates are that over 30 percent of those released rejoined the ranks of radical Islam. Currently, the Biden Administration conducts these assessments of detainee status via an interagency Guantanamo Review Task Force. The Task Force must approve release by unanimous consent and in accordance with Congressionally-mandated rules, the Biden Administration must inform Congress of its intent to transfer/release a detainee at least 15 days before their transfer.

AL-BIHANI v. OBAMA
United States Court of Appeals for the District of Columbia Circuit
No. 09-5051 (Jan. 5, 2010)

BROWN, *Circuit Judge*:

Ghaleb Nassar Al-Bihani appeals the denial of his petition for a writ of habeas corpus and seeks reversal or remand. He claims his detention is unauthorized by statute and the procedures of his habeas proceeding were constitutionally infirm. We reject these claims and affirm the denial of his petition.

I

Al-Bihani, a Yemeni citizen, has been held at the U.S. naval base detention facility in Guantanamo Bay, Cuba since 2002. He came to Guantanamo by a circuitous route. It began in Saudi Arabia in the first half of 2001 when a local sheikh issued a religious challenge to Al-Bihani. In response, Al-Bihani traveled through Pakistan to Afghanistan eager to defend the Taliban's Islamic state against the Northern Alliance. Along the way, he stayed at what the government alleges were Al Qaeda-affiliated guesthouses; Al-Bihani only concedes they were affiliated with the Taliban. During this transit period, he may also have received instruction at two Al Qaeda terrorist training camps, though Al-Bihani disputes this. What he does not dispute is that he eventually accompanied and served a paramilitary group allied with the Taliban, known as the 55th Arab Brigade, which included Al Qaeda members within its command structure and which fought on the front lines against the Northern Alliance. He worked as the brigade's cook and carried a brigade-issued weapon, but never fired it in combat. Combat, however—in the form of bombing by the U.S.-led Coalition that invaded Afghanistan in response to the attacks of September 11, 2001—forced the 55th to retreat from the front lines in October 2001. At the end of this protracted retreat, Al-Bihani and the rest of the brigade surrendered, under orders, to Northern

Alliance forces, and they kept him in custody until his handover to U.S. Coalition forces in early 2002. The U.S. military sent Al-Bihani to Guantanamo for detention and interrogation.

After the Supreme Court held in *Rasul v. Bush*, 542 U.S. 466, 483-84 (2004), that the statutory habeas jurisdiction of federal courts extended to Guantanamo Bay, Al-Bihani filed a habeas petition with the U.S. District Court for the District of Columbia, challenging his detention under 28 U.S.C. § 2241(a). The district court stayed the petition until the Supreme Court in *Boumediene v. Bush*, 128 S. Ct. 2229 (2008), held that the section of the Military Commissions Act of 2006 (2006 MCA), Pub. L. No. 109-366, 120 Stat. 2600 (codified in part at 28 U.S.C. § 2241 & note), that withdrew jurisdiction from the courts to entertain habeas petitions filed by Guantanamo detainees was an unconstitutional suspension of the writ. 128 S. Ct. at 2274. *Boumediene* held that detainees were entitled to proceed with habeas challenges under procedures crafted to account for the special circumstances of wartime detention. *Id*. at 2276.

Soon after the *Boumediene* decision, the district court, acting with admirable dispatch, revived Al-Bihani's petition and convened counsel to discuss the process to be used. The district court finalized the procedure in a published case management order. *See Al-Bihani v. Bush* (CMO), 588 F. Supp.2d 19 (D.D.C. 2008) (case management order). The order established that the government had the burden of proving the legality of Al-Bihani's detention by a preponderance of the evidence; it obligated the government to explain the legal basis for Al-Bihani's detention, to share all documents used in its factual return, and to turn over any exculpatory evidence found in preparation of its case. To Al-Bihani, the order afforded the opportunity to file a traverse and supplements to the traverse rebutting the government's factual return, to introduce new evidence, and to move for discovery upon a showing of good cause and the absence of undue burden on the government. The order reserved the district court's discretion, when appropriate, to adopt a rebuttable presumption in favor of the accuracy of the government's evidence and to admit relevant and material hearsay, the credibility and weight of which the opposing party could challenge. The order also scheduled status conferences to clarify any discovery and evidentiary issues with the government's factual return and to identify issues of law and fact prior to the habeas hearing where such issues would be contested. *See id*. at 20-21.

After the parties filed their cases in accordance with the case management order and the district court held a day and a half of hearings, the district court denied Al-Bihani's petition. Adopting a definition that allowed the government to detain anyone "who was part of or supporting Taliban or al Qaeda forces, or associated forces that are engaged in hostilities against the United States or its coalition partners,"[1] the district court found Al-Bihani's actions met the standard. *See Al-Bihani v. Obama* (Mem. Op.), 594 F. Supp.2d 35, 38, 40 (D.D.C. 2009) (memorandum opinion). It cited as sufficiently credible the evidence—primarily drawn from Al-Bihani's own admissions during interrogation—that Al-Bihani stayed at Al Qaeda-affiliated guesthouses and that he served in and retreated with the 55th Arab Brigade. *See id*. at 39-40. The district court declined to rely on evidence drawn from admissions—later recanted by Al-Bihani—that he attended Al Qaeda training camps on his way to the front lines. *See id*. at 39.

---

1. This was the initial definition offered by the government as the controlling standard. In its filings before this court, the government modified the definition in its initial habeas return to replace the term "support" with "substantially supported." *See* Brief for Appellees at 21-22. The district court adopted the initial definition. *See* Mem. Op. at 38.

Al-Bihani appealed the district court's denial to this court under 28 U.S.C. § 2253(a), alleging numerous substantive and procedural defects with the order. We review the district court's findings of fact for clear error, *DeBerry v. Portuondo*, 403 F.3d 57, 66 (2d Cir. 2005), its habeas determination *de novo*, *id.*, and any challenged evidentiary rulings for abuse of discretion, *Al Odah v. United States*, 559 F.3d 539, 544 (D.C. Cir. 2009).

II

Al-Bihani's many arguments present this court with two overarching questions regarding the detainees at the Guantanamo Bay naval base. The first concerns whom the President can lawfully detain pursuant to statutes passed by Congress. The second asks what procedure is due to detainees challenging their detention in habeas corpus proceedings. The Supreme Court has provided scant guidance on these questions, consciously leaving the contours of the substantive and procedural law of detention open for lower courts to shape in a common law fashion. *See Hamdi v. Rumsfeld*, 542 U.S. 507, 522 n.1 (2004) (plurality opinion of O'Connor, J.) ("The permissible bounds of the [enemy combatant] category will be defined by the lower courts as subsequent cases are presented to them."); *Boumediene*, 128 S. Ct. at 2276 ("We make no attempt to anticipate all of the evidentiary and access-to-counsel issues…and the other remaining questions [that] are within the expertise and competence of the District Court to address in the first instance."). In this decision, we aim to narrow the legal uncertainty that clouds military detention.

A

Al-Bihani challenges the statutory legitimacy of his detention by advancing a number of arguments based upon the international laws of war. He first argues that relying on "support," or even "substantial support" of Al Qaeda or the Taliban as an independent basis for detention violates international law. As a result, such a standard should not be read into the ambiguous provisions of the Authorization for Use of Military Force (AUMF), Pub. L. No. 107-40, § 2(a), 115 Stat. 224, 224 (2001) (reprinted at 50 U.S.C. § 1541 note), the Act empowering the President to respond to the attacks of September 11, 2001. Al-Bihani interprets international law to mean anyone not belonging to an official state military is a civilian, and civilians, he says, must commit a direct hostile act, such as firing a weapon in combat, before they can be lawfully detained. Because Al-Bihani did not commit such an act, he reasons his detention is unlawful. Next, he argues the members of the 55th Arab Brigade were not subject to attack or detention by U.S. Coalition forces under the laws of co-belligerency because the 55th, although allied with the Taliban against the Northern Alliance, did not have the required opportunity to declare its neutrality in the fight against the United States. His third argument is that the conflict in which he was detained, an international war between the United States and Taliban-controlled Afghanistan, officially ended when the Taliban lost control of the Afghan government. Thus, absent a determination of future dangerousness, he must be released. *See* Geneva Convention Relative to the Treatment of Prisoners of War (Third Geneva Convention) art. 118, Aug. 12, 1949, 6 U.S.T. 3316, 75 U.N.T.S. 135. Lastly, Al-Bihani posits a type of "clean hands" theory by which any authority the government has to detain him is undermined by its failure to accord him the prisoner-of-war status to which he believes he is entitled by international law.

Before considering these arguments in detail, we note that all of them rely heavily on the premise that the war powers granted by the AUMF and other statutes are limited by the international laws of war. This premise is mistaken. There is no indication in the AUMF, the Detainee Treatment Act of 2005, Pub. L. No. 109-148, div. A, tit. X, 119 Stat. 2739, 2741-43, or the MCA of 2006 or 2009, that Congress intended the international laws of war to act as extra-textual limiting principles for the President's war powers under the AUMF. The international laws of war as a whole have not been implemented domestically by Congress and are therefore not a source of authority for U.S. courts. *See* RESTATEMENT (THIRD) OF FOREIGN RELATIONS LAW OF THE UNITED STATES § 111(3)-(4) (1987). Even assuming Congress had at some earlier point implemented the laws of war as domestic law through appropriate legislation, Congress had the power to authorize the President in the AUMF and other later statutes to exceed those bounds. *See id.* § 115(1)(a). Further weakening their relevance to this case, the international laws of war are not a fixed code. Their dictates and application to actual events are by nature contestable and fluid. *See id.* § 102 cmts. b & c (stating there is "no precise formula" to identify a practice as custom and that "[i]t is often difficult to determine when [a custom's] transformation into law has taken place"). Therefore, while the international laws of war are helpful to courts when identifying the general set of war powers to which the AUMF speaks, *see Hamdi*, 542 U.S. at 520, their lack of controlling legal force and firm definition render their use both inapposite and inadvisable when courts seek to determine the limits of the President's war powers.

Therefore, putting aside that we find Al-Bihani's reading of international law to be unpersuasive, we have no occasion here to quibble over the intricate application of vague treaty provisions and amorphous customary principles. The sources we look to for resolution of Al-Bihani's case are the sources courts always look to: the text of relevant statutes and controlling domestic caselaw.

Under those sources, Al-Bihani is lawfully detained whether the definition of a detainable person is, as the district court articulated it, "an individual who was part of or supporting Taliban or al Qaeda forces, or associated forces that are engaged in hostilities against the United States or its coalition partners," or the modified definition offered by the government that requires that an individual "substantially support" enemy forces. The statutes authorizing the use of force and detention not only grant the government the power to craft a workable legal standard to identify individuals it can detain, but also cabin the application of these definitions. The AUMF authorizes the President to "use all necessary and appropriate force against those nations, organizations, or persons he determines planned, authorized, committed, or aided the terrorist attacks that occurred on September 11, 2001, or harbored such organizations or persons." AUMF § 2(a). The Supreme Court in *Hamdi* ruled that "necessary and appropriate force" includes the power to detain combatants subject to such force. 542 U.S. at 519. Congress, in the 2006 MCA, provided guidance on the class of persons subject to detention under the AUMF by defining "unlawful enemy combatants" who can be tried by military commission. 2006 MCA sec. 3, § 948a(1). The 2006 MCA authorized the trial of an individual who "engaged in hostilities or who has purposefully and materially supported hostilities against the United States or its co-belligerents who is not a lawful enemy combatant (including a person who is part of the Taliban, al Qaeda, or associated forces)." *Id.* § 948a(1)(A)(i). In 2009, Congress enacted a new version of the MCA with a new definition that authorized the trial of "unprivileged enemy belligerents," a class of persons that includes those who "purposefully and materially supported hostilities against the United States or its coalition partners." Military Commissions Act of 2009 (2009 MCA) sec. 1802, §§ 948a(7), 948b(a), 948c, Pub. L. No. 111-84, tit. XVIII, 123 Stat. 2190, 2575-76. The provisions of the 2006 and 2009 MCAs are illuminating in this case because the government's detention authority logically covers a category of persons no narrower than is covered by its military commission authority. Detention authority in fact sweeps wider, also extending at least to traditional P.O.W.s, *see id*. § 948a(6), and arguably to other categories of persons. But for this case, it is enough to recognize that any person subject to a military commission trial is also subject to detention, and that category of persons includes those who are part of forces associated with Al Qaeda or the Taliban or those who purposefully and materially support such forces in hostilities against U.S. Coalition partners.

Within these provisions of the 2006 and 2009 MCAs, the facts that were both found by the district court and offered by Al-Bihani in his traverse place Al-Bihani within the "part of" and "support" prongs of the relevant statutory definition. The district court found Al Qaeda members participated in the command structure of the 55th Arab Brigade, *see* Mem. Op. at 40, making the brigade an Al Qaeda-affiliated outfit, and it is unquestioned that the 55th fought alongside the Taliban while the Taliban was harboring Al Qaeda. Al-Bihani's evidence confirmed these points, establishing that the 55th "supported the Taliban against the Northern Alliance," a Coalition partner, and that the 55th was "aided, or even, at times, commanded, by al-Qaeda members." Brief for Petitioner-Appellant at 33. Al-Bihani's connections with the 55th therefore render him detainable. His acknowledged actions—accompanying the brigade on the battlefield, carrying a brigade-issued weapon, cooking for the unit, and retreating and surrendering under brigade orders—strongly suggest, in the absence of an official membership card, that he was part of the 55th. Even assuming, as he argues, that he was a civilian "contractor" rendering services, *see id*. at 32, those services render Al-Bihani detainable under the "purposefully and materially supported" language of both versions of the MCA. That language constitutes a standard whose outer bounds are not readily identifiable. But wherever the outer bounds may lie, they clearly include traditional food operations essential to a fighting force and the carrying of arms. Viewed in full, the facts show Al-Bihani was part of and supported a group—prior to and after September 11—that was affiliated with Al Qaeda and Taliban forces and engaged in hostilities against a U.S. Coalition partner. Al-Bihani, therefore, falls squarely[2] within the scope of the President's statutory detention powers.

The government can also draw statutory authority to detain Al-Bihani directly from the language of the AUMF. The AUMF authorizes force against those who "harbored... organizations or persons" the President determines "planned, authorized, committed, or aided the terrorist attacks of September 11, 2001." AUMF § 2(a). It is not in dispute that Al Qaeda is the organization responsible for September 11 or that it was harbored by the Taliban in Afghanistan. It is also not in dispute that the 55th Arab Brigade defended the Taliban against the Northern Alliance's efforts to oust the regime from power. Drawing from these facts, it

---

2. In reaching this conclusion, we need not rely on the evidence suggesting that Al-Bihani attended Al Qaeda training camps in Afghanistan and visited Al Qaeda guesthouses. We do note, however, that evidence supporting the military's reasonable belief of either of those two facts with respect to a non-citizen seized abroad during the ongoing war on terror would seem to overwhelmingly, if not definitively, justify the government's detention of such a non-citizen. *Cf.* NAT'L COMM'N ON TERRORIST ATTACKS UPON THE UNITED STATES, THE 9/11 COMMISSION REPORT 66-67.

cannot be disputed that the actual and foreseeable result of the 55th's defense of the Taliban was the maintenance of Al Qaeda's safe haven in Afghanistan. This result places the 55th within the AUMF's wide ambit as an organization that harbored Al Qaeda, making it subject to U.S. military force and its members and supporters—including Al-Bihani—eligible for detention.

...

A clear statement requirement is at odds with the wide deference the judiciary is obliged to give to the democratic branches with regard to questions concerning national security. In the absence of a determination by the political branches that hostilities in Afghanistan have ceased, Al-Bihani's continued detention is justified.

Al-Bihani also argues he should be released because the government's failure to accord him P.O.W. status violated international law and undermined its otherwise lawful authority to detain him. Even assuming Al-Bihani is entitled to P.O.W. status, we find no controlling authority for this "clean hands" theory in statute or in caselaw. The AUMF, DTA, and MCA of 2006 and 2009 do not hinge the government's detention authority on proper identification of P.O.W.s or compliance with international law in general. In fact, the MCA of 2006, in a provision not altered by the MCA of 2009, explicitly precludes detainees from claiming the Geneva conventions—which include criteria to determine who is entitled to P.O.W. status—as a source of rights. *See* 2006 MCA sec. 5(a). And the citation Al-Bihani gives to support his theory is not controlling. The section of Justice Souter's separate opinion in *Hamdi* in which he discusses a clean hands theory was part of his dissent in that case. *See* 542 U.S. at 553 (Souter, J., concurring in part, dissenting in part, and concurring in the judgment) ("For me, it suffices that the Government has failed to justify [detention] in the absence of...a showing that the detention conforms to the laws of war....[T]his disposition does not command a majority of the Court."). Moreover, Justice Souter's opinion fails to identify any other controlling authority that establishes or discusses this theory in any way. This leaves no foundation for Al-Bihani's clean hands argument, and it fails to persuade.

...

III

Al-Bihani's detention is authorized by statute and there was no constitutional defect in the district court's habeas procedure that would have affected the outcome of the proceeding. For these reasons, the order of the district court denying Al-Bihani's petition for a writ of habeas corpus is
Affirmed.

...

Predictably, although the 2008 *Boumediene* ruling only addressed the habeas rights of Guantanamo Bay detainees, another group of detainees quickly filed suit in federal court in Washington seeking habeas review for their cases—detainees designated as enemy combatants and held at Bagram Air Force Base, Afghanistan. Despite the Obama Administration's heated efforts to argue that these individuals should not receive federal court habeas review of their status determination, the D.C.

District Court in the consolidated cases entitled *Al Maqaleh v. Gates* ruled that those who were not Afghan citizens and not captured in Afghanistan were entitled to habeas review. The government immediately sought review of this determination to the D.C. Circuit Court of Appeals and won. Thus, President Obama could detain illegal enemy combatants without providing access to a federal judge if he detained them in Afghanistan.

AL MAQALEH v. GATES
United States Court of Appeals for the District of Columbia Circuit
No. 09-5265 (May 21, 2010)

Sentelle, Tatel, and Edwards, Circuit Judges

I. Background

A. The Petitioners

All three petitioners are being held as unlawful enemy combatants at the Bagram Theater Internment Facility on the Bagram Airfield Military Base in Afghanistan. Petitioner Fadi Al-Maqaleh is a Yemeni citizen who alleges he was taken into custody in 2003. While Al-Maqaleh's petition asserts "on information and belief" that he was captured beyond Afghan borders, a sworn declaration from Colonel James W. Gray, Commander of Detention Operations, states that Al-Maqaleh was captured in Zabul, Afghanistan. Redha Al-Najar is a Tunisian citizen who alleges he was captured in Pakistan in 2002. Amin Al-Bakri is a Yemeni citizen who alleges he was captured in Thailand in 2002. Both Al-Najar and Al-Bakri allege they were first held in some other unknown location before being moved to Bagram.

B. The Place of Confinement

Bagram Airfield Military Base is the largest military facility in Afghanistan occupied by United States and coalition forces. The United States entered into an "Accommodation Consignment Agreement for Lands and Facilities at Bagram Airfield" with the Islamic Republic of Afghanistan in 2006, which "consigns all facilities and land located at Bagram Airfield... owned by [Afghanistan,] or Parwan Province, or private individuals, or others, for use by the United States and coalition forces for military purposes." (Accommodation and Consignment Agreement for Lands and Facilities at Bagram Airfield Between the Islamic Republic of Afghanistan and the United States of America) (internal capitalization altered). The Agreement refers to Afghanistan as the "host nation" and the United States "as the lessee." The leasehold created by the agreement is to continue "until the United States or its successors determine that the premises are no longer required for its use." *Id.* (internal capitalization altered).

Afghanistan remains a theater of active military combat. The United States and coalition forces conduct "an ongoing military campaign against al Qaeda, the Taliban regime, and their affiliates and supporters in Afghanistan." These operations are conducted in part from Bagram Airfield. Bagram has been subject to repeated attacks from the Taliban and al Qaeda, including a

March 2009 suicide bombing striking the gates of the facility, and Taliban rocket attacks in June of 2009 resulting in death and injury to United States service members and other personnel.

While the United States provides overall security to Bagram, numerous other nations have compounds on the base. Some of the other nations control access to their respective compounds. The troops of the other nations are present at Bagram both as part of the American-led military coalition in Afghanistan and as members of the International Security Assistance Force (ISAF) of the North Atlantic Treaty Organization. The mission of the ISAF is to support the Afghan government in the maintenance of security in Afghanistan. *See* S.C. Res. 1386, U.N. Doc. S/RES/1386 (Dec. 20, 2001); S.C. Res. 1510, U.N. Doc. S/RES/1510 (Oct. 13, 2003); S.C. Res. 1833, U.N. Doc. S/RES/1833 (Sept. 22, 2008). According to the United States, as of February 1, 2010, approximately 38,000 non-United States troops were serving in Afghanistan as part of the ISAF, representing 42 other countries. *See* International Security Assistance Force, *International Security Assistance Force and Afghan National Army Strength & Laydown*, http://www.nato.int/isaf/docu/epub/pdf/placemat.pdf.

C. The Litigation

Appellees in this action, three detainees at Bagram, filed habeas petitions against the President of the United States and the Secretary of Defense in the district court. The government moved to dismiss for lack of jurisdiction, relying principally upon § 7(a) of the Military Commissions Act of 2006. The district court consolidated these three cases and a fourth case, not a part of these proceedings, for argument. After the change in presidential administrations on January 22, 2009, the court invited the government to express any change in its position on the jurisdictional question. The government informed the district court that it "adheres to its previously articulated position." …

II. Analysis

…

B. Application to the Bagram Petitioners

Our duty, as explained above, is to determine the reach of the right to habeas corpus and therefore of the Suspension Clause to the factual context underlying the petitions we consider in the present appeal. In doing so, we are controlled by the Supreme Court's interpretation of the Constitution in *Eisentrager* as construed and explained in the Court's more recent opinion in *Boumediene*....

At the outset, we note that each of the parties has asserted both an extreme understanding of the law after *Boumediene* and a more nuanced set of arguments upon which each relies in anticipation of the possible rejection of the bright-line arguments. The United States would like us to hold that the *Boumediene* analysis has no application beyond territories that are, like Guantanamo, outside the *de jure* sovereignty of the United States but are subject to its *de facto* sovereignty. As the government puts it in its reply brief, "[t]he real question before this Court, therefore, is whether Bagram may be considered effectively part of the United States in light of the nature and history of the U.S. presence there." Reply Br. of the United States at 7. We disagree.

…

The status of the Bagram detainees is determined not by a Combatant Status Review Tribunal but by an "Unlawful Enemy Combatant Review Board" (UECRB). As the district court correctly noted, proceedings before the UECRB afford even less protection to the rights of detainees in the determination of status than was the case with the CSRT. Therefore, as the district court noted, "while the important adequacy of process factor strongly supported the extension of the Suspension Clause and habeas rights in *Boumediene*, it even more strongly favors petitioners here." *Al Maqaleh*, 604 F. Supp. 2d at 227. Therefore, examining only the first of the Supreme Court's three enumerated factors, petitioners have made a strong argument that the right to habeas relief and the Suspension Clause apply in Bagram as in Guantanamo. However, we do not stop with the first factor.

The second factor, "the nature of the sites where apprehension and then detention took place," weighs heavily in favor of the United States. Like all petitioners in both *Eisentrager* and *Boumediene*, the petitioners here were apprehended abroad. While this in itself would appear to weigh against the extension of the writ, it obviously would not be sufficient, otherwise *Boumediene* would not have been decided as it was. However, the nature of the place where the detention takes place weighs more strongly in favor of the position argued by the United States and against the extension of habeas jurisdiction than was the case in either *Boumediene* or *Eisentrager*. In the first place, while *de facto* sovereignty is not determinative, for the reasons discussed above, the very fact that it was the subject of much discussion in *Boumediene* makes it obvious that it is not without relevance. As the Supreme Court set forth, Guantanamo Bay is "a territory that, while technically not part of the United States, is under the complete and total control of our Government." 128 S. Ct. at 2262. While it is true that the United States holds a leasehold interest in Bagram, and held a leasehold interest in Guantanamo, the surrounding circumstances are hardly the same. The United States has maintained its total control of Guantanamo Bay for over a century, even in the face of a hostile government maintaining *de jure* sovereignty over the property. In Bagram, while the United States has options as to duration of the lease agreement, there is no indication of any intent to occupy the base with permanence, nor is there hostility on the part of the "host" country. Therefore, the notion that *de facto* sovereignty extends to Bagram is no more real than would have been the same claim with respect to Landsberg in the *Eisentrager* case. While it is certainly realistic to assert that the United States has *de facto* sovereignty over Guantanamo, the same simply is not true with respect to Bagram. Though the site of detention analysis weighs in favor of the United States and against the petitioners, it is not determinative.

But we hold that the third factor, that is "the practical obstacles inherent in resolving the prisoner's entitlement to the writ," particularly when considered along with the second factor, weighs overwhelmingly in favor of the position of the United States. It is undisputed that Bagram, indeed the entire nation of Afghanistan, remains a theater of war. Not only does this suggest that the detention at Bagram is more like the detention at Landsberg than Guantanamo, the position of the United States is even stronger in this case than it was in *Eisentrager*. As the Supreme Court recognized in *Boumediene*, even though the active hostilities in the European theater had "c[o]me to an end," 23 at the time of the *Eisentrager* decision, many of the problems of a theater of war remained: In addition to supervising massive reconstruction and aid efforts the American forces stationed in Germany faced potential security threats from a defeated enemy. In retrospect the post-War occupation may seem uneventful. But at the time *Eisentrager* was decided, the Court was right to be concerned about judicial interference with the military's efforts to contain "enemy elements, guerilla fighters, and 'were-wolves.'" 128 S. Ct. at 2261 (quoting *Eisentrager*, 339 U.S. at 784).

In ruling for the extension of the writ to Guantanamo, the Supreme Court expressly noted that "[s]imilar threats are not apparent here." 128 S. Ct. at 2261. In the case before us, similar, if not greater, threats are indeed apparent. The United States asserts, and petitioners cannot credibly dispute, that all of the attributes of a facility exposed to the vagaries of war are present in Bagram. The Supreme Court expressly stated in *Boumediene* that at Guantanamo, "[w]hile obligated to abide by the terms of the lease, the United States is, for all practical purposes, answerable to no other sovereign for its acts on the base. Were that not the case, *or if the detention facility were located in an active theater of war*, arguments that issuing the writ would be 'impractical or anomalous' would have more weight." *Id.* at 2261-62 (emphasis added). Indeed, the Supreme Court supported this proposition with reference to the separate opinion of Justice Harlan in *Reid*, where the Justice expressed his doubts that "every provision of the Constitution must always be deemed automatically applicable to United States citizens in every part of the world." *See* 354 U.S. at 74 (Harlan, J., concurring in the result). We therefore conclude that under both *Eisentrager* and *Boumediene*, the writ does not extend to the Bagram confinement in an active theater of war in a territory under neither the *de facto* nor *de jure* sovereignty of the United States and within the territory of another *de jure* sovereign.

We are supported in this conclusion by the rationale of *Eisentrager*, which was not only not overruled, but reinforced by the language and reasoning just referenced from *Boumediene*. As we referenced in the background discussion of this opinion, we set forth more fully now concerns expressed by the Supreme Court in reaching its decision in *Eisentrager*:

> Such trials would hamper the war effort and bring aid and comfort to the enemy. They would diminish the prestige of our commanders, not only with enemies but with wavering neutrals. It would be difficult to devise more effective fettering of a field commander than to allow the very enemies he is ordered to reduce to submission to call him to account in his own civil courts and divert his efforts and attention from the military offensive abroad to the legal defensive at home. Nor is it unlikely that the result of such enemy litigiousness would be a conflict between judicial and military opinion highly comforting to enemies of the United States.

Eisentrager, 339 U.S. at 779. Those factors are more relevant to the situation at Bagram than they were at Landsberg. While it is true, as the Supreme Court noted in *Boumediene*, that the United States forces in Germany in 1950 faced the possibility of unrest and guerilla warfare, operations in the European theater had ended with the surrender of Germany and Italy years earlier. Bagram remains in a theater of war. We cannot, consistent with *Eisentrager* as elucidated by *Boumediene*, hold that the right to the writ of habeas corpus and the constitutional protections of the Suspension Clause extend to Bagram detention facility in Afghanistan, and we therefore must reverse the decision of the district court denying the motion of the United States to dismiss the petitions.

We do not ignore the arguments of the detainees that the United States chose the place of detention and might be able "to evade judicial review of Executive detention decisions by transferring detainees into active conflict zones, thereby granting the Executive the power to switch the Constitution on or off at will." Brief of Appellees at 34 (quotation marks and citation omitted). However, that is not what happened here. Indeed, without dismissing the legitimacy or sincerity of appellees' concerns, we doubt that this fact goes to either the second or third of the Supreme Court's enumerated factors. We need make no determination on the importance of this possibility, given that it remains only a possibility; its resolution can await a case in which the claim is a reality rather than a speculation. In so stating, we note that the Supreme Court did not dictate that the three enumerated factors are exhaustive. It only told us that "*at least* three factors" are relevant. *Boumediene*, 128 S. Ct. at 2259 (emphasis added). Perhaps such manipulation by the Executive might constitute an additional factor in some case in which it is in fact present. However, the notion that the United States deliberately confined the detainees in the theater of war rather than at, for example, Guantanamo, is not only unsupported by the evidence, it is not supported by reason. To have made such a deliberate decision to "turn off the Constitution" would have required the military commanders or other Executive officials making the situs determination to anticipate the complex litigation history set forth above and predict the *Boumediene* decision long before it came down.

Also supportive of our decision that the third factor weighs heavily in favor of the United States, as the district court recognized, is the fact that the detention is within the sovereign territory of another nation, which itself creates practical difficulties. Indeed, it was on this factor that the district court relied in dismissing the fourth petition, which was filed by an Afghan citizen detainee. *Al Maqaleh*, 604 F. Supp. 2d at 229-30, 235. While that factor certainly weighed more heavily with respect to an Afghan citizen, it is not without force with respect to detainees who are alien to both the United States and Afghanistan. The United States holds the detainees pursuant to a cooperative arrangement with Afghanistan on territory as to which Afghanistan is sovereign. While we cannot say that extending our constitutional protections to the detainees would be in any way disruptive of that relationship, neither can we say with certainty what the reaction of the Afghan government would be.

In sum, taken together, the second and especially the third factors compel us to hold that the petitions should have been dismissed.

Conclusion

For the reasons set forth above, we hold that the jurisdiction of the courts to afford the right to habeas relief and the protection of the Suspension Clause does not extend to aliens held in Executive detention in the Bagram detention facility in the Afghan theater of war. We therefore reverse the order of the district court denying the motion for dismissal of the United States and order that the petitions be dismissed for lack of jurisdiction. So ordered.

6.5 Military Commissions

Anyone even marginally aware of the War on Terror understands that the use of military commissions has always served as a lightning rod for political and legal debate. In fact, when President Obama first took office in 2009, he suspended the use of military commissions (except for the cases already in progress) but then restarted them for new trials by executive order in March 2011, while simultaneously continuing the old argument for trying unlawful enemy combatants in federal district courts.

Ostensibly, if the detainees are correctly designated as enemy combatants, the United States has six options which it may pursue against the detainees: (1) release the detainee to his country of origin (or any other country that will take him); (2) turn the accused over to an appropriate foreign criminal jurisdiction (e.g., the new government in Afghanistan); (3) turn the accused over to an International Tribunal; (4) try the accused in a United States federal district court; (5) try the accused in a United States military commission (so long as they are not a U.S. citizen); or (6) detain him indefinitely as an enemy combatant until the war is over. If one is only concerned with expediency, the first option is probably the most attractive and needs little discussion. Likewise, the use of an International Tribunal is attractive but probably not workable due to concerns over such issues as the absence of a death penalty and possible security compromises of "sources and techniques" that the United States employs for gathering intelligence.

The final forum available to prosecute those individuals taken from Afghanistan (or any other location) who are suspected of committing war crimes is the military commission. On November 13, 2001, President Bush signed an executive (military) order which authorized the creation of military commissions to try certain "non-citizens" for engaging in terrorist acts against the United States or aiding or abetting in terrorist acts against the United States. The Supreme Court in *Hamdan v. Rumsfeld* found that the military commissions were not consistent with the standards of Common Article 3 which required that the "passing of sentences" had to be "pronounced by a regularly constituted court affording all the judicial guarantees which are recognized as indispensable by civilized peoples." Further, the Court rejected the idea that the 2001 Congressional Authorization for Use of Military Force allowed the President to authorize military commissions. In fact, the majority decided that the President's military commissions order was not lawful because it was "not regularly constituted" as required by Common Article 3. In short, the Court seemed willing to accept a military commission to try enemy combatants, but only if it was authorized by Congress, not the President.

Because military commissions have not been used since the end of World War II, the efficacy of using this forum to prosecute the al-Qa'eda and Taliban fighters for war crimes mandates analysis from both legal and historical perspectives. Probably 10 or more detainees at Guantanamo Bay are now pending trial by military commission.

Military commissions are non-Article III courts. They derive their basic grant of authority from Articles I and II of the United States Constitution. Respectively, Congress has the power to "define and punish...offenses against the Law of Nations," and the President is the "Commander in Chief of the Army and Navy."

Historically, military commissions (and military tribunals) have been used in a variety of situations associated with urgent government needs related to war. In *Madsen v. Kinsella*, the Supreme Court spoke at some length on the history of military commissions and tribunals, stating: "Since our nation's earliest days, such commissions have been constitutionally recognized agencies for meeting many urgent governmental responsibilities relating to war." In addition, the Court has recognized the fact that military commissions have been used without Congress specifically "declaring war" (*Talbot v. Seeman*). For example, military tribunals were used in the War with Mexico, even though Congress never formally declared war. The War with Mexico lasted from 1846–1848, and broke out when Texas, an American settled province of Mexico that had broken away in 1836, was annexed as a State by the United States in 1845. Congress passed the Act of Congress of May 13, 1846, which did not declare war, but recognized "a state of war as existing by the act of the Republic of Mexico" (*Prize Cases*, 67 U.S. 365).

A military commission consists of a panel of military officers who are authorized to render a verdict and sentence. The historical concern in this instance is not whether military commissions can be used to prosecute United States citizens who may or may not be belligerents, but whether commissions are constitutionally able to prosecute non-citizen belligerents for offenses in violation of the law of war. Regarding the use of military tribunals to try United States citizens who are not belligerents, the Supreme Court rendered its opinion in 1866 in *Ex Parte Milligan*, where it held that as long as the civilian courts were operating, the use of military tribunals to try United States citizens who were not actual belligerents was unconstitutional. In December of 1866, the United States Supreme Court granted a writ of habeas corpus to a civilian noncombatant named Lambdin P. Milligan, a pro-Confederate Indiana resident who was convicted in October 1864 by a military tribunal convened in Indianapolis, Indiana. Milligan was convicted of treason and sentenced to be hanged. The lower federal court denied his petition for habeas corpus. In granting the writ for review, the Supreme Court held that although the American Civil War was still in progress at the time of the trial, the circumstances in Indiana, a Union State not in control by Confederate forces, did not justify the use of a military tribunal to prosecute a United States citizen because the civil courts were open and free to function. As to the use of military commissions to prosecute noncitizen and citizen belligerents for offenses in violation of the law of war, the standard is set out in the World War II case of *Ex Parte Quirin*.

In *Ex Parte Quirin*, the United States Supreme Court upheld the convictions of eight German saboteurs who had been captured in the United States and tried by a military commission ordered by President Franklin Roosevelt. The Germans had been sent to attack public and government facilities. At least one of the Germans claimed American citizenship. The Court upheld the jurisdiction of military commissions against all of the Germans, stating: "By the Articles of War, and especially Article 15, Congress has explicitly provided, so far as it may constitutionally do so, that military tribunals shall have jurisdiction to try offenders or offenses against the law of war in appropriate cases." The Court easily distinguished the case from *Ex Parte Milligan*, holding that offenses against the law of war by actual belligerents were constitutionally authorized to be tried by military commissions. Besides the trials of the German saboteurs during World War II, subsequent military commissions were used to prosecute approximately 2,600 members of the Axis for violations of the law of war, including the murder of captured American soldiers at the Battle of the Bulge. The surviving high-ranking war criminals in the German military and government were tried by a special international tribunal in Nuremberg, Germany, at the Nuremberg Trials. The senior Japanese leaders were tried at the International Military Tribunal for the Far East.

Although the Supreme Court has long held that the Constitution's Fifth and Sixth Amendment protections apply to non-United States citizens (*Wong Wing v. United States*, 163 U.S. 228), such protections do not extend to belligerents subject to trial in military commissions for war crimes. Seemingly, the use of military commissions has deeply seated historical and legal precedent as long as the accused are actual combatants charged with violations of the law of war. In *Application of Yamashita*, the Court traced the history of military commissions and concluded: "By thus recognizing military commissions in order to preserve their traditional jurisdiction over enemy combatants…Congress gave sanction, as we held in *Ex Parte Quirin* to any use of military commissions contemplated by the common law of war." In its January 2002 report on the lawfulness of using military commissions, the American Bar Association Task Force on Terrorism and Law found that the terror attacks of September 11, 2001, were arguably violations of the law of war that would justify the use of military commissions to prosecute accused terrorists.

Among the handful of detainees who have been convicted by military commissions in the War on Terror is Salim Ahmed Hamdan, of Yemen. Hamdan, who acknowledged that he was a former driver for Osama bin Laden, was charged with a variety of offenses including conspiracy to attack civilians. Although the military commissions process was halted by a district court ruling in 2004, the D.C. Circuit in July 2005 reversed, upholding the legality of the military commissions set up by Executive Order. Then, on June 29, 2006, a sharply divided Court in *Hamdan v. Rumsfeld* reversed the Court of Appeals ruling that the Military Commissions process established by President Bush violated Common Article 3 of the Geneva Conventions as well as the military Uniform Code of Military Justice.

Prompted by the Supreme Court's holding in *Hamdan*, an energized Congress understood that they could no longer remain on the sidelines in the War on Terror. In late 2006, Congress established the creation of military commissions, affirming quite satisfactorily that the Military Commissions Act (MCA) of 2006 was consistent with the requirements of Common Article 3 of the Geneva Conventions—the military commissions so established constituted a "regularly constituted court," affording all the necessary "judicial guarantees which are recognized as indispensable by civilized peoples." Indeed, with the passage of the 2006 MCA, Congress firmly committed itself to the view that the nation was at war and that the legislative branch of government had a significant role to play in a variety of legal issues associated with the "enemy combatants"—both legal and illegal—that seek to do great physical harm to the United States and its allies. While the Detainee Treatment Act of 2005 provided an advanced signal that Congress was at last willing to get involved in a limited manner in some of the thorny legal aspects of the War on Terror, the 2006 MCA represented a major Congressional shift in scope. In short, the 2006 MCA was a resounding statutory broadside that impacted forcefully and with great effect across the entire legal landscape.

Without question, the 2006 MCA certainly washed away all doubt regarding Congress' willingness to characterize the War on Terror as a real global war against real enemies who desire to murder and terrorize. Accordingly, Congress demonstrated that it was more than willing to employ the full weight of the rule of law pertaining to armed conflict against the enemies of the United States. In fact, the Democrat controlled Congress followed suit by amending portions of the MCA in its 2009 Military Commissions Act.

Not only did the 2006 MCA provide crystal clear guidance in the context of the establishment and operation of military commissions to try "any alien unlawful enemy combatant" (al-Qa'eda and al-Qa'eda-styled Islamic terrorists) it provided concrete statutory definitions concerning a wide variety of terms that had been previously hotly debated. The 2006 MCA also clearly placed a large legal "seal of approval" on many of the initiatives taken by the Bush Administration in the War on Terror. For instance, the 2006 MCA defined "unlawful enemy combatants" in precise language:

(i) a person who has engaged in hostilities or who has purposefully and materially supported hostilities against the United States or its co-belligerents who is not a lawful enemy combatant (including a person who is part of the Taliban, al Qaeda, or associated forces); or

(ii) a person who, before, on, or after the date of the enactment of the Military Commissions Act of 2006, has been determined to be an unlawful enemy combatant by a Combatant Status Review Tribunal or another competent tribunal established under the authority of the President or the Secretary of Defense.

While the 2009 MCA changed the 2006 MCA term "unlawful enemy combatant" to "unprivileged enemy belligerent" it still provided a similar detailed description of who qualified as the enemy in the War on Terror: "An individual (other than a privileged belligerent) who has engaged in hostilities against the United States or its coalition partners; or has purposefully and materially supported hostilities against the United States or its coalition partners; or an individual who was a member of al-Qaeda at the time the offense occurred."

In accordance with its constitutional power to "define and punish…offenses against the Law of Nations," the MCA also lists in detail the criminal offenses that fall within the jurisdiction of the military commissions. Apart from the traditional list of war crimes that one would expect to encounter, the MCA appropriately includes "conspiracy" and "providing material support for terrorism," drawing definitional language from the Material Support Act provisions at Section 2339A. While *Boumediene* struck down the 2006 MCA provisions restricting habeas corpus, the major thrust of the 2009 MCA serves as the centerpiece for an emerging rule of law in the War on Terror.

In the sphere of authorizing trial by military commissions, Congress wisely allows for military commissions to operate in the traditional manner of all previous military commissions (hundreds were tried by military commissions in World War II, some were even U.S. citizens) and consider, for example, hearsay evidence and information gathered without a search warrant. In terms of hearsay evidence, the 2009 MCA holds that evidence not otherwise admissible under the rules of evidence applicable in trial by general-courts-martial may still be admitted under certain circumstances should the military judge determine that the evidence would have probative value and the proponent provides advanced notice. However, the burden of persuasion to demonstrate unreliability or lack of probative value rests on the profferer of the evidence. Physical evidence seized outside the United States shall not be excluded on the grounds that it was seized without a search warrant or other authorization. The 2009 MCA also allows verbal and written statements from the accused so long as the statement was not obtained by the use of torture or by cruel, inhuman, or degrading treatment.

Ironically, some still view the common sense evidentiary provisions in the 2009 MCA as a violation of Common Article 3's requirement that the accused be afforded all the necessary "guarantees…recognized as indispensable by civilized peoples." Such ethnocentric views are quickly dispelled when one considers the day-to-day activity of most modern European criminal courts where hearsay is regularly considered and far different legal avenues regarding the introduction of evidence are regularly employed. Even the International Criminal Court, the icon of those who worship at the altar of internationalism, allows hearsay. In fact, earlier calls by some (including uniformed judge advocates who should have known better) that a military commission should include the same due process standards that American soldiers enjoy at a military courts-martial under the Uniform Code of Military Justice were wisely disregarded by Congress in 2006 and 2009. Obviously, these "relaxed" provisions in the MCA are necessary due to the exigencies of war—witnesses and victims may be dead, investigators are not able to get to the crime scene, etc. Nevertheless, the 2009 MCA provides more due process rights to the accused than any military commission in the history of military commissions in the history of war. In general frame, the 2009 MCA provides the following rights for the accused who is charged:

- a copy of the charges in English and a language he understands;
- right to a free military attorney or to hire a civilian attorney, may also have foreign consultants;
- a presumption of innocence for the accused;
- guilt must be proven by the government beyond a reasonable doubt;

- access to evidence that the prosecution plans to present at trial;
- access to evidence known or reasonably should be known to the prosecution tending to exculpate the accused;
- right to remain silent;
- no adverse inference for remaining silent;
- right to testify subject to cross-examination;
- right to obtain witnesses and documents for defense;
- right to present evidence and cross-examine witnesses;
- no statement obtained by torture or by cruel, inhuman, or degrading treatment is admissible;
- accused will see every piece of evidence that the panel sees (even classified);
- appointment of interpreters to assist defense;
- right to be present at every stage of trial (except when proceedings are closed for national security) unless disruptive;
- access to sentencing evidence;
- cannot be tried again by military commission once verdict is final;
- right to submit a plea agreement;
- a panel consists of at least five members (at least 12 members if death penalty case);
- challenges to members of the panel by the defense;
- two-thirds of the military officers on the panel must agree on findings of guilt;
- unanimous decision for death sentence;
- trial is open to the public (exceptions recognized for physical safety of participants);
- automatic appellate review by a Court of Military Commission Review (CMCR);
- further review by petition to the D.C. Court of Appeals and by writ of certiorari to the Supreme Court.

A final way to compare the procedures and rights of the accused is revealed in the following chart, which compares the current MCA with the processes used in current military courts-martial trials for American soldiers, federal district courts, and the International Criminal Courts. Clearly, the MCA process is well within the norm of other judicial forums.

Comparison Chart of Procedures and Rights for Persons Being Tried by Military Commissions, Courts-Martial, U.S. District Courts, and International Criminal Courts

Procedures and or Rights	Military Commissions Act 2009 Manual for Military Commissions	Uniform Code of Military Justice (UCMJ)	U.S. District Court	Nuremberg Trials (WWII)	International Criminal Courts
Presumption of Innocence	Defendant is presumed innocent	Same	Same	Not specified	Same
Burden of Proof	Burden of proof on government	Same	Same	Same	Same
Standard of Proof	Burden of proof is "beyond a reasonable doubt."	Same	Same	Not specified	Same
Right to Speedy Trial	Right to Speedy trial—arraignment in 30 days, assemble commission in 120; unknown for MCA	120 days after the earlier of preferral of charges, restraint or entry on active duty	Within 70 days of indictment	Expeditious	Without undue delay
Right to Be Informed of Charges	Defendant must be informed of charges as soon as practicable	As soon as practicable	After indictment	Reasonable time before trial	Promptly and to provide adequate time for defense
Assistance of Defense Counsel	Right to detailed defense counsel at no charge to accused	Detailed defense counsel, individual military counsel or civilian counsel	Public defender at no charge	Right to counsel	Choice of counsel from court list
Right to Be Present at Trial	Defendant entitled to be present at trial; may be removed for disruptive or dangerous conduct	Same	Same	Accused not entitled to be present at trial	Same
Right to Confront Witnesses	Right to cross-examine witnesses	Same	Same	Same	Same
Double Jeopardy	No double jeopardy	Same	Same	Not specified	Allowed
Right to Assistance of Interpreter	Right to interpreter	Same	Same	Same	Same
Right Against Self-Incrimination	Yes	Same	Same	No. Tribunal may interrogate any defendant	Same

Procedures and or Rights	Military Commissions Act 2009 Manual for Military Commissions	Uniform Code of Military Justice (UCMJ)	U.S. District Court	Nuremberg Trials (WWII)	International Criminal Courts
Judge/Jury Model; Panel of Judges	Military Judge and Members	Same	Judge and Jury	Panel of judges	Panel of judges
Pretrial Legal Review	Convening Authority reviews charges and decides whether to refer them to military commission for trial	Same	Grand Jury	Same	Same
Admissibility of Hearsay Evidence	Hearsay admissible if deemed probative	Hearsay not admissible unless a specific exception exists	Hearsay not admissible unless a specific exception exists	Hearsay admissible if deemed probative	Hearsay admissible if deemed probative, unless it is gathered in violation of ICC statute or internationally recognized human rights
Compulsory Process to Obtain Defense Witnesses	Defense has reasonable opportunity to obtain witnesses	Accused may obtain witnesses for defense	Accused may obtain witnesses for defense	Defense may apply for production of witnesses and will be granted, subject to certain requirements	Trial Chamber may require attendance and testimony of witness
Exclusionary Rules	Statements obtained through torture or ill treatment are not admissible. Fourth Amendment protections not available for evidence seized outside United States	Exclusionary rules apply	Exclusionary rules a apply	No exclusionary rule. Evidence of probative value admitted.	Exclusionary rules apply
Challenges to Court Members/Jury	Challenges to members of court permitted	Same	Same	Not permitted	Same
Public Trial	Public trial, subject to some exceptions	Same	Same	Not specified	Same
Votes Required to Convict	2/3 vote of members required to convict, 3/4 required for more than 10 years, unanimous for death	Same	Unanimous in all cases	3 of 4 members	Majority
Appellate Review	Four levels of appellate review, including review by Supreme Court	Three levels of appellate review, including review by Supreme Court	Two levels of appellate review, including Supreme Court	No appellate review	One level of appellate review

In 2008, the first contested military commission trial was completed for al-Qa'eda member Salim Hamdan (David Hicks was convicted in 2007 by military commission after a guilty plea). Clearly a rebuff to those that view the military commissions process a "rubber stamp" or "kangaroo court," Hamdan was convicted of only about half of the charges he was charged with:

Count 1: Conspiracy

Specification 1: conspiracy to commit a variety of offenses (attacks on civilians, etc.) — **acquitted**

Specification 2: conspiracy to commit murder in violation of the law of war by attacking US and coalition servicemen — **acquitted** (Judge Allred instructed the panel that the charge required proof that the conspiracy targeted "protected persons" — civilians or persons rendered hors de combat).

Count 2: Material Support

Specification 1: Providing himself as personnel to al Qaeda with knowledge or intent that this support would "be used for an act of terrorism" (a count analogous to 18 USC 2339A) — **acquitted**

Specification 2: Providing himself as personnel to al Qa'eda, period (a count analogous to 18 USC 2339B, which unlike 2339A does not require any linkage to another offense) — **CONVICTED**

Specification 3: Providing al Qa'eda with SA-7 surface-to-air missiles in November 2001, knowing they would be used for an act of terrorism (again along the lines of 2339A) — **acquitted**

Specification 4: Providing al Qa'eda with SA-7 surface-to-air missiles in November 2001, period (again along the lines of 2339B) — **acquitted**

Specification 5: Providing support to al Qa'eda through his service as a driver, knowing this would facilitate communications and planning for terrorist acts — **CONVICTED**

Specification 6: Similar to Specification 5 — **CONVICTED**

Specification 7: Providing support to al Qa'eda through service as a bodyguard, knowing this would facilitate communications and planning for terrorist acts — **CONVICTED**

Specification 8: Similar to Specification 7 — **CONVICTED**

As various legal challenges to portions of the 2009 MCA make their way through the lower courts, it is highly doubtful that the Supreme Court will strike down very much of the MCA as unconstitutional. Indeed, in time of war the Court has traditionally been most reluctant to intervene in matters of national security, particularly when the executive and legislative branches have joined together in such a seamless fashion.

With the exception of the 2005 Detainee Treatment Act legislation, that dealt with the treatment, interrogation, and trial of detainees, Congress at first seemed content to sit on the sidelines in the War on Terror. With the passage of the 2006 MCA and then the 2009 MCA, Congress has become properly energized in the War on Terror. While rational people understand that the unique threat of al-Qa'eda-styled terrorism against the United States can best be addressed by employing the laws established for armed conflict, it is equally true that the law of war needs to be updated to encompass the new paradigm. Since the international community will not act, this means that Congress must remain involved and informed.

6.6 Federal Courts

It is well settled that federal district courts of the United States have the legal authority under both domestic and international law to prosecute nonresident aliens for terrorist crimes committed on foreign soil as well as for war crimes. This power has been exercised many times against militant Islamic terrorists, both prior to and after 9/11. In contrast to military commissions, which can only try enemy combatants, federal courts can prosecute enemy combatants and Islamic terrorists who do not qualify as enemy combatants.

A widely cited precedent which amplifies just how far the jurisdictional reach extends in this regard is the case of *United States v. Yunis*. The *Yunis* case involved the federal criminal trial of Fawaz Yunis, an Arab terrorist who participated in the hijacking of a Royal Jordanian Airlines airplane at Beirut International Airport in June 1985. The only connection the act had with the United States was the fact that a handful of American citizens were on board the hijacked plane. After reviewing the pertinent international agreements relating to hostage taking and hijacking, the federal district court denied a defense motion to dismiss for lack of jurisdiction and Yunis was convicted of conspiracy, hostage taking and air piracy.

On appeal of his conviction, the Court of Appeals for the D.C. Circuit said the following about the concept of customary international law as it applied to certain criminal acts: "Nor is jurisdiction precluded by norms of customary international law. The district court [correctly] concluded that two jurisdictional theories of international law, the 'universal principle' and the 'passive personal principle,' (*United States v. Benitez*, 741 F.2d. 1312) supported assertion of United States jurisdiction to prosecute Yunis on hijacking and hostage-taking charges." According to the appellate court, the "universal principle" of jurisdiction allows States to prosecute those "offenses recognized by the community of nations as of universal concern, such as piracy, slave trade, attacks on or hijacking of aircraft, genocide, war crimes, and perhaps certain acts of terrorism." Under the "passive personal principle," a State may prosecute non-nationals for crimes committed against its nationals outside of its territory. Furthermore, the circuit court found that the conduct of the government in bringing Yunis (with some amount of violence to his person) into the United States would not be a bar to his prosecution. Under the Supreme Court's Ker-Frisbie rule, even the illegal arrest of a defendant is not sufficient to warrant a dismissal of charges. The illegal conduct must "shock the conscience of the court."

A constant problem for the government in dealing with the threat of al-Qa'eda-styled terrorism is expressed in the policy of "anticipatory prosecution," or "pre-emptive prosecution." Desiring to avoid another 9/11 attack on the United States, the government's policy in the first years after 9/11 was to arrest suspected terrorists at the earliest opportunity in a given investigation, as opposed to letting a particular terror plot mature. The down side to this policy was that the government was not able to prove the more serious terror offenses in a court of law, leaving the suspects charged with lesser offenses and sentenced to shorter terms. Responding to criticism that DOJ should wait longer before intervening with premature arrests in a terror investigation, a September 11, 2008 DOJ document entitled: Fact Sheet: Justice Department Counter-Terrorism Efforts Since 9/11 explains:

> In each of these cases, the Department has faced critical decisions on when to bring criminal charges, given that a decision to prosecute a suspect exposes the Government's interest in that person and effectively ends covert intelligence investigation. Such determinations require the careful balancing of competing interests, including the immediate incapacitation of a suspect and disruption of terrorist activities through prosecution, on the one hand; and the continuation of intelligence collection about the suspect's plans, capabilities, and confederates, on the other; as well as the inherent risk that a suspect could carry out a violent act while investigators and prosecutors attempt to perfect their evidence.
>
> While it might be easier to secure convictions after an attack has occurred and innocent lives are lost, in such circumstances, the Department would be failing in its fundamental mission to protect America and its citizens, despite a court victory. For these reasons, the Department continues to act against terror threats as soon as the law, evidence, and unique circumstances of each case permit, using any charge available. As Attorney General Mukasey has stated: "[W]hen it comes to deciding whether and when to bring charges against terrorists, I am comfortable knowing this: I would rather explain to the American people why we acted when we did, even if it is at a very early stage, than try to explain why we failed to act when we could have, and it is too late."

As the horror of 9/11 fades into history, the federal authorities have become more patient. For instance, the Fort Dix Six case where a cell of radical Islamic terrorists were planning to enter Fort Dix, New Jersey, and murder military personnel was allowed to mature for a year before the arrests were made. Also, in 2010, radical Islamic terrorists Mohamed Mahmood Alessa and Carlos Almonte were arrested for conspiracy to commit murder after over four years of surveillance by the FBI.

By law and custom, federal prosecutors are authorized the discretion to decline cases brought to them by investigative agencies. According to a 2009 Syracuse University study by the Transactional Records Access Clearinghouse, from 2004 to 2008 various federal investigative agencies initially characterized nearly 8,900 individuals arrested as "international terrorists." Of that number, only 2,302 individuals were convicted in federal district courts on either criminal statutes penalizing terrorist activity or other criminal statutes dealing with more general offenses, e.g., immigration violations, identity theft, or false statement charges. In turn, only 1,245 of the 2,302 received prison confinement, and only 52 were sentenced to 20 years or more in confinement. Reflecting the policy of anticipatory prosecution, although the 2,302 convicted persons were designated as "international terrorists" by the DOJ, the actual crimes they were charged with often had no direct connection to what courts normally deem to be terrorist activity. In fact, the primary lead charge was 18 U.S.C. § 1001 (fraud/false statements, identity theft). In labeling an individual as a terrorist, Courts generally turn to a group of 14 federal statutes determined to be "terrorist" offenses, such as 18 U.S.C. § 2332 (terrorism transcending national borders) and 18 U.S.C. § 2339 (providing material support to terrorists).

Interestingly, only one American, Adam Gadahn (aka Azzam al-Amriki), born Adam Pearlman, was charged with the crime of treason (seditious conspiracy charges were used against the terrorists who conducted the 1993 bombing on the World Trade Center). Raised in California, Gadahn converted to Islam in 1995 and later moved to Pakistan where he has since appeared in a series of videos, calling for terrorist attacks on Americans. Treason, the only crime spelled out in the Constitution, is codified at 18 U.S.C. § 2381. The indictment alleges that Gadahn, owing allegiance to the United States, knowingly adhered to al-Qa'eda and provided it aid-and-comfort, with intent to "betray the United States." The indictment provided extensive quotations from five separate al-Qa'eda videos in which he appeared and urged others to attack the United States. He was also charged with providing material support in violation of 18 U.S.C. § 2339B. In 2015, Gadahn was killed by a U.S. drone strike in Waziristan, Pakistan.

The violation of immigration laws served as the primary authority for the FBI and immigration officials to detain approximately 1,000 individuals across the United States in the wake of the 9/11 terrorist attacks. Many were detained at the Metropolitan Detention Center (MDC) in Brooklyn, New York. Within four months, about two-thirds of those detained accepted voluntary departure orders and were deported; others were convicted of lesser crimes and deported. It is unclear how many of these deported illegal aliens were actually terrorists or had firm links to militant Islamic groups. Predictably, many of those detained made allegations of abuse by guards and harsh conditions based on their race, religion, or national origin. The Supreme Court in *Ashcroft v. Iqbal* (2009) rejected an effort by a Pakistani detainee at the MDC, who served a 16 month sentence before being deported, to sue former high-ranking Bush Administration officials. In the 5-4 decision, Justice Kennedy ruled that the detainees were not purposefully detained and housed based on race, religion, or national origin, but "in the aftermath of a devastating attack [the government] sought to keep suspected terrorists in the most secure conditions available until the suspects could be cleared of terrorist activity."

In the past twenty years, the FBI has broken up numerous al-Qa'eda and radical jihadist Islamic cells in the United States. Fortunately, because of the hard work of law enforcement at all levels, the vast majority of the plots were unsuccessful, with the marked exception of the murder of 13 soldiers at Fort Hood, Texas, in 2009 and the Boston bombings in 2013. These plots included attacks on military installations, subway systems, famous landmarks, shopping malls, airports, airplanes, tunnels, bridges, and schools.

Charging considerations also raise unique issues, as do defenses of freedom of religion and privacy, as illustrated in the case of Sheik Omar Abdel Rahman, one of the most notorious Islamic militants prosecuted to date. The so-called blind Sheik was associated with the 1993 terror bombing of the World Trade Center.

UNITED STATES v. RAHMAN
United States Court of Appeals for the Second Circuit
189 F.3d 88 (2nd Cir. 1999)

NEWMAN, LEVAL, and PARKER, Circuit Judges.
PER CURIAM:

INTRODUCTION

These are appeals by ten defendants convicted of seditious conspiracy and other offenses arising out of a wide-ranging plot to conduct a campaign of urban terrorism. Among the activities of some or all of the defendants were rendering assistance to those who bombed the World Trade

Center, planning to bomb bridges and tunnels in New York City, murdering Rabbi Meir Kahane, and planning to murder the President of Egypt. We affirm the convictions of all the defendants. We also affirm all of the sentences, with the exception of the sentence of Ibrahim El-Gabrowny, which we remand for further consideration.

BACKGROUND

Defendants-Appellants Sheik Omar Abdel Rahman, El Sayyid Nosair, Ibrahim El-Gabrowny, Clement Hampton-El, Amir Abdelgani ("Amir"), Fares Khallafalla, Tarig Elhassan, Fadil Abdelgani ("Fadil"), Mohammed Saleh, and Victor Alvarez (collectively "defendants") appeal from judgments of conviction entered on January 17, 1996, following a nine-month jury trial in the United States District Court for the Southern District of New York (Michael B. Mukasey, District Judge).

The defendants were convicted of the following: seditious conspiracy (all defendants); soliciting the murder of Egyptian President Hosni Mubarak and soliciting an attack on American military installations (Rahman); conspiracy to murder Mubarak (Rahman); bombing conspiracy (all defendants found guilty except Nosair and El-Gabrowny); attempted bombing (Hampton-El, Amir, Fadil, Khallafalla, Elhassan, Saleh, and Alvarez); two counts of attempted murder and one count of murder in furtherance of a racketeering enterprise (Nosair); attempted murder of a federal officer (Nosair); three counts of use of a firearm in relation to a crime of violence (Nosair); possession of a firearm with an obliterated serial number (Nosair); facilitating the bombing conspiracy by shipping a firearm in interstate commerce and using and carrying a firearm in relation to a crime of violence (Alvarez); two counts of assault on a federal officer (El-Gabrowny); assault impeding the execution of a search warrant (El-Gabrowny); five counts of possession of a fraudulent foreign passport, and one count of possession with intent to transfer false identification documents (El-Gabrowny).

...

II. The Defense Case

The defendants presented their case for two months, calling 71 witnesses. Hampton-El, Elhassan, Alvarez, and Fadil Abdelgani each testified on his own behalf. The specific defenses put forth by the individual defendants will be set out below as they become relevant to particular claims on appeal. Siddig Ali, among others, was charged in the same indictment as the defendants but was not part of the trial because he pleaded guilty to all counts with which he was charged and cooperated, to a degree, with the Government.

III. Verdicts and Sentences

The jury trial in the case ran from January 9, 1995, to October 1, 1995. The jury returned verdicts finding defendants guilty on all submitted charges, except that Nosair and El-Gabrowny obtained not guilty verdicts on the Count Five bombing conspiracy charges. The defendants were sentenced as follows: Rahman and Nosair, life imprisonment; El-Gabrowny, 57 years; Alvarez, Hampton-El, Elhassan, and Saleh, 35 years; Amir Abdelgani and Khallafalla, 30 years; Fadil Abdelgani, 25 years. The sentences are more fully explained in Part IV(A), infra.

DISCUSSION
I. Constitutional Challenges

...

B. Seditious Conspiracy Statute and the First Amendment

Rahman, joined by the other appellants, contends that the seditious conspiracy statute, *18 U.S.C. § 2384*, is an unconstitutional burden on free speech and the free exercise of religion in violation of the First Amendment. First, Rahman argues that the statute is facially invalid because it criminalizes protected expression and that it is overbroad and unconstitutionally vague. Second, Rahman contends that his conviction violated the First Amendment because it rested solely on his political views and religious practices.

1. Facial Challenge

a. *Restraint on Speech. Section 2384 provides:* If two or more persons in any State or Territory, or in any place subject to the jurisdiction of the United States, conspire to overthrow, put down, or destroy by force the Government of the United States, or to levy war against them, or to oppose by force the authority thereof, or by force to prevent, hinder, or delay the execution of any law of the United States, or by force to seize, take, or possess any property of the United States contrary to the authority thereof, they shall be fined under this title or imprisoned not more than twenty years, or both.

18 U.S.C. § 2384.

As Section 2384 proscribes "speech" only when it constitutes an agreement to use force against the United States, Rahman's generalized First Amendment challenge to the statute is without merit. Our court has previously considered and rejected a First Amendment challenge to Section 2384.
...

2. Application of Section 2384 to Rahman's Case

Rahman also argues that he was convicted not for entering into any conspiratorial agreement that Congress may properly forbid, but "solely for his religious words and deeds" which, he contends, are protected by the First Amendment. In support of this claim, Rahman cites the Government's use in evidence of his speeches and writings.

There are two answers to Rahman's contention. The first is that freedoms of speech and of religion do not extend so far as to bar prosecution of one who uses a public speech or a religious ministry to commit crimes. Numerous crimes under the federal criminal code are, or can be, committed by speech alone. As examples: Section 2 makes it an offense to "counsel," "command," "induce" or "procure" the commission of an offense against the United States. *18 U.S.C. § 2(a)*. Section 371 makes it a crime to "conspire...to commit any offense against the United States." *18 U.S.C. § 371*. Section 373, with which Rahman was charged, makes it a crime to "solicit, command, induce, or otherwise endeavor to persuade" another person to commit a crime of violence. *18 U.S.C. § 373(a)*. Various other statutes, like Section 2384, criminalize conspiracies of specified objectives, see, e.g., *18 U.S.C. § 1751(d)* (conspiracy to kidnap); *18 U.S.C. § 1951* (conspiracy to interfere with commerce through robbery, extortion, or violence); *21 U.S.C. § 846* conspiracy to violate drug laws). All of these offenses are characteristically committed through speech. Notwithstanding that political speech and religious exercise are among the activities most jealously guarded by the First Amendment, one is not immunized from prosecution for such speech-based offenses merely because one commits them through the medium of political speech or religious preaching. Of course, courts must be vigilant to insure [sic] that prosecutions are not improperly based on the mere expression of unpopular ideas. But if the evidence shows that the speeches crossed the line into criminal solicitation, procurement of criminal activity, or conspiracy to violate the laws, the prosecution is permissible.

The evidence justifying Rahman's conviction for conspiracy and solicitation showed beyond a reasonable doubt that he crossed this line. His speeches were not simply the expression of ideas; in some instances they constituted the crime of conspiracy to wage war on the United States under Section 2384 and solicitation of attack on the United States military installations, as well as of the murder of Egyptian President Hosni Mubarak under Section 373.

For example:

Rahman told Salem he "should make up with God...by turning his rifle's barrel to President Mubarak's chest, and killing him."

On another occasion, speaking to Abdo Mohammed Haggag about murdering President Mubarak during his visit to the United States, Rahman told Haggag, "Depend on God. Carry out this operation. It does not require a fatwa.... You are ready in training, but do it. Go ahead."

The evidence further showed that Siddig Ali consulted with Rahman about the bombing of the United Nations Headquarters, and Rahman told him, "Yes, it's a must, it's a duty."

On another occasion, when Rahman was asked by Salem about bombing the United Nations, he counseled against it on the ground that it would be "bad for Muslims," but added that Salem should "find a plan to destroy or to bomb or to...inflict damage to the American Army."

Words of this nature—ones that instruct, solicit, or persuade others to commit crimes of violence—violate the law and may be properly prosecuted regardless of whether they are uttered in private, or in a public speech, or in administering the duties of a religious ministry. The fact that his speech or conduct was "religious" does not immunize him from prosecution under generally-applicable criminal statutes.

Rahman also protests the Government's use in evidence of his speeches, writings, and preachings that did not in themselves constitute the crimes of solicitation or conspiracy. He is correct that the Government placed in evidence many instances of Rahman's writings and speeches in which Rahman expressed his opinions within the protection of the First Amendment. However, while the First Amendment fully protects Rahman's right to express hostility against the United States, and he may not be prosecuted for so speaking, it does not prevent the use of such speeches or writings in evidence when relevant to prove a pertinent fact in a criminal prosecution. The Government was free to demonstrate Rahman's resentment and hostility toward the United States in order to show his motive for soliciting and procuring illegal attacks against the United States and against President Mubarak of Egypt. See *Mitchell, 508 U.S. at 487* ("The First Amendment...does not prohibit the evidentiary use of speech to establish the elements of a crime or to prove motive or intent."); *United States v. Hoffman, 806 F.2d 703, 708-09 (7th Cir. 1986)* (evidence of religious affiliation relevant to show defendant's motive to threaten President, because defendant leader of religious group was imprisoned by Government at time of threats).

Furthermore, Judge Mukasey properly protected against the danger that Rahman might be convicted because of his unpopular religious beliefs that were hostile to the United States. He explained to the jury the limited use it was entitled to make of the material received as evidence of motive. He instructed that a defendant could not be convicted on the basis of his beliefs or the expression of them—even if those beliefs favored violence. He properly instructed the jury that it could find a defendant guilty only if the evidence proved he committed a crime charged in the indictment.

We reject Rahman's claim that his conviction violated his rights under the First Amendment. …

CONCLUSION

The ten defendants were accorded a full and fair jury trial lasting nine months. They were vigorously defended by able counsel. The prosecutors conducted themselves in the best traditions of the high standards of the Office of the United States Attorney for the Southern District of New York. The trial judge, the Honorable Michael B. Mukasey, presided with extraordinary skill and patience, assuring fairness to the prosecution and to each defendant and helpfulness to the jury. His was an outstanding achievement in the face of challenges far beyond those normally endured by a trial judge.

We have considered all of the other claims raised on appeal by all of the defendants, beyond those discussed in this opinion, and conclude that they are without merit. The convictions of all ten defendants are affirmed. With the exception of the sentence of defendant El-Gabrowny, which is remanded for further proceedings as set forth in this opinion, the sentences of all the other defendants are affirmed.

A cornerstone law enforcement tool for prosecuting those accused of engaging in domestic terrorism is the so-called Material Support Act which first appeared in the Antiterrorism and Effective Death Penalty Act of 1996. The Material Support Act provides an independent substantive offense used as a basis for early intervention where the alleged terrorist activity is "nipped in the bud." Embodied in two sections, the law makes it a criminal offense for anyone to provide *material support or resources* in aid of terrorist offenses or to provide *material support or resources* to a foreign terrorist group so designated by the Secretary of State. This means that it is a federal crime to provide almost anything of value, including training, money, or personnel to such terror groups. If no deaths are involved, the maximum penalty is fifteen years in jail. On the other hand, if the death of any person results from the support activities, the offender can be incarcerated for any term or for life. The impact of the Material Support Act on law enforcement is significant. According to Norman Abrams, it "may be the most significant doctrinal development in the federal criminal law since the enactment of RICO and the other organizational crime statutes, the money laundering statutes, and the criminal forfeiture laws [because] [t]hey show how each new federal criminal 'war'—from Prohibition through the wars on organized crime, on illegal drugs, and now on terror—has spawned new laws or legal doctrines designed to expand the [grasp] of the federal government's criminal enforcement arm."

Despite concerns regarding the expansiveness of the Material Support Act and its effect on civil liberties (the Material Support Act was amended in the Intelligence Reform and Terrorism Protection Act of 2004 in response to a number of judicial decisions interpreting the previous language), there is no doubt that the Act has become a vital weapon in addressing the breakup of domestic terror cells in the War on Terror. Because many of the dozens of cases have been resolved by guilty pleas, relatively few have produced lower court opinions interpreting the provisions.

Providing Material Support To Terrorists
18 U.S.C.A. § 2339A

(a) Offense—Whoever provides material support or resources or conceals or disguises the nature, location, source, or ownership of material support or resources, knowing or intending that they are to be used in preparation for, or in carrying out, a violation of section 32, 37, 81, 175, 229, 351, 831, 842(m) or (n), 844(f) or (i), 930(c), 956, 1114, 1116, 1203, 1361, 1362, 1363, 1366, 1751, 1992, 1993, 2155, 2156, 2280, 2281, 2332, 2332a, 2332b, 2332f, or 2340A of this title, section 236 of the Atomic Energy Act of 1954 (42 U.S.C. 2284), section 46502 or 60123(b) of title 49, or any offense listed in section 2332b(g)(5)(B) (except for sections 2339A and 2339B) or in preparation for, or in carrying out, the concealment of an escape from the commission of any such violation, or attempts or conspires to do such an act, shall be fined under this title, imprisoned not more than 15 years, or both, and, if the death of any person results, shall be imprisoned for any term of years or for life....

(b) Definitions—As used in this section
(1) the term "material support or resources" means any property, tangible or intangible, or service, including currency or monetary instruments or financial securities, financial services, lodging, training, expert advice or assistance, safehouses, false documentation or identification, communications equipment, facilities, weapons, lethal substances, explosives, personnel, transportation, and other physical assets, except medicine or religious materials;
(2) the term "training" means instruction or teaching designed to impart a specific skill, as opposed to general knowledge; and
(3) the term "expert advice or assistance" means advice or assistance derived from scientific, technical or other specialized knowledge.

Providing Material Support or Resources to
Designated Foreign Terrorist Organizations
18 U.S.C.A. § 2339B

(a) Prohibited activities.
(1) Unlawful conduct. Whoever, within the United States or subject to the jurisdiction of the United States, knowingly provides material support or resources to a foreign terrorist organization, or attempts or conspires to do so, shall be fined under this title or imprisoned not more than 15 years, or both, and, if the death of any person results, shall be imprisoned for any term of years or for life....

(g) Definitions. As used in this section…

(4) the term "material support or resources" has the same meaning as in section 2339A;…

(6) the term "terrorist organization" means an organization designated as a terrorist organization under section 219 of the Immigration and Nationality Act.

The latest revisions to the Material Support Act provide the government with the ability to obtain convictions by proving a mens rea of "knowing or intending" for § 2339A violations, and "knowingly" for § 2339B violations. While the Clinton Administration era law does not penalize membership in a terror group, it does outlaw what is termed "material support." Thus, the government need only show that the individual knowingly provided the proscribed group with some material support, which in many of the cases so far adjudicated has involved attendance at a radical terror training camp in Afghanistan. To date, federal judges have largely upheld the legality of the statute and numerous members of terror sleeper cells have been convicted, including New York's Lackawanna Six.

Many have expressed concern that the Material Support Act, as it is currently enforced at § 2339B, grants the Secretary of State too much latitude in designating which organizations qualify as terrorist organizations. In contrast, some have argued that terrorist organizations savvy enough to compartmentalize themselves into different sub-organizations would still be able to receive contributions to assist their non-military activities. Nevertheless, the designation of a terrorist organization by the State Department under the statute remains subject to a rigorous administrative procedure which requires all conclusions to be supported with exhaustive fact finding, the opportunity for congressional members to object to the designation prior to its publication in the Federal Register, and the organization itself allowed to appeal its designation to the D.C. Circuit of the U.S. Court of Appeals. These facts alone demonstrate that the United States is determined to vigorously fight terror before it strikes without succumbing to a "Star Chamber" mentality that threatens the civil liberties of all in the name of security. The 2010 Supreme Court case of *Holder v. Humanitarian Law Project* (6-3) rejected the idea that the Material Support Act was unconstitutionally vague and that it required a mens rea element of specific intent as opposed to just knowledge of the identity of the terror organization. The Court also rejected the plaintiff's First Amendment argument and freedom of association argument.

In summary, United States federal district courts have jurisdiction to try individuals for terrorist-related offenses under a variety of statutes. However, instead of charging suspected al-Qa'eda war criminals with violations of the law of war, the federal courts apply parallel statutes related to the *malum in se* crime or apply the appropriate terrorist statute. Some of the al-Qa'eda members that were not designated as enemy combatants have been sent to federal court, such as Richard Reid and Zacarias Moussaoui, while other members that were designated as enemy combatants faced trial by military commissions. Confusion has occurred when a designated enemy combatant is sent to federal court for trial and not to a military commission, as was the ill-informed desire of the Obama Administration in November 2009 to send five al-Qa'eda enemy combatants to stand trial in New York City. Obviously, this disjointed policy allows a great amount of flexibility for the government, but also causes massive confusion to the public. Again, the vast majority of Islamic terrorists jailed in this nation had to be tried in federal court (over 350 since 9/11) because they were never labeled as enemy combatants by the President. These terrorists were clearly influenced and "infected" with the virus of radical Islam but they did not qualify as enemy combatants and therefore could not be tried by means of the military commissions process.

6.7 Investigating Terrorist Suspects

One of the first issues of concern that captured the attention of the public following the terrorist attacks of September 11, 2001, was the possibility that other al-Qa'eda terrorist cells were at large on American soil. Federal, State, and local law enforcement personnel were put on the highest alert and an immediate search for suspected terrorists associated with the attacks on America began under the direction of the DOJ.

If you are trying to stop terrorists at the airport, you are too late. If the most important weapon in the War on Terror is intelligence, then it is certain that America's first line of defense must be anchored on reliable intelligence. America's ability to gather and analyze intelligence is much greater than that of al-Qa'eda-styled terrorists and this advantage must be maintained. To better assist law enforcement to prevent future acts of terrorism against the United States, Congress passed the USA PATRIOT Act which contains a variety of criminal procedure provisions. Many of the revisions are related to the Foreign Intelligence and Surveillance Act (FISA) and the anonymous judges of the FISA court.

FISA codifies in federal law the procedures associated with how the intelligence community conducts electronic surveillance and physical searches for the acquisition of foreign intelligence for reasons of national security. Since its passage in 1978, FISA has withstood a variety of legal challenges, most related to concerns regarding violation of the Fourth Amendment to the Constitution.

In passing FISA, the intent of Congress was to strike an appropriate balance between the need to protect national security with the need to protect civil liberty rights of Americans. FISA was certainly never intended to impact adversely on American government intelligence community activities directed at places or people outside of the United States.

FISA created two layers of special courts: one to issue orders and the other to provide review. The Foreign Intelligence Surveillance Court (FISC) is a "secret" court comprised of eleven non-disclosed federal district court judges appointed by the Chief Justice of the Supreme Court. Since these appointed judges are federal district court judges the FISC court is a proper Article III court. A FISC judge rules on the submitted intelligence community applications for court orders authorizing or denying electronic surveillance and physical searches. The Foreign Intelligence Surveillance Court of Review (FISCR) is also a "secret" court and consists of three non-disclosed federal district or federal appellate judges with the power to review FISC actions.

The basic mechanics for how the FISC court order process works reveals a stringent system of agency checks and cross checks prior to submission to the FISC judge. An application to conduct an electronic surveillance is initiated by a federal intelligence community officer. After going through a variety of internal agency bureaucratic procedures and rules, culminating with the approval of the Attorney General, the application is then presented under oath to a FISC judge. The central language in the application must clearly address a number of issues to include the following: (1) the target of the electronic surveillance must be identified as well as the information relied on by the government to demonstrate that the target is either a "foreign power" or an "agent of a foreign power;" (2) the type of surveillance which will be used; (3) the minimization procedures to be employed; and (4) certification by a high-ranking Executive Branch official that he specially determines that the information sought is "foreign intelligence information" and that "a significant purpose" of the electronic surveillance or search is to obtain foreign intelligence information.

In order to issue a court order authorizing the surveillance, the FISC judge reviewing the application must specifically determine that there is probable cause to believe that the target of the surveillance or search is a foreign power or agent of a foreign power and that a significant purpose of the electronic surveillance or search is to collect foreign intelligence. Nevertheless, the representations in the application must be accepted unless he finds that they are "clearly erroneous." In the case of a United States person, the FISC judge must also determine that the target of the surveillance is not being considered an agent of a foreign power based on activities protected by the First Amendment.

In 2006, 2009, 2011, and 2019, Congress extended most all of the provisions in the original USA PATRIOT Act. Because almost all of the provisions in the USA PATRIOT Act amend or add language to existing federal statutes, it will be some time before the meaning and impact of many of the provisions can be fully evaluated in terms of constitutionality. For example, Section 203 of the Act amends the *Federal Rules of Criminal Procedure* (FRCP) to allow the sharing of grand jury information with other interested federal agencies if it relates to foreign intelligence. Section 203 also allows law enforcement and intelligence officers to break down the so-called "wall" that once prohibited the two agencies from sharing information in cases associated with national security. Amazingly, the ability to exchange terrorist-related information did not exist prior to the USA PATRIOT Act. Currently, federal law enforcement and federal intelligence officers share a wide variety of information associated with criminal investigations and foreign intelligence.

Similarly, Section 218 allows FISA court orders in cases where "a significant purpose" of the investigation is obtaining foreign intelligence. This provision also breaks down the wall between law enforcement and intelligence officers. In fact, Section 218 authority was instrumental in the disruption of the 2002 terror sleeper cell known as the Portland Seven out of Portland, Oregon. Six of these militant Islamic terrorists were convicted and sentenced to terms in prison ranging from three to 18 years; the remaining terror suspect was killed in a gun battle with Pakistani authorities in 2003.

Section 219 amends the FRCP to authorize nationwide search warrants for terrorism cases. Section 209 permits stored voicemail to be obtained by a search warrant and not a wiretap court order. Section 214 provides for FISA courts to issue pen-register and trap-and-trace orders in terrorist cases similar to the process used in the context of criminal investigations. Previously, the order could not be issued unless the subject was contacting a foreign power.

Section 215 amends the old "business records" authority of the FISA. At one time, Section 215 was perhaps the most controversial provision of the USA PATRIOT Act, which authorizes investigators to seek a court order compelling the production of any "tangible item" no matter who held it, relevant to certain counterintelligence and counterterrorism investigations. Despite the fact that the Justice Department indicated that, as of March 2005, the Section 215 authority had been used on only 35 occasions, some continued to raise a variety of civil rights concerns, e.g., it could be used to look at library cards (the Justice Department indicated in 2005 that Section 215 had never been used to secure library, bookstore, gun sale or medical records).

Section 213 adds a subsection to 18 U.S.C. § 3103a in order to authorize a delayed notice of execution of a search warrant (under specific conditions). The search warrant grants federal agencies the ability to conduct secret searches when armed with the appropriate probable cause judicial warrant. Section 213 of the USA PATRIOT Act simply codifies a law enforcement tool that has been in use for decades by federal judges. The statute eliminates the requirement that law enforcement provide a person subject to a search warrant with contemporaneous notice of the search. Known as "sneak-and-peek," these searches allow law enforcement officers the authority to search and seize any tangible object or record with delayed notification to the owner or possessor when the court finds necessity for action.

Sneak-and-peek authority has stirred debates over the provision's value to the defense of the nation and its attendant harm to civil liberties. Representative C.L. "Butch" Otter (R-Idaho) offered his view at a floor debate: "Sneak-and-peek searches give the government the power to repeatedly search a private residence without informing the residents that he or she is the target of an investigation. Not only does this provision allow the seizure of personal property and business records without notification, but it also opens the door to nationwide search warrants and allows the CIA and the NSA to operate domestically."

Despite the rhetoric of those who oppose the provision, sneak-and-peek searches cannot be carried out without a probable cause search warrant issued by a neutral and detached magistrate. In addition, in order to perform this type of search, the court must find "reasonable cause to believe that providing immediate notification of the execution of the warrant may have an adverse effect" on the investigation. Furthermore, the law does not allow for searches to be conducted without any notification; instead, it simply allows for a delay in notification when there is reasonable belief that prior notification could damage the investigation. Obviously, the sneak-and-peek provision is an extremely valuable tool because it allows the authorities to gather evidence without "tipping their hand." Often, many terrorists, or groups of terrorists in "sleeper cells," maintain only temporary domiciles and are known to move locations very quickly. This provision aids officials in gathering valuable information from a suspect's house or apartment without alerting the suspect of the investigation. In this context, the property that could possibly be seized (or copied) could include laptop computers and other computer records.

Section 206 allows the FISA court to authorize the use of roving wiretap surveillance, permitting the interception of any communications made to or by a suspect without identifying a specific telephone line or computer system to be monitored. In other words, the wiretap authorization is attached to the particular terrorist suspect as opposed to a particular communication technology. Because terrorists are likely to quickly change communication devices to avoid detection, Section 206 provides a vital tool to law enforcement in monitoring their activities. This provision had been used many times against international terrorists and spies. Similarly, Section 207 of the USA PATRIOT Act extends the initial FISA court order time duration from 90 days to 120 days, and such court orders can now be extended for up to one year as opposed to the former requirement of renewable 90 day periods.

Section 212 expands the original law which required that third parties, such as common carriers, be specified in a court order to provide any assistance necessary to conduct surveillance. The new law extends that obligation to any unnamed and unspecified third party. Those parties would include, for instance, any libraries that provide internet access to the public, university computer labs and internet cafes. This allows federal agencies the ability to monitor these facilities if they have probable cause to believe that a terrorist or intelligence target is using the facility to transmit communications. Furthermore, the FBI may issue so-called national security letters demanding a limited amount of information from financial or communication entities.

6.8 Use of the Military in Domestic Law Enforcement

There have been a number of new developments associated with the War on Terror that impact on the use of the United States military. While National Security Presidential Directive 5 designates the Department of Homeland Security as the lead federal agency for consequence management and support to law enforcement, with the FBI as the lead federal agency to handle a terrorist attack in the United States, the President as Commander in Chief retains the authority to directly employ the armed forces in any situation involving homeland defense. To be sure, the use of the military would be a tool of last resort prompted by exigent circumstances.

Recognizing the need to increase military preparedness to fight the War on Terror, Congress has increased defense spending by large percentages over the past five years. More importantly, in light of the War on Terror, for the first time the Pentagon's Congressionally mandated 2006 *Quadrennial Defense Review* (QDR), which is the official strategic policy of how the United States armed forces should be utilized, took into account the nation's war against terrorism and the acknowledgement that the War on Terror could be a "long war."

One area often revisited in the context of new missions for the American military is the question of whether a long-standing law prohibiting the use of the active military to support domestic law enforcement within the borders of the United States should be revoked or modified. This law is the 1878 Posse Comitatus Act (PCA), 10 U.S.C. § 375; 18 U.S.C. § 1385, which prohibits the use of the military to execute the civil laws of the United States. In full text, the PCA states:

> Whoever, except in cases and under circumstances expressly authorized by the Constitution or Act of Congress, willfully uses any part of the Army or the Air Force as a posse comitatus or otherwise to execute the laws shall be fined under this title or imprisoned not more than two years, or both.

Posse comitatus is Latin for "the force of the country," and refers to the English common law doctrine which empowered the local sheriff to summon able-bodied men to help enforce the law in an emergency situation. With the end of Reconstruction, federal troops employed as a standing army of occupation in the South were finally withdrawn in 1877. In 1878, Congress passed the PCA which stopped the practice of local or federal civilian law enforcement being able to conscript military troops into their posses. Thus, the root cause of the Act came about due to the use of federal troops in the Southern States to assist civilian law enforcement of the Reconstruction Act of 1867 pushed through by radical Republicans following the American Civil War. It originally only applied to the United States Army, but was extended in 1947 to the Air Force. Nevertheless, the DOD views the Act as applying to all services. However, the PCA does not apply to a member of the Reserve component when not on active federal duty, nor to a member of the State National Guard when not in federal service. Finally, the Act does not apply to the Coast Guard.

Apart from the Insurrection Act, which allows the President to deploy troops to "put down lawlessness, insurrection, and rebellion" (used in the 1992 Los Angeles Race Riots), several laws grant specific exceptions to the application of the PCA. United States Code, Title 18, Section 831, provides that if nuclear material is involved in an emergency, the Secretary of Defense may provide assistance to the Department of Justice, notwithstanding the PCA. The Act does not prevent the President from using the military in cases of civil disorders or emergencies. Section 831 defines emergencies as those "that pose a serious threat to the interests of the United States; and in which enforcement of the law would be seriously impaired if the assistance were not provided; and civilian law enforcement personnel are not capable of enforcing the law." In fact, the military has been used hundreds of times in such domestic operations. The Act also does not apply to the use of United States armed forces personnel who either arrest or assist in the arrest of international criminals outside the territory of the United States. In addition, a variety of United States courts have held that military support to domestic law enforcement, short of actual search, seizure, arrest, or similar confrontation with civilians, does not violate the PCA. Specific examples of permitted support to domestic law enforcement include traffic direction; the provision of information, equipment, and facilities; and even training. Violations of the PCA include a fine of $10,000 and/or two years imprisonment.

6.9 Immigration Issues

As of 2020, estimates place the number of illegal aliens living in the continental United States at over 15 million people. On the other side of the equation, there are about 3,000 Homeland Security personnel to police them. With the fact that many of the 9/11 murderers had false identity cards and were here illegally, many blamed the Immigration and Naturalization Service (INS) for the attacks. In 2002 Congress abolished the INS and replaced it with three separate agencies under the DHS: the Bureau of Citizenship and Immigration Services (BCIS), the Bureau of Immigration and Customs Enforcement (BICE), and the Bureau of Customs and Border Protection (BCBP).

Although an in-depth analysis of the new changes authorized by the USA PATRIOT Act is beyond the scope of this book, the provision giving the Attorney General broad powers to take into custody and detain illegal aliens suspected of terrorism will most likely prove to be the most controversial and bears analysis here. The power to indefinitely detain illegal aliens raises at the very least a constitutional due process issue under the Fifth Amendment, a matter which will most certainly require resolution by the federal judiciary.

Specifically, Section 412(a) of the USA PATRIOT Act adds Section 236A to the Immigration and Nationality Act, allowing the Attorney General to take into custody any alien certified to be inadmissible or deportable on one of six grounds: (1) espionage, (2) sabotage, (3) export restrictions, (4) attempt to overthrow the United States Government, (5) terrorist activities, and (6) any other "activity that endangers the national security of the United States." Section 412(a)(5) then requires the government to either begin criminal or deportation proceedings within seven days of the detention. Ostensibly, however, Section 412(a)(6) empowers the government to indefinitely detain certain certified illegal alien terrorists who are not likely to be deported in the foreseeable future due to the continuing nature of the investigation. The question of concern regards the matter of how long a certified individual terrorist may be detained and under what conditions.

The United States Supreme Court has yet to rule on the constitutionality of Section 412(a)(6). Nevertheless, because of a 2001 decision entitled *Zadvydas v. Davis*, it seems likely that the Court will probably find that Section 412(a)(6) is constitutional. In *Zadvydas*, the Court was concerned with the constitutionality of whether the government could detain a removable illegal alien beyond the removable period (i.e., indefinitely, or "only for a period reasonably necessary to secure the alien's removal from the country"). The Court construed the applicable section of the Immigration and Nationality Act narrowly, firmly disapproving the indefinite detention of aliens who were not likely to be deported. Still, the Court in *Zadvydas* did recognize in the opinion that suspected terrorists could be held for indefinite periods in preventive detention. The Supreme Court understood that illegal aliens detained for "terrorism or other special circumstances where special arguments might be made for forms of preventive detention," should not be affected by the general rule disapproving the indefinite detention of resident aliens not likely to be deported. *Zadvydas* seemingly exempted suspected alien terrorists as a "small segment of particularly dangerous individuals" that the government could subject to indefinite detention.

Concerns for security measures have caused the United States to revisit the issue of immigration laws regarding who is allowed into the country and under what conditions they are allowed to remain.

Each year tens of millions of visas are granted to foreign nationals to enter the United States. The reason for entry into the United States generally includes matters related to education, travel, or to conduct business. Of paramount concern in weighing this figure is the fact that about 40 percent of the nation's undocumented immigrants have overstayed their visas and millions of others simply cross the Mexican border illegally. Still, the government has done little to correct the problem.

One proposal to halt or slow illegal immigration is the creation of a national identity card (NIC), which is standard fare for all nations in Western Europe. Proponents of this highly debated concept argue that such a card would not only stop the flow of illegal aliens into the U.S., but also prevent terrorists from entering and then operating from within America's borders. Opponents not only worry that an NIC would violate the fundamental right of privacy guaranteed by the U.S. Constitution, but cite historical abuses as well ranging from "pass laws" used to enforce slavery in the North and South prior to the War Between the States, to the abuses of the Nazis towards Jews and others.

In 2010, the Democrat-controlled Senate proposed a new social security card to replace the paper blue and white social security card which is probably the simplest document to forge in the history of documents. The social security card was introduced in 1936. Despite President Roosevelt's promise that it would be a confidential document never to be used for identification purposes, the social security account number is *the* identifier for all, e.g., the IRS began to use it in 1962; Medicare in 1965; and DOD in 1967. Recognizing that since 1990, each newborn in America is now issued a social security number, which is recorded on the birth certificate, the 2010 Senate proposal was to create a new fool-proof type of social security card for all U.S. citizens and legal immigrants. The new card would be a high-tech, fraud-proof document with biometric identifiers. While the new social security card would not contain medical information or other personal information, the proposed law mandated that all employers would be responsible for swiping the card through a special machine to confirm the person's identity and immigration status. Those who were caught under the new law would be penalized with fines and community service and forced to the back of the line of prospective legal immigrants if they passed a background check. Senator Dick Durbin, who worked on the outline of the proposed bill and had long advocated a national identity card for all driver's licenses, cited the inevitability of a NIC saying: "For a long time it was resisted by many groups but now we live in a world where we take off our shoes at the airport and pull out our identification… people understand that in this vulnerable world we have to be able to present identification."

Perhaps in an ever shrinking world rooted in information and technology, the issue of whether Americans should be required to possess a national identity card that cannot be forged or faked is moot. In reality, the government already "knows" all about the people that are paying taxes and otherwise are here legally. As such, the only people that would potentially suffer harm are those that are illegally present. The question then is really about when and where the government can act on the information. In the 1983 Supreme Court case of *Kolender v. Lawson* the Court struck down a California statute that required individuals "who loiter or wander the streets to identify themselves and to account for their presence when requested by a peace officer" as unconstitutional because it violated the Due Process clause of the Fourteenth Amendment as vague for "failing to clarify what is contemplated by the requirement that a suspect provide 'credible and reliable' identification." The California law was struck down not because people were required to have identification (in the Democrat bill it would be near "full-proof" identification), but because it constituted an illegal request for said identification by the government which also violated the Fourth Amendment. In short, the government may only ask for identification from individuals in limited circumstances. Obviously, if the individual is requesting benefits or services from the government they must present valid identification specified by the government in order to receive said things. The government can demand and specify the type of identification that will be accepted. On the other hand, government agents, to include police, may only ask for valid identification pursuant to a limited set of circumstances. They may ask for valid identification if there is a "reasonable suspicion" that the person committed, is committing, or is about to commit a crime. This judge-made rule was established by the Supreme Court in *Terry v. Ohio* (1968). In all other cases, the police may demand valid identification based on a valid arrest as the Fourth Amendment only protects from unreasonable searches and seizures.

In the final analysis, whatever new changes Congress may make to existing immigration law, it is painfully obvious that a far better job has to be done. This critique extends from screening and background checks of individuals seeking visas to enter the borders of the United States to tracking the millions of illegal aliens who have overstayed their visas or simply have come here without a visa. Despite these troubling facts, concerns must be voiced in the public square that an inordinate tightening of immigration laws may promote "racial profiling" (racial profiling is the practice of targeting individuals solely on the basis of their race or ethnicity in the belief that a particular group is more likely to engage in certain unlawful behavior) or encourage an untoward atmosphere of bigotry and fear in the general population. Still, it is a fact that the vast majority of Islamic terror operatives do fit a certain profile. As Justice Kennedy wrote for the majority in *Ashcroft v. Iqbal* (2009): "It should come as no surprise that a legitimate policy directing law enforcement to arrest and detain individuals because of their suspected link to the attacks [9/11] would produce a disparate, incidental impact on Arab Muslims, even though the purpose of the policy was to target neither Arabs nor Muslims." Nevertheless, changes in the law should not negatively affect the vast majority of law-abiding aliens; no American wishes to see a return to the poisoned atmosphere that occurred when, for instance, President Franklin Roosevelt ordered the internment of American citizens of Japanese descent during World War II.

6.10 Privacy and New Information-Gathering Technologies

The revolutionary advancements in the field of technology have made the world a smaller place. Even without the threat of terror, the impact on privacy issues has been phenomenal. Nevertheless, if the ability to engage in preventive measures to defeat terrorism are to be realized, the government will most certainly seek to employ the latest information-gathering technologies which will include, at the very least, the increased use of video surveillance in public places, image-recognition modeling to scan faces, computer data mining, and eavesdropping on electronic message traffic. Within days after September 11, 2001, the Attorney General proposed a laundry list of new wiretap and electronic eavesdropping powers to enable law enforcement officials to "act more quickly in fast-moving cases [of terrorism]." Many of these requests, such as a revision of wiretapping laws pertaining to cell phones and so on, have already been enacted into law; many more issues are sure to be debated as the balance between privacy and security is stretched to the limit. While there exists no specific constitutional right to privacy in public places, some privacy advocates early on feared that the next wave of government requests might short-circuit constitutional safeguards under the guise of counterterrorism.

A survey of some of the new proposals for combating terrorism clearly adds to the discussion of where the line should be drawn between privacy and security. Indeed, it is largely uncertain where a terrorist attack will most likely originate. Attacks could come from outside an airplane in the form of surface to air missiles, or through the thousands of privately owned planes that can be easily rented. In addition, the 1995 attack on the Tokyo subway by the Aum Shinrikyo religious cult highlights the security challenge posed by terrorists using chemical or biological agents. Still, a favorite target of the radical Islamic terrorist remains commercial aviation as seen in the failed Christmas Day 2009 attack on Delta flight 253 over Detroit.

While metal detection technology has long been used to screen things and people who enter certain government facilities and airports, backscatter technology is now being used to screen airline travelers in most major American airports. The TSA is also using Backscatter "portals"—21-foot-high arch-like machines—for screening vehicles and containers. Backscatter technology uses beams of low-power energy that does not penetrate the subject (as does x-ray technology) to produce a detailed picture image. It is superior to metal detectors in that it can detect with great precision things such as non-metallic weapons, drugs, or bombs. On the other hand, it also reveals the traveler's breasts, buttocks, and genitalia with a detail that can count the number of hairs on a person's back. Does such an intrusion constitute a violation of the Fourth Amendment? Recalling that the Fourth Amendment does not create an absolute right to privacy, but a qualified one to protect individuals from "unreasonable searches," the courts will ultimately decide where the line is to be drawn. Although the Supreme Court has never directly ruled that airport administrative searches are proper, lower courts have. In *United States v. Aukai* (2007), the U.S. Court of Appeals for the Ninth Circuit held that an airport screening process did not violate the Fourth Amendment if conducted in a reasonable fashion.

UNITED STATES v. AUKAI
United States Court of Appeals for the Ninth Circuit
497 F.3d 955 (March 21, 2007)

BEA, Circuit Judge

More than 700 million passengers board commercial aircraft in the United States each year. FN1. The Transportation Security Administration ("TSA") is given the task of ensuring their safety, the safety of airline and airport personnel and, as the events of September 11, 2001, demonstrate, the safety of the general public from risks arising from commercial airplane flights. To do so, the TSA conducts airport screening searches of all passengers entering the secured area of the airport. We have previously held such airport screening searches are constitutionally reasonable administrative searches. Today we clarify that the reasonableness of such searches does not depend, in whole or in part, upon the consent of the passenger being searched.

On February 1, 2003, Daniel Kuualoha Aukai arrived at the Honolulu International Airport intending to take a Hawaiian Airlines flight from Honolulu, Hawaii, to Kona, Hawaii. He proceeded to check in at the ticket counter but did not produce a government-issued picture identification. Accordingly, the ticket agent wrote the phrase "No ID" on Aukai's boarding pass. Aukai then proceeded to the security checkpoint, at which signs were posted advising prospective passengers that they and their carry-on baggage were subject to search. He entered the security checkpoint at approximately 9:00 a.m., placed his shoes and a few other items into a plastic bin, and voluntarily walked through the metal detector or magnetometer. The parties agree that the magnetometer did not signal the presence of metal as Aukai walked through it. Nor did his belongings trigger an alarm or otherwise raise suspicion as they passed through the x-ray machine. After walking through the magnetometer, Aukai presented his boarding pass to TSA Officer Corrine Motonaga.

Pursuant to TSA procedures, a passenger who presents a boarding pass on which "No ID" has been written is subject to secondary screening even if he has passed through the initial screening without triggering an alarm or otherwise raising suspicion. As it was performed here, secondary screening consists of a TSA officer passing a handheld magnetometer, known as a "wand," near and around the passenger's body. If the wand detects metal, it sounds an alarm. The TSA officer then discerns the cause of the alarm, using techniques such as feeling the outside of the passenger's clothes in the area that caused the alarm and, if that area is near a pocket, directing the passenger to empty his pocket.

Because Aukai's boarding pass had the "No ID" notation, Motonaga directed Aukai to a nearby, roped-off area for secondary screening. Aukai initially complied but complained that he was in a hurry to catch his flight which, according to the boarding pass, was scheduled to leave at 9:05 a.m., just a few minutes later. Although Aukai went to the roped-off area as directed, he did not stay there. When Motonaga noticed that Aukai had left the area and was gathering his belongings from the plastic bin, she instructed Aukai that he was not allowed to retrieve his property and that he had to stay in the roped-off area.

Aukai then appealed to TSA Officer Andrew Misajon, who was to perform the secondary screening, explaining again that he was in a hurry to catch his flight. Misajon nonetheless had Aukai sit in a chair and proceeded to use the wand to detect metal objects. At some point, Misajon had Aukai stand, and when Misajon passed the wand across the front of Aukai's body, the wand alarm was triggered at Aukai's front right pants pocket. Misajon asked Aukai if he had anything in his pocket, and Aukai responded that he did not. Misajon passed the wand over the pocket a second time; again the wand alarm was triggered. Misajon again inquired whether Aukai had anything in his pocket; again Aukai said he did not. Misajon then felt the outside of Aukai's pocket and concluded that something was inside the pocket. Misajon could also see the outline of an unknown object in Aukai's pocket. At some point during this screening process, Aukai informed Misajon that he no longer wished to board a plane and wanted to leave the airport.

At this point, TSA Supervisor Joseph Vizcarra approached Misajon and asked whether he needed assistance. Misajon related the events and Vizcarra asked Misajon to pass the wand over Aukai's pocket again. When the wand alarm again was triggered, Vizcarra directed Aukai to empty his pocket. Aukai again protested that he had nothing in his pocket. Using the back of his hand, Vizcarra touched the outside of Aukai's pocket and felt something in the pocket. He again directed Aukai to empty his pocket. This time Aukai reached into his pocket and removed either his keys or change, but a bulge was still visible in his pocket. Vizcarra directed Aukai to remove all contents from his pocket. After claiming at first that there was nothing more, Aukai finally removed an object wrapped in some form of tissue paper and placed it on a tray in front of him.

Suspecting that the object might be a weapon, Vizcarra summoned a nearby law enforcement officer. Vizcarra then unwrapped the object and discovered a glass pipe used to smoke methamphetamine. The law enforcement officer escorted Aukai to a small office near the security checkpoint. Aukai was placed under arrest and was searched incident to his arrest. During the search, the police discovered in Aukai's front pants pockets several transparent bags containing a white crystal substance. Aukai eventually was taken into federal custody, where he was advised of and waived his *Miranda* rights, and then gave a statement in which he inculpated himself in the possession of methamphetamine.

Aukai was indicted for knowingly and intentionally possessing, with the intent to distribute, 50 grams or more of methamphetamine in violation of *21 U.S.C. § 841(a)* and *841(b)(1)(A) (viii)*. Aukai filed a motion to suppress the evidence found incident to his arrest at the airport and the statement he later made, which the district court denied. Aukai then pleaded guilty pursuant to a written plea agreement that preserved his right to appeal the denial of his suppression motion. The district court sentenced Aukai to a term of imprisonment of 70 months and a term of supervised release of 5 years. Aukai timely appealed.

We review de novo the district court's legal basis for denying a motion to suppress, but review the district court's findings of fact for clear error. *United States v. Marquez, 410 F.3d 612, 615 (9th Cir. 2005)* (as amended).

The *Fourth Amendment* requires the government to respect "[t]he right of the people to be secure in their persons…and effects, against unreasonable searches and seizures." *U.S. Const. amend. IV.* "A search or seizure is ordinarily unreasonable in the absence of individualized suspicion of wrongdoing. While such suspicion is not an 'irreducible' component of reasonableness, [the Supreme Court has] recognized only limited circumstances in which the usual rule does not apply." *City of Indianapolis v. Edmond, 531 U.S. 32, 37, 121 S. Ct. 447, 148 L. Ed. 2d 333 (2000)* (citations omitted). However, "where the risk to public safety is substantial and real, blanket suspicionless searches calibrated to the risk may rank as 'reasonable'—for example, searches now routine at airports and at entrances to courts and other official buildings." *Chandler v. Miller, 520 U.S. 305, 323, 117 S. Ct. 1295, 137 L. Ed. 2d 513 (1997)* (holding Georgia's requirement that candidates for state office pass a drug test did not fit within this exception) (citing *Nat'l Treasury Employees Union v. Von Raab, 489 U.S. 656, 674-76, 109 S. Ct. 1384, 103 L. Ed. 2d 685 & n.3 (1989)* (upholding warrantless drug testing of employees applying for promotion to positions involving drug interdiction)). Thus, "where a *Fourth Amendment* intrusion serves special governmental needs, beyond the normal need for law enforcement, it is necessary to balance the individual's privacy expectations against the Government's interests to determine whether it is impractical to require a warrant or some level of individualized suspicion in the particular context." *Von Raab, 489 U.S. at 665-66.*

Under this rationale the Supreme Court has repeatedly upheld the constitutionality of so-called "administrative searches." FN2. In *New York v. Burger, 482 U.S. 691, 107 S. Ct. 2636, 96 L. Ed. 2d 601 (1987)*, the Supreme Court upheld the warrantless search of a junkyard's records, permits, and vehicles. The Supreme Court reasoned: "Because the owner or operator of commercial premises in a 'closely regulated' industry has a reduced expectation of privacy, the warrant and probable-cause requirements, which fulfill the traditional *Fourth Amendment* standard of reasonableness for a government search have lessened application.…" *Id. at 702* (internal citation omitted). Thus, New York's interest in regulating the junkyard industry, in light of the rise of motor-theft and comprehensive motor vehicle insurance premiums, served as a "special need" allowing inspection without a warrant. *Id. at 708-09; see also id. at 702.* The regulatory statute also provided a "constitutionally adequate substitute for a warrant" because the statute informed junkyard operators that inspections would be made on a regular basis and limited the discretion of inspecting officers. *Id. at 711.*

In *Michigan Department of State Police v. Sitz, 496 U.S. 444, 110 S. Ct. 2481, 110 L. Ed. 2d 412 (1990)*, Sitz challenged the constitutionality of suspicionless sobriety checkpoints conducted on Michigan's highways, contending that the program violated the *Fourth Amendment's* protection against unreasonable seizures. *Id. at 447-48*. The Supreme Court upheld the sobriety checkpoints because "the balance of the State's interest in preventing drunken driving, the extent to which [the sobriety checkpoints] can reasonably be said to advance that interest, and the degree of intrusion upon individual motorists who are briefly stopped, weighs in favor of" finding the sobriety checkpoints constitutionally reasonable. *Id. at 455*.

Significantly, the Supreme Court has held that the constitutionality of administrative searches is not dependent upon consent. In *United States v. Biswell, 406 U.S. 311, 92 S. Ct. 1593, 32 L. Ed. 2d 87 (1972)*, the Supreme Court upheld the warrantless search of a pawn shop owner's gun storeroom. The search was authorized by a federal gun control statute. The Court held that, "[i]n the context of a regulatory inspection system of business premises that is carefully limited in time, place, and scope, the legality of the search depends not on consent but on the authority of a valid statute." FN3. *Id. at 315*. Thus, "[w]hen a [gun] dealer chooses to engage in this pervasively regulated business and to accept a federal license, he does so with the knowledge that his business records, firearms, and ammunition will be subject to effective inspection." *Id. at 316*.

The constitutionality of an airport screening search, however, does not depend on consent, *see Biswell, 406 U.S. at 315*, and requiring that a potential passenger be allowed to revoke consent to an ongoing airport security search makes little sense in a post-9/11 world. FN6. Such a rule would afford terrorists (FN7) multiple opportunities to attempt to penetrate airport security by "electing not to fly" on the cusp of detection until a vulnerable portal is found. This rule would also allow terrorists a low-cost method of detecting systematic vulnerabilities in airport security, knowledge that could be extremely valuable in planning future attacks. Likewise, given that consent is not required, it makes little sense to predicate the reasonableness of an administrative airport screening search on an irrevocable implied consent theory. Rather, where an airport screening search is otherwise reasonable and conducted pursuant to statutory authority, *49 U.S.C. § 44901*, all that is required is the passenger's election to attempt entry into the secured area of an airport. FN8. *See Biswell, 406 U.S. at 315*; *49 C.F.R. § 1540.107*. Under current TSA regulations and procedures, that election occurs when a prospective passenger walks through the magnetometer or places items on the conveyor belt of the x-ray machine. FN9. The record establishes that Aukai elected to attempt entry into the posted secured area of Honolulu International Airport when he walked through the magnetometer, thereby subjecting himself to the airport screening process.

Although the constitutionality of airport screening searches is not dependent on consent, the scope of such searches is not limitless. A particular airport security screening search is constitutionally reasonable provided that it "is no more extensive nor intensive than necessary, in the light of current technology, to detect the presence of weapons or explosives [ ] [and] that it is confined in good faith to that purpose." *Davis, 482 F.2d at 913*. We conclude that the airport screening search of Aukai satisfied these requirements.

The search procedures used in this case were neither more extensive nor more intensive than necessary under the circumstances to rule out the presence of weapons or explosives. After passing through a magnetometer, Aukai was directed to secondary screening because his boarding pass was marked "No ID." Aukai then underwent a standard "wanding procedure." When the wand alarm sounded as the wand passed over Aukai's front right pants pocket, TSA Officer Misajon did not reach into Aukai's pocket or feel the outside of Aukai's pocket. Rather,

Misajon asked Aukai if he had something in his pocket. When Aukai denied that there was anything in his pocket, Misajon repeated the wanding procedure. Only after the wand alarm again sounded and Aukai again denied having anything in his pocket did Misajon employ a more intrusive search procedure by feeling the outside of Aukai's pocket and determining that there was something in there.

...

Like the Third Circuit, we find these search procedures to be minimally intrusive. *See Hartwell, 436 F.3d at 180* (holding similar search procedures to be "minimally intrusive," explaining that the procedures are "well-tailored to protect personal privacy, escalating in invasiveness only after a lower level of screening disclosed a reason to conduct a more probing search").

The duration of the detention associated with this airport screening search was also reasonable. Witnesses testified that Aukai entered the checkpoint area at approximately 9:00 a.m. and that the entire search at issue—starting from when Aukai walked through the checkpoint until the TSA's efforts to rule out the presence of a weapon resulted in the discovery of drug paraphernalia—took no more than 18 minutes. Although longer than detentions approved in other cases, *see, e.g., Sitz, 496 U.S. at 448* (average delay of 25 seconds); *United States v. Martinez-Fuerte, 428 U.S. 543, 546-47, 96 S. Ct. 3074, 49 L. Ed. 2d 1116 (1976)* (average detention of 3-5 minutes), the length of Aukai's detention was reasonable, especially in light of Aukai's conduct, because it was not prolonged beyond the time reasonably required to rule out the presence of weapons or explosives. FN10. *See Illinois v. Caballes, 543 U.S. 405, 407, 125 S. Ct. 834, 160 L. Ed. 2d 842 (2005)* (stating that a seizure can become unlawful if it is "prolonged beyond the time reasonably required to complete [its] mission").
AFFIRMED.

A new idea currently in the mill involves the use of electronic profiling. Since the beginning of the War on Terror, the Pentagon has stepped up its testing of various image-recognition technology hardware, developing sophisticated technology that is superior to new automatic teller machines which can scan a customer's face for positive identification. This technology has already been tested in England where thousands of outdoor cameras are used to keep watch on "pedestrians and passerby, employing a facial-recognition system that can automatically pick out known criminals and alert local authorities to their presence." These cameras can compare hundreds of thousands of faces on file against a particular subject face within seconds.

Despite the complaints regarding invasion of privacy, "pod" cameras are rapidly becoming a part of the modern landscape. In fact, the 6,000 cameras set in London's subway system were pivotal in solving the July 7 and July 21, 2005, bombings by al-Qa'eda operatives. Private cameras in Boston also greatly assisted in flushing out the jihadists responsible for the 2013 bombings at the Boston marathon. Cities across the United States are following suit. In Chicago, for example, over 2,000 camera pods are now in place in high-crime areas and on transit and public buildings. In 2005, the Department of Homeland Security gave over $800 million to 50 cities for surveillance cameras. By 2010, New York City had installed thousands of cameras that record images of everyone who passes through a passenger turnstile or entrance gate for public transportation. The car bomb driven by Faisal Shahzad in the 2010 Times Square terror plot was caught on video.

6.11 Assassination

Osama bin Laden is quoted as saying that "[t]he confrontation that Islam calls for with these godless and apostate regimes does not know Socratic debates, Platonic ideals, nor Aristotelian diplomacy. But it knows the dialogue of bullets, the ideals of assassination, bombing and destruction, and the diplomacy of the cannon and the machine gun." In contrast, the United States is deeply concerned with fighting the War on Terror under the rule of law—domestically and internationally. From a domestic perspective, the continuing dilemma for democratic policymakers is how to protect the nation without curtailing long-recognized civil liberties. From an international perspective, American policymakers are likewise concerned with following all those international laws associated with both the lawfulness of the use of force and the appropriate application of that force. Without question, the most pressing issue in the international realm centers on the Obama Administration's promotion of a legal rationale for the preemptive use of military force against al-Qa'eda-styled terrorists or rogue States who pose a direct or gathering threat to the United States.

Juxtaposed to the issue of crafting a legal basis for the use of preemptive military force is the recurring issue of whether certain individuals—such as high level al-Qa'eda or leaders of totalitarian States which support or sponsor terrorism—can be legally targeted for "assassination." In other words, if preemptive military force is an acceptable addition to the rule of law, can the United States simply kill selected high-level leaders without having to employ large-scale military forces against the offending rogue nation or terrorist organization?

Currently, there are two principle documents associated with these two legal concerns. Respectively, they are the groundbreaking 2002 National Security Strategy of the United States of America released by the Bush White House on September 17, 2002, and the Presidential Executive Order 12333 banning assassination.

The purpose of this section is to provide a policy and legal analysis of the United States' position regarding assassination as viewed in the context of the lawful use of preemptive military force. In doing so, this section examines the deficiencies of the current Executive Order 12333 and suggests that it should be replaced by a new executive order which clearly defines the circumstances under which individuals may be lawfully targeted for death by military forces—either in peacetime or war. Alternatively, if a new and more precise executive order is not issued to replace Executive Order 12333, there are two interlocking principles that argue against overturning Executive Order 12333. The first of these reasons regards properly understanding the most common definition of assassination and the second relates to the proper use of armed force under the rule of law. Taken together, those who advocate that the ban on assassination should be lifted without modification in order to allow the United States to engage in assassination are essentially advocating that the United States should be able to engage in unlawful killing, or murder.

In the days following the September 11, 2001, attacks on the United States the question of retaliation and self-preservation weighed heavily on the minds of policymakers. Instinctively, many in Washington called for an immediate response to the perpetrators behind the attacks, even if it meant engaging in assassination which some clearly viewed to be in violation of longstanding Executive Order 12333, prohibiting assassination by agents of the United States government. Then, prior to the March 2003 war in Iraq, many expressed the idea of toppling the dictator Saddam Hussein by simply killing him. Currently, the Obama Administration utilizes unmanned drone aircraft to kill suspected enemies in such places as Afghanistan, Pakistan, Sudan, Yemen, Somali, and other locations. Some have called these Obama killings illegal and acts of assassination. Accordingly, a proper understanding of Executive

Order 12333 and the legal basis for responding to aggression is required.

The genesis of Executive Order 12333 can be traced back to 1977, when President Gerald Ford issued the first executive order prohibiting political assassination. President Ford was prompted to action by a 1975 Congressional Report (commonly known as the Church Commission) headed by Senator Frank Church which held hearings on the question of whether or not the United States had engaged in assassination or assassination plots against certain foreign leaders. The most damning portion of the report found that between 1960 and 1965, "the United States was implicated in several assassination plots to kill Fidel Castro," the ruler of Communist Cuba.

The Church Commission found that the CIA's Operation Mongoose sought to eliminate Castro with a number of unlikely weapons, such as poison tipped pens and cigars, and an exploding seashell that was to be placed near Castro's favorite scuba spots. Issuing a document consisting of hundreds of pages, the Church Commission was unable to make a finding that "assassination plots were authorized by the Presidents or other people above the governmental agency or agencies involved," but the commission did find that the "system of executive command and control was so ambiguous that it [was] difficult to be certain at what levels assassination activity was known and authorized." The Church Commission strongly concluded that assassination was both legally and morally repugnant to a democratic people and should never be associated with the United States of America: "[A]ssassination is incompatible with American principles, international order, and morality. It should be rejected as a tool of foreign policy."

Curiously, despite the exhaustive research done by the Church Commission on assassination and the call for "intervention by Congress to proscribe it as a matter of law," Congress never enacted legislation to legally ban the use of assassination as an instrument of foreign policy, leaving the matter to the Executive Branch via an executive order. Although presidential executive orders are policy and not law, this distinction is functionally irrelevant, particularly in regard to the politically charged issue of assassination.

President Ford's executive order on assassination read: "Prohibition of Assassination. No employee of the United States Government shall engage in, or conspire to engage in, political assassination." Shortly thereafter, President Jimmy Carter followed suit with his own slightly modified version which deleted the term "political," and in 1981, President Ronald Reagan issued Executive Order 12333 on assassination. It reads in full text: "No person employed by or acting on behalf of the United States government shall engage in, or conspire to engage in, assassination." Subsequent presidents have not changed the Reagan order banning assassination by agents of the United States. Executive Order 12333 remains in effect in the Obama Administration.

A common and reoccurring theme of frustration runs across the arguments of those who seek the repeal of Executive Order 12333. This frustration actually reflects a lack of understanding of what assassination actually means or entails, not what Executive Order 12333 actually prohibits. In short, the central problem is that people use the same word—assassination—and assume that everyone is talking about the same meaning. Of course, this situation is aggravated both by the brevity of the executive order, which provides no definition whatsoever for the term assassination, and the fact that it makes no attempt to distinguish between instances of lawful killing verses instances of assassination, or unlawful killing.

Former conservative United States Senator Jesse Helms from North Carolina amplified this confusion when he remarked on September 11, 2001, that he was in favor of taking whatever action was necessary, to include assassination, to punish those responsible for the attacks on the United States: "I hope I will live to see the day when it will once again be the policy of the United States of America to go after the kind of sneaky enemies who created this morning's mayhem." Then, just over a week after the terrorist attacks, liberal minded National Public Radio senior news correspondent, Daniel Schorr, forcefully urged policymakers to do away with the ban on assassination. Schorr wrote: "A 25 year old executive order reflecting the reaction to mindless cold war plotting against President Castro and other third world leaders, seems completely anachronistic after the Sept. 11th. It is time to rescind an assassination ban that has no more reason for existing." In fact, in the days immediately after the attacks on America, Congressman Bob Barr of Georgia proposed a bill in the House of Representatives which would have nullified Executive Order 12333.

Fortunately, cooler heads prevailed and Congress passed no legislation regarding Executive Order 12333. Shortly thereafter, then White House spokesman, Ari Fleischer correctly related to reporters that the assassination ban "does not limit America's ability to act in self-defense." The elimination of terrorists could require, Fleischer remarked, "acts which involve the lives of others."

Although Fleischer rightly understood in September 2001 that the ban on assassination did not prohibit the United States from taking actions in self-defense against specific threats, he later seemed to have lapsed into misunderstanding. At an October 1, 2002, press conference, Fleischer voiced support for non-American actors assassinating Saddam Hussein. When asked about the cost of a possible war with Iraq, spokesman Fleischer remarked, "I can only say that the cost of a one-way ticket is substantially less than that [the estimated cost of nine billion dollars a month]. The *cost of one bullet*, if the *Iraqi people* take it on themselves, is substantially less than that [emphasis added]." While the assassination of Saddam Hussein by his own people would not violate Executive Order 12333, reporters immediately asked Fleischer if the Bush Administration was encouraging assassination. Fleischer shrewdly stopped short of using the term assassination in reference to Saddam Hussein, perhaps remembering that such a call to the Iraqi people would violate the customary law on assassination.

In January 2020, President Trump authorized the targeted killing of Iranian general Qasem Soleimani, a known terror leader behind numerous murders throughout the Middle East to include actions against American soldiers in Iraq. His death was justified by the United States under the doctrine of self-defense.

Without question, the traditional concept of assassination absolutely prohibits one nation from encouraging others, in this case the Iraqi people, to murder the leader of an unfriendly government. Nevertheless, as the United States geared up for possible war with Iraq, national news media sources continued to speculate about the assassination of the Iraqi dictator. Numerous newspapers cited "senior intelligence reports" that Saddam Hussein would probably be assassinated by "members of his inner circle in the final days or hours before U.S. forces launch a major ground attack."

Those who call the loudest for abandoning Executive Order 12333 mistakenly feel that it might impede the expeditious prosecution of the War on Terror—either against al-Qa'eda leaders or the senior leaders of those handful of totalitarian regimes that back terrorism. To date, however, neither Congress nor the President have taken steps that would blunt the ban on assassination. The reason for this inactivity rests in a mixed bag of historical, legal, and policy considerations. Still, there are several strong arguments for abandoning the current executive order on assassination, not because it impedes the War on Terror but because it is more confusing than helpful in defining the application of the lawful use of military force against legitimate targets—whether in peacetime or war—to include the senior leadership of hostile governments or terrorist groups.

Before a thing can be properly discussed it must be properly defined. Nowhere is this more applicable than in addressing the issue of assassination *vis-à-vis* Executive Order 12333. Assassination is defined in leading dictionaries as follows:

- *Webster's Dictionary*: "The act of killing or murdering by surprise or secret assault."
- *American Heritage College Dictionary*: "1. To murder (a prominent person) by surprise attack, as for political reasons. 2. To destroy or injure treacherously."
- *Black's Law Dictionary*: "The act of deliberately killing someone, especially a public figure, usually for hire or political reasons."
- *Random House Dictionary*: "1. To kill suddenly or secretively. Murder premeditatedly and treacherously. 2. To destroy or denigrate treacherously and viciously."

A comparison of most definitions reveals that the common meaning associated with the term assassination is that it is "murder by surprise" usually carried out for "political purposes." In a law review article on the topic, Tyler Harder believes that the best way to capture the meaning of assassination is to view it as a combination of three essential elements: "(1) a murder, (2) of a specifically targeted figure, (3) for a political purpose." Thus, an assassination must contain all three elements or the killing will not meet the requirements of an assassination. Harder's approach is a good starting point because it focuses on the elements of murder—always an illegal concept—and politics—a concept generally reserved for activities not in the sphere of warfare.

Since assassination is universally regarded as murder, it is important to distinguish the concept of murdering another human being, which is always illegal *per se*, from the concept of killing another human being, which may or may not be illegal. Unfortunately, the distinction between murder and killing is often blurred in modern society contributing to a lack of clarity on the subject of assassination. Many postmodernists erroneously believe, for example, that it is somehow immoral for the State to take the life of another human being under any circumstances. For them, the concept of *nullen crimen sine poena* (no crime without punishment) does not extend to taking the life of another human. Hence, in their minds, all killing is both immoral and illegal.

Interestingly, definitional problems regarding the lawfulness of killing another human being can be traced back to the Biblical prohibition on this matter found in the Decalogue at Exodus 20:13 and Deuteronomy 5:17, which many widely regarded English translations, such as the King James version of the Bible, incorrectly render as: "Thou shalt not kill." In fact, the correct translation of the Hebrew into the English is: "Thou shalt not *murder* [emphasis added]." The Hebrew word for kill is not used in the prohibitions of Exodus 20:13 and Deuteronomy 5:17. The Hebrew word that is used is *lo tirtzach* and, according to Biblical scholar R.B. Thieme, Jr., "refers only to the criminal act of homicide, not [for instance] taking the life of enemy soldiers in legitimate warfare." In fact, the Mosaic law is filled with detailed laws that specifically mandate that the State should lawfully kill certain humans convicted under the rule of law for such crimes as murder, kidnapping, etc. The Old Testament principle is properly seen as centering on the duty of the State to protect its citizens from domestic criminal behavior.

In turn, the Mosaic law also sets out a detailed law of war codex which provides for the protection of citizens on exterior lines by specifically authorizing the killing of enemy combatants. From the Judeo tradition, killing enemy combatants in battle is not murder.

Assassination, then, is clearly identified and properly classified as a type of killing that is unlawful, i.e., a form of murder, and murder is always defined as the unlawful killing of a human being with malice aforethought. Although Executive Order 12333 does not define assassination, this silence certainly provides no legitimacy to advocating a "new" definition of assassination which would somehow characterize the concept as anything other than what it is—murder. Furthermore, since murder is an intrinsically illegal act, the definitional problem automatically defeats any reasoned advancement of the proposition that murder, e.g., assassination, can somehow be made lawful.

In other words, if murder is a violation of both domestic United States law and international law, Executive Order 12333 really does not make illegal something that was not already illegal. Therefore, doing away with Executive Order 12333 would not allow the United States to engage in assassination, either in peace or war. Indeed, revoking Executive Order 12333 would only send a negative signal, suggesting to the world that the United States did away with the ban so that it could commit an illegal act of murder.

The word "assassination" is derived from the Arabic word *hashishiyyin*, which refers to the practice of an eleventh century Muslim "brotherhood" that was specifically devoted to killing their religious and political enemies in any manner available. To be sure, the concept of assassination is far more ancient and can apply with equal validity to various infamous incidents in history to include the murder by surprise for political purposes of Gaius Julius Caesar by Brutus and his fellow plotters in 44 B.C., as well as to Hebrew Zealots who conducted random acts of assassination against the occupying Romans and those who supported the Romans in Judea prior to the fall of Jerusalem by the legions of Rome under Titus in A.D. Because American history has witnessed the assassination of several presidents by assassins, to include President Abraham Lincoln, most Americans view assassination as something that is carried out against political figures.

There are even historical instances where the concept of assassination was incorporated as an integral part of certain religious beliefs. For example, when the British entered India in the nineteenth century, they encountered a Hindu cult devoted to the goddess Kali that required its members to commit murder by surprise upon random victims as a form of worship. In contrast to other assassinations, these murders by surprise were not for political purposes, but for religious purposes.

Early Western scholars discussed the matter of assassination both in the context of war and peace. They all viewed assassination as an act directed against the leader of a country. Interestingly, some of the earliest commentators, such as theologian and philosopher Thomas Aquinas, felt that killing an evil sovereign for the common good might be legally justified. However, Aquinas' view held little sway with subsequent scholars, particularly following the 1648 Peace of Westphalia and the rise of the nation-state.

In fact, extremely sensitive to the concept of reciprocity as the key element in international intercourse between nation-states, most seventeenth century scholars rejected the idea of assassinating a leader in peacetime under any circumstances and equally frowned on the use of assassination as a legitimate use of armed force during war. Regardless of the method of attack employed during warfare, the attack should never involve treachery, a term commonly associated with assassination but seldom defined. Influenced by Europe's Code of Chivalry, many international jurists in the area felt that assassination should not be employed in order that the "honor of arms be [sic] preserved and public order and safety of sovereigns and generals not be unduly threatened."

Hugo Grotius, the so-called father of international law and author of the first real codification of rules relating to the conduct of warfare, spent a great deal of time exploring the matter of assassination in the context of war. Grotius used treachery or treacherous murder as an analytical starting point in his commentaries. Understanding the issue of reciprocity, he discussed assassination as something that violates an express or tacit obligation between countries. For Grotius, a violation of natural law or the law of nations certainly occurred if a leader was killed by those that had an obligation to him; such an act of assassination would be treacherous. Conversely, if an enemy leader is ambushed or tricked into a trap by opposing soldiers and killed, then natural law was not violated. Grotius wrote, "It is in fact permissible to kill an enemy in any place whatsoever. According to the law of nations, not only those who do such deeds, but also others who instigate others who do them, are considered free from blame." In any event, Grotius strongly disapproved of putting a monetary price on the head of an enemy leader, reasoning that this would encourage the leader's subjects to kill him treacherously, i.e., by assassination.

The early American position on the matter held assassination as an illegal tool in both peacetime and wartime. The first significant mention of assassination occurred during the American Civil War with the adoption by Union forces of a codification of the law of war known as the Lieber Code. On April 24, 1863, the Lieber Code was promulgated as Army General Orders Number 100 by the Secretary of War, E.D. Townsend. In a merger of peacetime and wartime scenarios, Section IX, paragraph 148 states:

> The law of war does not allow proclaiming either an individual belonging to the hostile army, or a citizen, or a subject of the hostile government an outlaw, who may be slain without trial by any captor, any more than the modern law of peace allows such international outlawry; on the contrary, it abhors such an outrage. The sternest retaliation should follow the murder committed in consequence of such proclamation, made by whatever authority. Civilized nations look with horror upon offers of rewards for the *assassination of enemies* as relapses into barbarism [emphasis added].

Since the somewhat confusing definition of the Lieber Code, subsequent American legal views on assassination have improved only slightly. Surprisingly, the next significant mention of the concept of assassination is not found until 1956, in FM 27-10, The Law of Land Warfare. Paragraph 31 of FM 27-10, entitled Assassination and Outlawry, quotes Article 23, paragraph b of the Annex to the Hague Convention Number IV, dated 18 October 1907: "It is especially forbidden to kill or wound treacherously individuals belonging to the hostile nation or army." The current version of the Army's manuel is FM 6-27 (replacing FM 27-10 in 2019) then goes on to describe this sentence in the context of American military law:

> This article is construed as prohibiting assassination, proscription, or outlawry of an enemy, or putting a price upon an enemy's head, as well as offering a reward for an enemy "dead or alive." It does not, however, preclude attacks on individual soldiers or officers of the enemy whether in the zone of hostilities, occupied territory, or elsewhere.

To date, one of the very best efforts to handle the legal aspects of assassination *vis-à-vis* Executive Order 12333 is contained in a 1989 legal memorandum written by H. Hays Parks, the Chief of the International Law Branch, International Affairs Division, Office of the Judge Advocate General. In his memorandum entitled, "Executive Order 12333 and Assassination," Parks does an excellent job explaining the term assassination "in the context of military operations across the conflict spectrum." In essence, Parks correctly concludes that the targeting and killing of hostile or enemy leaders in an act of self-defense is not an act of assassination, even if by surprise.

It is well settled in modern international law that no nation may engage in aggression against any other nation. The definition of aggression is spelled out in the 1957 General Assembly's United Nations Definition of Aggression and certainly includes the act of assassination. According to Article 2(4) of the

Charter of the United Nations (U.N. Charter), all member states: "[s]hall refrain in their international relations from the threat or use of force against the territorial integrity or the political independence of any state, or in any manner inconsistent with the Purposes of the United Nations." With this premise so stated, it is equally well recognized that the legitimate use of force is rooted in the inherent right of every nation to act in self-defense if it is the object of aggression.

It is also important to realize that aggressive acts are often carried out by one nation against another without the intent to provoke full scale hostilities or war. Likewise, the nation that is attacked with aggressive force will respond in self-defense with proportional military action with no intention of going to war.

Article 51 of the U.N. Charter codifies the right of a nation attacked with aggressive violence to engage in self-defense. The doctrine of self-defense, of course, is a customary right of ancient origin not created by the United Nations Charter. In pertinent part, Article 51 reads: "Nothing in the present Charter shall impair the inherent right of individual or collective self-defense if an armed attack occurs against a Member of the United Nations." Thus, the State that engages in acts of aggression, or the unlawful use of force, may never claim that it is acting under the self-defense provisions of Article 51 of the U.N. Charter. Furthermore, apart from the fundamental requirement of proportionality in the employment of violence in self-defense, the use of self-defense can occur in times of peace as well as war. In other words, even if a state of armed conflict does not exist, the customary principle of self-defense is a separate basis for the use of force. As long as the use of force in self-defense adheres to the customary standards of necessity and proportionally it is lawful.

On numerous occasions, the United States has lawfully exercised the inherent right of self-defense against individuals or States in both peacetime and wartime environments. President Bill Clinton, for example, sent cruise missiles against several al-Qa'eda terrorist training camps in Afghanistan following the 1998 al-Qa'eda attack on the United States embassies in Africa. This military action occurred during peacetime and was permitted under the rule of law regarding self-defense. Even if the leader Osama bin Laden was targeted in the attacks, President Clinton's actions would not be classified as attempted assassination.

Similarly, in the 1991 Gulf War (and the 2003 campaign), Saddam Hussein himself was a legitimate military target and his death by coalition forces would not have been an assassination. As the commander in chief of the Iraqi military, Saddam Hussein could have been legally targeted and killed. In war, enemy combatants are legitimate targets for attack so long as the hostile forces are not killed with treachery, e.g., while legitimately visiting a protected place such as a hospital. The fact that Hussein was not specifically targeted was clearly a political decision, although President George H. Bush is said to have remarked: "We're not in the position of targeting Saddam Hussein, but no one will weep for him when he is gone." Despite the lawfulness of killing the enemy leader in wartime, there often exists an unwillingness to specifically target that individual.

Parks correctly recognizes that a State may use military force in peacetime if it is acting in self-defense. Such acts are not assassination:

> Historically, the United States has resorted to the use of military force in peacetime where another nation has failed to discharge its international responsibilities in protecting U.S. citizens from acts of violence originating in or launched from its sovereign territory, or has been culpable in aiding and abetting international criminal activities.

After listing several historical examples of the United States' use of military force in self-defense, including the 1986 bombing of "terrorist related targets in Libya," Parks concludes: "Hence there is historical precedent for the use of military force to capture or kill individuals whose peacetime actions constitute a direct threat to U.S. citizens or U.S. national security."

Indeed, immediately following the terrorist attacks of September 11, 2001, the Congress of the United States clearly recognized the inherent right of self-defense. Again, while Congress never "declared war" under the provisions of Article I of the Constitution, they quickly passed a joint resolution which left no doubt as to their desire to authorize the President of the United States to use military force in self-defense. Among other things, the Congressional Resolution recognized the inherent right of self-defense,

> [U]nder the Constitution to take action to deter and prevent acts of international terrorism against the United States…[and] authorized [the President] to use all necessary and appropriate force against those nations, organizations, or persons he determines planned, authorized, committed, or aided the terrorist attacks that occurred on September 11, 2001, or harbored such organizations or persons, in order to prevent any future acts of international terrorism against the United States by such nations, organizations or persons.

Congress clearly understood that targeting individual terrorists associated with the attacks on the United States was not assassination, but the appropriate response in self-defense to unlawful aggression. President Obama has most certainly fully embraced this concept.

From a legal perspective, the most challenging issue associated with the continuing War on Terror is the fact that both the nature of the enemy and the nature of the threat has changed dramatically, and so the response under the rule of law has to change. In his State of the Union message of January 29, 2002, President George W. Bush signaled his resolve that the United States of America would "not permit the world's most dangerous regimes to threaten us with the world's most destructive weapons."

In the context of killing individuals, can the United States go beyond the rhetoric and target for death a known terrorist or individual leader of a nation that sponsors or supports terrorism? If the use of a weapon of mass destruction by a fanatical terrorist is on the near horizon, do the traditional international rules related to the use of force, i.e., only used in self-defense, actually work in the real world of the al-Qa'eda virtual State? In other words, must the United States idly wait for a catastrophic terrorist attack before it can respond, or does a threatened nation have the right to engage in preemptive self-defense against those individuals that are planning the attack?

As previously covered, the most striking instance in modern history occurred in the 1967 Six Day War when Israel, anticipating a full-scale armed attack from Egypt, Syria, Jordan, and others, attacked Arab airfields first. The doctrine of preemptive self-defense holds that when a State is faced with an imminent armed attack it may resort to proportional acts of preemptive self-defense. Other scholars view the concept of anticipatory self-defense as inconclusive. For example, one textbook on national security law writes: "Past practice is inconclusive, but it suggests that a state facing an imminent and potentially devastating armed attack may escape condemnation for a preemptive response."

Parks lists three forms of self-defense that the United States recognizes as appropriate for unilateral action under the inherent right of self-defense: "(a) Against an actual use of force, or hostile act. (b) Preemptive self defense against an imminent use of force. (c) Self defense against a continuing threat." Parks agrees that the preemptive use of military force against terrorists would be permissible and would not be assassination. Parks specifically asserts:

This right of self defense would be appropriate to the attack of terrorist leaders where their actions pose a continuing threat to U.S. citizens or the national security of the United States. As with an attack on a guerrilla infrastructure, the level to which attacks could be carried out against individuals within a terrorist infrastructure would be a policy rather than a legal decision.

Nevertheless, the fact that a nation is acting under the rubric of self-defense does not allow that nation to employ military force in any manner it so desires. The State acting in self-defense is still required to adhere to a set of binding international rules associated with how that force is employed. In time of war, these rules are known as the law of war or the law of armed conflict. However, in the modern era, where the line between war and peacetime is inexorably blurred, many of the most basic rules regarding military necessity, unnecessary suffering and proportionality apply equally to the peacetime use of military force.

The law of armed conflict describes lawful targets which can be destroyed in the proper context of military operations. The general principle is that the nation acting in self-defense—whether in a peacetime or wartime environment—may kill the enemy, whether lawful combatants or unprivileged belligerents, and may include in either category civilians who take part in the hostilities. An enemy combatant, whether part of an organized military or a civilian who undertakes military activities, is a legitimate target at all times and may be lawfully killed, even if by surprise. This includes the leader of the hostile forces.

Thus, unannounced attacks involving the element of surprise do not preclude the use of violence. All "combatants are subject to attack if they are participating in hostilities through fire, maneuver and assault; providing logistic, communications, administrative, or other support." In addition, there is "no distinction made between an attack accomplished by aircraft, missile, naval gunfire, artillery, mortar, infantry assault, ambush, land mine or booby-trap, a single shot by a sniper, a commando attack, or other, similar means." It is not an act of assassination to kill individuals in this context.

In turn, the law of armed conflict absolutely prohibits the killing of noncombatants, except as a matter of collateral damage where civilians may be killed ancillary to the lawful attack of a military objective. Civilians that maintain close proximity to a military objective assume the risk of being killed by enemy fire. Since they are neither specifically targeted individuals nor are they killed by the use of treachery, the killing of such civilians is not assassination. On the other hand, specifically targeting innocent civilians as a military objective is always illegal and criminal.

During President Obama's eight years in office, CIA drone attacks (unmanned aircraft) on suspected enemy combatants in Afghanistan, Pakistan, Yemen, and other locations killed well over 1,000 people. The vast majority of them were low-level fighters linked to the Taliban, al-Qa'eda, or ISIS. The collateral deaths of civilians in these "death from above" attacks is unknown, although the Obama Administration in 2013 finally admitted to killing four Americans.

In this context, of particular note is President Obama's 2011 authorization to kill American-born Anwar al-Awlaki, a notorious al-Qa'eda cleric. While the general legal basis for targeted killing is rather elementary, the application in the War on Terror is often clouded due to the utter failure of the government to set out the authority with a sense of clarity. For instance, the confusion associated with whether the 2011 drone killing in Yemen of al-Qaeda cleric and leader, American-born Anwar al-Awlaki, was "legal" or not, reflects very poorly on the Obama Administration. Due to the inability of the commander-in-chief to lucidly articulate a legal justification divorced from political overtones, even people in the United States found it quite easy to accuse the country of wrongdoing. The *New*

York Times editorial page of October 4, 2011, carried six letters to the editor on the topic of al-Awlaki's death. Of those six letters, only one of them understood that the killing was an entirely lawful act carried out under the law of war. All the others reflected varying degrees of confusion that included sentiments that the United States was: (1) wrong for not operating under domestic criminal law to arrest al-Awlaki; (2) wrong for killing a U.S. citizen; or (3) that the rule of law didn't really matter because al-Awlaki was a "bad guy" and "we have to do what we have to do (the law of the jungle)."

Amazingly, not a single voice in the Obama Administration took the time to defend the action as lawful under a simple set of legal parameters related to the law of war. Instead, the White House issued statements associated with the fact that we were "defending" ourselves against a terrorist, even though the foundational rule of law justification has nothing to do with the fact that al-Awlaki was a "terrorist" or a bad person. The justification for America's lawful use of force against al-Awlaki was as follows: (1) the United States is at war with al-Qaeda; (2) the law of war rule of law applies to this war, not the domestic criminal law rule of law; (3) the law of war allows the United States to kill on sight any unlawful enemy combatant, detain indefinitely any unlawful enemy combatant, or use military commissions when appropriate (unless the nation imposes self-restrictions).

In fact, it took a full seven months after the killing of al-Awlaki before Attorney General Holder finally offered his "thoughts" on targeted killing at his March 5, 2012 address at Northwestern School of Law. Holder indicated that the United States would kill by drone or otherwise when: (1) the subject is located abroad; (2) the subject is a senior operational figure; (3) the subject is a member of al-Qaeda, Taliban, or associated forces; (4) the subject is involved in planning operations focused on killing Americans; (5) the threat is imminent and an opportunity to kill is open; (6) there is no feasible option for capture; and (7) the use of violence will comply with the law of war.

In the case of Anwar al-Awlaki, if he was a member of al-Qaeda (and he was), then he qualified for treatment under the full parameters of the law of war. Thus, it is not a violation of the law of war for the United States to kill an American citizen al-Qaeda member without warning. In addition, if that American citizen is an unlawful enemy combatant, then the United States can use the law of war as the proper rule of law to deal with him. While it is true that the 2006 (as well as the updated 2009) Military Commissions Act did exclude American citizen al-Qaeda members from trial by military commissions, this is a self-imposed rule, not a rule mandated by the law of war.

In summary, assassination is an unlawful killing in violation of the rule of law. Whether conducted in peacetime or wartime, assassination is absolutely forbidden under international law even in the absence of an executive order supposedly banning the practice. Anyone who carries out an act of assassination would be guilty of either murder or a war crime, depending on the circumstances. Furthermore, anyone who ordered the assassination would be guilty of either murder or a war crime under the concept of command responsibility.

At the end of the day, the use of force in legitimate acts of self-defense does not qualify as assassination. Those who think that the United States is somehow restricted by Executive Order 12333 from targeting terrorists or rogue nations that threaten to conduct terrorist acts are mistaken. If it is the case that Executive Order 12333 causes more confusion than not in understanding the applicable rule of law, should it be repealed? One commentator has argued that the "failure of the executive order to outline exactly what it prohibits has set planners and operators adrift." But a stronger case can be made by pointing out that it is the public, politicians, and commentators that are most confused by the executive order, not the military planners and operators. The military generally understands that the proper application of force in self-defense does not violate Executive Order 12333. Politicians and commentators seem most susceptible to succumbing to the temptation to associate an overbroad interpretation to the ban on assassination.

As a practical matter, it is fundamentally obvious that no American president will ever repeal Executive Order 12333 unless he immediately replaces it with a better product. The resulting negative repercussions in the sphere of public relations alone would render such a move remarkably insensate. America's enemies as well as Its friends and allies need to understand that the United States of America operates under the rule of law. As Professor John Norton Moore of Virginia so aptly put it:

> Law, however, is vitally important. Even in the short run, law serves as a standard of appraisal for national actions and as a means of communicating intentions to both friend and foe, and perceptions about lawfulness can profoundly influence both national and international support for particular actions.

6.12 The Constitution and the War on Terror

To some, the War on Terror produced a society in which the rights of the individual were pressed by ever increasing security measures designed to vindicate the expanding desire of protecting the safety of the public from global terrorism. On the other hand, edhe all too real specter of mass casualties, billions of dollars in physical damage, and civil disorder absolutely demands that the federal government fulfill its primary mission of ensuring the safety and viability of its citizens. As Supreme Court Justice Robert Jackson remarked in *Terminiello v. Chicago*, "[t]he constitutional Bill of Rights...[is not] a suicide pact." Jackson went on to say: "The choice is not between order and liberty. It is between liberty with order and anarchy without either."

In summary, the government has always taken steps to curtail civil liberties in times of crisis. In the past, some of the measures have been clearly unconstitutional, e.g., President Lincoln's suspension of the writ of habeas corpus for jailed "Northern" American citizens, or President Roosevelt's internment of thousands of U.S. citizens of Japanese descent. Compared with these abuses, the government's efforts in the War on Terror are hardly extreme. In fact, the American people have overwhelmingly approved of the overall performance of the government in finding a working balance between defending their freedoms and protecting their freedoms. Nevertheless, as the federal government makes policy and moves the nation in the War on Terror, it is prudent to well recall the caution of George Washington: "[T]he price of freedom is eternal vigilance." Accordingly, all measures employed to combat terrorism must be within the bounds of democratic principles and the rule of law. More importantly, so-called extraordinary laws should be proportionate to the terrorist threat and frequently reviewed, revised, and rescinded if no longer needed. For instance, the London bombings of July 2005 caused the British to develop new security laws that seriously challenge the foundation of freedom of speech by making it illegal to glorify or indirectly incite terrorism. Obviously, the line between free speech and security is greatly stressed in the War on Terror because this is not a war in the classic sense. This war will not end with a formal surrender. Thus, changes in law that appear necessary in the name of security for the moment may become an unwanted fabric of our society for future generations. If one is to avoid the slippery slope, then marked and clear legal notches must be set out beyond which we as Americans will not pass.

6.13 Questions for Discussion

1. *Legitimate targets*. A major debate exists surrounding the relationship terrorist agents must have to a terrorist organization in order to be considered legitimate military targets in the War on Terror. Considering the different classifications for terrorism, who is a legitimate target in the War on Terror: individuals or countries? Should individual terrorists be targeted militarily or judicially? Why might the favored response for a nation to a terrorist attack be to use military force as opposed to other methods? If the events of September 11, 2001, had not occurred, would your answer be the same?

2. *Financing terrorism*. The United States Code provides: "Whoever knowingly provides material support or resources to a foreign terrorist organization, or attempts or conspires to do so, shall be fined under this title or imprisoned not more than 15 years, or both, and, if the death of any person results, shall be imprisoned for any term of years or for life." 18 U.S.C.A. § 2339B(a) (1). In *United States v. Hammoud*, 381 F.3d at 316. (4th Cir. 2004) defendant, Mohammed Hammoud challenged his conviction in district court after he was found to have given aid to the foreign terrorist organization, Hizballah. Can this law aimed at criminalizing financial contributions to terrorist organizations do more to deter terrorism than laws which punish terrorist acts?

3. *Why did the United States refuse to sign Protocol I to the Geneva Conventions*? The United States is not a signatory to Protocol Additional to the Geneva Conventions of August 12, 1946, and Relating to the Protection of Victims of International Armed Conflicts, June 8, 1977, 1125 U.N.T.S. 3. Protocol I seeks to extend coverage to non-international conflicts in which "peoples are fighting against colonial domination and alien occupation and against racist regimes in the exercise of their right to self-determination." See generally Abraham Sofaer, *The U.S. Decision Not to Ratify Protocol I to the Geneva Conventions on the Protection of War Victims*, 82 AM. J. INT'L. L. 784 (1988).

4. *Lawful detention*? In September 1868, the U.S. District Court for the Southern District of Florida denied a writ of habeas corpus for Dr. Samuel Mudd, a civilian citizen of Maryland, who had been convicted by a military tribunal for his part in the Lincoln assassination of April 14, 1865. *Ex Parte Mudd*, 17 F. Cas. 954 (S.D. Fla. 1868) (No. 9,899). On June 30, 1865, the military tribunal convicted Dr. Mudd and sentenced him to life in prison. Dr. Mudd was transferred to a prison in Florida where he filed a writ of habeas corpus relying on *Ex Parte Milligan*. In denying the petition, Judge Thomas J. Boynton distinguished the murder of Lincoln as a military crime, even though the war had arguably ended prior to the assassination of Lincoln. The appeal of this decision reached the United States Supreme Court in February 1869, but was dismissed by Chief Justice Chase as moot due to the fact that President Andrew Johnson had pardoned Dr. Mudd and two other civilians. Was Mudd's detention lawful?

5. *Defining enemy combatants.* DOD Directive 2310.01E, entitled *The Department of Defense Detainee Program,* dated September 5, 2006, describes an enemy combatant as "a person engaged in hostilities against the United States or its coalition partners during *armed conflict* [emphasis added]." Is the DOD term "armed conflict" consistent with the 2009 Military Commissions Act definition of unprivileged enemy belligerents?

6. *Military commission or federal court?* Ahmed Ghailani, was labeled by President Bush as an enemy combatant and detained at Guantanamo Bay. He was involved in the 1998 East African embassy bombings. In 2009 President Obama ordered Ghailani released and had him transferred for criminal trial in a federal court in New York. Should Ghailani have been transferred out of military custody and not tried by military commission? Is it appropriate or legal for the Obama Administration to process some al-Qa'eda members through federal district courts while others are processed through military commissions per the 2009 Military Commissions Act? Should U.S. citizenship really make a difference?

7. *Free speech vs. material support.* In October 2006, Adam Yahiuye Gadahn, an American citizen from California was indicted by a federal grand jury and charged with treason and providing material support to al-Qa'eda per 18 USC § 2339B. Gadahn has appeared in numerous al-Qa'eda videos where he praises the terror group and calls on others to participate in murder and violence against the United States. The form of support is identified as "personnel" and "services." Presumably the theory is that Gadahn provided himself as personnel to al-Qa'eda. Can 2339B lawfully function as the equivalent of a membership prohibition? Due to the expansive reach of the Material Support Act, Professor Norman Abrams urges legal observers to "ask whether and to what extent the residual and preventative uses of these sections are beginning to trespass upon fundamental values of liberty." (Norman Abrams, *The Material Support Terrorism Offenses: Perspectives Derived from the (Early) Model Penal Code*, 1 J. NAT'L SEC. L. POL. 5, 6-7 (2005). Do you agree?

8. *Privacy concerns.* Bomb-sniffing dogs that are trained to smell bomb components that screening devices might miss are being employed at some airports. Is this approach more or less objectionable than the use of TSA airport screeners trained to spot "suspicious behavior" among passengers? What privacy issues are raised?

9. *Advancing the proper rule of law.* In February 2006, the U.N. Commission on Human Rights issued a joint report on the situation of the detainees at Guantanamo Bay. Based on interviews of "former Guantanamo Bay detainee's currently residing or detained in France, Spain and the United Kingdom," lawyers for detainees and "information available in the public domain" (the Rapporteurs refused to visit the detention facility at Guantanamo Bay for a first hand inspection) they concluded that the United States was engaging in "torture" in violation of international law. The Rapporteurs also found that the detention itself was illegal and that the "United States Government should either expeditiously bring all Guantanamo Bay detainees to trial [via domestic criminal or an international tribunal] or release them without further delay." What premise did the Rapporteurs reject in making the second finding? Why is the first finding flawed?

Selected Bibliography

Aquinas, St. Thomas. ON POLITICS AND ETHICS, (Paul E. Sigmund trans. 1988).

Bank, Aaron. OSS TO GREEN BERETS, 1986.

Chesney, Robert M., *Federal Prosecution of Terrorism-Related Offenses: Conviction and Sentencing Data in Light of the "Soft-Sentence" and "Data-Reliability Critiques*, 11 LEWIS & CLARK L. REV. 862 (Winter 2007).

De Vattel, E. THE LAW OF NATIONS OR THE PRINCIPLES OF INTERNATIONAL LAW APPLIED TO THE CONDUCT AND TO THE AFFAIRS OF NATIONS AND OF SOVEREIGNS, (Charles G. Fenwick trans. 1916).

Dep't of Army, Field Manual 27-10. *The Law of Land Warfare* (July 1956).

Dunoff, Jeffrey L., Steven R. Ratner, and David Wippman. INTERNATIONAL LAW NORMS, Actors Process, 2002.

Elliott, H.W. THE TRIAL AND PUNISHMENT OF WAR CRIMINALS IN THE "NEW WORLD ORDER." (unpublished doctoral of juridical science thesis 1996) (available at the Rare Book Room, U. of Virginia School of Law).

Ford, Franklin L. POLITICAL MURDER: FROM TYRANNICIDE TO TERRORISM, 1985.

Franck, Thomas M., and Michael J. Glennon. FOREIGN RELATIONS AND NATIONAL SECURITY LAW, 1993.

Geneva Convention of August 12, 1949, Relative to the Treatment of Prisoners of War, 6 U.S.T. 3316, T.I.A.S. No. 3364, 75 U.N.T.S. 135.

Gentili, Alberico. DE IURE BELLI LIBRI TRES, John C. Rolfe trans., 1933.

Grotius, Hugo. THE LAW OF WAR AND PEACE (1625), *reprinted in* THE LAW OF WAR: A DOCUMENTARY HISTORY. L. Freidman. (ed.) 1972.

Hartigan, Richard Shelly. LIEBER'S CODE AND THE LAW OF WAR, 1983.

Heddings, Raymond E. U.S. ROLES IN PROVIDING HUMANITARIAN ASSISTANCE FOLLOWING NBC ACCIDENTS/INCIDENTS: THE LEGAL CONSIDERATIONS, 1999.

Kerwin, Cornelius M. RULEMAKING: HOW GOVERNMENT AGENCIES WRITE LAW AND MAKE POLICY, 1999.

McHugh, William. *Forcible Self-help in International Law*, 25 NAVAL WAR C. REV. 61 (1972).

Moore, John Norton. LAW AND THE GRENADA MISSION, 1984.

Parks, W. Hays. *Memorandum of Law: Executive Order 12333 and Assassination*. THE ARMY LAWYER, Dec.1989, at 4.

Pumphrey, Carolyn W. (ed.) TRANSNATIONAL THREATS: BLENDING LAW ENFORCEMENT AND MILITARY STRATEGIES, available at http://carlisle-www.army.mil/usassi/welcome.htm. 2000.

Rosen, Richard D., *America's Professional Military Ethic and the Treatment of Captured Enemy Combatants in the Global War on Terror*, 5 GEORGETOWN J. OF LAW & PUB. Pol. 113 (Winter 2007).

Scales, Robert H., Jr. FUTURE WARFARE, 1999.

Schindler, Dietrich, and Jiai Toman. THE LAWS OF ARMED CONFLICT 3, 1988.

Schmitt, Michael N. *State Sponsored Assassination in International and Domestic Law*. 17 YALE J. INT'L L. 679 (1992).

Sloan, Steven. BEATING INTERNATIONAL TERRORISM, 1986.

Thieme, R.B., Jr., FREEDOM THROUGH MILITARY VICTORY, 1977.

Chapter 7

Interrogation Techniques

If interrogators step over the line from coercion to outright torture, they should be held personally responsible. But no interrogator is ever going to be prosecuted for keeping Khalid Sheikh Mohammed awake, cold, alone and uncomfortable. Nor should he be.

—Mark Bowden

With the start of the 2001 "War on Terror," the interrogation of detainees engaged in conducting or plotting terrorism has long been a source of much consternation—both from a legal and policy standpoint. While all can agree that the goal of these interrogations is to glean meaningful intelligence to prevent future terror attacks against the U.S. or its allies, far too often, meaningful debate about lawfulness and efficacy is mired in ideological or political dogma, making it difficult, if not impossible, to establish a clear understanding of the issues at hand. Illustrations of this point over the past 20 years are numerous. For instance, in May 2009, the United States Senate Committee on the Judiciary, Subcommittee on Administrative Oversight and the Courts conducted a public hearing regarding the Bush-era Department of Justice-approved interrogation techniques for certain "unlawful enemy combatants" that was titled: "*What Went Wrong: Torture and the Office of the Legal Counsel in the Bush Administration*." Clearly, the Democratic party-chaired hearing was not a fact-finding exercise; the minds of the majority were already made up.

In discussing the issue of American interrogation practices, most are reminded of the Abu Ghraib prison abuse incident or the spurious "water boarding is torture" allegation. In the former case, was the prison abuse a reflection of a systemic policy—either *de jure* or *de facto*—on the part of the United States to illegally extract information from detainees, or was the abuse simply isolated acts of criminal behavior on the part of a handful of soldiers amplified by a grossly incompetent tactical chain of command at the prison facility? In the later case, did the Department of Justice approve CIA interrogation techniques, to include water boarding, which constituted torture?

Along with Abu Ghraib and water boarding, the central concern associated with interrogation methodologies centers on the time period from 2002-2005, the years before the enactment of a series of laws and the Supreme Court *Hamdan* ruling causing serious limitations on the use of various forms and levels of physical and physiological force to extract information from certain detainees. In turn, juxtaposed to all this is the matter of rendition, where it is alleged that the United States purposefully sent detainees to other nations knowing that they were going to be subjected to interrogations that employed torture or other illegal techniques.

Without question, numerous elements of the government have direct roles to play in gathering timely intelligence about terrorist networks. The primary responsibilities are shared by the CIA, the FBI, and the DOD. The CIA has the lead for terrorist matters outside the United States and the FBI has lead for terrorist matters in the United States. The DOD relies chiefly on the Defense Intelligence Agency (DIA), a DOD support agency with over 7,000 military and civilian employees stationed throughout the world.

Starting in 2005 three important developments have shaped U.S. policy and law in terms of interrogation techniques. In the context of enemy combatants under the control of the U.S. government, the Detainee Treatment Act of 2005 adopted international human rights terminology in setting out interrogation limits. In short, American interrogators could not engage in "cruel, inhuman and degrading treatment or punishment of persons under detention, custody, or control of the United States Government." Pursuant to the so-called McCain Amendment, "cruel, unusual, and inhuman treatment or punishment" covers all those acts prohibited by the Fifth, Eighth, and Fourteenth Amendments to the Constitution, language stated in the U.S. reservations to the Torture Convention. The second development was the *Hamdan* case and the resulting 2006 Military Commissions Act which applied the provisions of Common Article 3 of the Geneva Conventions to all detainees. Finally, Executive Order 13441 issued by President Obama in January 2009, now requires all U.S. agencies (to include the CIA) to comply with the new Bush-era Army Field Manual on interrogations (FM 2-22.3) which specifically outlaws: (1) forcing the detainee to be naked, perform sexual acts, or pose in a sexual manner; (2) placing hoods or sacks over the head of the detainee, or using duct tape over the eyes; (3) applying beatings, electric shock, burns, or other forms of physical pain; (4) water boarding; (5) using military working dogs; (6) inducing hypothermia or heat injury; (7) conducting mock executions; and (8) depriving the detainee of necessary food, water, or medical care. Still, President Obama's order does allow federal agencies to employ non-coercive techniques and established a High-Value Detainee Interrogation Group (HIG), composed of experienced interrogators and support personnel from law enforcement, the DOD, and the intelligence community. The HIG still functions under President Trump.

Allegations of torture roll off the tongue with ease. In the context of American interrogation practices and treatment of detainees, charges of torture are regularly raised by a variety of individuals and interest groups often associated with fixed political agendas. Recognizing that not every alleged incident of mistreatment necessarily satisfies the legal definition of torture, it is imperative that one views such allegations with a clear understanding of the applicable legal standards set out in law and judicial precedent. In this manner, claims of illegal interrogation practices can be properly measured as falling above or below a particular legal threshold. Only then can one hope to set aside the shrilly voiced rhetoric by such groups as the American Civil Liberties Union (ACLU) or Amnesty International, who once called the Guantanamo detention facility the "gulag of our time," and objectively establish whether or not the United States stands in violation of the rule of law.

In tandem with investigating American interrogation practices, the matter of how authorities should deal with the so-called "ticking time bomb" terrorist merits serious scrutiny in America's war against the unrestrained savagery of fanatical al-Qa'eda suicide bombers bent on using weapons of mass destruction. The concern is so great that a number of prominent voices both in and outside of the government have advocated that a judicial exception should be carved out to allow torture as an interrogation tool in special instances. Perhaps one of the most prominent and unexpected voices to advocate such a position is Professor Alan Dershowitz of Harvard Law School.

While some may claim that Dershowitz is reluctantly reflecting a new and ugly pragmatism associated with fighting terrorism, America cannot allow itself to slip into a Star Chamber mentality where torture is mandated by the State as a necessary evil. Understanding the need to find the appropriate balance between civil liberties and security concerns, the purpose of this chapter is twofold. First, the interrogation practices used by the United States to get information from various categories of detainees will be measured in light of both the domestic and international laws on torture and other forms of mistreatment. Bluntly put, did the United States employ illegal interrogation methods in the War on Terror, particularly between the years 2002-2005, as some have charged? Second, in the special case of the ticking time bomb terrorist, should the United States openly disregard the rule of law and officially sanction the use of torture?

The American position on the question of illegal interrogation practices is that the United States does not engage in torture or other ill-treatment, either in questioning or housing detainees. During the Bush Administration, U.S. National Security Council spokesman, Sean McCormack, exemplified the official stand: "The United States is treating enemy combatants in U.S. government control, wherever held, humanely and in a manner consistent with the principles of the Third Geneva Convention of 1949." Of course, this is not to say that the United States did not then and does not now fully question detainees at a variety of levels. Government officials responsible for gathering information from detainees certainly employ the full range of permissible interrogation tactics measured against the existing law at the time. In other words, some "legal" interrogation practices from 2002-2005 would be clearly "illegal" today.

7.1 Defining Torture

Torture as an instrument of the State to either punish or extract information from certain individuals has a long and dark history which need not be fully recounted here. Suffice it to say that in the West, the practice can be traced to the Romans who codified the use of torture as part of the Roman criminal law (Roman citizens were generally exempt).

In England, the earliest authoritative records regarding State use of torture appears in the Privy Council registers in the year 1540, which extends, with some gaps in the reports, for a hundred years. (Anyone familiar with the reign of Henry VIII knows that the State practice of torture surely predated these official warrants.) The number of official warrants issued by the Crown during this period was less than 100, an amazingly low figure relative to the number of felony investigations which occurred in any given year. This low statistic demonstrates that the predominant use of torture was interrogational in nature and not for punishment. The 1597 case of Jesuit priest John Gerard typifies the goal of torture. The Crown's warrant directed Gerard's torture in the Tower of London by means of "the manacles" and other "such torture" in order to make Gerard "utter directly and truly his uttermost knowledge" concerning certain traitors to the Crown.

In the modern era, by fixed law and customary practice, the prohibition on torture is now universal in nature; a majority of States have ratified the various international agreements associated with banning torture. Nevertheless, even though no State allows torture in its domestic law, the practice continues to flourish. It is estimated that one in four States regularly engages in the torture of various prisoners and detainees. Added to this paradox is the dilemma that some of the acts that should clearly constitute torture do not enjoy a uniformity of definition within the international community. As one legal commentator rightly pointed out, "The prohibition of torture…is not, itself, controversial. The prohibition in application, however, yields endless contention as each perpetrator [State actor] seeks to define its own behavior so as not to violate the ban."

Before exploring the common international legal definition of torture, it is useful to survey the general understanding of the term. Torture comes from the Latin verb "torquere" (to twist) and is defined in leading Anglo-Saxon dictionaries as follows: "Infliction of severe physical pain as a means of punishment or coercion;" "[t]he act of inflicting excruciating pain, as punishment or revenge, as a means of getting a confession or information, or for sheer cruelty;" "[t]he infliction of intense pain to the body or mind to punish, to extract a confession or information, or to obtain sadistic pleasure."

Certainly the red thread in these definitions is a combination of two essential elements: (1) the infliction of severe physical pain to the body or mind used to; (2) punish or obtain information. International law adopts this formula but sharpens it by stipulating that a State actor must carry out the act of torture and that the act must be intentional. Thus, one may describe certain criminals as torturing their victims during the commission of a particularly gruesome murder, but such criminal acts carried out by non-State actors are not violations of the international law on torture. In addition, international law expands the prohibition of torture to include other less abusive acts commonly designated in the world community as "other acts of cruel, inhuman, or degrading treatment or punishment," which is shortened simply to "ill-treatment."

7.2 The Torture Convention

Like the concept of human rights, international law really had little to say about the practice of State torture until the close of World War II. With the establishment of the United Nations in 1945, the prohibition of torture and ill-treatment are now core rights found in all of the most important international documents and treaties.

Article 5 of the 1948 Universal Declaration of Human Rights serves as the foundation for all subsequent efforts outlawing torture. Article 5 of the Declaration consists of only one brief sentence: "No one shall be subjected to torture or to cruel, inhuman, or degrading treatment or punishment." Later, the widely influential and legally binding International Covenant on Civil and Political Rights tracked the Universal Declaration of Human Rights. In pertinent part, Article 7 of the Covenant utilizes the exact same language found in the Universal Declaration on Human Rights: "No person shall be subjected to torture or to cruel, inhuman or degrading treatment or punishment." In binding itself to the International Covenant on Civil and Political Rights, the United States Senate sought to clarify the meaning of Article 7 and attached a reservation which defined "cruel, inhuman or degrading treatment or punishment" as meaning "the cruel and unusual treatment or punishment prohibited by the Fifth, Eighth, and Fourteenth Amendments to the Constitution of the United States."

In 1975, the United Nations adopted the Declaration on the Protection of all Persons from Being Subjected to Torture or Other Cruel, Inhuman or Degrading Treatment or Punishment. Although this document was a declaration only, it served as the basis for the 1984 United Nations Convention Against Torture, and Other Cruel, Inhuman or Degrading Treatment or Punishment (Torture Convention), the primary international agreement governing torture and ill-treatment. As suggested by the title, the point which had served as a source of controversy was more fully addressed in the Torture Convention—the distinction between "torture" and "other acts of cruel, inhuman, or degrading treatment or punishment." While both acts were previously prohibited in other documents, for the first time, the Torture Convention spelled out the obligations and consequences attendant to each type of act. Still, the Torture Convention did not exhibit the same care in defining what it meant by "other cruel, inhuman or degrading treatment or punishment" as it did with regard to torture. Without question, the Torture Convention devoted far more attention to crafting the meaning of the term torture, which it defined as:

> [A]ny act by which severe pain or suffering, whether physical or mental, is intentionally inflicted on a person for such purposes as obtaining from him or a third person information or a confession, punishing him for an act he or a third person has committed or is suspected of having committed, or intimidating or coercing him or a third person, or for any reason based on discrimination of any kind, when such pain or suffering is inflicted by or at the instigation of…a public official or other person acting in an official capacity. It does not include pain or suffering arising only from, inherent in or incidental to lawful sanctions.

According to the Torture Convention, for torture to exist in the context of an interrogation the following criteria must be present: (1) the behavior must be based on an intentional act; (2) it must be performed by a State agent; (3) the behavior must cause severe pain or suffering to body or mind; and (4) it must be accomplished with the intent to gain information or a confession. In adopting the Torture Convention, the United States Senate provided the following reservations which require specific intent and better define the concept of mental suffering:

> [T]he United States understands that, in order to constitute torture, an act must be *specifically intended* to inflict severe physical or mental pain or suffering and that mental pain or suffering refers to *prolonged mental harm* caused by or resulting from: (1) the intentional infliction or threatened infliction of severe physical pain or suffering; (2) the administration or application, or threatened administration or application, of mind altering substances or other procedures calculated to disrupt profoundly the senses or the personality; (3) the threat of imminent death; or (4) the threat that another person will imminently be subjected to death, severe physical pain or suffering, or the administration or application of mind altering substances or other procedures calculated to disrupt profoundly the senses or personality [emphasis added].

Article 2 of the Torture Convention absolutely excludes the notion of exceptional circumstances to serve as an excuse to the prohibition of torture. "No exceptional circumstances whatsoever, whether a state of war or a threat of war, internal political instability or any other public emergency, may be invoked as a justification for torture."

As noted, the phrase "other acts of cruel, inhuman, or degrading treatment or punishment," e.g., ill-treatment, is not defined in the Torture Convention. It is just stated. The Torture Convention certainly obliges each State party to the document to "undertake to prevent…other acts of cruel, inhuman, or degrading treatment or punishment," but Article 16 of the Torture Convention is the only part of the entire treaty that addresses ill-treatment.

Since the Torture Convention desires to "make more effective the struggle against torture and other cruel, inhuman or degrading treatment or punishment throughout the world," the distinction rests in the fact that torture and ill-treatment are viewed as two limbs of the same formula with torture, quite understandably, being predominant. Thus, while all acts of torture must necessarily encompass ill-treatment, acts of ill-treatment do not constitute torture. Clearly, a greater stigma is associated with the insidious evil of torture so that all intuitively realize that international law forbids torture, even if few are cognizant of the fact that ill-treatment is also prohibited. In turn, interrogation practices that do not rise to the level of ill-treatment may be repugnant by degree, but may be perfectly legal under international law. This being the case, it is efficacious to carefully note the differences between torture and ill-treatment as they have significant ramifications regarding State Party obligations.

Article 4 requires each State Party to ensure that torture is a criminal offense under its domestic criminal law and Article 12 dictates that each State Party investigate any allegations of torture under its jurisdiction when reasonable grounds exist to believe that such acts have occurred. Article 7 further requires the State Party to either extradite the alleged torturer or "submit the case to competent [domestic] authorities for the purpose of prosecution." Also, Article 15 excludes all statements elicited through torture from evidence in a court of law, while Article 14 requires the State Party to make compensation to the victims of torture.

In contrast, Article 16 has no similar requirements mandating that ill-treatment be criminalized in domestic penal codes, requiring the prosecution of individuals charged with ill-treatment, or limitations on rendition. In addition, Article 16 has no requirement that victims of ill-treatment be compensated or that statements obtained as the fruit of ill-treatment must be excluded from evidence at a criminal trial. According to commentator Matthew Lippman, "[t]he failure to strengthen article [sic] 16 appears to have been based on a belief that the concept of cruel, inhuman or degrading treatment or punishment was too vague a legal standard upon which to base legal culpability and judgments."

Once one understands the basic statutory language prohibiting torture, the question of whether certain acts constitute torture or ill treatment can only be addressed by looking at leading judicial decisions and extrapolating the facts in those cases to the particulars at hand. Thus, while many individuals may cavalierly brand the CIA's practice of water boarding as "torture," the question can only find resolution in a competent judicial ruling on the matter. In this context, the inherent vagueness of ill-treatment and the reluctance of the Torture Convention to fully define the concept or to provide even a minimum level of sanction to the practice are further amplified by the leading international case dealing with unlawful interrogation practices. The most influential and widely recognized international court in the world is the European Court of Human Rights. The court's ruling in *Ireland v. United Kingdom* provides the most useful barometer of the international legal view concerning what acts would and would not amount to torture.

The *Ireland* court found certain interrogation practices of English authorities to investigate suspected terrorism in Northern Ireland to be "inhuman and degrading," i.e., ill-treatment, under the European Convention on Human Rights, but not severe enough to rise to the level of torture. According to the Court, the finding of ill-treatment rather than torture "derives principally from a difference in the intensity of the suffering inflicted." In *Ireland*, the Court considered the use of five investigative measures known as "the five techniques" which were practiced by British authorities for periods of "four or five" days pending or during interrogation sessions. By a lopsided vote of 13-4, the Court ruled that the interrogation techniques *did not* constitute torture.

Although *Ireland* was decided prior to the 1984 Torture Convention, the language of the European Convention on Human Rights is identical to the Torture Convention's definition of torture and ill-treatment. Furthermore, in *Selmouni v. France* (1999), the European Court of Human Rights cited *Ireland* with approval.

In order to determine whether a particular form of ill-treatment should be qualified as torture, the Court must have regard to the distinction, embodied in Article 3, between this notion and that of inhuman or degrading treatment. As the European Court has previously found, it appears that it was the intention that the Convention should, by means of this distinction, attach a special stigma to deliberate inhuman treatment causing very serious and cruel suffering (see the *Ireland v. the United Kingdom* judgment cited above …).

IRELAND v. UNITED KINGDOM
European Court of Human Rights
2 EHRR 25 (1978)

PANEL: Judge Balladore Pallieri (President), Judges, Wiarda, Zekia, Cremona, O'Donoghue, Pedersen, Thsr Vilhjalmsson, Ryssdal, Ganshof Van Der Meersch, Sir Gerald Fitzmaurice, Bindschedler-Robert, Evrigenis, Teitgen, Lagergren, Liesch, Gvlc Kl, Matscher, Mr M-A Eissen, Registrar, and Mr H Petzold, Deputy Registrar.

AS TO THE FACTS
I. The Emergency Situation and its Background
The tragic and lasting crisis in Northern Ireland lies at the root of the present case. In order to combat what the respondent Government describe as "the longest and most violent terrorist campaign witnessed in either part of the island of Ireland," the authorities in Northern Ireland exercised from August 1971 until December 1975 a series of extrajudicial powers of arrest, detention and internment. The proceedings in this case concern the scope and the operation in practice of those measures as well as the alleged ill-treatment of persons thereby deprived of their liberty.

…

15. Northern Ireland is not a homogeneous society. It consists of two communities divided by deep and long-standing antagonisms. One community is variously termed Protestant, Unionist or Loyalist, the other is generally labeled as Catholic, Republican or Nationalist. About two-thirds of the population of one and a half million belong to the Protestant community, the remaining third to the Catholic community. The majority group is descended from Protestant settlers who emigrated in large numbers from Britain to Northern Ireland during the seventeenth century. The now traditional antagonism between the two groups is based both on religion and on social, economic and political differences. In particular, the Protestant community has consistently opposed the idea of a united Ireland independent of the United Kingdom, whereas the Catholic community has traditionally supported it.

16. The Irish Republican Army (IRA) is a clandestine organisation with quasi-military dispositions. Formed during the troubles prior to the partition of the island and illegal in the United Kingdom as well as in the Republic of Ireland, the IRA neither accepts the existence of Northern Ireland as part of the United Kingdom nor recognizes the democratic order of the Republic. It has periodically mounted campaigns of terrorism in both parts of the island of Ireland and in Great Britain. After 1962, the IRA was not overtly active for some years.

During the time covered by the complaints of the applicant Government, that is from 1971 to 1975, virtually all those members of the IRA living and operating in Northern Ireland were recruited from among the Catholic community.

...

47. At the beginning of 1972, despite a small drop, the level of violence remained higher than at any time before 9 August 1971. On 30 January 1972, 13 people were killed by army gunfire in the course of disorders taking place in the predominantly Catholic town of Londonderry. This incident led to a new upsurge in support for the IRA amongst the Catholic community.

In the first three months of 1972, 87 people were killed, including 27 members of the security forces. Two assassinations carried out in March, one of a Protestant and the other of a Catholic, were the only deaths attributed to Loyalist activity. 421 explosions, the vast majority attributed to the IRA, were caused during the same period.

48. From August 1971 until 30 March 1972 there had been in Northern Ireland 1,130 bomb explosions and well over 2,000 shooting incidents. 158 civilians, 58 soldiers and 17 policemen had been killed, and 2,505 civilians, 306 soldiers and 107 RUC members injured.

Throughout these months the numbers held under detention or internment orders proceeded to rise until a total of over 900 persons, all suspected of involvement with the IRA, were held at the end of March 1972. At the same time, the ordinary processes of the criminal law continued to be used, against Protestants as well as Catholics, whenever there was thought to be sufficient evidence to ground a criminal conviction. Thus, between 9 August 1971 and 31 March 1972, over 1,600 people were charged with "terrorist-type" offences.

49. In March 1972, in view of the deteriorating circumstances, the Government in London decided that they should assume direct responsibility for the administration of law and order in Northern Ireland if there was to be any hope of political progress. This decision was unacceptable to the Government of the province and accordingly it was announced on 24 March 1972 that direct rule from Westminster not only on law and order but on all matters was to be introduced.

Under the Northern Ireland (Temporary Provisions) Act 1972 (hereinafter referred to as the "Temporary Provisions Act"), which was passed by the United Kingdom Parliament and came into force on 30 March 1972, temporary provision was made for the exercise of the executive and legislative powers of the Northern Ireland Parliament and Government by the United Kingdom authorities. The Belfast Parliament was prorogued and the Queen empowered to legislate in its stead by Order in Council. The executive powers of the Belfast Government were transferred to the Secretary of State for Northern Ireland. This was a new office created for the purpose; its holder was a member of the United Kingdom Government and answerable to the United Kingdom Parliament. The legislation was enacted for a period of one year but was subsequently extended.

...

68. On 8 August 1973, the Northern Ireland (Emergency Provisions) Act 1973 (hereafter abbreviated to the "Emergency Provisions Act") came into force. This Act, which was based mainly on the recommendations of the Diplock Commission (see paras. 58 and 59 above), repealed the 1922 Special Powers Act, Regulations 10 and 11(1) and the 1972 Terrorists Order, while retaining in substance the procedure laid down in the latter Order. Briefly, the extrajudicial powers introduced under the Emergency Provisions Act were:

(i) arrest and detention for 72 hours;

(ii) interim custody for 28 days; and

(iii) detention (see paras. 88 and 89 below for a fuller explanation). These emergency powers remained in force for a period of one year unless renewed. The Act also dealt with the trial and punishment by the ordinary courts of certain scheduled offences, for the most part offences concerned with violence. One provision, s.6, is referred to below at para. 136.

69. Between 1 February 1973 and 31 October 1974, interim custody orders were served on 99 Protestants and 626 Catholics; at all times many more Catholics than Protestants were actually held. Shortly before Christmas 1973, 65 detainees, 63 of whom were Catholics, were released.

70. During the same period, 2,478 persons were charged with "terrorist-type offences", the total being made up as follows: 1,042 Protestants, 1,420 Catholics and 16 soldiers. These figures included 60 Protestants and 66 Catholics charged with murder. In addition, searches were being conducted and arms recovered in relation to both sides.

...

III. Allegations of Ill-Treatment

A. Introduction

92. As recounted above at paras. 39 and 41, on 9 August 1971 and thereafter numerous persons in Northern Ireland were arrested and taken into custody by the security forces acting in pursuance of the emergency powers. The persons arrested were interrogated, usually by members of the RUC, in order to determine whether they should be interned and/or to compile information about the IRA. In all, about 3,276 persons were processed by the police at various holding centres from August 1971 until June 1972. The holding centres were replaced in July 1972 by police offices in Belfast and at Ballykelly Military Barracks.

93. Allegations of ill-treatment have been made by the applicant Government in relation both to the initial arrests and to the subsequent interrogations. The applicant Government submitted written evidence to the Commission in respect of 228 cases concerning incidents between 9 August 1971 and 1974....

96. Twelve persons arrested on 9 August 1971 and two persons arrested in October 1971 were singled out and taken to one or more unidentified centres. There, between 11 to 17 August and 11 to 18 October respectively, they were submitted to a form of "interrogation in depth" which involved the combined application of five particular techniques.

These methods, sometimes termed "disorientation" or "sensory deprivation" techniques, were not used in any cases other than the fourteen so indicated above. It emerges from the Commission's establishment of the facts that the techniques consisted of:

(a) wall-standing: forcing the detainees to remain for periods of some hours in a "stress position," described by those who underwent it as being "spread-eagled against the wall, with their fingers put high above the head against the wall, the legs spread apart and the feet back, causing them to stand on their toes with the weight of the body mainly on the fingers;"

(b) hooding: putting a black or navy coloured bag over the detainees' heads and, at least initially, keeping it there all the time except during interrogation;

(c) subjection to noise: pending their interrogations, holding the detainees in a room where there was a continuous loud and hissing noise;

(d) deprivation of sleep: pending their interrogations, depriving the detainees of sleep;

(e) deprivation of food and drink: subjecting the detainees to a reduced diet during their stay at the centre and pending interrogations.

97. From the start, it has been conceded by the respondent Government that the use of the five techniques was authorized at "high level." Although never committed to writing or authorized in any official document, the techniques had been orally taught to members of the RUC by the English Intelligence Centre at a seminar held in April 1971....

104. T 6 and T 13 were arrested on 9 August 1971 during Operation Demetrius. Two days later they were transferred from Magilligan Regional Holding Centre to an unidentified interrogation centre where they were medically examined on arrival. Thereafter, with intermittent periods of respite, they were subjected to the five techniques during four or possibly five days; neither the Compton or Parker Committees nor the Commission were able to establish the exact length of the periods of respite.

The Commission was satisfied that T 6 and T 13 were kept at the wall for different periods totaling between twenty to thirty hours, but it did not consider it proved that the enforced stress position had lasted all the time they were at the wall. It stated in addition that the required posture caused physical pain and exhaustion. The Commission noted that, later on during his stay at the interrogation centre, T 13 was allowed to take his hood off when he was alone in the room, provided that he turned his face to the wall. It was not found possible by the Commission to establish for what periods T 6 and T 13 had been without sleep, or to what extent they were deprived of nourishment and whether or not they were offered food but refused to take it.

The Commission found no physical injury to have resulted from the application of the five techniques as such, but loss of weight by the two case-witnesses and acute psychiatric symptoms developed by them during interrogation were recorded in the medical and other evidence. The Commission, on the material before it, was unable to establish the exact degree of any psychiatric after-effects produced on T 6 and T 13, but on the general level it was satisfied that some psychiatric after-effects in certain of the fourteen persons subjected to the techniques could not be excluded.

...

107. T 13 and T 6 instituted civil proceedings in 1971 to recover damages for wrongful imprisonment and assault; their claims were settled in 1973 and 1975 respectively for £15,000 and £14,000. The twelve other individuals against whom the five techniques were used have all received in settlement of their civil claims compensation ranging from £10,000 to £25,000.

...

PROCEEDINGS BEFORE THE COMMISSION

144. In their original application, lodged with the Commission on 16 December 1971, and later supplemented, the Irish Government made various allegations of violations by the United Kingdom of Articles 1, 2, 3, 5, 6 and 14 of the Convention.

145. On 1 October 1972, the Commission declared the application inadmissible as regards Article 2 but accepted the allegations that:

> — the treatment of persons in custody, in particular the methods of interrogation of such persons, constituted an administrative practice in breach of Article 3;

...

147. In its report, the Commission expressed the opinion:

> (i) unanimously, that the powers of detention and internment without trial as exercised during the relevant periods were not in conformity with Article 5(1) to (4), but were "strictly required by the exigencies of the situation" in Northern Ireland, within the meaning of Article 15(1);
>
> ...
>
> (iv) unanimously, that the combined use of the five techniques in the cases before it constituted a practice of inhuman treatment and of torture in breach of Article 3;
>
> (v) unanimously, that violations of Article 3 occurred by inhuman, and in two cases degrading, treatment of
>
> —T 6, in an unidentified interrogation centre in August 1971,
>
> —T 2, T 8, T 12, T 15, T 9, T 14 and T 10 at Palace Barracks, Holywood, in September, October and November 1971,
>
> —T 16, T 7 and T 11, at various places in August, October and December 1971;
>
> (vi) unanimously, that there had been at Palace Barracks, Holywood, in the autumn of 1971, a practice in connection with the interrogation of prisoners by members of the RUC which was inhuman treatment in breach of Article 3 of the Convention;

...

DECISION-1:
AS TO THE LAW

148. Paragraph (d) of the application of 10 March 1976 states that the object of bringing the case before the Court (r.31(1)(d)) of the Rules of Court) is:

> "to ensure the observance in Northern Ireland of the engagements undertaken by the respondent Government as a High Contracting Party to the Convention and in particular

of the engagements specifically set out by the applicant Government in the pleadings filed and the submissions made on their behalf and described in the evidence adduced before the Commission in the hearings before them."

"To this end," the Court is invited:

"to consider the report of the Commission and to confirm the opinion of the Commission that breaches of the Convention have occurred and also to consider the claims of the applicant Government with regard to other alleged breaches and to make a finding of breach of the Convention where the Court is satisfied that a breach has occurred."

...

149. The Court notes first of all that it is not called upon to take cognizance of every single aspect of the tragic situation prevailing in Northern Ireland. For example, it is not required to rule on the terrorist activities in the six counties of individuals or of groups, activities that are in clear disregard of human rights. The Court has only to give a decision on the claims made before it by the Irish Republic against the United Kingdom. However, in so doing, the Court cannot lose sight of the events that form the background to this case.

I. On Article 3

150. Article 3 provides that "no one shall be subjected to torture or to inhuman or degrading treatment or punishment."

...

C. Questions concerning the merits

162. As was emphasized by the Commission, ill-treatment must attain a minimum level of severity if it is to fall within the scope of Article 3. The assessment of this minimum is, in the nature of things, relative; it depends on all the circumstances of the case, such as the duration of the treatment, its physical or mental effects and, in some cases, the sex, age and state of health of the victim, etc.

163. The Convention prohibits in absolute terms torture and inhuman or degrading treatment or punishment, irrespective of the victim's conduct. Unlike most of the substantive clauses of the Convention and of Protocols Nos. 1 and 4, Article 3 makes no provision for exceptions and, under Article 15(2), there can be no derogation there from even in the event of a public emergency threatening the life of the nation.

164. In the instant case, the only relevant concepts are "torture" and "inhuman or degrading treatment", to the exclusion of "inhuman or degrading punishment".

...

165. The facts concerning the five techniques are summarized at paras. 96-104 and 106-107 above. In the Commission's estimation, those facts constituted a practice not only of inhuman and degrading treatment but also of torture. The applicant Government ask for confirmation of this opinion which is not contested before the Court by the respondent Government.

166. The police used the five techniques on fourteen persons in 1971, that is on twelve, including T 6 and T 13, in August before the Compton Committee was set up, and on two in October whilst that Committee was carrying out its enquiry. Although never authorized in writing in any official document, the five techniques were taught orally by the English Intelligence Centre to members of the RUC at a seminar held in April 1971. There was accordingly a practice.

167. The five techniques were applied in combination, with premeditation and for hours at a stretch; they caused, if not actual bodily injury, at least intense physical and mental suffering to the persons subjected thereto and also led to acute psychiatric disturbances during interrogation. They accordingly fell into the category of inhuman treatment within the meaning of Article 3. The techniques were also degrading since they were such as to arouse in their victims feelings of fear, anguish and inferiority capable of humiliating and debasing them and possibly breaking their physical or moral resistance.

On these two points, the Court is of the same view as the Commission.

In order to determine whether the five techniques should also be qualified as torture, the Court must have regard to the distinction, embodied in Article 3, between this notion and that of inhuman or degrading treatment.

In the Court's view, this distinction derives principally from a difference in the intensity of the suffering inflicted.

The Court considers in fact that, whilst there exists on the one hand violence which is to be condemned both on moral grounds and also, in most cases, under the domestic law of the Contracting States, but which does not fall within Article 3 of the Convention, it appears on the other hand that it was the intention that the Convention, with its distinction between "torture" and "inhuman or degrading treatment," should by the first of these terms attach a special stigma to deliberate inhuman treatment causing very serious and cruel suffering.

Moreover, this seems to be the thinking lying behind Article 1 in fine of Resolution 3452 (XXX) adopted by the General Assembly of the United Nations on 9 December 1975, which declares: "Torture constitutes an aggravated and deliberate form of cruel, inhuman or degrading treatment or punishment."

Although the five techniques, as applied in combination, undoubtedly amounted to inhuman and degrading treatment, although their object was the extraction of confessions, the naming of others and/or information and although they were used systematically, they did not occasion suffering of the particular intensity and cruelty implied by the word torture as so understood.

168. The Court concludes that recourse to the five techniques amounted to a practice of inhuman and degrading treatment, which practice was in breach of Article 3.

(b) Ill-treatment alleged to have accompanied the use of the five techniques
169. The applicant Government claim that the fourteen persons subjected to the five techniques, or some of those persons including T 6 and T 13, also had to undergo other kinds of treatment contrary to Article 3.

The Commission has found such treatment only in the case of T 6, although it regarded it as probable that the use of the five techniques was sometimes accompanied by physical violence (see para. 105 above).

170. As far as T 6 is concerned, the Court shares the Commission's opinion that the security forces subjected T 6 to assaults severe enough to constitute inhuman treatment. This opinion, which is not contested by the respondent Government, is borne out by the evidence before the Court.

...

FOR THESE REASONS, THE COURT

I. On Article 3

1.   holds unanimously that, although certain violations of Article 3 were not contested, a ruling should nevertheless be given thereon;

2.   holds unanimously that it has jurisdiction to take cognisance of the cases of alleged violation of Article 3 to the extent that the applicant Government put them forward as establishing the existence of a practice;

3.   holds by sixteen votes to one that the use of the five techniques in August and October 1971 constituted a practice of inhuman and degrading treatment, which practice was in breach of Article 3;

4.   holds by thirteen votes to four that the said use of the five techniques did not constitute a practice of torture within the meaning of Article 3;

5.   holds by sixteen votes to one that no other practice of ill-treatment is established for the unidentified interrogation centres;

6.   holds unanimously that there existed at Palace Barracks in the autumn of 1971 a practice of inhuman treatment, which practice was in breach of Article 3;

7.   holds by fourteen votes to three that the last-mentioned practice was not one of torture within the meaning of Article 3;

...

Another source of guidance to distinguish a reasonable interrogation from an interrogation that crosses the line into ill-treatment or torture is found in the 1999 Israeli High Court decision entitled, *Public Committee Against Torture v. State of Israel (Public Committee)*. In the context of outlawing certain interrogation practices by Israeli officials, the High Court considered how otherwise reasonable interrogation practices could become illegal if taken to an extreme point of intensity. Playing music to disorient a subject prior to questioning is not illegal per se, but if the music is played in a manner that causes undue suffering, it is arguably a form of ill-treatment or torture. Depriving subjects of sleep during a lengthy interrogation process may be legitimate, but depending on the extent of sleep deprivation, could also constitute ill-treatment or torture. The use of handcuffing for the protection of the interrogators is a common and acceptable practice, so long as the handcuffs are not unduly tightened so as to cause excess pain. Similarly, the use of blindfolds is acceptable if done for legitimate security reasons, while the use of sacks over the head without proper ventilation is unacceptable.

The backdrop for *Public Committee* is as follows. The General Security Service of Israel (GSS) is responsible for conducting investigations of suspected terrorists who commit crimes against the State of Israel. As part of this responsibility, the GSS engages in the detention and interrogation of suspected terrorists. Up until the late 1980s, the official position of the government of Israel was that GSS interrogators did not use "coercive" methods during terrorist interrogations. In 1987, the government appointed the Landau Commission to investigate the methods of interrogation used by the GSS. In November 1987, the Landau Commission issued its report, recognizing the terrorist threat to the nation and the attendant necessity for the GSS to engage in what it termed euphemistically as "a moderate measure of physical pressure" during interrogations of suspected terrorists. In a separate secret part of the report, the Landau Commission set out limits in the types of physical pressure that the GSS might employ. In the publicly released section of the report, the commission advised that GSS agents should combine "non-violent psychological pressure of a vigorous and extensive interrogation… with…a moderate amount of physical pressure." In short, the Landau Commission provided the green light for the GSS to use "moderate…physical pressure" when conducting interrogations.

Adopting the recommendations of the Landau Commission, the Israeli government issued directives authorizing the GSS to use various physical means in certain cases. In taking the unprecedented step of trying to regulate the use of physical pressure during the interrogation of suspected terrorists, the government contended that such methods did not constitute torture. The Supreme Court of Israel found that the primary techniques used by the GSS (which had until then remained secret) involved the following:

- Shaking: The practice of shaking was deemed to be the most brutal and harshest of all the interrogation methods. The method is defined as "the forceful shaking of the suspect's upper torso, back and forth, repeatedly, in a manner which causes the neck and head to dangle and vacillate rapidly."
- Shabach Position: The practice of binding the subject in a child's chair "tilted forward towards the ground, in a manner that causes him real pain and suffering." Other reports amplify the method and add that the subject's head is "covered in a hood while powerfully deafening music is emitted within inches of the suspect's head."
- Frog Crouch: The practice of making the subject crouch on the tips of their toes for five-minute intervals.
- Excessive Tightening of Handcuffs: The practice of inflicting injury to a suspect by excessive tightening of handcuffs or through the use of small handcuffs.
- Sleep Deprivation: The practice of intentionally keeping the subject awake for prolonged periods of time.

In ruling that there existed an absolute prohibition on the use of torture or ill-treatment as a means of interrogation, the Supreme Court held some of the practices of the GSS violated Israel's Basic Law—Human Dignity and Liberty. Specifically, the Court found that shaking, the use of the shabach, the use of the frog crouch, and, in certain instances, the deprivation of sleep, were all illegal and prohibited investigation methods. The fact that the Court did not characterize any of these techniques as having the severity of pain or suffering indicative of torture indicates that the Court viewed them as ill-treatment only, as in *Ireland*.

7.3 Rendition

In tandem with the issue of targeted killing, the matter of rendition has been a lightning rod for debate when used in the context of the War on Terror. Simply put, rendition refers to the long-standing practice of one state sending a non-citizen individual to another state. The practice is not illegal per se and the government's authority to engage in rendition stems from the president's authority under Article II. The act of rendition only becomes illegal under a limited set of circumstances. The seminal legal instrument in this regard is the 1984 Torture Convention. Article 3 of the Torture Convention prohibits any state party to "expel, return ("*refouler*") or extradite any person to another State where there are substantial grounds to believe that he would be in danger of being subjected to torture." The more common euphemism for this illegal practice is "extraordinary rendition," although it should be properly categorized as "illegal rendition."

In making the determination as to whether an illegal rendition has occurred, the state party is required by Article 3(2) to "take into account all relevant considerations" with particular regard to whether or not there exists "a consistent pattern of gross, flagrant or mass violations of human rights" in the receiving state. Even though the Torture Convention's combined factors of "substantial grounds," coupled with "a consistent pattern of gross, flagrant or mass violations of human rights," provide considerable flexibility for a state party to justify a particular rendition, at least the prohibition is established and a standard is established, albeit a subjective one. Surprisingly, Article 16 has no similar requirement regarding rendition to a state that engages in "other cruel, inhuman or degrading treatment," shortened to the term "ill-treatment." For all practical purposes, this means that a state is free to turn over an individual to a state that it actually knows engages in ill-treatment. In practice, the United States relies heavily on assurances from the host state via diplomatic channels that the non-citizen will not be subjected to torture or ill-treatment.

Because the Senate's ratification of the Torture Convention expressly mandated that the treaty was not "self-executing," Congress passed legislation to implement Article 3 of the Torture Convention as part of the Foreign Affairs Reform and Restructuring Act of 1998 (FARRA). Curiously, however, in terms of rendition the FARRA only provided a policy statement without legal effect. The pertinent provision states:

> It shall be the policy of the United States not to expel, extradite, or otherwise effect the involuntary return of any person to a country in which there are substantial grounds for believing that person would be in physical danger of being subjected to torture, regardless of whether the person is physically present in the United States.

In the War on Terror, the concern over illegal rendition centered on the transfer of an individual from the United States to another country. Since detainees are unlawful enemy combatants, they are not prisoners of war and thus not subject to protection of the Geneva Conventions as a bar to any transfer whatsoever. Law Professor Robert Chesney argues quite persuasively that because of the definition of "protected persons" in the Fourth Geneva Convention, the al-Qaeda, Taliban, and associated forces are not covered and thus are all candidates for rendition.

While the Clinton Administration engaged in rendition of terror suspects prior to 9/11, the Bush Administration engaged in lawful rendition of detainees as well. According to the left-leaning Center for Human Rights and Global Justice, however, the United States engaged in illegal rendition by sending non-citizens to such countries as "Egypt, Jordan, Morocco, Saudi Arabia, Yemen, and Syria. Although candidate Obama strongly condemned rendition in the Bush Administration when running for office in 2007, he quickly reversed his position after the election and as a practical matter adopted the entire rendition policy that he had so strongly condemned as torture and illegal. The 2009 Obama executive order condoned the practice of rendition but promised more oversight in the process to ensure that torture does not occur. As a practical matter, over the past six years, the Obama Administration has utilized the practice sparingly, if at all.

In terms of American legal jurisprudence related to rendition, the Ninth Circuit case of *Bellout v. Ashcroft* provides a typical view of the standard legal burden and how it is evaluated. Not only is the burden on the defendant, the concept of what constitutes an illegal rendition which would violate the Torture Convention is also set at a high level.

BELLOUT v. ASHCROFT
United States Court of Appeals for the Ninth Circuit
363 F.3d 975 (April 12, 2004)

SILVERMAN, Circuit Judge:

Mouloud Bellout, a native and citizen of Algeria, petitions for review of the BIA's summary affirmance of the IJ's denial of Bellout's application for asylum, withholding of removal, and protection under the Convention Against Torture (CAT). The IJ found Bellout statutorily ineligible for relief from deportation because he engaged in terrorist activity when he joined "Armed Islamic Group (GIA)," a State Department-recognized terrorist organization, in 1995 and lived in GIA camps in Algeria for three years. Bellout has been removed to Algeria.

We hold as follows: First, because the IJ found that there are reasonable grounds to believe that Bellout engaged in or is likely to engage in terrorist activity under *8 U.S.C. § 1158(b)(2)(a) (v)*, we lack jurisdiction to review the IJ's determination that Bellout is ineligible for asylum by virtue of *8 U.S.C. § 1158(b)(2)(D)*. Second, substantial evidence supports the IJ's conclusion that Bellout is ineligible for withholding of removal. Finally, substantial evidence supports the IJ's denial of deferral of removal under CAT.

I. FACTS

Bellout attempted to enter the United States at Los Angeles International Airport on January 6, 1999, using a fraudulent Belgian passport. After the INS initiated removal proceedings, Bellout applied for asylum, withholding of deportation, and relief under CAT, alleging that he would be tortured by terrorists or police if he returned to Algeria. At his hearing, Bellout testified that he joined GIA in 1995, lived in GIA mountain camps, made friends with other members, read GIA's pamphlets and literature, discussed ideology with other members of the group, and carried weapons and ammunition. When GIA divided into a second group in 1996, Bellout went with the second group—"Algamma El-Salafia Lel-Daawa Wal Ketal." He remained with this group until 1998, when he left Algeria.

The IJ found that Bellout was statutorily barred from asylum, withholding of removal and relief under CAT as an alien "who the Attorney General knows, or has reasonable grounds to believe, is engaged in or is likely to engage after entry in any terrorist activity."

8 U.S.C. § 1189(a) authorizes the Secretary of State to designate foreign terrorist organizations by providing notice and findings to congressional leaders and publishing the designation in the Federal Register. Unless Congress disapproves the designation, it becomes effective upon publication in the Federal Register. *Id. § 1189(a)(2)(B)*. Although the designation is effective for two years, the Secretary may redesignate a foreign terrorist organization after the two years expire. *Id. § 1189(a)(4)*.

The Secretary has designated and redesignated the "Armed Islamic Group (GIA)" as a terrorist organization under *8 U.S.C. § 1189. Designation of Foreign Terrorist Organizations, 62 Fed. Reg. 52650 (Oct. 8, 1997); 64 Fed. Reg. 55112 (Oct. 8, 1999); 66 Fed. Reg. 51088 (Oct. 5, 2001); 68 Fed. Reg. 56860 (Oct. 2, 2003).* According to the State Department Office of Counterterrorism's 1999 Report of Foreign Terrorist Organizations, GIA is an extremely violent terrorist group that frequently and brutally attacks and kills civilians, journalists, and foreign residents. The Report says that GIA uses assassinations and bombings and favors kidnapping victims and slitting their throats. According to the Report, GIA's activities are not limited only to Algeria; GIA hijacked an Air France flight in December 1994 and is suspected of a series of bombings in France in 1995.

Because Bellout had been a member of a State Department-designated terrorist organization, the IJ found that Bellout engaged in terrorist activity and, in the alternative, posed a danger to security in the United States. He was therefore ineligible for asylum. He likewise was ineligible for withholding of deportation. The IJ also concluded that Bellout was not entitled to deferral of removal under CAT because he had failed to establish that he would more likely than not be tortured if he returned to Algeria. The BIA affirmed the IJ's decision, adopting that decision as the final agency determination pursuant to 8 C.F.R. § 3.1(a)(7) (2002).

Bellout argues that the IJ erred in finding that he was ineligible for asylum and withholding of removal because he engaged in terrorist activity, and in denying him relief under CAT.

…

IV. RELIEF UNDER CAT

Bellout argues that the IJ should have granted him deferral of removal under the Convention Against Torture because, he claims, the police will torture him if he returns to Algeria. Article 3 of the United Nations Convention Against Torture or Punishment prohibits removal to a state where there are substantial grounds to believe the alien would be tortured. *Al-Saher v. INS, 268 F.3d 1143, 1146 (9th Cir. 2001).* Although barred from "withholding of removal" under CAT, Bellout remains eligible for "deferral of removal" under CAT. *8 C.F.R. § 1208.17(a) (2003).* We review the denial of relief under CAT for substantial evidence. *Zheng v. Ashcroft, 332 F.3d 1186, 1194 (9th Cir. 2003).*

To be eligible for deferral of removal under CAT, Bellout must establish that he "is more likely than not to be tortured" if he returns to Algeria. *8 C.F.R. § 1208.17(a) (2003); see also Zheng, 332 F.3d at 1194.* Bellout testified to one incident of abuse by the police in 1994 before he joined GIA. There is no evidence in the record that the Algerian government is aware that Bellout joined GIA or is interested in him. The IJ found that there was no evidence that members of militant groups who leave Algeria will be persecuted or tortured upon return and that Bellout did not meet his burden of establishing it is more likely than not that he will face torture if returned to Algeria. The evidence does not compel a contrary conclusion. *Zheng, 332 F.3d at 1194.*

PETITION FOR REVIEW DISMISSED IN PART AND DENIED IN PART.

Real world enforcement mechanisms to ensure compliance with the Torture Convention's prohibition of torture and ill-treatment are wholly inadequate. This is because the individual State Party is expected to self-police and, if this fails, the only remaining hope for meaningful pressure is international condemnation from the court of world opinion. While the Torture Convention did create an investigatory body called the Committee Against Torture, its responsibilities revolve around a complex maze of reports and recommendations which, as one might anticipate, have generally accomplished very little. In fact, the biggest stick that the Committee Against Torture wields is the threat that it may provide an unfavorable summary of a particular country in its yearly report. As always, the chief enforcement tool in a democracy is the rule of law coupled with the judgment of its citizens; civilized peoples are repulsed by the concept of torture. Levels of compliance in totalitarian regimes are dismal, and the minimal progress that is achieved occurs only through the economic and political pressure applied by democracies.

7.4 United States Domestic Law

The American experience has not been guiltless in terms of the sanctioned use of torture and ill-treatment to elicit confessions in domestic criminal investigations, particularly in the early part of the last century. By 1931, the appalling practice of torture by local law enforcement had become so common throughout the nation that a special government fact-finding commission was set up to investigate the matter. The Wickersham Commission issued a report on abusive police interrogation practices that not only educated the public, but also energized the United States Supreme Court to hand down a string of cases in which police interrogation abuses that "shocked the conscience" of the Court were equated with torture.

Currently, torture is defined in 18 U.S.C. § 2340 as:

[A]n act committed by a person acting under the color of the law specifically intended to inflict severe physical or mental pain or suffering (other than pain or suffering incidental to lawful sanctions) upon another person within his custody or physical control.

While domestic acts of torture are punished as common law crimes, 18 U.S.C. § 2340A makes it a federal offense for an American national to either commit or attempt to commit torture outside the United States. In 1992, Congress passed the Torture Victim Protection Act of 1991, which opened United States courts to civil law damage suits by any individual "who, under actual or apparent authority, or color of law, of any foreign nation," violates international law regarding torture.

In the context of what techniques would be lawful for interrogators to use in the United States, a 2003 United States Supreme Court decision entitled *Chavez v. Martinez* provides some current guidance. The central issue in *Chavez* involved the issue of coercive questioning by a police officer.

The facts of the case are as follows. While "investigating suspected narcotics activity" near a vacant lot, police in Oxnard, California, stopped Oliverio Martinez as he was riding his bike down a darkened path. The police conducted a *Terry* patdown frisk of Martinez and discovered a knife in his waistband. An altercation ensued and police officers claim that Martinez took one of the officer's "gun from its holster and pointed it at them." Officer Pea then drew her service pistol and shot Martinez five times, leaving him blinded and paralyzed. Martinez was placed under arrest and taken by ambulance to the hospital. Sergeant Ben Chavez, the patrol supervisor, "accompanied Martinez to the hospital and then questioned Martinez while he was receiving treatment from medical personnel." The interrogation in the emergency room of the hospital "lasted a total of about 10 minutes, over a 45-minute period, with Chavez leaving the emergency room for periods of time to permit medical personnel to attend to Martinez."

During the interrogation, Chavez never read Martinez his *Miranda* warnings. There can be no question that Martinez was disoriented and in extreme pain throughout the process of interrogation. At first Martinez was uncooperative. "At one point, Martinez said 'I am not telling you anything until they treat me,' yet Chavez continued the interview." Later, Martinez admitted taking the gun and pointing it at police. This act resulted in Martinez being shot by Pea.

Although Martinez was never charged with any crime and his statements were never used against him in a criminal proceeding, he subsequently filed a claim for damages in the United States District Court for the Central District of California under 42 U.S.C. § 1983, alleging that Sergeant Chavez had violated his Fifth Amendment right against self-incrimination as well as his Fourteenth Amendment substantive due process right. The Court of Appeals for the Ninth Circuit affirmed the District Court's denial of Chavez's defense of qualified immunity and entered summary judgment in favor of Martinez for both claims. With Justice Thomas delivering the opinion for the majority, the Supreme Court granted certiorari and reversed and remanded the case.

In seeking guidance for questioning suspected terrorists within the United States, the case is significant for two reasons. First, by overturning the Ninth Circuit's ruling that "the mere use of compulsive questioning, without more, violates the Constitution," the Court clearly established that the Fifth Amendment is not violated when law enforcement agents who do not intend to use statements in subsequent criminal proceedings interrogate with coercion an unwilling suspect without providing *Miranda* warnings. The Court related that "mere coercion does not violate the text of the Self-Incrimination Clause absent the use of compelled statements in a criminal case against the witness." Thus, the Court held that "the absence of a 'criminal case' in which Martinez was compelled to be a 'witness' against himself defeats his core Fifth Amendment claim" and voids any § 1983 action. Still, the Court was quick to note that they were not condoning the use of torture or ill-treatment by law enforcement:

> [O]ur views of the proper scope of the Fifth Amendment's Self-Incrimination Clause do not mean that police torture or other abuse that results in a confession is constitutionally permissible so long as the statements are not used in trial; it simply means that the Fourteenth Amendment's Due Process Clause, rather than the Fifth Amendment's Self Incrimination Clause, would govern the inquiry in those cases and provide relief in appropriate circumstances.

Second, the ruling left in place the subjective "shock the conscience" standard, taken from the 1952 case of *Rochin v. California*, for determining when the police cross the threshold for conduct that violates the Fourteenth Amendment. In *Rochin*, police officers witnessed the defendant swallow two capsules which they suspected were illegal substances. Rochin was handcuffed and taken to a hospital where a doctor forced an emetic solution through a tube into Rochin's stomach and against Rochin's will. Rochin vomited two morphine capsules and was subsequently convicted. Overturning the conviction, the Supreme Court held that obtaining evidence by methods that are "so brutal and so offensive to human dignity" stands in violation of the Fourteenth Amendment's due process clause:

> [W]e are compelled to conclude that the proceedings by which this conviction was obtained do more than offend some fastidious squeamishness or private sentimentalism about combating crime too energetically. This is conduct that *shocks the conscience*....They are methods too close to the rack and screw to permit of constitutional differentiation [emphasis added].

As to whether the facts of *Chavez* would constitute a violation of the Fourteenth Amendment, the Court remanded that issue back to the lower court although at least five of the justices apparently were not "shocked" that Sergeant Chavez engaged in a repetitive interrogation even though Martinez was suffering "excruciating pain." Despite the fact that Sergeant Chavez may have indeed benefited from the situation if Martinez subjectively thought that he had to answer questions as a condition of getting medical treatment, this was not the case and medical personnel were treating Martinez throughout the interrogation period. Justice Thomas wrote that "we cannot agree with Martinez's characterization of Chavez's behavior as egregious or conscience shocking." The fact that Chavez did not interfere with medical treatment and did not cause the pain experienced by Martinez (the bullet wounds to Martinez occurred prior to and totally apart from the questioning process) were certainly important factors which influenced some, but not all, of the justices.

Expressing an opposite view, Justice Stevens dissented and saw the interrogation conducted by Sergeant Chavez as tantamount to torture and a clear violation of the Fourteenth Amendment:

> As a matter of fact, the interrogation of respondent was the functional equivalent of an attempt to obtain an involuntary confession from a prisoner by torturous methods. As a matter of law, that type of brutal police conduct constitutes an immediate deprivation of the prisoner's constitutionally protected interest in liberty.

Unfortunately, the Court did not provide any new approaches to assist in defining what would constitute interrogation behavior that would "shock the conscience." The Court was content to cite previous examples from past cases, traced from the 1936 case of *Brown v. Mississippi*.

In *Brown*, the Court ruled that convictions based on confessions extracted by law enforcement through methods tantamount to torture violated the Fourteenth Amendment. The facts of the case involved the hanging and whipping of a murder suspect by local police until a confession was obtained. Other defendants were also tortured—they "were made to strip and…were laid over chairs and their backs were cut to pieces with a leather strap with buckles on it…and in this manner the defendants confessed to the crime." All of the defendants were convicted of murder and sentenced to death. In reversing the convictions, the Supreme Court stated the following:

> [The] state is free to regulate the procedure of its courts in accordance with its own conceptions of policy, unless in so doing it offends some principle of justice so rooted in the traditions and conscience of our people as to be ranked as fundamental. But freedom of the state in establishing its policy is the freedom of constitutional government and is limited by the requirement of due process of law. Because a state may dispense with a jury trial, it does not follow that it may substitute trial by ordeal. The rack and torture chamber may not be substituted for the witness stand.

Not all fact patterns are as easy to associate with torture as *Brown*, which is clearly torture. Indeed, those familiar with the "shock the conscience" test understand that the Court has often interpreted the test with a great degree of flexibility, particularly when judging the actions of law enforcement officers faced with exigent circumstances related to governmental needs such as public safety issues. For example, in the 1998 case of *County of Sacramento v. Lewis* the Court denied a § 1983 claim based on an alleged substantive due process violation. In *Lewis*, a passenger on a motorcycle was killed as the result of a high-speed police chase ending when the fleeing motorcycle tipped over and a police car in close pursuit struck and killed the respondent's sixteen-year-old son.

In discussing the threshold for shocking the conscience, the *Lewis* decision "made it clear that the due process guarantee does not entail a body of constitutional law imposing liability whenever someone cloaked with state authority causes harm." Indeed, "[i]n a due process challenge to executive action, the threshold question is whether the behavior of the governmental officer is so egregious, so outrageous, that it may fairly be said to shock the contemporary conscience."

Interestingly, an equally important aspect of *Lewis* centered on the Court's view that not only does the conduct have to be egregious, but that "conduct intended to injure in some way unjustifiable by any government interest is the sort of an official action most likely to rise to the conscience-shocking level." This means that the Court will provide greater deference if the government can demonstrate a justification for its conduct based on the totality of the circumstances. The stronger the justification, the more flexibility allowed.

This deference factor certainly played out in a 1966 Ninth Circuit case entitled *Blefare v. United States*. In a fact pattern similar to *Rochin*, the appellants were suspected of swallowing narcotics which were lodged in their rectums or stomachs. Appellants were searched by U.S. officials at a border crossing from Mexico into the United States where they consented to a rectal probe by a doctor. When the rectal probe found no drugs, a "saline solution was…given the appellants to drink to produce vomiting." Blefare, one of the suspects, "was seen by the doctor to have regurgitated an object and reswallowed it." Then, without Blefare's consent the doctor forcefully passed a soft tube into the "nose, down the throat and into the stomach," through which fluid flowed in order to induce vomiting. This resulted in the discovery of packets of heroin and the subsequent conviction of Blefare.

The Ninth Circuit refused to hold that the involuntary intrusion into Blefare's stomach shocked the conscience. The Court attempted to distinguish the case from *Rochin* by noting that Blefare had at first consented to the rectal probe and the drinking of saline, and that, in any event, the actions to induce vomiting were not brutal. Arguably, the ruling hinged on the fact that the State had an important governmental interest in keeping heroin from entering the United States. In the Court's view, it would have been shocking had they overturned the conviction based on the due process clause. The Court felt that it would "shock the conscience" if Blefare's conviction were set aside:

> It would shock the conscience of law abiding citizens if the officers, with the knowledge these officers had, were frustrated in the recovery and use of this evidence. It is shocking to know that these appellants swallowed narcotics to smuggle it into and through the United States for sale for profit.…If we were mechanically to invoke Rochin to reverse this conviction, we would transform a meaningful expression of concern for the rights of the individual into a meaningless mechanism for the obstruction of justice.

To be sure, there are a number of cases that proponents of coercive questioning techniques can cite to buttress the view that in exigent circumstances the police may be obliged to use force to get life saving information. For instance, in *Leon v. Wainwright* the Eleventh Circuit brushed aside the fact that police officers had used "force and threats" on kidnap suspect Jean Leon in order to get the suspect to reveal the location of his kidnap victim. When apprehended by a group of police officers in a Florida parking lot, Leon refused to reveal the location of his kidnap victim (the victim, Louis Gachelin, had been taken by gunpoint to an apartment where he was undressed and bound to a chair). In order to get the suspect to talk, police officers physically abused Leon by twisting his arm and choking him until he revealed where the victim was being held. Later, Leon was taken to the police station where he made a second confession which the Court ruled as admissible at his trial. In speaking to the use of brutal force to get the information needed to protect the victim, the Court deemed that the action of the officers was reasonable given the immediate concern to find the victim and save his life.

We do not by our decision sanction the use of force and coercion by police officers. Yet this case does not represent the typical case of unjustified force. We do not have an act of brutal law enforcement agents trying to obtain a confession in total disregard of the law. This was instead a group of concerned officers acting in a reasonable manner to obtain information they needed in order to protect another individual from bodily harm or death.

Returning to *Chavez*, the government brief attempted to draw together the concept of governmental interest by arguing that the Court in *Chavez* should take the opportunity to create a "terrorist exception" which would accord protection to police officers from § 1983 suits when questioning suspected terrorists. This matter was not directly addressed by the justices. Nevertheless, if one adds *Chavez* to *Lewis* and its progeny, certain constitutional parameters for interrogating a terrorist suspect can now be staked out. Simply put, even if a terrorist suspect asks for a lawyer and demands that all questioning cease, law enforcement may justifiably refuse these requests and engage in interrogation that may consist of coercive techniques so long as the techniques utilized fall below the threshold of shocking the conscience (which equates to actions not in violation of the Torture Convention). In addition, under the concept of governmental interest, the more the suspected terrorist matches the scenario of the ticking time bomb terrorist, the more deference given to police interrogators under the umbrella of public safety.

Critics of *Chavez* such as Brooklyn law professor and President of the ACLU, Susan Herman, fear that allowing the use of coercive interrogation techniques short of the ambiguous "shock the conscience" standard leaves open the door for abuse to those not suspected of terrorism. Others are dismayed that the *Chavez* Court refused to even acknowledge the existence of the Torture Convention and its place in the matter of coercive interrogations.

7.5 Allegations of United States Sanctioned Torture

Keeping in mind that the goal of any antiterrorism effort is to stop or eliminate the terrorists before they commit murderous attacks, there are four general law enforcement means that mesh together in this effort: (1) using informants and undercover agents to infiltrate the terror cell (known as HUMINT sources); (2) using surveillance, searches, and wiretaps to learn of locations, organizational structure and plans for future attacks; (3) arresting and detaining individuals before they commit a terrorist attack; and (4) interrogation of individuals. Only the last category, interrogating those detained as suspected foot soldiers of terrorism, is discussed herein.

Since the advent of the War on Terror, the United States has detained thousands of individuals which can be grouped into one of four categories: (1) those suspected of having links to the al-Qa'eda, or a similar radical Islamic fundamentalist, terror movement; (2) those designated by the President as enemy combatants; (3) those detained as prisoners of war in the Iraq military campaign; and (4) those who were apprehended in Iraq and Afghanistan and designated as "security detainees." Most of those detained in the first category were apprehended by federal law enforcement personnel on the heels of the attacks of September 11, 2001, and, after questioning, the majority were deported as illegal aliens. Those in the third group have since been released.

Detainees in the second group were members of the al-Qa'eda network or Taliban captured on the battlefields of Afghanistan, although the United States also included other suspected members of al-Qa'eda apprehended in places other than the military combat zone of Afghanistan. Along with Yaser Esam Hamdi, at least two enemy combatants, Ali Saleh Kahlah Al-Marri and Jose Padilla, were arrested in the United States. With the 2006 release of the 14 detainees held by the CIA in "undisclosed" locations, almost all of the individuals in the second category are currently being housed in Guantanamo Bay, Cuba, since Bagram Air Force Base in Afghanistan is no longer operational. Some of the detainees have been held in detention as enemy combatants since 2002 without being charged with a crime. With the drawdown of American combat forces from Iraq, all those in the fourth group were turned over to the Iraqi government and the Afghan government in Afghanistan. Some detainees in the second and fourth group of individuals—enemy combatants and security detainees—were subjected to extended interrogation by programs administered by the DOD and the CIA.

Once a terrorist suspect is detained, what do American interrogators do? In the first few years following 9/11 (2002-2005) the answer to that question was difficult to ascertain. It was not until the passage of the Detainee Treatment Act of 2005 that uniform standards for interrogation of individuals in the custody of the DOD were set out. The Detainee Treatment Act expressly prohibited cruel, inhuman, or degrading treatment of detainees in the custody of any U.S. agency. Then, in 2006, the Supreme Court in *Hamdan* ruled that the detainees must be given all the provisions set out at Common Article 3 of the Geneva Conventions. Common Article 3 of the Geneva Conventions requires the following, with special reference to (1) (c) below:

ARTICLE 3 COMMON TO THE GENEVA CONVENTIONS OF 1949

In the case of armed conflict not of an international character occurring in the territory of one of the High Contracting Parties, each Party to the conflict shall be bound to apply, as a minimum, the following provisions:

(1) Persons taking no active part in the hostilities, including members of armed forces who have laid down their arms and those placed *hors de combat* by sickness, wounds, detention, or any other cause, shall in all circumstances be treated humanely, without any adverse distinction founded on race, colour, religion or faith, sex, birth or wealth, or any other similar criteria.

To this end, the following acts are and shall remain prohibited at any time and in any place whatsoever with respect to the above-mentioned persons:

(a) violence to life and person, in particular murder of all kinds, mutilation, cruel treatment and torture;

(b) taking of hostages;

(c) outrages upon personal dignity, in particular humiliating and degrading treatment;

(d) the passing of sentences and the carrying out of executions without previous judgment pronounced by a regularly constituted court, affording all the judicial guarantees which are recognized as indispensable by civilized peoples.

(2) The wounded and sick shall be collected and cared for.

An impartial humanitarian body, such as the International Committee of the Red Cross, may offer its services to the Parties to the conflict.

The Parties to the conflict should further endeavour to bring into force, by means of special agreements, all or part of the other provisions of the present Convention.

The application of the preceding provisions shall not affect the legal status of the Parties to the conflict.

The quickly enacted 2006 Military Commissions Act also provided similar protections:

(c) Additional Prohibition on Cruel, Inhuman, or Degrading Treatment or Punishment—

(1) IN GENERAL—No individual in the custody or under the physical control of the United States Government, regardless of nationality or physical location, shall be subject to cruel, inhuman, or degrading treatment or punishment.

(2) CRUEL, INHUMAN, OR DEGRADING TREATMENT OR PUNISHMENT DEFINED—In this subsection, the term 'cruel, inhuman, or degrading treatment or punishment' means cruel, unusual, and inhumane treatment or punishment prohibited by the Fifth, Eighth, and Fourteenth Amendments to the Constitution of the United States, as defined in the United States Reservations, Declarations and Understandings to the United Nations Convention Against Torture and Other Forms of Cruel, Inhuman or Degrading Treatment or Punishment done at New York, December 10, 1984.

(3) COMPLIANCE—The President shall take action to ensure compliance with this subsection, including through the establishment of administrative rules and procedures.

Returning to the time period of 2002-2005, the reluctance to release the exact interrogation techniques early on centered on the fear that the release of such information would allow enemy forces to develop counter-intelligence techniques to frustrate American efforts to get meaningful intelligence. Consequently, U.S. officials remained silent about the techniques, telling the public that its agents were employing the full range of robust interrogation tactics to include offering various incentives such as money or engaging in trickery.

Perhaps the most well-known official source available to the public early on regarding the need for secrecy in the use of interrogations in the War on Terror was the Jacoby Declaration. The Jacoby Declaration consisted of a nine page sworn statement issued to the District Court for the Southern District of New York in the case of *Padilla v. Bush* by Vice Admiral Lowell E. Jacoby (USN), the Director of the DIA.

In a section of the declaration entitled "Interrogation Techniques," Jacoby stated that the "approach to interrogation is largely dependent upon creating an atmosphere of dependency and trust between the subject and the interrogator." Creating this atmosphere can take a prolonged period of time. Then, in a section entitled "Use of Interrogations in the War on Terrorism," Jacoby devoted several paragraphs describing asymmetric warfare and the unique threats posed by terrorists who "have also clearly demonstrated their willingness—and in fact have expressed their intent—to use any type of potential weapon, including weapons of mass destruction" against the United States. Still, Jacoby refused to provide any information as to the methods used by American interrogators. Jacoby stated only that the "United States is now engaged in a *robust* program of interrogating individuals who have been identified as enemy combatants in the War on Terrorism [emphasis added]." Then, in a last amplification he stated: "As detainees collectively increase their knowledge about United States detention facilities and *methods of interrogation*, the potential risk to national security increases *should those methods be released* [emphasis added]."

Suggestions by various ideologues and other "unnamed" government sources that American interrogators might be forced to engage in physical pressure, e.g., torture or ill-treatment, to get information from suspected terrorists surfaced almost immediately after the terror attacks of September

11, 2001. In October 21, 2001, a *Washington Post* article served as the information source of choice to those who accuse the United States of engaging in torture. The article quoted the perennial "unnamed" FBI agent as stating:

> We are known for humanitarian treatment, so basically we are stuck....Usually there is some incentive, some angle to play, what you can do for them. But it could get to that spot where we could go to pressure…where we don't have a choice, and we are probably getting there.

Then, in March of 2002, the *Washington Post* once again relied on "unnamed sources" to alert its readers that the United States government had turned over dozens of suspected terrorists "to countries, including Egypt and Jordan, whose intelligence services have close ties to the CIA and where they can be subjected to interrogation tactics—including torture and threats to their families—that are illegal in the United States." As previously noted, rendition is a common practice which is only improper under international law if, for instance, the United States knowingly delivers a suspect to a nation that it has substantial grounds to believe engages in "a consistent pattern of gross, flagrant or mass violations of human rights." While an "unnamed source" in a media article may view a particular country as a nation that satisfies this test, it is ultimately a question for the government of the United States and the international community to answer.

Without more evidence than that provided by unnamed sources, it is impossible to accurately gauge what interrogation methods are being used in a particular State. In addition, from a legal perspective, there is no international prohibition against rendering a suspected terrorist to a nation that engages in interrogation practices that would constitute ill-treatment. For example, assuming for the sake of argument that Jordan does use some amount of physical or physiological pressure in its interrogation practices, one would need to determine whether or not the type of pressure rises to the level of torture, or is ill-treatment only.

It was not until December 26, 2002, that the public was alerted to the concept of "stress and duress" tactics allegedly used by American interrogators. According to the initial story in the *Washington Post*, various unnamed government sources suggested that the United States was using a laundry list of questionable techniques to get uncooperative detainees housed outside the United States to talk. The article stated: "At times they [uncooperative detainees] are held in awkward, painful positions and deprived of sleep with a 24-hour bombardment of lights—subject to what are known as 'stress and duress'." Other examples of stress and duress listed were so-called "false flag" operations in which the detainee is deceived into believing he has been turned over to a "country with a reputation for brutality," or having female interrogators question the detainee, "a psychologically jarring experience for men reared in a conservative Muslim culture where women are never in control."

The article also alleged that when detainees were first apprehended, "MPs [military police] and U.S. Army Special Forces troops…[would] beat them [detainees] up and confine them in tiny rooms." To buttress this view, the article then quoted another unnamed American official as saying: "[O]ur guys may kick them around a little bit in the adrenaline of the immediate aftermath [of the arrest]."

Ultimately, if such stress and duress tactics failed to glean meaningful results, the article reported that the detainees were rendered to third countries where they could be subjected to mistreatment or "mind-altering drugs such as sodium pentothal." However, the *Washington Post* article piece placed a caveat on its claims about rendition practices by noting that the CIA's "Directorate of Operations instructions, drafted in cooperation with the general counsel, tells case officers in the field that they may not engage in, provide advice about or encourage the use of torture by cooperating intelligence services from other countries." As expected, with the publication of the stress and duress story, similar secondhand reports also found their way into the media, most of them parroting the mantra that America tortures detainees as an official policy.

Throughout the War on Terror, the Red Cross regularly criticized the United States for alleged violations of international law by conducting interrogations of non-uniformed combatants and terrorists taken into custody. The legal basis that the Red Cross asserted was Additional Protocol I to the Geneva Conventions of August 12, 1949, which would accord prisoner of war status to these people. The problem with this charge was that the United States has never ratified Protocol I. On the contrary, the United States specifically rejected Protocol I for the very reason that it bestowed a legal status on non-uniformed combatants. Thus, the idea that Protocol I is binding on the United States as a principal of "customary international law" is correct only in part. The United States is not bound by Protocol I in this regard and is perfectly within its legal rights to interrogate non-uniformed combatants; these individuals are not entitled to the protections given to prisoners of war. The Red Cross is unquestionably a valuable early warning system for any democracy that wants to respect the rule of law, but its credibility is weakened each time it uses the guise of Protocol I to criticize the United States.

7.6 DOD Interrogation Practices 2002-2005

With the breaking of the Abu Ghraib prison abuse story in mid 2004 the question of American interrogation techniques could no longer remain in the dark; the public could no longer be left to wonder whether the techniques used by the military were lawful or actually involved torture. The propaganda value of Abu Ghraib demanded transparency to combat the negative press. In June 2004 the government released a 10-centimeter pile of previously classified internal memos and documents from senior policymakers in the Bush Administration detailing the approved interrogation tactics for conducting interrogations of uncooperative detainees at Guantanamo Bay by the military. Much later, with the advent of the Obama Administration, the public was also given access to portions of the DOJ memorandums concerning the interrogation practices of the CIA.

The volume of information now available to the public makes it possible to set out a fairly detailed chronology of the what, when, where, and how of interrogation practices. The discussion is best divided between the DOD's military interrogation actions at Guantanamo Bay and the CIA's interrogation actions at undisclosed locations overseas (not Guantanamo Bay).

First, in terms of the military's interrogation practices, under the law of war the purpose of detaining enemy combatants is to ensure that they do not return to join enemy forces and, in this unique situation, to allow American officials the opportunity to gather any necessary intelligence about the terrorists' organizational infrastructure, financial network, communication system, weapon supply lines, and plans for future terror attacks. As is the practice in all wars, the purpose of detention is not to punish the enemy combatant, but to protect the host nation from future acts of violence by the enemy. In this light, over 450,000 German and Italian enemy combatants were held in the United States during World War II. They were not charged with crimes, afforded lawyers, or allowed access to U.S. courts to file habeas corpus petitions.

The precise status of enemy combatant is pivotal in determining what interrogation techniques can be used to gather information from the subject detainee. Article 17 of the Third Geneva Convention provides that prisoners of war are only required to give their "surname, first names and rank, date of birth, and army regimental, personal or serial number, or failing this, equivalent information." The prisoner of war is not required to give any further information upon questioning. To leave no doubt on this point, Article 17 goes on to provide the following:

> No physical or mental torture, nor any other form of coercion, may be inflicted on prisoners of war to secure from them information of any kind whatever. Prisoners of war who refuse to answer may not be *threatened, insulted, or exposed to any unpleasant or disadvantageous treatment of any kind* [emphasis added].

Certainly, if the full provisions of the Third Geneva Convention covered the detainees, American authorities would not be entitled to interrogate them or obtain additional information. Conversely, enemy combatants who are not prisoners of war do not fall under the full protections of the Third Geneva Convention and may therefore be questioned by American interrogators on additional topics of interest.

By far the group that has received the most attention consists of the almost 800 men once held at Guantanamo Bay, Cuba (GITMO), at a specially built facility named Camp Delta. As of 2020, the less than 40 detainees at GITMO continue to receive regular visits by ICRC, diplomats from their respective nations, military attorneys, and various other fact finding groups.

Again, the majority of the illegal enemy combatants were captured on the battlefields of Afghanistan. Although all of the detainees were said to be participants in the War on Terror, initially the Bush Administration did not recognize these detainees as eligible for prisoner of war status under the Third Geneva Convention, nor did the Bush Administration apply Common Article 3 of the Geneva Conventions. The reason that the Bush Administration did not apply the Third Geneva Convention was because both the Taliban fighters and the al-Qa'eda fighters failed to qualify as lawful enemy combatants under the applicable provisions of international law. Specifically, prisoner of war status is only conferred on persons who are "[m]embers of armed forces of a Party to the conflict" or "members of other militias and members of other volunteer corps, including those of organized resistance movements, belonging to a Party…provided that such…fulfill[s]" four specific conditions:

- That of being commanded by a person responsible for his subordinates;
- That of having a fixed distinctive sign recognizable at a distance;
- That of carrying arms openly; and
- That of conducting their operations in accordance with the laws and customs of war.

Despite the fact that the Third Geneva Convention was not applied to these enemy combatants, the Bush Administration pledged that all detainees were treated in accordance with the humanitarian concerns set out in the Geneva Conventions. Nevertheless, they were all subject to being interrogated.

A review of the 2004 memorandums show that the most severe technique that was approved by Secretary of Defense Rumsfeld for Guantanamo Bay detainees was the use of "mild, non-injurious physical contact—poking, grabbing, lightly shoving" against selected high-value detainees, like one Guantanamo detainee named al-Qahtani.

The documents reveal that on October 11, 2002, Major General Michael Dunleavy, the Joint Task Force Commander for Guantanamo Bay, submitted a request for approval to use non-standard interrogation techniques on three detainees held at Guantanamo Bay. The requested interrogation techniques were divided into three categories:

Category I:
1. Yelling at the detainee;
2. Deceiving the detainee by:
   a. Using multiple interrogators; or
   b. Posing as interrogators from a country with a reputation for harsh treatment of detainees;

Category II:
1. Placing the detainee in stress positions;
2. Using falsified documents or reports to deceive the detainee;
3. Placing the detainee in isolation;
4. Interrogating detainees in non-standard interrogation environments or booths;
5. Depriving detainee of light and auditory stimuli;
6. Hooding detainee during interrogation;
7. Interrogating detainee for twenty-hour sessions;
8. Removing all "comfort items" (including religious items);
9. Switching detainee from hot food to cold rations;
10. Removing all clothing;
11. Forced grooming (shaving facial hair);
12. Exploiting individual phobias (such as fear of dogs) to induce stress;

Category III:
1. Convincing the detainee that death or severe pain is imminent for him or his family;
2. Exposing the detainee to cold weather or water (with medical monitoring);
3. Water boarding;
4. Using light physical contact, such as grabbing, pushing, or poking with a finger.

On December 2, 2002, Rumsfeld authorized all Category I and II techniques, but only a single Category III approval was given for interrogators to use "mild, noninjurious physical contact" (grabbing or pushing). According to the released documents, some FBI agents who were cooperating with the military interrogators as well as other military personnel themselves objected to the approved techniques and voiced those concerns up their respective chains of command. Six weeks later, on January 15, 2003, Rumsfeld rescinded the approval of the use of all Category II techniques and the one Category III technique. In doing so, Rumsfeld ordered: "In all interrogations, you should continue the humane treatment of detainees, regardless of the type of interrogation technique employed." In April 2003, Rumsfeld issued a new set of directives that applied only to the detainees in Guantanamo Bay, Cuba. This memorandum set out dozens of interrogation techniques that essentially tracked the guidelines of then Army FM 34-52, Intelligence Interrogation.

In relation to "security detainees" in Iraq, the then head of U.S. forces, Lieutenant General Ricardo Sanchez, issued a one-page directive in October 2003, titled "Interrogation Rules of Engagement" which would be applicable to non-POWs. This directive allowed for practices, vetted by Army lawyers as lawful under the Fourth Geneva Convention and Common Article 3, that included silence, repetition of questioning, emotional love/hate techniques, and the use of fear (where the interrogator behaves in a heavy overpowering manner by yelling or throwing things).

In September 2006, the DOD issued its new military detainee and terror suspect treatment guidelines. The DOD Directive 2310.01E is entitled: The Department of Defense Detainee Program. In addition, Army Field Manual (FM) 2-22.3, Human Intelligence Collector Operations (September 2006), supersedes FM 34-52, Intelligence Interrogation. FM 2-22.3 absolutely prohibits the use of torture or physical stress techniques in conducting interrogation.

7.7 CIA Interrogation Policies 2002-2005

In announcing the new interrogation rules, President Bush also informed the public that 14 "high value" terror suspects had been transferred from undisclosed CIA locations overseas to GITMO. This speech was the first official acknowledgement of the existence of the previously secret CIA detainee program. President Bush said that the CIA program had been authorized by a secret presidential directive issued on September 17, 2001. Relating that the program was subject to internal legal review, the Bush Administration promoted the legal view that the CIA detainees were wartime detainees held under the law of war; international human rights law, which applies in peacetime, was not applicable. Believing that the CIA program had "saved lives," President Bush confirmed that with the transfer of the 14 there were "now no terrorists in the CIA program." Further, the Bush Administration denied that any of the CIA detainees were subjected to interrogation techniques that violated international or domestic law. The water boarding interrogation technique used on a handful of detainees in the CIA program was viewed as constituting a level of force that did not rise to the level of torture under the Torture Convention.

The clandestine "black-site" detention facilities were established by the CIA in order to interrogate suspected high value al-Qa'eda leaders. The interrogations were initially conducted jointly by the CIA and FBI. With the capture of senior al-Qa'eda leader Abu Zubaydah during a raid in Pakistan in late March 2002, the CIA determined that it needed permission to use more aggressive interrogation techniques. The CIA psychologists proposed 12 so-called "enhanced interrogation techniques" (EITs) which they modeled entirely from practices used in the U.S. military's Survival, Evasion, Resistance, and Escape (SERE) training program (except for the use of non-poisonous insects).

The SERE program is used to train pilots and special operations forces to withstand harsh and abusive treatment by the enemy should they be captured. Begun after the Korean War, tens of thousands of military personnel have gone through the program which subjects the participants to such things as stress positions, sleep deprivation, exposure to extreme cold or heat, and water boarding.

Understanding that the CIA would use the EITs on only senior members of al-Qa'eda who had knowledge of imminent terrorist threats against the United States, on August 1, 2002, the Office of the Legal Counsel (OLC), Department of Justice, issued two legal memorandums under the signature Jay S. Bybee, Assistant Attorney General, OLC. The classified version issued to the CIA, was entitled: Memorandum for John Rizzo, Acting General Council of the Central Intelligence Agency, Interrogation of al-Qa'eda Operative (classified Bybee memo). After reviewing the applicable international and domestic law to include statutes and case law, the classified Bybee memo concluded that "because the acts inflicting torture are extreme, there is sufficient range of acts that though they might constitute cruel, inhuman, or degrading treatment or punishment [ill-treatment] fail to rise to the level of torture." In addition, the classified Bybee memo concluded that the infliction of severe physical or mental pain or suffering must be the "defendant's precise objective." Thus, noting that the SERE techniques produced no prolonged mental harm that would violate the Torture Convention, the classified Bybee memo authorized the CIA to use 10 of the 12 proposed EITs. Each technique was carefully described in the legal memorandum, along with restrictions and safeguards which required, for instance, the presence of psychologists and medical personnel along with the interrogator. The approved techniques were:

(1) Attention grasp: The interrogator grasps the subject with both hands, with one hand on each side of the collar opening, in a controlled and quick motion, and draws the subject toward the interrogator.

(2) Walling: The subject is pulled forward and then quickly and firmly pushed into a flexible wall so that his shoulder blades hit the wall. His head and neck are supported with a rolled towel to prevent whiplash.

(3) Facial hold: The Interrogator holds the subject's head immobile by placing an open palm on either side of the subject's face, keeping fingertips well away from the eyes.

(4) Facial or insult slap: With fingers slightly spread apart, the interrogator's hand makes contact with the area between the tip of the subject's chin and the bottom of the corresponding earlobe.

(5) Cramped confinement: The subject is placed in a confined space, typically a small or large box, which is usually dark. Confinement In the smaller space lasts no more than two hours and in the larger space, up to 18 hours.

(6) Insects: A harmless insect is placed in the confinement box with the detainee.

(7) Wall standing: The subject may stand about four to five feet from a wall with his feet spread approximately to his shoulder width. His arms are stretched out in front of him and his fingers rest on a wall to support all of his body weight. The subject is not allowed to reposition his hands or feet.

(8) Stress positions: These positions may include having the detainee sit on the floor with his legs extended straight out in front of him with his arms raised above his head or kneeling on the floor while leaning back at a 45 degree angle.

(9) Sleep deprivation: The subject is prevented from sleeping, not to exceed 11 hours at a time.

(10) Waterboard: The subject is restrained on a bench with his feet elevated above his head. His head is immobilized and an interrogator places a cloth over his mouth and nose while pouring water onto a cloth. Airflow is restricted for 20 to 40 seconds; the technique produces the sensation of drowning and suffocation.

Later, other OLC legal memorandums were issued in 2005 and 2007. The 2005 so-called Bradbury legal memorandum superseded the classified Bybee memo, but confirmed the basic conclusions of the classified Bybee memo regarding the use of EITs. The Bradbury memo held that 13 EITs would not constitute torture: (1) dietary manipulation; (2) nudity; (3) attention grasp; (4) walling; (5) facial hold; (6) facial slap or insult slap; (7) abdominal slap; (8) cramped confinement; (9) wall standing; (10) stress positions; (11) water dousing; (12) sleep deprivation (more than 48 hours); and (13) water boarding.

Despite the many gross distortions which continue to circulate about the CIA program in general, and water boarding in particular (which was deemed to be the worst of the EITs), the water boarding approved EIT was only used on three of the high value detainees in CIA hands: Abu Zubaydah, Abd Al-Rahim Al-Nashiri (captured in November 2002), and Khalid Sheik Muhammed (captured in March 2003). Abu Zubaydah was waterboarded 83 times, the majority of which lasted less than ten seconds and Khalid Sheik Muhammed was waterboarded 180+ times. Apparently, however, there is evidence that some of the interrogators may have engaged in illegal conduct in their individual capacities. Allegations of verbal threats to Abu Zubaydah and pointing an unloaded pistol next to Al-Nashiri's head have surfaced and are being investigated by the Obama Administration. In any event, in the fall of 2005, as Congress was crafting the Detainee Treatment Act of 2005, the CIA removed water boarding from the list of EITs. No one has been waterboarded (with the exception of US military personnel) since 2005. Although the 2006 Military Commissions Act attempted to circumvent the ruling in *Hamdan* as applying to the CIA (by redefining certain abuses that could be considered to constitute a war crime under the War Crimes Act, 18 U.S.C. § 2441) President Obama's Executive Order 13491 issued in January 2009, directs the CIA and all federal agencies to proceed with interrogations "strictly in accord with the principles, processes, conditions, and limitations [FM 2-22.3] prescribed." Today there is no difference between what the military and other federal agencies can do in terms of conducting an interrogation.

In July 2009, the DOJ Office of Professional Responsibility (OPR) issued a report entitled: Investigation into the Office of Legal Counsel's Memoranda Concerning Issues Relating to the Central Intelligence Agency's Use of "Enhanced Interrogation Techniques" of Suspected Terrorists. The OPR report concluded that former OLC lawyers "John Yoo and Jay Bybee had engaged in professional misconduct by failing to provide 'thorough, candid, and objective' analysis in memoranda regarding the interrogation of detained terrorist suspects." The OPR indicated that it would refer its findings of misconduct to the State legal bar for disciplinary action. In January 2010, however, the DOJ Office of the Deputy Attorney General issued its own memorandum objecting to the findings of the OPR report and refused to "authorize OPR to refer its findings to the state [sic] bar disciplinary authorities in the jurisdictions where Yoo and Bybee are licensed." In short, the DOJ determined that Yoo and Bybee had not engaged in professional misconduct in advising the CIA on the legality of EITs based on existing law at the time.

In summary, given the following facts, it is clear that the CIA did not engage in unlawful interrogation practices during the time frame 2002-2005. First, existing international case law such as *Ireland* and *Public Committee* clearly set an extremely high bar for what would constitute torture. Even the worst of the CIA EITs, water boarding, is clearly not torture when measured against *Ireland*. Second, the techniques used by the CIA (with the exception of the harmless insect) are all used on American military personnel in SERE training courses. If the techniques were torture as claimed by some then the Torture Convention would demand that the SERE interrogators and those who approved the program be prosecuted. There is no exception in the Torture Convention for military "training."

7.8 The Ticking Time Bomb Scenario

Those associated with the art of interrogation know that the initial goal is to get the suspect to start talking and that the best way to get reliable and useful information is to treat the subject humanely; in other words, to not engage in torture or ill-treatment. In fact, when faced with torture, individuals will most likely say anything to stop the pain, making their statements sometimes questionable. According to a former Colonel in Army intelligence, "Anything you can do to disconnect someone is going to help...[b]ut it's a myth that torture is effective. The best way to win someone over is to treat them kindly." On the other hand, to say that torture never produces accurate information is simply naive. In fact, if the subject has information, he will at some point "break." Recognizing this reality, the DOD only requires American soldiers in the military's Code of Conduct to resist torture to the best of their ability. The fact is that torture does work on someone who has information.

Many legal scholars who understand the threat of al-Qa'eda-styled terrorism often paraphrase with approval former Supreme Court Justice Jackson's observation that "the Constitution is not a suicide pact." One issue that gains a tremendous amount of attention in this debate is how to deal with a suspected terrorist in a ticking time bomb scenario. Even noted civil rights advocates like Harvard law professor Laurence Tribe understand that the landscape has changed. After 9/11 he wrote: "The old adage that it is better to free 100 guilty men than to imprison one innocent describes a calculus that our Constitution—which is no suicide pact—does not impose on government when the 100 who are freed belong to terrorist cells that slaughter innocent civilians, and may well have access to chemical, biological, or nuclear weapons."

Different commentators have varying turns on the theme of the ticking time bomb, but it commonly goes something like this. Suppose a terrorist suspect is taken into custody in a major city and is found to be in possession of nuclear bomb-making materials and detailed maps of the downtown area. The terrorist blurts out to police that he is a member of al-Qa'eda and that a nuclear car bomb is on a timer set to detonate in ten hours (the time he had estimated he could safely get away from the blast). The suspect then demands a lawyer and refuses to answer any more questions. Of course, law enforcement may legitimately ignore his demands and conduct a reasonable interrogation as long as they do not engage in torture, ill-treatment or employ techniques that would shock the conscience. But what if reasonable interrogation techniques yield no information—the suspect refuses to talk? This Hobson's choice poses one of the strongest arguments for the use of non-lethal torture.

Given the premise of the ticking time bomb scenario, it is difficult to portray oneself as a centrist—either one uses whatever means necessary to get the information to stop the blast or one simply allows the slaughter of innocent civilians. Should a reasonable law enforcement officer with a spouse and children residing in the blast zone simply resign himself to the fact that they are all going to perish since it is unlawful under both international and domestic law to use torture? Or is it more likely that the law officer faced with this scenario would in fact engage in torture and then raise the defense of necessity at a subsequent criminal trial?

Alternatively, one might attempt to overcome the moral dilemma if the government created a justification defense which sanctioned the use of torture in special circumstances. In this manner one could eschew hypocrisy—the government would sanction the use of torture and the law officer would not face prosecution for his acts.

As noted in the *Public Committee* decision, the Supreme Court of Israel was clearly apprehensive about the sweeping scope of its decision, particularly in the context of a ticking time bomb terrorist. In rendering its decision, the Court strongly signaled that the Knesset (legislative branch of Israel) might find it efficacious at some point to "sanction physical means in interrogations…provided, of course, that a law infringing upon a suspect's liberty…is enacted for a proper purpose, and to an extent no greater than is required." To date, the Israeli legislature has not enacted any such legislation.

In addition, despite its absolute stance rejecting the legality of moderate physical pressure and the associated administrative directives promulgated to regulate the use of moderate physical pressure *vis-à-vis* the interrogation of terrorist suspects, the Supreme Court of Israel went on to recognize the defense of necessity if individual GSS investigators were charged with employing such prohibited interrogation techniques in the case of a ticking time bomb scenario. Citing Israeli penal law regarding necessity—engaging in illegal conduct in order to promote a greater good—the Court recognized that GSS interrogators would have the right to raise the defense of necessity in a subsequent prosecution. The Court stated that "[o]ur decision does not negate the possibility that the 'necessity' defense be available to GSS investigators [in ticking time bomb scenarios]…if criminal charges are brought against them, as per the Court's discretion." The Court said that "if a GSS investigator—who applied physical interrogation methods for the purpose of saving human life—is criminally indicted, the 'necessity' [defense] is likely open to him in the appropriate circumstances."

Indeed, the Court seemed to anticipate that any reasonable GSS investigator, charged with protecting innocent lives, would apply "physical interrogation methods for the purpose of saving human life" when confronted with a ticking time bomb terrorist. In other words, GSS investigators would use whatever means necessary to avert the explosion of the bomb. The Court noted, however, that the threat of the explosion must be a "concrete level of imminent danger:"

> [The] "necessity" exception is likely to arise in instances of "ticking time bombs," and that the immediate need...refers to the imminent nature of the act rather than that of the danger. Hence, the imminence criteria is satisfied even if the bomb is set to explode in a few days, or perhaps even after a few weeks, provided the danger is certain to materialize and there is no alternative means of preventing its materialization. In other words, there exists a concrete level of imminent danger of the explosion's occurrence.

The defense of necessity is a doctrine well-known to the common law. It is defined as "[a] justification defense for a person who acts in an emergency that he or she did not create and who commits a harm that is less severe than the harm that would have occurred but for the person's actions." Professor Wayne Lafave's criminal law text amplifies this definition by explaining that "the harm done is justified by the fact that the action taken either accomplished a greater good or prevented a greater harm."

The general understanding of the necessity defense at common law was that it was in response to circumstances emanating from the forces of nature and not from people. "With the defense of necessity, the traditional view has been that the pressure must come from the physical forces of nature (storms, privations) rather than from human beings." When the pressure is from human beings, the defense, if applicable, is duress, not necessity.

In the modern era, the distinction between the pressure coming from nature or human beings has merged. According to Lafave, defense of necessity extends to both instances.

> [T]he reason is of public policy: the law ought to promote the achievement of high values at the expense of lesser values, and sometimes the greater good for society will be accomplished by violating the literal language of the criminal law....The matter is often expressed in terms of choice of evils: when the pressure of circumstances presents one with a choice of evil, the law prefers that he avoid the greater evil by bringing about the lesser evil.

Still, the defense of necessity is not available to a defendant in situations where the legislature has previously made a determination of values. This concept is clearly stated in the Model Penal Code: "Neither the Code nor other law defining the offense provides exceptions or defenses dealing with the specific situation involved; and a legislative purpose to exclude the justification claimed does not otherwise plainly appear." For instance, a person may not take a human life in order to save himself.

It is no secret to those familiar with the debate on civil liberties in the War on Terror that Harvard Law School's Alan Dershowitz has publicly advocated a far more aggressive approach to dealing with such things as the ticking time bomb terrorist. Dershowitz opposes the use of a necessity defense because relying on a necessity defense allows for torture to be carried on "below the radar screen," which invites greater abuse by law enforcement agents. Without bantering words, Dershowitz acknowledges the utility of nonlethal torture to get life saving information from a ticking time bomb terrorist. To be sure, Dershowitz's views spawned a firestorm of debate, not because he has advocated something new, but because it was Alan Dershowitz, the well-known civil libertarian, who made the case for State approved torture.

According to Dershowitz, such instruments of non-lethal torture could include the use of "a sterilized needle inserted under the fingernails to produce unbearable pain without any threat to health or life." The authority to engage in non-lethal torture would come from a torture warrant issued by a judge. In this manner, Dershowitz argues that the process of torture is judicially sanctioned and the chances of abuse by individual investigators is thereby reduced. "I believe…that a formal requirement of a judicial warrant as a prerequisite to nonlethal torture would decrease the amount of physical violence directed against suspects."

Those who oppose the use of torture under any circumstance whatsoever, to include the ticking time bomb scenario, invariably attempt to change or avoid the premise. Those who flatly reject Dershowitz's proposal for judicial torture warrants for a ticking time bomb terrorist are prone to engage in avoidance. For example, a recent law review article noted that "[b]y expanding the narrow framework of Dershowitz's inquiry, it is possible to focus our debate on alternative means of maintaining national security that do not violate [the] human dignity [of the terrorist]." Of course, the only way to lessen the likelihood of a ticking time bomb scenario is to neutralize the bomb before the fuse is lit, i.e., increasing police powers to break up the terrorist organizations and to prevent the unthinkable from coming to fruition.

No one can disagree that the rule of law and democracy are cherished values that must be protected. However, Dershowitz counters that in time of war it is sometimes necessary to, as Abraham Lincoln advocated, suspend our liberties to protect our liberties. In fact, Lincoln denied habeas corpus and unilaterally jailed thousands of American citizens (in the North) who expressed dissent.

Interestingly, Dershowitz's argument would require lawyers to chart a legal course around the Fourth, Fifth, and Fourteenth Amendment protections of the United States Constitution, while simultaneously ignoring the binding obligations of the Torture Convention which clearly states in Article 2: "No exceptional circumstances whatsoever, whether a state of war or a threat of war, internal political instability or any other public emergency, may be invoked as a justification for torture."

Dershowitz also fails to consider the matter of war crimes in his argument. To add judicial torture warrants to the corpus of America's rule of law would not only make a mockery of the rule of law, it would subject the United States to allegations of international war crimes. As noted, all of the existing international laws relating to armed conflict—to include the Geneva Conventions, the Hague Conventions, and customary principles—are codified by the military in FM 27-10, Law of Land Warfare. Violations of the law of war are labeled as war crimes. FM 27-10, paragraph 499 defines the term war crime as a "technical expression for a violation of the law of war by a person or persons, military or civilian." War crimes are divided into simple breaches and grave breaches. Grave breaches are set out in the Geneva Conventions to include such acts as torture or inhuman treatment, including biological experiments, or willfully causing great suffering or serious injury to body or health. FM 27-10, paragraph 502 defines the following acts as "grave breaches" of the Geneva Convention of 1949 if committed against persons or property protected by the Conventions: willful killing, torture or inhuman treatment, including biological experiments, willfully causing great suffering or serious injury to body or health, and extensive destruction and appropriation of property, not justified by military necessity and carried out unlawfully and wantonly.

Each nation is under a strict legal obligation to search for all persons alleged to have committed war crimes and to investigate all allegations of war crimes. If a grave breach of the law of war is discovered, that nation has the obligation to either prosecute or extradite the accused offender. FM 6-27, paragraph 498 indicates that:

> [a]ny person, whether a member of the armed forces or a civilian, who commits an act which constitutes a crime under international law is responsible therefore and liable to punishment. Such offenses in connection with war comprise: a. Crimes against peace, b. Crimes against humanity, and c. War crimes.

The United States policy is that American soldiers accused of violations of the law of war will be prosecuted under the provisions of the Uniform Code of Military Justice (UCMJ) for the substantive offense. For example, killing unarmed civilians is a war crime and also a substantive crime of murder. A deliberate attack on noncombatant civilians clearly violates the codified and customary laws of war. Indeed, the law of war was designed to protect innocent civilians.

Acts of torture constitute a grave breach of the law of war and the United States has an obligation to investigate and, if allegations of torture are valid, to either prosecute or extradite the offender to a nation that desires to prosecute. There are no exceptions for a ticking time bomb terrorist. The al-Qa'eda are clearly illegal enemy combatants, but that does not provide the United States with a license to torture them.

It is easy to choose between a right and a wrong, but the ticking time bomb scenario forces one to choose between the lesser of two wrongs. Disregarding the legal issues associated with torturing a ticking time bomb terrorist, is it possible to morally justify the use of torture to extract information? Those who believe so point to the so-called utilitarian principle best developed by philosopher Jeremy Bentham. Under the concept of utilitarianism, the pain inflicted on the ticking time bomb terrorist by means of otherwise prohibited interrogation techniques is weighed against the potential pain and death that would be inflicted on the community. Accordingly, the utilitarian argument is cited with approval by those who believe that the community's welfare is of greater value than the welfare of the terrorist who seeks to destroy the community.

There are a great number of words in the English language to describe a person who not only does the *right thing* in a given situation, but performs that action in the *right way*. Such a person may be described as exhibiting virtue, integrity, honor, courage, etc. The formula of doing a right thing in a right way is an essential ingredient for the establishment and development of a just and democratic society based on the rule of law. Conversely, deviations from the formula are destructive to the individual and to society. For instance, I regularly inform my students that getting an "A" on a Civil Procedure exam in law school is a right thing, but cheating to accomplish this goal can only be characterized as a wrong way to achieve the "A." Thus, doing a right thing (getting an "A") must be done in a right way (by studying and not cheating) or the result is wrong.

In dealing with the ticking time bomb terrorist scenario, the right thing is simple enough to appreciate—law enforcement must get the information that could save the lives of thousands or, if the bomb is a weapon of mass destruction, tens of thousands. The more difficult part of the formula is the second half—getting the needed information in the right way.

Prior to *Public Committee*, the government of Israel had taken the unusual step of trying to regulate the use of torture if not by means of a judicial torture warrant, then by administrative rules. In short, the government directives had provided a justification defense to an interrogator who engaged in torture. This practice was struck down as unlawful. A similar move to regulate torture in the United States would certainly meet the same end—a democracy cannot sanction torture. Once it does, it has abandoned the moral high ground; it is no longer a democracy. Whether justification flows from the legislative, executive, or judicial branch, it is anathema to a freedom loving people.

If an interrogator engages in torture, he must be charged for his crimes. Drawn from the Israeli approach in *Public Committee*, a defense of necessity would require him to satisfy a four pronged test: (1) the investigator had reasonable grounds to believe that the suspect had direct knowledge which could be used to prevent the weapon from detonating; (2) that the weapon posed an imminent danger to human life; (3) that there existed no alternative means of preventing the weapon from exploding; and (4) that the investigator was acting to save human life. Accordingly, while there could very well exist an emergency ticking time bomb scenario in which torture of a particular terrorist is necessary, the interrogator must face criminal liability. To approach the issue in any other manner would send the wrong signal to friends and foe alike. Those who believe that the United States can defend freedom by subverting our own values are as misguided as those who demand that the government fight the War on Terror without altering civil liberties by jot or tittle. Torture is illegal and must remain on the books as such.

7.9 Abu Ghraib and the Search for the Smoking Gun

This chapter would not be complete without a section on the so-called Abu Ghraib scandal and the associated implications for the War on Terror. While the end to major combat operations was declared by President Bush on May 1, 2003, a new and deadly chapter in the Iraq War quickly took hold—coalition forces and Iraqi civilians were now targeted for murder by various groups of sectarian guerrilla fighters, common criminals and al-Qa'eda linked terrorists. Even the capture of the dictator Saddam Hussein on December 15, 2003, did not stem the growing volume of terrorist attacks.

The rising intensity of the insurgency in mid 2003 also mandated that the large number of detainees that were being apprehended had to be categorized and housed. As already detailed, the United States grouped the detainees into one of three categories: (1) Iraqi soldiers who qualified as prisoners of war (POWs) under the Geneva Conventions; (2) those suspected of having links to a variety of terrorist groups (to include Saddam loyalists and radical Islamic fundamentalists), called "security detainees;" and (3) common criminals.

Those in the first category were quickly processed and released back into Iraqi society within a few months. While most of the prisoners were treated in accordance with the protections of the Geneva Conventions, the U.S. military reported some incidents of physical abuse by American guards. The most common type of abuse seemed to occur at or near the point of capture and included physical assaults and petty larceny. In general terms, however, the vast majority of POWs were treated in accordance with international law protections. Most importantly, as POWs, this particular class of detainees was not required to give any further information upon additional questioning by American forces.

Those in the second category were held for indefinite periods of time pending interrogation and eventual transfer to the nascent Iraqi judicial system. The reason that these security detainees were not given the protections of the Third Geneva Convention was because they failed to qualify as lawful enemy combatants. Again, prisoner of war status is conferred only on those persons who are "[m]embers of armed forces of a Party to the conflict" or "members of other militias and members of other volunteer corps, including those of organized resistance movements, belonging to a Party...provided that such...fulfill[s]" four specific conditions: (a) being commanded by a person responsible for his subordinates; (b) having a fixed distinctive sign recognizable at a distance; (c) carrying arms openly; and (d) conducting their operations in accordance with the laws and customs of war.

Unless a detainee in the post major combat phase of the Iraq War met these requirements, he was not entitled to the status of prisoner of war but was rather a security detainee. At most, such an individual would be protected only by the Fourth Geneva Convention covering civilians held during the occupation and the humanitarian protections provided by Common Article 3 of the Geneva Conventions. Common Article 3 protects all unlawful combatants taken captive from "(a) violence to life and person, in particular murder of all kinds, mutilation, cruel treatment and torture; (b) taking hostages; [and] (c) outrages upon personal dignity, in particular humiliating and degrading treatment...." Essentially, the detainee must be treated humanely, but can be questioned to gain information.

The establishment of detention facilities to house the detainees was aggravated by the sheer number of detainees. This required the coalition to utilize prison structures that had been used in the Saddam era to include the infamous prison at Abu Ghraib, located about 20 miles west of Baghdad. Abu Ghraib was the largest U.S. run detention facility and, at a high point in the tempo of operations, housed up to 7,000 detainees in October 2003. It was a vast complex of six separate compounds on a 280 acre site circled by over 2 miles of fences and 24 guard towers. The Red Cross reported that they made regularly scheduled visits to a total of 14 U.S. run facilities to include the infamous Tier 1 (cellblock 1a), "a darkened, two-story isolation wing used for interrogations" and the site of the prisoner abuse at Abu Ghraib. During the visit to Tier 1 at Abu Ghraib, they reported that they did not notice anything "as bad as the abuses portrayed in the...photos." About 35 people were held in Tier 1 during the Red Cross visit.

The public was first shown the infamous photographs taken inside of the U.S. military run prison at Abu Ghraib in a CBS show called *60 Minutes II* which aired on April 28, 2004. The widely circulated photos showed a handful of U.S. military police soldiers engaged in a variety of abusive and sexually sadistic acts against mostly blindfolded Iraqi detainees. Among other things, the photos showed naked prisoners stacked in pyramids, connected by wires, on dog leashes, and threatened by dogs. In addition, a handful of U.S. military police charged in the abuse scandal had forced naked prisoners to simulate sex acts.

The chronology of how the Abu Ghraib abuse story was revealed began on January 13, 2004, when Army Specialist Joseph Darby, a military policeman at Abu Ghraib, gave a computer disc containing the abuse photos to a military investigator. On January 14, 2004, the Army immediately initiated a criminal investigation and the United States Central Command (the four-star combatant command located in Florida) informed the media in a press release on January 16, 2004, that it was investigating detainee abuse at an unspecified U.S. prison in Iraq. On February 23, 2004, the military informed the U.S. press that 17 Army personnel had been suspended of duty pending further criminal investigations about the detainee abuse. Then, on March 20, 2004, the military reported to the media that it had charged six soldiers with detainee abuse to include criminal charges of assault, cruelty, indecent acts, and mistreatment. Interestingly, however, the press did not fully respond to the growing story as the mere fact that soldiers were being punished for misconduct did not constitute news that was out of the ordinary—the military regularly punishes soldiers who violate the law. In fact, the media only became energized on April 28, 2004, when *60 Minutes II* aired the photos.

Pursuant to evidence of criminal misconduct contained in a U.S. Army Criminal Investigation Division (CID) Report, seven enlisted reserve soldiers, all from the 372nd Military Police Company, 320th Military Police Battalion, 800th Military Police Brigade, were charged with an assortment of violations of provisions of the UCMJ. The central figure in the scandal was a reservist Private First

Class (PFC) named Lynndie England who is known for poses in which "she pointed at the genitals of a naked detainee while a cigarette dangled from her lips" and "holding a [dog] leash around a naked prisoner's neck." The other soldiers were Specialist Charles Graner, Staff Sergeant Ivan Frederick, Sergeant Javal Davis, Specialist Jeremy Sivits, Specialist Sabrina Harman, and Specialist Megan Armbuhl. All of those charged were reservists and all worked the night shift at Tier 1 in Abu Ghraib, where the abuses took place in the last months of 2003.

The particulars relating to the Abu Ghraib abuse story are now well settled thanks to the CID's criminal investigation and a number of collateral administrative investigations. In chronological order they are: (1) the April 2004 Taguba Report, prepared by Major General Antonio Taguba; (2) the July 2004 Army Inspector General Report, prepared under Lieutenant General Paul Mikolashek; (3) the August 2004 Fay Report, prepared by Major General George Fay; and (4) the August 2004 Schlesinger Report, headed by the former Secretary of Defense in the Nixon administration, James Schlesinger. In addition, there are other related examinations to include: (1) Vice Admiral Albert Church, Navy Inspector General, looking into interrogation and detention rules in Iraq, Afghanistan and elsewhere; (2) Secretary of Defense Donald Rumsfeld, looking into all prisoner operations and interrogation procedures; (3) CID investigation, looking into prisoner deaths in Iraq and Afghanistan; and (4) Lieutenant General James Helmly, Chief of the Army Reserve, looking into Army Reserve training procedures with special attention to military police and military intelligence.

The overriding question regarding the prisoner abuse echoes the thoughts of Senator Lindsey Graham (R-S.C.), a member of the Armed Services Committee: "How could we let this prison melt down and become the worst excuse for a military organization I've seen in my life?" None of the reports found that there was an official policy—either written or oral—to torture or abuse prisoners. According to the Schlesinger Report, the most far reaching investigation to date and the one which the *Wall Street Journal* deemed the "definitive assessment of what went wrong," "no approved procedures called for or allowed the kinds of abuse that in fact occurred." In fact, the Schlesinger Report found "no evidence of a policy of abuse promulgated by senior officials or military authorities." In addition, none of the Reports cite any direct abuse of prisoners by officers or by superiors ordering subordinates to commit the abuses. In short, the Schlesinger Report concurs with all the Reports to date in finding that the individuals that conducted the sadistic abuse are personally responsible for their acts.

Nevertheless, taking a broader examination of what happened at Abu Ghraib, the Schlesinger Report did find fault with the senior levels of command; there were "fundamental failures throughout all levels of command, from the soldiers on the ground to [the United States] Central Command and to the Pentagon" that set the stage for the abuses to occur.

The Schlesinger Report agreed with the calls for disciplinary action in the Fay Report for a number of officers in the immediate tactical chain of command who knew, or should have known, about the abuses at Abu Ghraib. "The commanders of both brigades—800 Military Police Brigade Commander Janis Karpinski and Military Intelligence Brigade Commander Thomas Pappas—either knew, or should have known, abuses were taking place and taken measures to prevent them." Certainly, however, this would include not only Brigadier General Karpinski and Colonel Pappas, but those subordinate commanders and on down the chain of command to the battalion, company, and platoon level. The chaotic environment at the prison existed in large part due to the dereliction of tactical commanders on the ground at Abu Ghraib.

The Schlesinger Report and all other investigations found that the culpability of commanders rested at the tactical level. The Schlesinger Report found "no evidence that organizations above 800th MP

Brigade—or the 205 MI Brigade—level" were directly involved in the incidents at Abu Ghraib.

While all the Reports talked about a number of factors that contributed to an atmosphere that allowed the abuses at Abu Ghraib to occur, the Schlesinger Report did the best job of providing a clear summation. These factors included:

- A lack of planning for detainee operations—from the Pentagon to the commanders on the ground in Iraq—and an inability to react to the marked spike in the insurgency that occurred in the summer of 2003;
- A confusing chain of command at Abu Ghraib where a military intelligence officer, Colonel Pappas, was placed in command of military police units;
- Lack of equipment and troops at Abu Ghraib; and
- A failure of the immediate chain of command to supervise and train soldiers under their command.

Finally, the Schlesinger Report did an excellent job of placing the problem of detainee abuse in a wider "real world" perspective. Noting that the U.S. military has handled about 50,000 detainees from all theaters of conflict since the start of combat operations in Afghanistan in 2001, the Schlesinger Report then compared that figure with the number of reported allegations of abuse, including some deaths. With around 300 cases of abuse reported, the Schlesinger Report noted that about one-third of the allegations occurred at the "point of capture or [at a] tactical collection point." As of August 2004, about half of the 300 cases had been investigated with 66 substantiated cases.

At the end of the day, it is simply false that the American military engaged in command directed torture or ill-treatment at Abu Ghraib, particularly when it was the military itself that self-reported to the media the fact that individual soldiers were being investigated and punished in accordance with the rule of law for wartime abuses at the prison. Clearly, the best indicator that the senior leadership is not culpable (with the exception of the direct tactical chain of command for dereliction of duty) is found in its continuing commitment to criminally investigate and prosecute those soldiers accused of committing detainee abuses. Numerous soldiers have already been prosecuted and sentenced for their crimes, and criminal trials will continue for others.

When one considers that the number of detainees in the War on Terror—including Afghanistan, Iraq, and other operations—is well over 50,000, it is unrealistic to expect that abuses will not occur. Violations of rules occur in every human endeavor, to include war. In an interview with the *Wall Street Journal*, Mr. James Schlesinger correctly noted that the "behavior of our troops is so much better than it was in World War II." The so-called "bad apple" syndrome is in fact the primary causative issue at Abu Ghraib—a handful of closely knit reserve personnel engaged in acts of sadism as they worked the night shift from October to December of 2003.

It is equally true that the Abu Ghraib story has been devastating to the United States war effort. While each and every case of abuse is repulsive to American standards of decency and justice, the terrorists have certainly become "media-savvy" in their quest to parlay these individual cases into marketable propaganda. For example, many nations that are opposed to the United States are quick to exploit the individual cases of abuse at Abu Ghraib by painting the entire conduct of all American soldiers as immoral and illegal. Of course, Americans do not need to be told that the abuses are beyond the pale of conduct expected of its military. A CNN Gallup poll taken in May 2004 showed that three in four Americans agreed that the abuses at Abu Ghraib could not be justified.

The investigative reports have done a great service to the American people and the world by dispelling the shrill cries of those who blame a secret Pentagon "culture of permissiveness" for the abuses at Abu Ghraib. While the Schlesinger Report found institutional and even personal responsibility in the tactical chain of command for allowing conditions for abuse to occur at Abu Ghraib, the Report specifically found that "[n]o approved procedures called for or allowed the kinds of abuse that in fact occurred. There is no evidence of a policy of abuse promulgated by senior officials or military authorities." The investigative reports exonerate the military from any charges of a systemic use of abuse to gain intelligence.

The abuses at Abu Ghraib should not have happened. The damage to American credibility and the War on Terror is incalculable. In the long run, the fact that the military prosecuted the Abu Ghraib offenders speaks volumes to the world about the true character of the United States and its military. To its great credit, the senior military leadership certainly learned the lessons of My Lai. Understanding that the best approach to dealing with criminal events is to act with alacrity and transparency, the tragedy at Abu Ghraib by a few has been thoroughly investigated and justice has been handed out to the perpetrators and, as the process moves forward, it is hopeful that the sword of justice will turn to those in the tactical chain of command. Two quotes sum up the entire affair: Senator Ben Nighthorse Campbell: "I don't know how the hell these people got into our Army;" and Secretary of Defense Donald Rumsfeld: "I failed to identify the catastrophic damage that the allegations of abuse could do to our operations in the theater, to the safety of our troops in the field, to the cause to which we are committed."

7.10 The HIG

The 2017 case of *U.S. v Ahmed Salim Faraj Abu Khatallah*, provides an excellent opportunity to review what the current rule of law deems to be permissible in terms of so-called "dual interrogations" for certain "high value" terrorists arrested for federal crimes. The Islamist terrorist Ahmed Salim Faraj Abu Khatallah was charged with the murder of U.S. Ambassador Christopher Stevens and three other U.S. government employees in the September 11, 2012 terror attack in Benghazi, Libya. Khatallah was apprehended in Libya, placed on a Navy ship, and subjected to two different interrogations. The first interrogation of the arrested suspect was conducted by a special intelligence squad created under the Obama Administration called the High-Value Detainee Interrogation Group (HIG). The second interrogation of the terror suspect was conducted by FBI agents after he waived his *Miranda* rights [*Miranda v. Arizona*, 384 U.S. 436 (1966) holding that detained criminal suspects, prior to police questioning, must be informed of their constitutional right to an attorney and against self-incrimination].

Given the still-real need to gather actionable intelligence from terrorists, President Obama also established a special interagency task force to review the entire interrogation process. In August 2009, the task force recommended to the Obama Administration the creation of the HIG. Composed of experienced interrogators and support personnel from law enforcement, the Department of Defense, and the intelligence community, Obama's National Security Council authored the HIG's Charter in 2010. While much about the HIG is classified, including the Charter itself, we do know that the Obama-created HIG is authorized to employ non-coercive techniques to gather intelligence. The FBI states the following facts about the HIG:

The High-Value Detainee Interrogation Group (HIG) is a three-agency entity—FBI, Central Intelligence Agency (CIA), and the Department of Defense (DoD)—established in 2009 that brings together intelligence professionals from the U.S. Intelligence Community to conduct interrogations that strengthen national security and that are consistent with the rule of law. High-value targets are nominated by U.S. intelligence agencies and must be approved by appropriate partner (FBI, CIA, and DoD) agency leadership.

The director of the HIG is an FBI representative and is assisted by two deputies—one from the DoD and the other from the CIA. Full-time HIG members are augmented by part-time HIG-trained professionals from U.S. Intelligence Community agencies.

Though the HIG is administered by the FBI, it is a multiagency organization whose principal function is intelligence-gathering—not law enforcement—and it is subject to oversight through the National Security Council, Department of Justice, and Congress. However, the actions of HIG teams are carefully documented, evidence is preserved in the event of a criminal prosecution, and its members are prepared to testify in court if necessary.

The HIG deploys expert Mobile Interrogation Teams (MITs) to collect intelligence that will prevent terrorist attacks and protect national security. Since the HIG's creation, MITs have been deployed both within the United States and abroad. Deployment teams generally consist of a team leader, interrogators, analysts, subject matter experts, linguists, and other personnel as needed. HIG interrogators are chosen for—among other attributes—their extensive interviewing and interrogation experience and their willingness to adapt to evolving interrogation techniques based on the latest scientific research.

Again, HIG personnel may not engage in any unlawful interrogation practices. They use authorized, lawful, non-coercive techniques that are designed to elicit voluntary statements and that do not involve the use of force, threats, or promises. The unclassified parameters of the program are set out in the HIG's August 2016 Interrogation Best Practices Report, which summarizes best practices for terrorist interrogations. The HIG is instructed to focus specifically on "High-Value Individuals," which are defined as:

An individual who is assessed by the HIG to possess information about: terrorist threats to the United States or its allies; the location of high-value terrorism subjects, particularly the leadership of terrorist groups that pose a threat to the United States or its allies; strategic-level plans or intentions of any terrorist or insurgent entity directing operations against deployed U.S. or allied forces; or strategic level knowledge of the organization, structure, leadership and key operatives, financial support, and communications methods of designated foreign terrorist organizations.

The HIG has functioned in the context of both domestic and foreign jihadists including Faishal Shahzad (Times Square car bomber), Dzhokhar Tsarnaev (Boston Marathon Bomber suspect), Umm Sayyaf (wife of an ISIS militant killed in Syria), Ahmed Abu Khattallah (Benghazi terror suspect), and others. But Ahmed Abu Khattallah is only one of two arrested terrorists to face criminal charges in federal court for participation in the coordinated terror attacks on the U.S. Special Mission compound in Benghazi. On July 15, 2013, "a criminal complaint and arrest warrant were issued for him" and, on

June 15, 2014, Khattallah was arrested in Benghazi by a specially formed and trained capture team consisting of an FBI agent and seven Navy SEALs. The American arrest team took Khattallah to the USS *New York* off the coast of Libya to transport him to the U.S. where he was presented before a federal judge in Washington D.C.

While on board the USS *New York*, Khattallah was subjected to two separate types of interrogations. The HIG team conducted the first interrogation, which lasted five days. In accordance with the HIG Charter, interrogations were conducted humanely but without any *Miranda* warnings. The government's purpose in using the HIG was to obtain actionable intelligence and, therefore, did not require advising Khattallah of his *Miranda* rights. Nevertheless, the HIG questioning was preceded by reading Khattallah the provisions of Article III of the Geneva Conventions, which were also posted in writing on his cell wall.

After a break of two days, during which no interrogations took place, an entirely new team consisting solely of FBI agents conducted a second interrogation. This second interrogation also lasted five days and was for prosecutorial purposes. Each day, Khattallah was read his *Miranda* rights before questioning began.

On August 16, 2017, after conducting an eight-day evidentiary hearing to consider Khattallah's assertion that the dual interrogation process undermined the voluntariness of his *Miranda* waiver, federal district judge Christopher Cooper issued a detailed 59-page pre-trial ruling, rejecting the defense argument. Without suggesting which legal test was used in determining his decision on the lawfulness of the dual interrogation process, the court applied two different tests to evaluate the legality of dual interrogations in Khattallah's case. Both tests are found in *Missouri v Seibert*, the first in the *Seibert* Plurality Test and the second in Justice Kennedy's concurrence in *Seibert*.

The *Seibert* Plurality Test is one of effectiveness – "whether it would be reasonable to find that in these circumstances the [*Miranda*] warnings could function 'effectively' as *Miranda* requires." The factors considered in this effectiveness evaluation were purely objective in nature and included:

> The completeness and detail of the questions and answers in the first round of interrogation [by the HIG], the overlapping content of the two statements [one given to the HIG and the other to FBI agents], the timing and setting of the first and the second, the continuity of police personnel, and the degree to which the interrogator's questions treated the second round as continuous with the first.

Based on the *Seibert* Plurality Test, the court easily concluded that the HIG intelligence-based interrogation was much broader than the second FBI *Miranda* interrogation, which focused on Khatallah's involvement in the Benghazi attack. The court also found that there was a significant break between the two types of interrogations where "Khatallah had two days entirely free of interviews, and during that break, he began receiving an extra daily meal and more regular shower privileges." Finally, the court noted that, before the second *Miranda* interrogation, the FBI agents made it clear to Khatallah that they were conducting a different and separate interrogation centered on intelligence-gathering. Moreover, "[t]he FBI agents also did not reference any information from the prior interviews, nor could they have, as they did not know what was discussed." After considering these factors, the court rejected Khatallah's argument that the dual interrogations violated his rights based on the *Seibert* Plurality Test.

Similarly, Justice Kennedy's test, which focused on the actual intent of the HIG interrogation, was also satisfied.

When an interrogator uses [a] deliberate, two-step strategy, predicated upon violating *Miranda* during an extended interview, postwarning statements that are related to the substance of prewarning statements must be excluded absent specific, curative steps.

The court also cited numerous judicial precedents that focused on several factors in determining "deliberateness"—such as overlapping content, continuity of interrogators, and the completeness of any prewarning interrogations. Applying these factors, the court found the government did not violate *Miranda* with deliberate intent. Indeed, from beginning to end, Khatallah was viewed as an international terrorist during the first HIG interrogation:

The interrogation plan was thus intended to optimize the amount of intelligence obtained from Abu Khatallah, and the intelligence officers were following orders from above … on how to achieve this goal.

Finally, the intelligence-gathering purpose was demonstrated in the information yielded from the interviews, which was logged by reports and daily summaries that were distributed to the intelligence community. The purpose, therefore, of the first HIG interrogation was to protect national security and not to undermine *Miranda*.

The use of the dual interrogation process did not undermine the voluntariness of Khatallah's *Miranda* waiver. Khatallah's HIG interrogation was properly performed and perfectly executed. In fact, the way in which the HIG interrogation was conducted *vis a vis* Khatallah represents the gold standard for how the HIG process should function.

In no way was the second FBI interrogation, which was properly conducted after waiting two full days and obtaining written and verbal waivers of Khatallah's *Miranda* rights, tainted by the HIG interrogation. Focused entirely on the Benghazi attack, the second interrogation was intended to obtain incriminating statements that could be used to prosecute Khattallah to the full extent of U.S. domestic law.

7.11 Conclusion

The story of "Half-Dead Bob" reported by *U.S. News and World Report* typifies the al-Qa'eda mindset while illustrating the American policy of humane treatment of detainees in accordance with the principles of the Geneva Conventions. An Arab captured on the battlefield of Afghanistan was nicknamed "Half-Dead Bob" by the Americans when he arrived at Guantanamo Bay. His nickname derived from the fact that he came to the detention center weighing 66 pounds, suffering from tuberculosis, shrapnel wounds, and having only one lung. The article states:

Army Maj. Gen. [Major General] Michael Dunlavey vividly remembers his first encounter with "Bob." Dunlavey ran interrogations at the base until November of last year. By the time they met, Bob was making a rapid recovery. He had put on 50 pounds and, sitting across a table from Dunlavey, he thanked him for the food and medical treatment. "General, you are probably a good Christian," Dunlavey recalls him saying. "And you are probably a good man. But, if I ever get free, I will kill you."

In the early years following 9/11, weighing the credibility of charges that the United States engaged in torture or ill-treatment as a standard practice was difficult at best. On the one hand, suggestions of torture generally came from media reports based on unnamed sources and anecdotal evidence. On the other hand, the government's penchant for secrecy regarding interrogation tactics made it next to impossible to make an independent assessment. Today, it is now clear that the United States did not engage in a systemic command directed interrogation regime that violated international or domestic law. In tandem with the June 2004 document release, President Bush declared, "Look, let me make very clear the position of my government and our country. We do not condone torture. I have never ordered torture. The values of this country are such that torture is not a part of our soul and being."

Again, apart from the moral argument and speaking strictly from a legal perspective, the United States cannot engage in torture. This is in violation of the Torture Convention and is penalized under domestic law. This is the baseline legal consideration. Following 9/11 both the military and CIA employed tactics that entered an ambiguous legal zone from 2002-2005. As foreboding as some of the outlined techniques may have appeared, there were many techniques that involved acts which were clearly permissible under any analysis. For example, one would be hard pressed to argue that the reported use of female interrogators, trickery, or a day long interrogation session would have ever constituted a prima facie case of even ill-treatment as some have suggested. Further, one could not automatically conclude that the use of awkward positioning of a particular detainee violated legal norms.

Accordingly, from 2002-2005 top legal advisors concluded that the United States could legitimately engage in interrogation practices that did not rise to the level of torture. By late 2005, however, the law quickly changed and continued to the point of absurdity where interrogators today may essentially not question a detainee without the express permission of the detainee. In fact, at Guantanamo Bay, it is forbidden for an American soldier who is not a Muslim to hand any religious object to a detainee as this would be "degrading" and in violation of Common Article 3! In short, our interrogation programs are now driven by "political correctness."

A factor that lends a tremendous amount of credibility to the government's contention that it abides by the international law prohibiting torture is the military's continuing commitment to criminally investigate and prosecute those soldiers accused of torture or ill-treatment. From the beginning of the War on Terror, the United States has responded well to verifiable instances of criminal activity that could be even remotely interpreted as torture or ill-treatment with relentless criminal investigation, prosecution, and punishment. For instance, a number of convictions have been handed down in a variety of cases as a result of the Army's criminal investigations. Indeed, if the government is sincere about prohibiting torture and ill-treatment, one would certainly expect that those who engaged in such illegal acts would be investigated and punished to the full extent of the law. The sincerity of the United States to reject the practice of illegal interrogations is further boosted by the fact that the initial stories concerning abuse are generally made by military officials. Again, the initial story about the prisoner abuse at Abu Ghraib was by the military, not the media. The media simply paid no attention to the March 2004 self reported information that several soldiers were going to be punished under UCMJ until a media source was given the photographs in April of 2004. The military's prompt and thorough investigation of the Abu Ghraib scandal and the transparency of the trials of the soldiers who were involved in these atrocities should reassure observers that the military command structure will not allow torture or ill-treatment tactics to become institutionalized.

Of course, to the naive the most direct source of information on torture would obviously come from those detainees who claim to have been tortured by the Americans. Consequently, as small groups of detainees are released from custody, Western reporters have attempted to glean first hand testimony as to the issue of torture. As one would expect from the mouths of ruthless terrorists devoted to a

Nazi-like ideology of hate (if one can murder innocent civilians, one can certainly lie), many of these newly released members of the Taliban and al-Qa'eda alleged that they were horribly tortured by their American captors.

Unexpectedly, others in the same group are sometimes quite open in proclaiming that all the detainees were treated well and not tortured. For instance, in a group of 27 detainees released from Guantanamo Bay in July 2003, 16 Afghans were interviewed by *Associated Press* correspondents as they were transferred to a Red Cross bus in Afghanistan. Those who alleged they were tortured complained in general terms of "cold rooms," "crowded rooms" and "beatings." Only one in the group, Abdul Rahman, specifically alleged that he had been "badly punished 107 times," and had been chained and beaten with "a metal rod on his legs and back." Interestingly, when pressed by reporters to show any scars or evidence left by the torture, Rahman "refused to show scars that may have resulted from any abuse."

In contrast, another detainee in the group, Nate Gul, told reporters that none of the detainees were beaten during interrogation: "They didn't beat us during the interrogation. They wrote down anything we said. They interrogated me about 30 to 40 times." In fact, as terrorist expert Mark Bowden revealed in the following comments from two former Pakistani detainees at Guantanamo, Americans do not engage in abuse as a fixed policy:

> Shah Muhammad and Sahibzada Osman Ali told me that except for some roughing up immediately after they were captured they were not badly treated at Camp X-Ray. They both felt bored, lonely, frustrated, angry, and helpless (enough for Shah Muhammad to attempt suicide), but neither believed that he would be harmed by his American captors, and both regarded the extreme precautions (shackles, handcuffs, hoods) that so outraged the rest of the world as comical.

At the end of the day, the reasonable observer must conclude that allegations that the United States condones and uses torture and ill-treatment as interrogation tools are vastly overstated and often simply taken for granted even by those who should know better. For instance, in his book, *The Case for Israel*, Dershowitz charged that the United States engages in "modified forms of torture that include physical and psychological components."

The purpose of detainee interrogation is to glean as much intelligence as possible from individuals who have information associated with the al-Qa'eda terrorist network and all associated terror networks. The goal is to apprehend as many of the terrorists as possible and to prevent future acts of terror on our people with particular concern for the likelihood that our enemies will surely use weapons of mass destruction against us. To date, interrogations have yielded much valuable information. According to the Jacoby Declaration the United States thwarted over 100 terrorist attacks worldwide based on information provided in part from detainee interrogations conducted in 2002. Hopefully, subsequent administrations will release similar reports showing how many lives were saved because of the CIA interrogation program.

One matter is fundamentally certain: if al-Qa'eda-styled terrorism is to be kept at bay, the United States must rely on detainee interrogation as an integral antiterrorist tool. The need for the interrogator to get information to protect the lives of innocents is a legitimate and perfectly lawful exercise. By its very nature, even the most reasonable interrogation places the detainee in emotional duress and causes stress to his being—both physical and mental. Still, a reasonable interrogation must necessarily be free of torture or ill-treatment.

Those who regularly claim that the United States oversteps the line regarding interrogation techniques tend to invoke the worn slippery slope argument, but that does not mean the potential for abuse does not exist. The old saw attributed to Lord Acton that "power tends to corrupt" has great validity.

7.12 Questions for Discussion

1. *Is it wise to advocate the use of an advance judicial approval for nonlethal torture?* Alan Dershowitz, WHY TERRORISM WORKS: UNDERSTANDING THE THREAT, RESPONDING TO THE CHALLENGE 141, 148 (2002). Dershowitz writes: "When I respond by describing the sterilized needle being shoved under the fingernails, the reaction is visceral and often visible—a shudder coupled with a facial gesture of disgust."

2. *Do we need rules?* In a FOX NEWS channel interview on *DaySide with Linda Vestor* (Oct. 31, 2003), Professor Addicott supported the pending criminal charges against an Army Lieutenant Colonel charged with assault in the interrogation of an Iraqi detainee. The Colonel allegedly threatened the Iraqi detainee with a pistol to get information about a future ambush of American soldiers. The live audience was largely opposed to the military's criminal investigation of the officer and displayed displeasure with the author's legal support for the referral of courts martial charges. *See also* Rowan Scarborough, *Colonel in Iraq Refuses to Resign*, WASH. TIMES, Oct. 31, 2003, at A3. Why?

3. *Does politics trump reason?* Professor Addicott provided oral and written testimony before the Senate Committee on the Judiciary, Subcommittee on Administrative Oversight and the Courts hearing entitled: "*What Went Wrong Torture and the Office of the Legal Counsel in the Bush Administration*," Washington, DC. The Democrat Senators used the 1983 case of *U.S. v. Lee* (744 F.2d 1124 (5th Cir. 1984) to conclude that the CIA's use of the waterboard was torture. While the *Lee* case used the term "water torture" as one of the things that four Texas police officers did to obtain confessions from prisoners, the court never described the technique. In turn, the Democrat Senators used the fact that several Japanese soldiers were convicted by American war crimes trials after World War II for engaging in "water torture" of American POWs. They failed, of course, to mention that the Japanese technique caused either death or unconsciousness when used and was nothing like the CIA technique. Professor Addicott was the only witness called to testify that defended the CIA's program. The text can be viewed in entirety at: http://jurist.law. pitt.edu/paperchase/2009/05/bush-era-interrogation-techniques.php.

4. *Releasing enemy combatants.* What dangers face a nation if it releases enemy combatants now that the War on Terror is essentially over? Following the end of WW II, the United States and its allies continued to detain German POWs, not releasing some until 1947. American news media have confirmed U.S. official findings that some detainees released from GITMO returned to Afghanistan and Pakistan in order to rejoin their comrades in fighting the United States and its allies. *See* John Mintz, *Released Detainees Rejoining the Fight*, WASH. POST, Oct. 22, 2004 at A01.

Selected Bibliography

42 U.S.C. § 1983.

> Every person who, under color of any statute, ordinance, regulation, custom, or usage, of an State or Territory or the District of Columbia, subjects or causes to be subjected, any citizen of the United States or other person within the jurisdiction thereof to the deprivation of any rights, privileges, or immunities secured by the Constitution and laws, shall be liable to the party injured in an action at law, suit in equity, or other proper proceeding for redress, except that in any action brought against a judicial officer for an act or omission taken in such officer's judicial capacity, injunctive relief shall not be granted unless a declaratory decree was violated or declaratory relief was unavailable.

Balz, Dan. *Durbin Defends Guantanamo Comments*, WASH. POST, June 17, 2005, at A11 (discussing the reactions of the White House and other politicians to Illinois Senator Richard J. Durbin's speech on the Senate floor, comparing interrogation procedures and conditions for detainees at Guantanamo Bay to those of Nazi concentration camps and Soviet gulags).

Bowden, Mark. *The Dark Art of Interrogation*, ATLANTIC MONTHLY, Oct. 2003, at 76.

Cohn, Marjorie. *Dropping the Ball on Torture: The U.S. Supreme Court Ruling in Chavez v. Martinez*, June 10, 2003, available at http://jurist.law.pitt.edu/forum/forumnew113.php.

Commission of Inquiry Into the Methods of Investigation of the General Security Service Regarding Hostile Terrorist Activity, reprinted in 23 ISR. L. R. 146 (1989).

Cooperman, Alan. *CIA Interrogation Under Fire; Human Rights Group Say Techniques Could Be Torture*, WASH. POST, Dec. 28, 2002, at A9 (detailing Human Rights Watch's accusations that the United States violated international law by torturing detainees and turning detainees over to states that engaged in torture).

Dershowitz, Alan. THE CASE FOR ISRAEL, 2004.

Dershowitz, Alan. WHY TERRORISM WORKS: UNDERSTANDING THE THREAT, RESPONDING TO THE CHALLENGE, 2002.

Gellman, Barton, and Dana Priest. *U.S. Decries Abuse But Defends Interrogations; 'Stress and Duress' Tactics Used On Terrorism Suspects Held in Secret Overseas Facilities*, WASH. POST, Dec. 26, 2002, at A1.

Langbein, John H. TORTURE AND THE LAW OF PROOF, 1987.

Schofield, Phillip. FIRST PRINCIPLES PREPARATORY TO CONSTITUTIONAL CODE: COLLECTED WORKS OF JEREMY BENTHAM, 1989.

Chapter 8

Cyber Warfare

We have learned from the tragedy of September 11 that our enemies will increasingly strike where they believe we are vulnerable...our cyberspace infrastructure is ripe for attack today.

—Senator Joseph Lieberman

While many trace the beginning of the War on Terror to September 11, 2001, it is now clear to all that the United States has been a primary target for terrorist attacks by radical Islamic terrorist groups for many years. Unfortunately, in hindsight, it is equally apparent that the United States was not adequately prepared to defend the homeland from the innovative al-Qa'eda terror attacks of September 11, 2001. The 9/11 Commission described the lack of preparedness of American intelligence and law enforcement agencies as a "failure of imagination." The government simply did not take seriously the possibility of terrorists using commercial airlines as precision weapons to attack buildings. The failure to appreciate the sophistication of the al-Qa'eda terrorist network opened the door for devastating attacks. Consequently, the United States was caught completely by surprise, resulting in the loss of 3,000 lives and billions of dollars in property loss.

Since the attacks of September 11, 2001, the government has crafted a variety of robust antiterrorism responses designed to disrupt terrorist networks and lessen the probability of future al-Qa'eda-styled terrorist attacks. Trying to anticipate emerging threats, these responses include the passage of the National Strategy to Secure Cyberspace, the National Strategy for the Physical Protection of Critical Infrastructure and Key Assets and the passage of the USA PATRIOT Act. Without question, shifting the tactical focus from punishing those individuals, organizations, or nations who commit terrorist crimes or engage in aggression to new broad methodologies designed to thwart such criminal acts in the first place has caused "a sea of change" in how the government approaches terrorism prevention.

Nevertheless, a new and deadly threat called cyber warfare is now emerging that may, as many commentators predict, catch the United States totally off guard. The same failure of recognition and lack of awareness prior to the terrorist air attacks of September 11, 2001, might be mimicking itself in the cyber world, and the attacks could prove to be more crippling and deadly than anything imaginable.

Fortunately, some in the government have recognized that if portions of our physical world could be destroyed as it was in the attacks of 9/11, a *fortiori*, our cyber world, which regulates all aspects of modern society, is an extremely vulnerable sector of our society, ripe for attack by a hostile nation (or even a sophisticated terror group).

Until the April-May 2007 coordinated cyber attacks which shut down the entire nation of Estonia, the full destructive potential of cyber warfare was something that the world had not adequately appreciated. As stated, while the major concern rests with the use of cyber weapons from a hostile nation, when one considers that terrorist organizations have been using computers, e-mail, and encryption to support and finance their organizations for years, it is only logical to conclude that they are fully aware that cyber offers a low cost method of inflicting major damage that is very difficult to trace.

While the line between cyber disruption and cyber warfare is not exact, ultimately, the real issue is one of cybersecurity. Does a sufficient cybersecurity framework exist that can adequately protect cyberspace and the information it contains, processes, and transmits? While the government has embarked on a variety of initiatives with private and public entities to protect against the threat of cyberterrorism, a growing number of legal and policy issues remain unanswered. The purpose of this chapter is to provide a basic framework for understanding the threat of cyber attacks and to explore the current state of preparedness from government and private industry perspectives to adequately respond to all forms of cyber threats to include cyber warfare.

8.1 Defining Cyber Terms

The modern world we have created is totally dependent on the workings of the Internet, computer databases and software of the cyber world. Without question, the cyber realm is fully incorporated into our everyday lives and touches almost everything we do or think. Apart from serving as a fantastic communication medium, the cyber world regulates all aspects of our infrastructure to include water, electricity, banking, transportation, technology, agriculture, medical, nuclear facilities, waste management, government services, etc. This fact has not only spawned the era of cyber crime, costing billions of dollars a year, but it has also given rise to the specter of cyberterrorism.

Dozens of new and unfamiliar terms associated with cyberspace have now entered the lexicon. Accordingly, before one can fully discuss the dangers associated with cyberterrorism, certain foundational terms require definition.

Cyberspace. The term cyberspace has many connotations and is used in a variety of contexts. Synonyms include the terms virtual space and cyber world (sometimes spelled cyberworld). In common understanding cyberspace refers to the entire function of computer-centric information technology—hardware and software—as it is created, stored and transmitted in the non-physical and physical terrain. A 2005 Congressional Research Service Report (CRS) (Creating a National Framework for Cybersecurity: An Analysis of Issues and Options) refers to cyberspace as "the combination of the virtual structure, the physical components that support it, the information it contains, and the flow of that information within it." The 2008 Department of Defense Dictionary of Military and Associated Terms defines cyberspace as: "A global domain within the information environment consisting of the interdependent network of information technology infrastructures, including the Internet, telecommunications networks, computer systems, and embedded processors and controllers." As a global phenomenon, cyberspace is largely controlled by private companies.

Cyberterrorism. Similar to the problem of obtaining universal agreement on defining the term space there is no generally accepted definition for cyberterrorism (sometimes spelled cyber terrorism). All intentional attacks on a computer or computer network involve actions that are meant to disrupt, destroy, or deny information. These attacks may be motivated by monetary gain, vandalism, terrorism, or as acts of war. Thus, most cyber attacks may be categorized as cyber crimes, but not all cyber attacks are deemed to be an act of cyberterrorism or war. Clearly, the key difference between cyber crime and cyberterrorism is the concept of *terror*. If a universal definition of the term terrorism does not exist, one can at least list four key characteristics of terrorism that better reflect the nature of the activity:

1. The illegal use of violence directed at civilians to produce fear in a target group.
2. The continuing threat of additional future acts of violence.
3. A predominately political or ideological character of the unlawful act.
4. The desire to mobilize or immobilize a given target group.

Combining these four key characteristics, then Secretary General of the United Nations, Kofi Annan, offered a succinct 2005 definition for terrorism:

[A]ny action constitutes terrorism if it is intended to cause death or serious bodily harm to civilians or non-combatants, with the purpose of intimidating a population or compelling a Government or an international organization to do or abstain from doing any act.

Adopting the general definitional theme of terrorism set out above, cyberterrorism is the improper use of various computing technology to engage in terrorist activity. Since the terror motivated cyber attack would most likely be against the critical infrastructure of a nation to intimidate or coerce another (usually a nation) in furtherance of specific political objectives, one commentator has defined cyberterrorism as "the premeditated, politically motivated attack against information, computer systems, computer programs, and data which results in violence against non combatant targets by sub-national groups or clandestine agents." On the other hand, some commentators like Rollins and Wilson contend that the use of the term cyberterrorism to describe an attack on the critical infrastructure is inappropriate "because a widespread cyber attack may simply produce annoyances, not terror, as would a bomb, or other chemical, biological, radiological, or nuclear explosive (CBRN) weapon."

Nevertheless, given the nation's complete dependency on cyberspace, if a cyber attack caused widespread damage to computer networks associated with the critical infrastructure, the level of fear from the resulting economic disaster and/or civilian fatalities would easily qualify as terrorism and perhaps as an act of war. Certainly the digital fears that emerged from the month-long denial of service (DDoS) cyber attack on the small Baltic country of Estonia (orchestrated from Russian sources apparently in response to the removal of a bronze statue of a World War II era Soviet soldier from a park) would qualify as cyberterrorism and perhaps, as some argued, as an act of war. The Estonian cyber attacks resulted in a digital infrastructure disaster as websites for government officials, government agencies, daily newspapers, and Estonia's biggest banks were overwhelmed and shut down due to the cyber onslaught of "unknown" digital information attacks.

Perhaps a more useful way to encapsulate the term cyberterrorism can be found in a 2005 CRS Report where the authors present cyberterrorism in two related categories:

- Effects-based: Cyberterrorism exists when computer attacks result in effects that are disruptive enough to generate fear comparable to a traditional act of terrorism, even if done by criminals [as opposed to terrorists].
- Intent-based: Cyberterrorism exists when unlawful or politically motivated computer attacks are done to intimidate or coerce a government or people to further a political objective, or to cause grave harm or severe economic damage.

Critical Infrastructure. The predominate concern that most drives the discussion of cyberterrorism is that a cyber attack will target one or more of the nation's critical infrastructures. The term critical infrastructure is defined with more or less uniformity in a variety of documents and laws. The 2003 National Strategy for the Physical Protection of Critical Infrastructure and Key Assets provides a detailed list of assets of national importance and critical infrastructure to include: information technology; telecommunications; chemicals; transportation; emergency services; postal and shipping services; agriculture and food; public health and healthcare; drinking water/water treatment; energy; banking and finance; national monuments and icons; defense industrial base; key industry/technology sites; and large gathering sites. The Department of Homeland Security (DHS) lists five general types of critical infrastructure:

(1) production industries: energy, chemical, defense industrial base;
(2) service industries: banking and finance, transportation, postal and shipping;
(3) sustenance and health: agriculture, food, water, public health;
(4) federal and state: government, emergency services;
(5) Information Technology (IT) and cyber: information and telecommunications.

Section 1016(b)(2) of the Critical Infrastructures Protection Act (CIPA) of 2001 specifically identifies as critical infrastructures "telecommunications, energy, financial services, water, and transportation sectors," all of which have not only physical components, but cyber components as well. In addition, section 1016(e) of CIPA expands the concept of critical infrastructure to mean all "systems and assets, whether physical or virtual, so vital to the United States that the incapacity or destruction of such systems and assets would have a debilitating impact on security, national economic security, national public health or safety, or any combination of those matters." Both the Uniting and Strengthening America by Providing Appropriate Tools Required to Intercept and Obstruct Terrorism Act of 2001 (USA PATRIOT Act) (renewed in 2006) and the Homeland Security Act of 2002 adopt the same definition set out below:

SEC. 1016. CRITICAL INFRASTRUCTURES PROTECTION

(a) SHORT TITLE.--This section may be cited as the "Critical Infrastructures Protection Act of 2001."

(b) FINDINGS.--Congress makes the following findings:

(1) The information revolution has transformed the conduct of business and the operations of government as well as the infrastructure relied upon for the defense and national security of the United States.

(2) Private business, government, and the national security apparatus increasingly depend on an interdependent network of critical physical and information infrastructures, including telecommunications, energy, financial services, water, and transportation sectors.

(3) A continuous national effort is required to ensure the reliable provision of cyber and physical infrastructure services critical to maintaining the national defense, continuity of government, economic prosperity, and quality of life in the United States.

(4) This national effort requires extensive modeling and analytic capabilities for purposes of evaluating appropriate mechanisms to ensure the stability of these complex and interdependent systems, and to underpin policy recommendations, so as to achieve the continuous viability and adequate protection of the critical infrastructure of the Nation.

(c) POLICY OF THE UNITED STATES.—It is the policy of the United States—

(1) that any physical or virtual disruption of the operation of the critical infrastructures of the United States be rare, brief, geographically limited in effect, manageable, and minimally detrimental to the economy, human and government services, and national security of the United States;

(2) that actions necessary to achieve the policy stated in paragraph (1) be carried out in a public-private partnership involving corporate and non-governmental organizations; and

(3) to have in place a comprehensive and effective program to ensure the continuity of essential Federal Government functions under all circumstances.

(d) ESTABLISHMENT OF NATIONAL COMPETENCE FOR CRITICAL INFRASTRUCTURE PROTECTION.

(1) SUPPORT OF CRITICAL INFRASTRUCTURE PROTECTION AND CONTINUITY BY NATIONAL INFRASTRUCTURE SIMULATION AND ANALYSIS CENTER.—There shall be established the National Infrastructure Simulation and Analysis Center (NISAC) to serve as a source of national competence to address critical infrastructure protection and continuity through support for activities related to counterterrorism, threat assessment, and risk mitigation.

(2) PARTICULAR SUPPORT.—The support provided under paragraph (1) shall include the following:

(A) Modeling, simulation, and analysis of the systems comprising critical infrastructures, including cyber infrastructure, telecommunications infrastructure, and physical infrastructure, in order to enhance understanding of the large-scale complexity of such systems and to facilitate modification of such systems to mitigate the threats to such systems and to critical infrastructures generally.

(B) Acquisition from State and local governments and the private sector of data necessary to create and maintain models of such systems and of critical infrastructures generally.

(C) Utilization of modeling, simulation, and analysis under subparagraph (A) to provide education and training to policymakers on matters relating to--

(i) the analysis conducted under that subparagraph;

(ii) the implications of unintended or unintentional disturbances to critical infrastructures; and

(iii) responses to incidents or crises involving critical infrastructures, including the continuity of government and private sector activities through and after such incidents or crises.

(D) Utilization of modeling, simulation, and analysis under subparagraph (A) to provide recommendations to policymakers, and to departments and agencies of the Federal Government and private sector persons and entities upon request, regarding means of enhancing the stability of, and preserving, critical infrastructures.

(3) RECIPIENT OF CERTAIN SUPPORT.—Modeling, simulation, and analysis provided under this subsection shall be provided, in particular, to relevant Federal, State, and local entities responsible for critical infrastructure protection and policy.

(e) CRITICAL INFRASTRUCTURE DEFINED.—In this section, the term "critical infrastructure" means systems and assets, whether physical or virtual, so vital to the United States that the incapacity or destruction of such systems and assets would have a debilitating impact on security, national economic security, national public health or safety, or any combination of those matters.

SCADA. As previously stated, the primary concern is that a cyber attack will target the electronic control systems that regulate the operational functions of a critical infrastructure so that the flow of essential services are disrupted. Such a scenario is possible because the thousands of interconnected computers, servers, routers, and switches associated with the myriad physical and virtual tasks inherent in operating and maintaining the nation's most important critical infrastructures, such as defense systems, chemical and hazardous materials, water supply systems, transportation, energy, finance systems, and emergency services are no longer predominately handled by people, but are rather electronically monitored and controlled by centralized computer networks called Industrial Control Systems (ICS), Supervisory Control and Data Acquisition (SCADA) systems, or any equivalent system in function such as distributed control systems or programmable logic control systems.

SCADA systems, or their equivalent, digitize and automate almost every imaginable task associated with a given critical infrastructure—from opening and closing valves in nuclear facilities, to operating circuit breakers on electrical power grids, to managing air traffic in the sky. Since SCADA systems provide the "brain power" to manage critical infrastructures a successful cyberterrorist attack on even a single SCADA could cause massive economic and physical damage across broad sections of the country.

Approximately 85 percent of the nation's critical infrastructures are owned and operated by private business where the predominate emphasis for SCADA is on maintaining system reliability and efficiency, not cybersecurity. In most cases, the SCADAs are connected to their associated private corporate networks which are in turn primarily connected directly or indirectly to the Internet. This cyberspace vulnerability presents an open door for a terrorist with the necessary skills to hack into a SCADA and, for example, disable the valves at the nuclear facility, shut down an entire electrical power grid, or redirect air traffic to harmful flight patterns.

Techniques Employed in Cyber Attacks. Not all disruptions of an information system's confidentiality, integrity, or availability (CIA) constitute a cyber attack. In fact, most disruptions of information systems are caused by unintentional human error and are called cyber incidents. A cyber attack refers only to the intentional disruption of an information system's CIA. The National Institute of Standards and Technology Federal Information Processing Standards Publication 200, Minimum Security Requirements for Federal Information and Information Systems, March 2006, defines a cyber incident as:

An occurrence that actually or potentially jeopardizes the confidentiality, integrity, or availability (CIA) of an information system or the information the system processes, stores, or transmits or that constitutes a violation or imminent threat of violation of security policies, security procedures, or acceptable use policies. Incidents may be intentional or unintentional.

Taken from a Government Accountability Office Report, GAO-07-705, dated June 2007, the chart below lists the most common techniques employed in conducting a cyber attack, along with a brief description. The individuals making such attacks range from juveniles (so-called "script-kiddies"), to disgruntled ex-employees, to thieves, to competitors, to terrorists, to agents of foreign governments. Terrorists wishing to launch a cyberterror attack would employ one or more of the tools listed below:

Type	Description
Spamming	Sending unsolicited commercial e-mail advertising for products, services, and websites. Spam can also be used as a delivery mechanism for malware and other cyber threats.
Phishing	A high-tech scam that frequently uses spam or pop-up messages to deceive people into disclosing their credit card numbers, bank account information, Social Security numbers, passwords, or other sensitive information. Internet scammers use e-mail bait to "phish" for passwords and financial data from the sea of Internet users.
Spoofing	Creating a fraudulent website to mimic an actual, well-known website run by another party. E-mail spoofing occurs when the sender address and other parts of an e-mail header are altered to appear as though the e-mail originated from a different source. Spoofing hides the origin of an e-mail message.
Pharming	A method used by phishers to deceive users into believing that they are communicating with a legitimate website. Pharming uses a variety of technical methods to redirect a user to a fraudulent or spoofed website when the user types in a legitimate Web address. For example, one pharming technique is to redirect users—without their knowledge—to a different website from the one they intended to access. Also, software vulnerabilities may be exploited or malware employed to redirect the user to a fraudulent website when the user types in a legitimate address.

Denial-of-service attack	An attack in which one user takes up so much of a shared resource that none of the resource is left for other users. Denial-of-service attacks compromise the availability of the resource.
Distributed denial-of-service	A variant of the denial-of-service attack that uses a coordinated attack from a distributed system of computers rather than from a single source. It often makes use of worms to spread to multiple computers that can then attack the target.
Virus	A program that "infects" computer files, usually executable programs, by inserting a copy of itself into the file. These copies are usually executed when the infected file is loaded into memory, allowing the virus to infect other files. A virus requires human involvement (usually unwitting) to propagate.
Trojan horse	A computer program that conceals harmful code. It usually masquerades as a useful program that a user would wish to execute.
Worm	An independent computer program that reproduces by copying itself from one system to another across a network. Unlike computer viruses, worms do not require human involvement to propagate.
Malware	Malicious software designed to carry out annoying or harmful actions. Malware often masquerades as useful programs or is embedded into useful programs so that users are induced into activating them. Malware can include viruses, worms, and spyware.
Spyware	Malware installed without the user's knowledge to surreptitiously track and/or transmit data to an unauthorized third party.
Botnet	A network of remotely controlled systems used to coordinate attacks and distribute malware, spam, and phishing scams. Bots (short for "robots") are programs that are covertly installed on a targeted system allowing an unauthorized user to remotely control the compromised computer for a variety of malicious purposes.

A review of the listed techniques point to four general types of attack. First, the most common type of cyber attack is service disruption or the distributed denial of service (DDoS) attack, which aims to flood the target computer with data packets or connection requests, thereby making it unavailable to the user or, in the case of a website, unavailable to the website's visitors. DDoS attacks are often conducted utilizing "zombies"—computer systems controlled by a "master" through the utilization of "bots" or "botnets." Service disruption could directly affect any aspect of the critical infrastructure causing regional or even global damage. A second, but related, type of cyber attack is designed to capture and then control certain elements of cyberspace in order to use them as actual weapons. The third category of cyber attack is aimed at theft of assets from, for example, financial institutions. This activity includes not only theft, but also extortion and fraud. Finally, a cyber attack can also manifest itself in a conventional explosive attack on a physical structure, such as a building that houses a SCADA.

Cybersecurity. There is no commonly accepted definition for the term cybersecurity (sometimes spelled cyber security). Obviously, responding to the task of protecting cyberspace requires, at a minimum, the adoption of a unified government definition. Different uses of the term cybersecurity can be found in a wide variety of federal laws, executive orders, presidential directives, and other agency directives. Taken together, cybersecurity is concerned with protecting the basic security of computerized systems from unauthorized access. The central focus of cybersecurity is protection of an information system's CIA. According to the 2005 CRS Report, Creating a National Framework for Cybersecurity: An Analysis of Issues and Options, cybersecurity refers to:

> [A] set of activities and other measures intended to protect—from attack, disruption, or other threats—computers, computer networks, related hardware and devices software [sic], and the information they contain and communicate, including software data, as well as other elements of cyberspace. The activities can include security audits, patch management, authentication procedures, access management, and so forth. They can involve, for example, examining and evaluating the strengths and vulnerabilities of the hardware and software used in the country's political and economic electronic infrastructure. They also involve detection and reaction to security events, mitigation of impacts, and recovery of affected components. Other measures can include such things as hardware and software firewalls, physical security such as hardened facilitates, and personnel training and responsibilities.

8.2 Cyber Threats

A cyber attack could be used to destroy not only the electronic, but also the physical infrastructures that hold the nation together. Such a scenario is possible because some of the nation's most important infrastructures, such as defense systems, chemical and hazardous materials, water supply systems, transportation, energy, finance systems, and emergency services are electronically controlled by centralized computer networks ICSs or SCADAs. A successful cyber attack on even a single ICS of SCADA could cause massive economic and physical damage throughout large portions of the United States. For example, in 2002, the FBI uncovered information emanating out of the Middle East that certain hackers were studying the electrical generation, transmission, water storage, distribution and gas facilities of SCADA digital systems used to control the utilities of the San Francisco Bay area in California. Theoretically, hackers could disrupt the SCADA or even take command of the system in order to disable the flood gates or control hundreds of thousands of volts of electric energy. In fact, this type of activity has already occurred.

Along with the growth in cyberspace is a growth in cyber attacks. The almost seamless interconnectivity of the Internet presents a readily available and inexpensive opportunity for computer network cyber attack. Each day uncountable numbers of people gain access, or attempt to gain access, without authorization to computers in order to read, modify, or destroy information. Although the vast majority of harmful cyber attacks on U.S. interests to date—both government and private—have involved criminal activity, common sense and reason dictate that cybersecurity must better prepare for the real possibility of an Estonian-styled cyberterror attack. New forms of digital attacks are constantly emerging so that future cyber attacks will result from vulnerabilities in software that hackers find and exploit. During the week of July 17, 2006, alone, the United States Computer Emergency Response Team (US-CERT) listed more than 30 new vulnerabilities in cyberspace that fell in what they deemed a "high risk" category. Some of the security breaches that actually caused widespread damage received much publicity and still linger in the collective memory of society, e.g., computer worms such as the Love Bug, Slammer, and Blaster. The Log Bug virus, which caused billions of dollars in losses, was caused by a single university student in the Philippines.

In 2000, a hacker was arrested in Australia for breaking into the SCADA of an Australian sewage and water treatment plant and directing the pumping of one million liters of sewage into the environment. The culprit, Vitek Boden, was apprehended during a routine traffic stop in Queensland, Australia. Boden was found in possession of a stolen computer and radio transmitter which he used to turn his vehicle into a mobile "command center." Boden had breached the SCADA system of an Australian water and sewage treatment plant off Australia's Sunshine Coast. Over the course of two months, Boden directed the system, on forty-six separate occasions, to pump massive amounts of raw sewage into the local environment. This was the first reported instance of a hacker successfully breaking into a critical infrastructure, causing massive damage and being apprehended. It is a harbinger of things to come.

To be sure, the activity of all kinds of cyber crime is on the increase. A study released in March 2019 found that cyber attacks on financial institutions have more than doubled from the previous year. Tom Kellermann and Bill Young, Modern Bank Heists: The Bank Robbery Shifts to Cyberspace, CARBON BLACK (Mar. 5, 2019), https://www.carbonblack.com/blog/modern-bank-heists-the-bank-robbery-shifts-to-cyberspace. Studies regularly demonstrate that the majority of Internet professionals believe a major attack on Wall Street or other banking institutions is imminent. It is well known that criminals and terror groups are especially attracted to financial institutions where they can steal funds, disrupt day-to-day business, or even create a major assault on the system to cause panic. A coordinated cyber attack could mean far more than the inconvenience of shutting down an ATM machine. It could encompass the transfer of millions of dollars from banking accounts.

Other possibilities for attack are equally possible. In a 2004 article in *Computerworld* magazine, security expert Peiter Zatka expressed concerns about a different type of cyber threat. Zatka warned that the real destruction might not occur from cyber attacks, but from insider threats. An insider threat exists when a hacker infiltrates an internal network and then, instead of causing an immediate denial of service or other type of harm, remains invisible inside the network in order to spy. The infiltrators use a technique called "sniffing" in order to acquire account information needed to access the network. This allows the interceptors the ability to obtain all the information that passes along the network line, including usernames and passwords.

Remaining undetected, the insider often alters encryption and communication applications in order to copy input and output data from the control terminals to various hidden sections on the system. Universities and network service providers are tempting targets for the harvesting of accounts and credentials. In testimony before the United States Senate in 2004, the Deputy Director of the FBI's cyberterrorism division stated: "The FBI predicts that terrorist groups will either develop or hire hackers, particularly for the purpose of complementing large scale attacks with cyberattacks." There is no doubt that al-Qa'eda-styled terrorists are studying means to attack the West's infrastructure by means of cyber space. If they are successful, the world could suffer an "electronic Pearl Harbor."

Representing the tip of the cyber jihad iceberg, one recent case from England illustrates what is occurring across the world in growing intensity. In 2007, a 21-year-old biochemistry student named Tariq al-Daour, a 24-year-old law student named Waseem Mughal and 23-year-old Younes Tsouli were convicted in the United Kingdom of using the Internet to incite murder. These Islamic terrorists employed a wide range of computer viruses and stolen credit card accounts to set up a sophisticated network of communication links and websites that hosted videos of al-Qa'eda suicide bombings, beheadings, and detailed tutorials on computer hacking and bomb-making. Tsouli was the administrator of the online jihadist website, "Muntada al-Ansar al-Islami," the once main Internet propaganda outlet for Abu Musab al-Zarqawi, al-Qa'eda's notorious chief lieutenant in Iraq (Zaraqwi was killed by American forces in 2006). According to British investigators, the trio used scores of stolen credit card accounts to register almost 200 website domains at 95 different Web service providers in the U.S. and Europe. A single computer found in the London apartment of al-Daour had 37,000 stolen credit card numbers with detailed personal information cross-referenced for each holder.

In summary, the threat domain can come from outside by means of communications channels or from inside by those with knowledge and ability to access the systems. Actors include individuals and hostile nations.

UNITED STATES v. MITRA
United States Court of Appeals for the Seventh Circuit
405 F.3d 492 (April 18, 2005)

EASTERBROOK, Circuit Judge. Wisconsin's capital city uses a computer-based radio system for police, fire, ambulance, and other emergency communications. The Smartnet II, made by Motorola, spreads traffic across 20 frequencies. One is designated for control. A radio unit (mobile or base) uses the control channel to initiate a conversation. Computer hardware and software assigns the conversation to an open channel, and it can link multiple roaming units into "talk groups" so that officers in the field can hold joint conversations. This is known as a "trunking system" and makes efficient use of radio spectrum, so that 20 channels can support hundreds of users. If the control channel is interfered with, however, remote units will show the message "no system" and communication will be impossible.

Between January and August 2003 mobile units in Madison encountered occasional puzzling "no signal" conditions. On Halloween of that year the "no system" condition spread citywide; a powerful signal had blanketed all of the City's communications towers and prevented the computer from receiving, on the control channel, data essential to parcel traffic among the other 19 channels. Madison was hosting between 50,000 and 100,000 visitors that day. When disturbances erupted, public safety departments were unable to coordinate their activities because the radio system was down. Although the City repeatedly switched the control channel for the Smartnet system, a step that temporarily restored service, the interfering signal changed channels too and again blocked the system's use. On November 11, 2003, the attacker changed tactics. Instead of blocking the system's use, he sent signals directing the Smartnet base station to keep channels open, and at the end of each communication the attacker appended a sound, such as a woman's sexual moan.

By then the City had used radio direction finders to pin down the source of the intruding signals. Police arrested Rajib Mitra, a student in the University of Wisconsin's graduate business school. They found the radio hardware and computer gear that he had used to monitor communications over the Smartnet system, analyze how it operated, and send the signals that took control of the system. Mitra, who in 2000 had received a B.S. in computer science from the University, possessed two other credentials for this kind of work: criminal convictions (in 1996 and 1998) for hacking into computers in order to perform malicious mischief. A jury convicted Mitra of two counts of intentional interference with computer-related systems used in interstate commerce. See *18 U.S.C. § 1030(a)(5)*. He has been sentenced to 96 months' imprisonment. On appeal he says that his conduct does not violate *§ 1030*—and that, if it does, the statute exceeds Congress's commerce power.

Section 1030(a)(5) provides that whoever

(A)

(i) knowingly causes the transmission of a program, information, code, or command, and as a result of such conduct, intentionally causes damage without authorization, to a protected computer;

(ii) intentionally accesses a protected computer without authorization, and as a result of such conduct, recklessly causes damage; or

(iii) intentionally accesses a protected computer without authorization, and as a result of such conduct, causes damage; and

(B) by conduct described in clause (i), (ii), or (iii) of subparagraph (A), caused (or, in the case of an attempted offense, would, if completed, have caused)—

(i) loss to 1 or more persons during any 1-year period (and, for purposes of an investigation, prosecution, or other proceeding brought by the United States only, loss resulting from a related course of conduct affecting 1 or more other protected computers) aggregating at least $5,000 in value;

(ii) the modification or impairment, or potential modification or impairment, of the medical examination, diagnosis, treatment, or care of 1 or more individuals;

(iii) physical injury to any person;

(iv) a threat to public health or safety; or

(v) damage affecting a computer system used by or for a government entity in furtherance of the administration of justice, national defense, or national security...

shall be punished as provided in subsection (c) of this section.

Subsection (e)(1) defines "computer" as "an electronic, magnetic, optical, electrochemical, or other high speed data processing device performing logical, arithmetic, or storage functions, and includes any data storage facility or communications facility directly related to or operating in conjunction with such device, but such term does not include an automated typewriter or typesetter, a portable hand held calculator, or other similar device." Subsection (e)(2)(B) defines a "protected computer" to include any computer "used in interstate or foreign commerce or communication." Finally, subsection (e)(8) defines "damage" to mean "any impairment to the integrity or availability of data, a program, a system, or information."

...

Mitra concedes that he is guilty if the statute is parsed as we have done. But he submits that Congress could not have intended the statute to work this way. Mitra did not invade a bank's system to steal financial information, or erase data on an ex-employer's system, see *United States v. Lloyd, 269 F.3d 228 (3d Cir.2001)*, or plaster a corporation's website with obscenities that drove away customers, or unleash a worm that slowed and crashed computers across the world, see *United States v. Morris, 928 F.2d 504 (2d Cir.1991)*, or break into military computers to scramble a flight of interceptors to meet a nonexistent threat, or plant covert programs in computers so that they would send spam without the owners' knowledge. All he did was gum up a radio system. Surely that cannot be a federal crime, Mitra insists, even if the radio system contains a computer. Every cell phone and cell tower is a "computer" under this statute's definition; so is every iPod, every wireless base station in the corner coffee shop, and many another gadget. Reading § *1030* to cover all of these, and police radio too, would give the statute wide coverage, which by Mitra's lights means that Congress cannot have contemplated such breadth.

Well of course Congress did not contemplate or intend this particular application of the statute. Congress is a "they" and not an "it"; a committee lacks a brain (or, rather, has so many brains with so many different objectives that it is almost facetious to impute a joint goal or purpose to the collectivity). See Kenneth A. Shepsle, *Congress is a "They," Not an "It": Legislative Intent as Oxymoron, 12 Int'l Rev. L. & Econ. 239 (1992)*. Legislation is an objective text approved in constitutionally prescribed ways; its scope is not limited by the cerebrations of those who voted for or signed it into law.

Electronics and communications change rapidly, while each legislator's imagination is limited. Trunking communications systems came to market after 1984, when the first version of *§ 1030* was enacted, and none of the many amendments to this statute directly addresses them. But although legislators may not know about trunking communications systems, they *do* know that complexity is endemic in the modern world and that each passing year sees new developments. That's why they write general statutes rather than enacting a list of particular forbidden acts. And it is the statutes they enacted—not the thoughts they did or didn't have—that courts must apply. What Congress would have done about trunking systems, had they been present to the mind of any Senator or Representative, is neither here nor there. See *West Virginia University Hospitals, Inc. v. Casey, 499 U.S. 83, 100-01, 111 S.Ct. 1138, 113 L.Ed.2d 68 (1991)*.

Section 1030 is general. Exclusions show just *how* general. Subsection (e)(1) carves out automatic typewriters, typesetters, and handheld calculators; this shows that other devices with embedded processors and software are covered. As more devices come to have built-in intelligence, the effective scope of the statute grows. This might prompt Congress to amend the statute but does not authorize the judiciary to give the existing version less coverage than its language portends. See *National Broiler Marketing Ass'n v. United States, 436 U.S. 816, 98 S.Ct. 2122, 56 L.Ed.2d 728 (1978)*. What protects people who accidentally erase songs on an iPod, trip over (and thus disable) a wireless base station, or rear-end a car and set off a computerized airbag, is not judicial creativity but the requirements of the statute itself: the damage must be intentional, it must be substantial (at least $5,000 or bodily injury or danger to public safety), and the computer must operate in interstate or foreign commerce.

Let us turn, then, to the commerce requirement. The system operated on spectrum licensed by the FCC. It met the statutory definition because the interference affected "communication." Mitra observes that his interference did not affect any radio system on the other side of a state line, yet this is true of many cell-phone calls, all of which are part of interstate commerce because the electromagnetic spectrum is securely within the federal regulatory domain. See, e.g., *Radovich v. National Football League, 352 U.S. 445, 453, 77 S.Ct. 390, 1 L.Ed.2d 456 (1957); Federal Radio Commission v. Nelson Brothers Bond & Mortgage Co., 289 U.S. 266, 279, 53 S.Ct. 627, 77 L.Ed. 1166 (1933)*. Congress may regulate all channels of interstate commerce; the spectrum is one of them. See *United States v. Lopez, 514 U.S. 549, 558, 115 S.Ct. 1624, 131 L.Ed.2d 626 (1995); United States v. Morrison, 529 U.S. 598, 608-09, 120 S.Ct. 1740, 146 L.Ed.2d 658 (2000)*. Mitra's apparatus was more powerful than the Huygens probe that recently returned pictures and other data from Saturn's moon Titan. Anyway, the statute does not ask whether the person who caused the damage acted in interstate commerce; it protects computers (and computerized communication systems) used in such commerce, no matter how the harm is inflicted. Once the *computer* is used in interstate commerce, Congress has the power to protect it from a local hammer blow, or from a local data packet that sends it haywire. (Indeed, Mitra concedes that he could have been prosecuted, consistent with the Constitution, for broadcasting an unauthorized signal. See *47 U.S.C. § 301, § 401(c)*.) Section 1030 is within the national power as applied to computer-based channel-switching communications systems.

Mitra offers a fallback argument that application of *§ 1030* to his activities is so unexpected that it offends the due process clause. But what cases such as *Bouie v. Columbia, 378 U.S. 347, 84 S.Ct. 1697, 12 L.Ed.2d 894 (1964)*, hold is that a court may not apply a clear criminal statute in a way that a reader could not anticipate, or put a vague criminal statute to a new and unexpected use. Mitra's problem is not that *§ 1030* has been turned in a direction that would have surprised reasonable people; it is that a broad statute has been applied *exactly as written*, while he wishes that it had not been. There is no constitutional obstacle to enforcing broad but clear statutes. See *Rogers v. Tennessee, 532 U.S. 451, 458-62, 121 S.Ct. 1693, 149 L.Ed.2d 697 (2001)* (discussing *Bouie's* rationale and limits). The statute itself gives all the notice that the Constitution requires.

During deliberations the jury inquired about the meaning of the word "intentionally." The judge referred them to the instructions, which included a definition. Mitra says that the judge should have drafted a new definition, because the first must have been confusing (though he concedes that it was correct). This sort of problem is one for the district judge to resolve on the spot; there would be little point in Monday morning quarterbacking....

8.3 Government and Private Sector Partnership

Starting with the Clinton Administration and continuing to the Biden Administration, the government's approach to cybersecurity for owners/operators of private computer systems has been one of cooperative engagement and not mandatory regulation. The general feeling was that since the civilian sector invented and developed cyberspace, security should be left to market forces. In short, despite the rapidly expanding reliance on the Internet by American businesses, consumers, and government agencies, the government provides extremely little affirmative regulatory laws in terms of cybersecurity functions for non-government computer systems. Instead, the concept of engagement stresses the promotion of voluntary public-private alliances to combat cyber attacks of all kinds with particular regard to protecting the nation's critical infrastructure. With but minor exceptions, aimed at government computer systems, the theme of engagement predominates all of the federal laws, executive orders and presidential directives associated with cyberspace. These include the following: Internet Integrity and Critical Infrastructure Protection Act (2000); Cyber Security Research and Development Act; National Strategy to Secure Cyberspace (2003); National Strategy for the Physical Protection of Critical Infrastructures and Key Assets (2003); Presidential Decision Directive (PDD) 63; Executive Order 13821, Critical Infrastructure Protection in the Information Age; and Homeland Security Presidential Directive No. 7 (HSPD-7). The two strategies are designed to help America secure the cyber world by establishing three main objectives: (1) prevent cyber attacks against America's critical infrastructure; (2) reduce national vulnerability to cyber attacks; and (3) reduce damage and recovery time from cyber attacks when they do occur.

DHS also encourages the development of voluntary partnerships with the private sector through information sharing and analysis centers (ISACs). Currently DHS lists 14 ISACs across the nation. The Cyber Security Research and Development Act authorizes a multi-year grant effort to promote computer security measures from private sources as well as universities and the establishment of multi-disciplinary Centers for Computer and Network Security Research. US-CERT is another joint endeavor between DHS and the public and private sectors. It is charged generally with protecting the nation's infrastructure and is responsible for coordinating defense and response against cyber attacks nationwide.

In February 2006, DHS hosted the first ever government-led real world cyber exercise called Cyber Storm (Cyber Storm 2 was held in 2008). Costing over 3 million dollars, this invitation-only exercise provided over 100 public and private agencies from over 60 locations in five countries with a platform to address a variety of technical and cooperative issues associated with a realistic "staged" mega cyber attack against large-scale critical infrastructure elements to include energy, transportation and information technology. Considering that reviews of the exercise showed that many of the participants did not even know of the existence of the National Cyber Response Coordination Group, which serves as the primary federal organization to respond to major cyber attacks, it is evident that a key component of the engagement strategy demands increased training exercise. In addition, considering that 90 percent of the threat from cyberterrorism exists in the private sector, it is equally evident that relying on voluntary engagement practices may not be adequate—regulatory mandates are needed.

There can be absolutely no question that the threat of cyber attack is a grave concern that has the potential for significant damage to vast areas of the public domain. Indeed, because of cyberterrorism's great potential for harm to the basic pillars of society many commentators argue that cyberspace has passed into the realm of a societal "commons" that obliges the government to exert greater protection. If cyberspace is considered a commons, *a fortiori*, cybersecurity demands that the government provide solid protection and regulation for the common good of the general public. From this perspective many question the wisdom of a federal policy to secure cyberspace that fails to incorporate strict cybersecurity standards or regulations on the private sector as part of the strategy.

Because it is impossible to immediately determine the source of a cyber attack—it may be an amateur "script kiddie," a terrorist, or even a nation-state—the so-called "response baton" will originate with the private sector and then may be passed to law enforcement and next, perhaps, to the military. Clearly, the main thrust of a commons oriented cybersecurity strategy would involve two key elements: (1) a program that required the sharing of timely and accurate information all along the continuum from private to government and (2) the adoption of industry-specific cybersecurity standards and certification for all information systems.

The concept of "standards" is defined by the National Standards Policy Advisory Committee as: "a prescribed set of rules, conditions, or requirements concerning definitions of terms; classification of components; specification of materials, performance, or operations; delineation of procedures; or measurement of quantity and quality in describing materials, products, systems, services, or practices." As suggested by the government's current engagement strategy, the federal government only promulgates cybersecurity standards for federal computer systems, except national security systems. The federal standards are developed by the National Institute of Standards and Technology (NIST) and set out as Federal Information Processing Standards (FIPS). FIPS are promulgated under the simple rule-making procedures (notice and comment) of the Administrative Procedure Act.

In accordance with National Security Directive 42, standards regarding national security systems are developed and controlled by the Committee on National Security Systems. The Federal Information Security Act of 2002, defines a national security system as:

Any computer system (including any telecommunications system, used or operated by an agency or by a contractor of an agency, or other organization on behalf of an agency...
(i) the function of which—

    (I)   involves intelligence activities;

    (II)   involves cryptologic activities related to national security;

    (III)   involves command and control of military forces;

    (IV)   involves equipment that is an integral part of a weapon or weapons system;

    (V)   ...is critical to the direct fulfillment of military or intelligence missions; or

(ii) is protected at all times by procedures established for information that have been specially authorized under criteria established by an Executive Order or an Act of Congress to be kept classified in the interest of national defense or foreign policy.

To be sure, numerous public and private studies offer various proposals for sound security and best practices needed to reduce vulnerabilities from cyber attack. The studies usually prescribe a standardized integration of cybersecurity technology associated with all critical infrastructure systems in order to ensure an acceptable national level of cybersecurity. While various approaches have been advanced, the 2005 CRS report RL32777, observed that none of them are "likely to be widely adopted in the absence of sufficient economic incentives for cybersecurity."

Those who believe that the federal government should not require the development and enforcement of mandatory cybersecurity standards in the private sector, often argue that apart from issues of intrusiveness and technical feasibility, that such requirements would simply be too costly. Although the argument related to cost would be dwarfed into insignificance when measured against the monetary damage incurred in the event of a mega cyberterrorist attack, technical matters ranging from how to develop said standards in the rapidly changing world of cyberspace to how the government would measure compliance pose significant challenges.

Those who critique the engagement strategy argue that absent the impetus that would be provided by a massive cyberterrorist attack on the nation's critical infrastructure, efforts to actually create a meaningful cooperative proactive and reactive strategy between the government and private industry are piecemeal. Even the more immediate negative consequences to businesses caused by the impact of cyber crime (which drains billions of dollars from consumers and private industry each year) have not resulted in the necessary strides to produce stronger and more secure computer networks.

8.4 Cyber Attacks and War

In July 2009, a multi-day DDoS cyber attack on American and South Korean websites occurred at the same time that North Korea was conducting ballistic missile tests over the Sea of Japan. This incident made headlines worldwide and caused many to consider the use of cyber as a weapon of war. In 2012, Saudi Aramco, one of the world's most powerful oil companies, was hacked by Iran destroying or seriously damaging over 35,000 computers and in 2016 the Justice Department accused Iran of attempting to hack into the SCADA system of a damn in New York. Indeed, in 2010, Mike McConnell who served as the Director of National Intelligence under President Bush, testified before Congress that the threat America faces from cyber warfare "rivals nuclear weapons in terms of seriousness."

A number of nation-states, to include the United States, are rapidly developing the operational doctrine and functional tools necessary to conduct what is termed cyber warfare. There is no doubt that cyber warfare with its non-kinetic use of force will be the next area for weapon development by militaries around the world. In fact, according to a variety of open source documents, the People's

Republic of China openly boasts that it intends to develop the capability to win a cyber war by the mid-21st century. In fact, scores of nation-states are actively involved in developing cyber war capabilities. In keeping with the Obama theme of internationalism, the Obama Cyberspace Policy Review states that "the United States needs to develop a strategy … to shape the international environment and bring like-minded nations together on a host of issues, including acceptable norms regarding territorial jurisdiction, sovereign responsibility and the use of force."

Cyber warfare involves the action of conducting a cyber information attack on the computer network of an adversary in order to limit their ability to obtain or use information. Of course, this matter is not restricted to the activity of nation-states—hackers and terrorists are not constrained by any rule of law and might engage in coordinated cyber attacks that could equally disrupt a nation's computer network system. Nevertheless, since the rule of law would certainly encompass the use of cyber information activity conducted by a nation-state, it is necessary to examine the law and policy issues related to cyber warfare.

The use of "information warfare" or cyber warfare is a new concept; the use of cyber tactics are emerging as a key component of 21st century warfighting. For instance, the U.S. military conducted successful cyber attacks in both the 1991 Gulf War and the 2003 Iraq War (to a lesser degree) to disrupt Iraqi command and control networks and the operation of other essential physical facilities. Currently, the Joint Functional Component Command for Network Warfare (JFCCNW) functions under the United States Strategic Command (STRATCOM), to coordinate cyber information actions for the DOD. In 2008, the U.S. Air Force established a Cyber Command to prepare its forces for fighting wars in cyberspace by protecting those information systems which operate U.S. critical infrastructures and to be able, if tasked, to attack an adversary's computer networks. The U.S. Navy has the Naval Network Warfare Command in Norfolk, Virginia. Furthermore, President Trump launched a new branch of military service in December 2019, called the United States Space Force (USSF). Established within the Department of the Air Force, the USSF is responsible for all U.S. ground and space-based systems monitoring a global network of surveillance sensors, satellites, telecommunications, and air and fleet operations. In short, DOD is developing both offensive and defensive capabilities to conduct war in cyberspace.

Like a number of legal issues that have emerged in the post-9/11 world, the question of addressing cyber attacks from an international law of war perspective remains unsettled. The central legal issue poses the following question: Does the use of a cyber attack constitute a sufficient "use of force" in the context of the law of war to be deemed an "armed attack" or an "act of war?"

The use of the term "act of war" traditionally refers to the use of aggressive force against a sovereign State by another State in violation of the United Nations (U.N.) Charter and/or customary international law. In almost every instance in the modern era, such illegal acts occur without a formal declaration of war and the aggressive act itself triggers the ensuing armed conflict, i.e., war. The application of the traditional law of war principles (also known as the law of armed conflict) was developed by the international community in response to readily recognized deliberate armed attacks by soldiers, aircraft, or vessels on the military, citizens, or territory of another nation-state. At the time of the development of the law of war, cyberspace did not exist. Thus, the question of whether or not a computer network attack is an act of war requires extrapolation from the existing norms related to the law of war.

Any analysis of the matter must begin with the U.N. Charter. The goal of the U.N. Charter is to restrict the unfettered power of member States to pursue activities and policies that threatened international peace and security. Understanding that the U.N. Charter does not outlaw the use of force—it only outlaws the use of *aggressive* force—there are four primary provisions of the U.N. Charter under which the use of force is analyzed.

First, Articles 2(3) and (4) set out the general obligations of all member States to settle disputes in a peaceful manner and to refrain from "the threat or use of force." U.N. Charter Article 2(3) requires that, "[a]ll Members shall settle their international disputes by peaceful means in such a manner that international peace and security, and justice are not endangered." U.N. Charter Article 2(4) states, "[a]ll Members shall refrain in their international relations from the threat or use of force against the territorial integrity or political independence of any State, or in any other manner inconsistent with the purposes of the United Nations." In 1970, the General Assembly elaborated on Article 2(4), with U.N. General Assembly Resolution 2625, Declaration on Principles of International Law Concerning Friendly Relations and Cooperation among States in Accordance with the Charter of the United Nations. Although General Assembly resolutions are considered as non-binding recommendations they often prove useful, particularly to the extent that they contain authoritative restatements of customary international law. General Assembly Resolution 2625 states:

> Every State has the duty to refrain from organizing, instigating, assisting, or participating in acts of civil strife or terrorist acts in another State or acquiescing in organized activities within its territory directed towards the commission of such acts, when the acts referred to in the present paragraph involve a threat or use of force.

Second, if a State engages in the use of aggressive force, Article 24 of the U.N. Charter gives the Security Council the "primary responsibility for the maintenance of international peace and security" and Article 27 requires that all permanent members of the U.N. Security Council (China, France, Russia, the United States, and Britain) must agree on enforcement provisions, e.g., authorizing member States to engage in the defensive use of armed force.

The third element in the analytical framework is Article 51 of the U.N. Charter, which expresses the "inherent right of self-defense" in the case of an armed attack. The inherent right of self-defense refers to the ancient customary right of a country to unilaterally engage in acts of self-defense in response to an armed attack regardless of what any other nation or organization, to include the United Nations, may or may not do.

Article 51 of the U.N. Charter states:

> Nothing in the present Charter shall impair the inherent right of individual or collective self-defense if an armed attack occurs against a Member of the United Nations, until the Security Council has taken measures to maintain international peace and security. Measures taken by Members in the exercise of the right of self-defense shall be immediately reported to the Security Council and shall not in any way affect the authority and responsibility of the Security Council under the present Charter to take at any time such action as it deems necessary in order to maintain or restore international peace and security.

While a cyber attack has the potential to do great harm to the critical infrastructure of a given nation-state, would such an action rise to the level of what Article 51 deems as an "armed attack"? Clearly, a cyber attack of sufficient scope on either the military network or the critical infrastructure could constitute a violation of Article 2(3) and 2(4), but would that be considered enough to constitute an armed attack triggering the customary right of self-defense now codified under Article 51 of the U.N. Charter?

Common sense would dictate that a cyber attack of sufficient magnitude should be considered an armed attack, but when the U.N. Charter was drafted in 1945, the founders clearly did not foresee the potential for devastation that could come from cyberspace. For instance, Article 41 of the U.N. Charter views the "complete or partial interruption of…telegraphic, radio, and other means of communication" as measures not rising to the level of the use of armed force. In turn, the definition of aggression as adopted by the 1974 General Assembly Resolution 3314, excludes the concept of cyber attacks as an act of aggression that would constitute an armed attack (see Chapter 2.3).

Finally, because there is no absolute requirement that a "threat to the peace, breach of the peace, or act of aggression," take the form of a traditional styled armed attack, Article 39 of the U.N. Charter ultimately provides the Security Council with the final authority to determine whether a particular cyber attack would constitute a breach of the peace, and to what degree. Obviously, for the Security Council to take action, the cyber attack would have to be extensive in nature. In other words, the consequences of a cyber attack would be a central ingredient in their decision making process. Article 39 of the U.N. Charter states:

> The Security Council shall determine the existence of any threat to the peace, breach of the peace, or act of aggression and shall make recommendations, or decide what measures shall be taken in accordance with Articles 41 and 42, to maintain or restore international peace and security.

A related issue in the analysis is the issue of State-sponsorship. The law of war recognizes acts of self-defense in the context of the acts of a hostile nation-state, not of individual actors or groups of individuals that act in their private capacity. The expectation is that the aggrieved State will notify the nation-state where the private actors are located and then request assistance and cooperation. If the host nation is unwilling or unable to provide assistance and cooperation, then the aggrieved State may be justified to use force as was the case with the United States *vis-à-vis* the Taliban's support for the terrorist al-Qa'eda network in Afghanistan. On the other hand, if the cyber attack cannot be traced to a nation-state, the matter of retaliation is greatly limited.

Clearly, the international laws associated with the use of force are woefully inadequate in terms of addressing the threat of cyber warfare. Without a clear set of rules addressing cyber warfare, individual nation-states will no doubt operate within the framework of existing legal norms by extrapolation, much like the North Atlantic Treaty Organization (NATO) did when it invoked the NATO collective self-defense clause under Article 5 of its Charter, declaring that the terror attacks of 9/11 constituted an "armed attack" under international law despite the fact that al-Qa'eda is not a nation-state.

The international community needs to agree on the application of cyber warfare to the international rules of armed conflict. To date, however, periodic calls for the development of international rules dealing with information warfare have gone unanswered. In 1998 and 1999, for example, Russia was unsuccessful in its bid to get the United Nations to explore the need for an information warfare weapons arms control protocol. The Russian resolution asked member States to provide input on the "advisability of elaborating international legal regimes to ban the development, production and use of particularly dangerous information weapons."

The only real significant international agreement on cyber matters to date is the 2001 Council of

Europe Convention on Cybercrime, which has been ratified by at least 26 nations, including the United States (July 1, 2004). There is hope that this convention, which focuses on cyber crime and not cyber warfare, may at least present a starting point for future efforts in the realm of cyber warfare.

Currently, DOD views the use of cyber technology in military operations as a part of what is termed Information Operations (IO). IO consists of five subcategories: Psychological Operations (PSYOP); Military Deception (MILDEC); Operations Security (OPSEC); Computer Network Operations (CNO); and Electronic Warfare (EW). While the domestic guidelines that detail how and when the United States would conduct a computer network attack is classified information in National Security Presidential Directive 16 (February 2003), there are a number of unclassified DOD policy directives that speak to IO operations which would certainly have impact on cyber warfare. For instance, in regard to PSYOP, only non-domestic audiences can be targeted. This restriction would certainly apply to electronic warfare.

From a military perspective, the use of cyber technology in warfare is something that is clearly viewed as a new and powerful weapon. Cyber warfare offers a cheap method of employing targeted force against an adversary—it requires no deployment of soldiers, vehicles, or vessels. As is the case for all weapons, however, the American military command structure responds to lawful commands from the government and uses force in accordance with the Standing Rules of Engagement (SROE). Depending on the objective of the military operation, the SROE are further amplified by multiple levels of Rules of Engagement (ROE) which are developed by commanders and their lawyers. Designed for offensive and defensive uses of force, these rules ensure compliance with the law of war as well as domestic law. Even though no review has yet been produced, the DOD has recommended a legal review to determine what level of data manipulation constitutes an attack. In addition, because cyber weapons can transit global networks and produce far-reaching and unforeseen results, considerations need to be addressed regarding the impact on neutrals.

At the end of the day, if directed by lawful authority, DOD can and will attack an adversary's computer system—private or government. No new authority is needed. The issue that is seldom discussed centers on the mechanics—the U.S. military relies significantly on the computer systems of the private sector and would presumably have to use those private assets in any large scale cyber attack.

8.5 Conclusion

America's technological advances in cyber technology are unmatched. As often is the case, however, a country's greatest strength can also prove to be a critical weakness. America's dependency on the cyber world opens new vulnerabilities to a different type of terrorist attack. A cyber attack can target an actual computer networking system that can cripple a critical infrastructure. It can also manifest itself in a conventional explosive attack on physical structures. Former FBI Director Louis Freech claimed that "the FBI believes cyber-terrorism, the use of cyber-tools to shut down, degrade, or deny critical national infrastructures, such as energy, transportation, communications, or government services, for the purpose of coercing or intimidating a government or civilian population, is clearly an emerging threat."

The use of ICSs and SCADAs to digitize and automate almost every aspect of the workings of electric utilities; chemical, gas, and oil refineries; public transportation; or hospital services makes them a tempting target for cyber terrorists who desire to cripple some component(s) of the nation's critical infrastructure. Since American ICS and SCADA systems are designed for efficiency not security—SCADAs are predominately linked to the Internet—the opportunity for a significant cyber attack is greatly enhanced. Making ICS and SCADA systems safe and secure is further frustrated by the absence of a strong federal strategy that mandates information sharing and cybersecurity standards. In addition, the widespread technical ignorance of security managers and the false sense of security due to the absence of a major cyber incident on America's infrastructure contribute to the vulnerability equation. Again, the threats can come from hostile foreign nations, terror groups, hackers, criminal organizations, and embittered inside employees. The impact can include massive human casualties, wide-scale economic damage, wide-scale disruption to public order, and significant disruption of national readiness for war.

The cyber threat must be met with the same recognition and gravity as a physical attack. In order to properly secure the nation security officials must not be lured into believing that our enemies lack the necessary equipment and knowledge needed to implement such an attack. Sadly, cyber security has not benefited from the increase in dollars seen elsewhere in homeland security. Collaborating the private industry with the government is in its infancy but it is imperative that long-term research and development continue. Eventually, the government may be forced to implement programs to ensure that private industry shares information and develops security systems that provide greater levels of security. Unfortunately, the complacent habit of dealing only with realized threats has not imparted a sense of urgency that will ultimately be necessary to protect the cyber world.

8.6 Questions for Discussion

1. *Applying the "terrorism" label to a cyber attack.* In *R v. Boden*, The Supreme Court of Queensland in Australia upheld 20 of the 26 convictions that Vitek Boden was sentenced to for his cyber attacks on the SCADA system of an Australian water and sewage treatment plant in the year 2000. 2002 WL 969399 (QCA), [2002] QCA 16. In his appeal, Boden contended that he was not a terrorist, but a disgruntled ex-employee, and the severe sentencing he received hurt his future marketability in the workplace. Boden was not found to have had any known connections to a terrorist organization. Does the fact Boden was a disgruntled ex-employee mean he should have been granted leniency? Was Boden a terrorist?

2. *Developing new tools to fight cyber attacks.* Locating the source of a DDoS attack is important for purposes of criminal prosecution, deploying effective countermeasures and development of new defense tools. Southwest Research Institute (SwRI) and CIAS are partnered on a project to develop an automated IP traceback solution to combat DDoS attacks. Although the IP Traceback concept faces additional challenges such as the need for cooperation among Internet Service Providers (ISPs) and the future potential for government regulation, there are legal concerns as well. What specific legal issues should the project's managers be concerned with? Why?

3. *Hostile Nation Cyber Attack.* How much disruption to the American cyberspace would have to occur to rise to the level of an "armed attack." Should the Biden Administration draw a line in the sand?

Selected Bibliography

Cyberspace Policy Review (May 2009)

Eldar Haber & Tal Zarsky, Cybersecurity for Infrastructure: A Critical Analysis, 40 FLA. ST. U.L. REV. 516 (2017).

Kellermann, Tom and Bill Young, *Modern Bank Heists: The Bank Robbery Shifts to Cyberspace*, CARBON BLACK (Mar. 5, 2019), https://www.carbonblack.com/blog/modern-bank-heists-the-bank-robbery-shifts-to-cyberspace.

Malcolm, John. *Virtual Threat, Real Terror: Cyberterrorism in the 21st Century*. Testimony of the Deputy Assistant Attorney General John G. Malcolm on Cyberterrorism, Senate Judiciary Committee, Subcommittee on Terrorism, Technology and Homeland Security, February 24, 2004.

Rollins, John, and Clay Wilson. *Terrorist Capabilities for Cyberattack: Overview and Policy Issues*. CRS Report RL33123. Oct. 20, 2005.

Sanger, David E., The Perfect Weapon: War, Sabotage, and Fear in the Cyber Age (2018).

USSF Capabilities, United States Space Force, https://www.spaceforce.mil/About-Us/About-Space-Force/Space-Capabilities/.

Zatko, Peiter. *Inside the Insider Threat*, COMPUTER WORLD, June 10, 2004.

Chapter 9

War Avoidance

Before we bring all the U.S. troops and all the coalition troops out of here [Afghanistan]… we must set conditions that prevent a reintroducing of the sorts of people that caused us to be standing where you and I are standing right now.

—General Tommy Franks

Synopsis

Apart from the fact that the United States emerged from the Cold War as the sole remaining superpower, a promising by-product of the disintegration of the Communist dictatorship was the addition of dozens of nascent democracies into the community of nations. At the time, little thought was given to the long-term effect of this phenomenon. Nevertheless, some recognized very quickly that the world was more secure, not only because an evil system of government had been swept into the dust bin of history, but because it witnessed a series of new governments that earnestly wanted to embark on the road to democracy and free market economy. Strongly advocating the need for the "world community" to foster the development of these new and struggling democracies, the Director of the Center for International Studies at New York University School of Law noted the utopian ideal: "The world will certainly miss the boat if it does not use the end of the cold war to create a global system for the new millennium, one which preserves peace, fosters economic growth, and prevents the deterioration of the human physical and environmental condition." Other scholars were happy to settle on advancing a very simple truth in both war and terrorism avoidance. As previously noted, this truth was best summed up in the words of Anthony Lake: "[D]emocracies tend not to wage war on each other and they tend not to support terrorism—in fact, they don't. They are more trustworthy in diplomacy and they do a better job of respecting the environment and human rights of their people." This hopeful theme was the heart and soul of the Bush Administration's war aims. President Bush best summed up this ideal in his second Inaugural Address in 2005: "The best hope for peace in our world is the expansion of freedom in all the world."

Although it is true that the Islamic and Arab community of nations are plagued with non-democratic governments, it is erroneous to label that corner of the globe as a monolithic conglomerate of countries that embrace the radical Nazi-like totalitarianism of Iran, Syria, and the virtual-State of the al-Qa'eda and ISIS movement. In addition, it is equally erroneous to assume that the vast majority of people who live under the tyranny of these dictatorships do so with any welcomed degree of loyalty or enthusiasm. In the words of former Secretary of State Condoleezza Rice: "We reject the condescending view that freedom will not grow in the soil of the Middle East—or that Muslims somehow do not share in the desire to be free." Basic denials of human rights are not a matter of "cultural heritage." Given the choice between freedom and dictatorial rule, rational humans—those who have not been brainwashed in "Hitler youth camps"—will always choose freedom.

The international community, especially the well-established democracies led by the United States, have a critical role to perform in the promotion of democratic values and human rights. The task of promoting genuine democratic standards of behavior in whatever new governments take hold will not be a simple undertaking. In far too many instances, forces of intolerance—ethnic, nationalistic, racial, and religious—permeate both the new governments and the societies from which they are formed. For instance, the new government in Iraq may desire the concepts associated with democracy, but a general pattern of ethnic and sectarian fragmentation has introduced an escalating and often uncontrollable level of disorder and violence. Thus, if nations do not find realistic ways to promote and foster at least the most fundamental categories of democratic values and human rights, the flames of terrorism and aggressive war will burn bright once again. Totalitarianism always stands hungrily at the door of freedom.

9.1 The Causes of Aggression

The most troubling aspect of all in addressing terrorism and war avoidance begins with the question of what causes people, or more precisely governments, to commit gross violations of human rights and unlawful violence. Clearly, this is a critical issue as it is directly related to the attendant matter of how to best halt terrorism and aggression. Thus, the question becomes whether there is a way to rid the planet of these scourges apart from the use of armed force.

In reviewing the human experience of the last six thousand years, one could list a host of factors related to a country's use of aggression against both its own people and its neighbors to include such things as religious conflict, ethnic strife, territorial disputes, population pressures, and competition for limited resources. While all of these external factors may be catalysts for aggression, any discussion that fails to examine the basic nature of man can never capture more than a part of the real truth. Biblical theologians who understand the Bible Doctrine of the "total depravity of man," such as the late R. B. Thieme, Jr., often stressed that the root of the matter centers on the makeup of Man, a morally flawed being: "In our beings are all the seeds of great conflicts." Holocaust victim Anne Frank also amplified this point in her diary:

> I don't believe that the big men, the politicians and the capitalists alone, are guilty of war. Oh no, the little man is just as guilty, otherwise the peoples of the world would have risen in revolt long ago. There's in people simply an urge to destroy, an urge to kill, to murder and rage, and until all mankind, without exception, undergoes a great change, wars will be waged, everything that has been built up, cultivated, and grown will be destroyed and disfigured, after which mankind will have to begin all over again.

Moreover, nations are made up of people. The troubles of the world are not beamed onto earth from some hostile alien force. Since violations of the rule of law in terms of aggression and terrorism are generally associated with corresponding human lusts for power and approbation, one must put the responsibility for violations not only on the external factors created by Man, but on the darker angles of mankind itself. Although numerous excuses are always voiced by the perpetrator, violations are ultimately a reflection of the problems that rest inside each individual, who, according to the basic tenets of every major religion, is morally flawed. Thus, the question of what causes a person to commit a *malum in se* crime can be asked collectively of a government that engages in a consistent pattern of aggression and human rights violations.

On the individual level, observations about the sinister side of some societies strongly reinforce the Judeo-Christian doctrine of the total depravity of Man. However, the view that there will always be aggressive warfare and terrorism in the world, like crime in society, is only partially correct. Crime on the national level and aggressive violence on the international level can be controlled. The concept of the total depravity of Man voiced by Anne Frank applies primarily to theological questions, e.g., the mechanics of salvation. The concept does not mean that mankind is in a state of total helplessness and wickedness *vis-à-vis* other people. On the contrary, operating under the principles of freedom and self-determination, freedom-oriented peoples have come together to form national entities so that they might produce the by-products of privacy, justice, and economic prosperity.

Under such a model, nation-states have prospered and flourished, but only to the extent that they have recognized the collateral need to protect those rights on interior and exterior lines. On interior lines, States must recognize the legitimate functions of a police and judicial system to punish criminal behavior; on exterior lines, nation-states must recognize the need for a strong military establishment to protect the nation from the aggressive behavior of dictatorships and international terrorism.

Objectively, much of what we know about the nature of governments created by Man comes from the record of our histories, records written in streams of blood. For example, to observe that various governments have engaged in horrendous acts of aggression against their own people and others simply describes their behavior, but only partially explains it. In fact, no one has ever satisfactorily explained why certain societies—ancient Assyria, Soviet Russia, Nazi Germany, North Vietnam, Communist China, or Saddam's Iraq—turned into aggressive war machines that committed murderous human rights violations against their own people and engaged in war with neighboring countries.

What has been established are the characteristics of those nations that have a high propensity for engaging in aggressive war, terrorism, and human rights abuses. National Security law expert and Director of the Center for National Security Law, Professor John Norton Moore, argues that totalitarian regimes like the Taliban and Saddam's Iraq are considerably more likely to resort to aggressive violence than democracies. Professor Moore terms this phenomenon the "radical regime" syndrome:

A radical totalitarian regime…seems to blend together a mixture of a failing centrally planned economy, severe limitations on economic freedom, a one-party political system, an absence of an independent judiciary, a police state with minimal human rights and political freedoms at home, a denial of the right to emigrate, heavy involvement of the military in political leadership, a large percentage of the GNP devoted to the military sector, a high percentage of the population in the military, leaders strongly motivated by an ideology of true beliefs including willingness to use force, aggressively anti-Western and antidemocratic in behavior, and selective support for wars of national liberation, terrorism, and disinformation against Western or democratic interests.

Tyrants seek the destruction of freedom loving people. Some, like the Taliban and current Iranian regime, cloak themselves in radicalized versions of Islam; others, like Saddam's Iraq and the current regime in Syria, have no driving religious affiliation. All of these regimes are linked, however, by a common bond of hate, power lust, and aggression to gain, maintain, and extend power. Human rights, the rule of law, capitalism, and civilian control of the military are alien concepts to totalitarian governments because the freedom inherent in these concepts cannot coexist with tyranny.

9.2 Religion and the War on Terror

Some have tried to depict the War on Terror as a war against all of Islam. This is simply not true. The War on Terror is a term that is generally used to describe the ongoing armed conflict against a select group of fanatics that embrace a highly radicalized Islam—a view of Islam that encourages and directs aggressive violence against the United States of America as well as all who do not share their militant jihadism. In 1996, Osama bin Laden, the founder of al-Qa'eda, issued his first declaration that he was at war with the United States. After listing a rambling series of so-called grievances against the "Zionist-Crusaders," he stated:

> The walls of oppression and humiliation cannot be demolished except in a rain of bullets. The freeman does not surrender leadership to infidels and sinners. My Muslim Brothers of the World: Your brothers in Palestine and in the land of the two Holy Places are calling upon your help and asking you to take part in fighting against the enemy—your enemy and their enemy—the Americans and the Israelis.

As even the novice student of history knows, the relationship between religion and war has existed for a very long time. A brief review of human history reveals that various individuals, groups, and nations have wrongfully used religious dogma as a pretext to engage in aggression against others. For instance, reflecting the idea that God was on their side, the Nazis in World War II issued a metallic military belt buckle to their infantry that was stamped with the phrase: Gott Mit Uns ("God With Us"). Accordingly, it is no surprise that the Islamic radicalism that fuels the War on Terror employs what it calls the "true" Moslem religion in order to cloak a lust for domination through despicable expressions of unlawful violence, primarily targeting innocent civilians (Muslims, Christians, and Jews). In short, al-Qa'eda-styled militants claim that their religious beliefs justify the use of illegal and aggressive violence.

On the other hand, when it comes to confronting the forces of al-Qa'eda-styled aggression, it is not surprising that democracies like the United States of America will also employ religious ideology, i.e., Christianity, and other religious symbolism to support the necessary use of force in self-defense. However, despite the fact that all American presidents, to include George W. Bush, have invoked religious themes in time of war, the use of religion in this context is generally subordinate to the more predominant and commonsense themes of self-defense and national patriotism.

When Karl Marx (1818-1883) wrote that religion is the "opium of the people," he was referring to the fact that religion has long been used by those in power to control the social, political, and cultural behavior of the masses, with little or no concern for the content or validity of the underlying theological principles. Indeed, to any serious student of history, there is no question that the psychological forces associated with religion have played a powerful role in controlling and channeling human behavior across a broad spectrum, even to the point where monstrous horrors have been committed in the name of God. People of all religions are guilty. This does not mean that the religion itself is at fault; only the people that have used (or misused) the religion are at fault.

In general terms, all of the major religions discourage the use of aggressive violence, to include terrorism; the moral codes of all religions are the same. Clearly, the basic themes of the various religious beliefs are not the problem. Even without religion, groups intent on aggression and terror would find some excuse to justify their unlawful use of violence.

In the War on Terror various individuals and groups engaged in aggressive violence against innocent civilians in the name of Islam. The response by the United States took the form of the use of violence in self-defense, but was generally not cloaked in any specific religious ideology. Paradoxically, the voices in the West that have most loudly employed religious beliefs in this context have been those that seek to tie Christianity with pacifism. In their search for the panacea of "universal brotherhood," these voices intentionally blur the difference between lawful and unlawful uses of force. While voices of restraint, proportionality, and negotiation must always be considered in the equation of responding to aggression, the use of lawful force under the rule of law must remain as a primary option. Just as it is wrong that al-Qa'eda-styled terrorists and the dictators that harbor them murder in the name of religion, it is wrong to ignore or excuse these voices of appeasement who cry out in the name of religion.

Like many words, the term "religion" is subject to a variety of meanings. According to the American Heritage College Dictionary, the most ordinary definition would mean "[b]elief in and reverence for a supernatural power or powers regarded as creator and governor of the universe," but it also means, "[a] set of beliefs, values, and practices based on the teachings of a spiritual leader." Interestingly, however, a generalized comparative study of the world's major religions reveals that one can actually subdivide the term into two categories—"works-religion" and "grace-religion."

Each day, around the world, there are those who begin and end their day by turning to the "sacred" writings of their religious traditions for comfort and guidance, understanding, and enlightenment. In the brief sojourn of mankind, seven major world religions have arisen and set out their beliefs in writing. These works are Hinduism's *Bhagavad Gita*, Judaism's *Tanakh*, Confucianism's *Analects*, Taoism's *Tao Te Ching*, Buddhism's *Dhammapada*, Christianity's *New Testament*, and Islam's *Koran*.

Religious books are not texts for the study of life sciences, but rather books that claim to be about God and His plan and purpose for mankind. In this regard, Hindus, Jews, Confucians, Taoists, Buddhists, Christians, and Muslims each claim that their book best reveals God(s) and offers the better—or, in some cases, the only—answer to the meaning of life. Such being the case, critics ask how it is possible to know which religion, if any, is correct. This, of course, sums up the real intellectual challenge associated with religion and raises the most profound question one can ask: What is the truth? The Roman governor of Judea asked this very question in AD 30, but only in a rhetorical sense. He did not desire an answer.

Surprisingly, a predominating factor one encounters in studying this matter revolves around an astonishing amount of apathy; most people simply have no desire to challenge themselves to even frame the question: which religion is true? Content to incorporate as their own whatever religious belief system they were born into—no matter how illogical or ill-conceived—independent thinking and reasoning have little, if anything, to do with how the mass of humanity comes to personalize a religious belief. For instance, you are a Hindu for no other reason except that your parents were Hindus. Or, you are a Lutheran, because your parents were Lutheran.

Still, people have free will, and in each generation there are those who find this follow-the-leader approach to religion wholly unsatisfactory. These are the *truth seekers*: men and women who base their personal religious beliefs not on the happenstance of their cultural birthright or other environmental factors (such as religious conversion due to a marriage partner of a different faith), but on a foundation which evaluates the full range of religious options and then makes an informed decision. Clearly, for someone who insists a concern for truth, there is absolutely no subject more important to which the human mind can address itself. Unlike the infamous Pontius Pilate who disingenuously asked, "What is [the] truth?" and then refused to intellectually consider the answer, the truth-seeker is not discouraged by the fact that various world religions compete for consideration. Of necessity, truth should encourage honest scrutiny. Truth will always prevail.

So what can be said about the origin of religion? As long as humans have looked out into the night sky, it seems apparent that some have set aside the obvious social and cultural forces associated with "religion" and given a great deal of careful thought about what constitutes the true nature of God. Accordingly, if one accepts the premise that God exists, it is entirely reasonable to assume two points. First, God makes sense. And second, He purposefully reveals Himself in a sensible fashion— in the language and culture of the particular time frame in which any human resides—to those individuals who desire to know Him. As Thieme notes from his study of the Bible, God does not "hide the ball" to the truth seeker.

Unfortunately, from a historical perspective, much of this God-directed activity towards people is difficult to chronicle, as the vast majority of the human experience in this regard has been based on oral traditions, leaving few traces of record. We can only say with certainty that archeological evidence associated with some of the earliest human sites unequivocally demonstrates that humans have always held some kind of belief in an afterlife. Therefore, meaningful information about God's revelations can only be found in the historic period of Man's sojourn, when people developed writing. This era did not begin until, at most, a mere 5,000 years ago in the Euphrates River valley. Since that time, seven major religions have emerged, each leaving written records to stand for consideration.

Anyone who has taken the time to engage in the study of comparative religion realizes that it is impossible to catalogue all the many variations and sub-groupings that reside in each of the major religions. Nevertheless, certain broad generalities can be drawn. Thus, apart from all the things that can be said about Hinduism, Buddhism, Confucianism, Taoism, Islam, Judaism, or Christianity, when one boils each of them down to their bottom lines—to their basic beliefs—there emerge four central themes that are shared as base commonalities:

(1) All religions agree that the nature of each human either is, or becomes, tainted with sin. Man is a morally flawed creature relative to God(s).

(2) All religions share a common moral code that reflects similar, if not identical, values for human behavior. For all practical purposes, the basic moral laws for how all members of any religion should behave are identical to the moral and ethical laws found in all other major religions and, for that matter, in any significant human social structure. It is a fundamental commonality that all religions prohibit the evils of murder, larceny, lying, brawling, and hatred, while encouraging love, self-control, self-discipline, charity, and helping the less fortunate.

(3) All religions share a system of rituals designed to assist the adherent in some fashion associated with the belief system.

(4) All religions proclaim that the primary goal of the religion is for the human soul to obtain eternal union with God(s) or some other supreme sublime force in the afterlife.

The real issue that sharply and forever divides the major religions rests in the mechanics of how one achieves the goal of obtaining this eternal relationship with God under the fourth commonality listed above. In this regard, there are two, and only two, diametrically opposed answers to how this is achieved—(1) by a system of *human merit*, or (2) through a system of unmerited *grace*. Those religions that teach that the mechanics by which Man achieves eternal union are via human merit, effort, or works (human morality coupled with the performance of various rituals) are properly classified as *works-religion*. All religions except Biblical Christianity fall into the camp of works-religion. In contrast, Biblical Christianity rejects the concept that Man can achieve relationship with perfect God based on any system of morality, ritual, or human effort. Christian dogma states that relationship with God is automatically and irrevocably achieved when one accepts the salvation work of the God/man Jesus Christ on the cross by a simple act of non-meritorious faith. Thus, only Biblical Christianity is properly termed as *grace-religion*.

Islam is a works-religion. Islam was introduced into the Middle East in AD 622 by an Arab named Muhammad (570-632). Muhammad was born into the Koreish tribe in Mecca, in what is now Saudi Arabia. Although he was orphaned young and grew up poor and disadvantaged, Muhammad married a wealthy older widow and entered a life of ease at the age of 25. Freed from the need to work, Muhammad spent long hours in a mountain cave outside the city. Here he claimed to have received a series of revelations from Allah, the leading god worshipped in the polytheistic city of Mecca. Muhammad soon declared that Allah was the only god in existence and that all the other gods were false. An illiterate, Muhammad attracted a small band of followers to document everything he said. At the age of forty Muhammad began to preach in public, only to be greeted with skepticism and hostility by the ruling merchants of Mecca. Eventually, he was forced to flee about 300 miles to the rival city of Yathrib, later called Medina, where he raised an army of 10,000 warriors. After a series of violent battles between Medina and Mecca lasting several years, Muhammad took the city of Mecca by force and the surviving inhabitants converted to Islam. From Mecca, the new religion spread rapidly, primarily on the wings of military expansionism.

When Muhammad died in 632, he left behind a battle-hardened army, ready to move into Europe. A disagreement about his successor led to a split in the religion which exists today—Sunni and Shiite. Over 80% of Muslims are Sunni. Sunnis disagree that Muhammad's successor should be a blood relative. Accordingly, Muhammad's primary military chief, Abu Bakr (573-634), swiftly took control of the ever-expanding Islamic army and violently crushed all opposition to his claim as successor. Abu Bakr was the first caliph of Mecca and launched the Islamic forces on a blitzkrieg across Arabia, conquering region after region in the name of the new religion. By 710, the Arab Muslims had even entered Spain, only to be turned back from France by the Frankish ruler Charles Martel (688-741) and his knights at the Battle of Tours in 732.

Abu Bakr was also responsible for collecting all of the sayings of Muhammad and incorporating them into a book called the *Koran*. The *Koran*, more than any other item, is central to the Muslim religion. Under Muslim dogma, in order for the soul of the deceased to go to heaven or paradise, one must strictly follow the dictates of the *Koran*.

The religion is divided into Five Pillars of Islam and Six Pillars of Faith. The pillars focus on various rituals and beliefs that every Muslim must accept and perform. In general terms, to be a Muslim requires the following:

(1) One must confess the core Islamic beliefs in the proper manner. The *shahada*, that Allah is god and that Muhammad the Prophet is his messenger: "*La ilaha illa Allah; Muhammad rasul Allah*." Although Islam recognizes that there have been "prophets" before him (e.g., Moses and Jesus), Muhammad is the culmination and no legitimate prophets will succeed him. (Some Sunni's look for a Mahdi and some Shiites look for a missing 12th Imam, to appear).

(2) One must pray in a particular manner that requires the faithful to prostrate himself in the direction of Mecca five times a day. A caller delivers the call to prayer from a tall tower, a symbol to all that the nation is strictly tied to a communion with god and to a social brotherhood.

(3) One must give money to the poor and to the religious organization in compliance with a set mathematical formula. The *Koran* is explicit on this matter; annually, two and one-half percent of the Muslim's property must be given to the poor.

(4) One must fast once a each year, during the month of Ramadan.

(5) One must go on a sacred pilgrimage; the greatest—required for all during their lifetime, if at all possible—is the trip to Mecca. The annual pilgrimage to Mecca is called the *Hajj*.

(6) One must take part in "holy" war, if required. The holy war concept can apply in the real sense of taking up arms against an enemy, but it also speaks of an inner spiritual cleansing of wicked thoughts and deeds. As such, the *Koran* lays down a meticulous code of moral and ethical behavior. Drinking intoxicants, gambling, larceny, lying, eating pork, and unlawful sexual relations (a man can be married to several wives) are just a few of the sins detailed in the *Koran*.

In conclusion, Muhammad founded a religion that prescribes an extremely strict moral, social, political, and legal code, coupled with a series of demanding rituals. Muhammad stressed that he was not divine; he was only a human whom God had chosen to be the messenger. His message was that one must strictly follow all of the Islamic moral laws and codes of behavior and then stand at a final judgment tribunal conducted by Allah where the follower will be evaluated as to whether or not he is deemed worthy enough to enter into heaven. The alternative is hell.

Of all the major religions, Christianity has the largest number of followers and is the most widespread. Christians claim a direct extension from Judaism (Genesis 15:6), and the Christian Bible incorporates with its New Testament all of the books of the *Tanakh* (the Old Testament). The testimony of Christ's person and work is recorded in the New Testament, a series of documents written by either eyewitnesses or those directly associated with eyewitnesses, from circa A.D. 40 (the earliest estimate for the book of Matthew) to circa A.D. 96 (the latest estimate for the book of Revelation). Although there are three major divisions—Roman Catholicism, Eastern Orthodoxy, and Protestantism—Christianity is a system of belief that begins and ends with the person of Jesus of Nazareth. Biblical Christianity holds that Jesus is the promised Messiah written extensively about in the Old Testament—the Christ, the God/man—who, while suspended on a Roman cross, willingly bore God's judgment for all human sins (Isaiah 53; Psalm 22). The necessity for the sacrifice rests in the simple but often ignored fact that since God is absolutely perfect in His essence, He cannot allow imperfect man to have an eternal fellowship/relationship. Perfection rejects imperfection. Thus, the penalty of human sin had to be dealt with by means of Christ taking the judgment in His own body for all human sin during the last three hours while He hung on the cross. This unlimited atonement which covers each human's sin—past, present, and future—provides instantaneous and irrevocable salvation to any member of the human race who accepts the free gift by belief in Him, regardless of personal merit or moral worthiness in his mortal life span. Since entrance into a relationship with God in time and eternity requires only a single speck of non-meritorious faith alone in Christ alone, this central doctrine for salvation is called the "gospel" or "good news" (John 3:16).

Unlike other religions, whose founders could be entirely removed without destroying the noetic (intellectual) aspects of the religion, without the person and work of Jesus Christ, Christianity would cease to be. This is because the path set forth by Christianity to an eternal relationship with God (salvation) is not based on any system or formula of human works (morality, rituals, and so on) or philosophy, as all other types of works-religion dictate. Rather, it is based on the work of Jesus Christ while on the cross. R.B. Thieme, Jr., encapsulates this point in his book, *The Plan of God*: "Biblical Christianity asserts that only the work of God through Jesus Christ provides the means of salvation and eternal relationship with God (John 8:12). Christianity proclaims God's way of salvation for the human race."

In the early years of Christianity, when the Roman persecution was heaviest, believers would use the symbol of the fish as a recognition sign. As an encapsulated illustration to what Biblical Christians believe—then and now—the Greek letters that spell "fish" correspond to the words "Jesus Christ God's Son [the] Savior."

In summary, in Christianity one's eternal relationship with God is based absolutely and solely on a single act of personal belief in the redeeming work of the God/man Jesus Christ on the death-cross where He suffered "spiritual death" and became the substitute sacrifice for mankind's sin. Since Jesus Christ is the perfect God/man, He was qualified to bear the sins of the world and provide salvation to all who believe. This grace policy excludes all human merit as a means of salvation and thus stands in sharp contrast to all of the other major religions. Ephesians 2:8-9: "For by grace are you saved through faith; and that not of yourselves, it is the gift of God: Not of works lest any man should boast."

Although the grace system of belief revealed in Christianity is totally antithetical to the works formula for salvation found in the other world religions, the concept of human morality and works as a vehicle to gain the approbation of God is a constant plague to the Biblical Christian doctrine. To be sure, Christians are commanded to be good citizens and follow the moral laws set out in the Bible, but this obligation is not a requirement for salvation. Salvation is appropriated freely based on a one-shot decision in a moment of time to believe in Christ. For example, when a Roman official asked what he had to do to be saved, Acts 16:31 records that Paul and Silas said: "Believe on the Lord Jesus Christ, and thou shalt be saved, and thy house [should also do the same]."

In his multi-volume work on systematic theology, Dr. Lewis Sperry Chafer, late president and professor of systematic theology at Dallas Theological Seminary, wrote:

> The idea that man will stand on a basis of personal worthiness has been the chief heresy, opposing the central doctrine of grace, from the time of Christ's death to the present hour. It so permeates the church that few who preach are able to exclude it from their attempts at gospel preaching. It is safe to say that wherever the element of human merit is allowed to intrude into the presentation of the plan of salvation, the message is satanic to that extent.

Thus, grace-religion is all that God is free to do for Man on the basis of the work of Jesus Christ on the cross. For Biblical Christians, grace is God's policy and plan. Works-religion is a progressive process; grace is non-meritorious and instantaneous.

Of course, as previously discussed radical Islam rejects the works-religion system of main-stream

Islam and asserts that those who die in "jihad" do not go before the Judgment Seat of Allah for evaluation on their worthiness to enter heaven. Instead, these martyrs by-pass the judgment of Allah and automatically enter paradise to receive their eternal rewards. While some may find a "grace" element to this belief, it is not the grace concept of Biblical Christianity—the adherent has to kill themselves, a substantial "work" which is done to gain the approbation of Allah.

In sum, regardless of the fact that Christianity and Islam are diametrically opposed as to the means of salvation, it is vitally important that the West understand that the War on Terror was never a religious conflict that pitted Islam against Christianity. It was rather a war against religious fanatics who wrongfully invoked the Islamic religion as a justification for aggression. History has seen these fanatics many times before as they have pillaged and murdered in the name of the other major religions, to include Christianity. In the short term these fanatics must be killed or detained, in the long term the "Hitler Youth Camps" that preach jihadist murder must be shut down.

9.3 The New Paradigm for War Avoidance

Recognizing a nexus between the nation that mistreats its own citizens and the nation that fosters aggression against its neighbors, "[b]oth the preamble and Article 1 of the United Nations Charter make crystal clear that the drafters were under the impression that the unleashing of aggressive war occurred at the hands of those States in which the denial of the value...of the individual human being...was most evident." Furthermore, with the outstanding research of eminent scholars such as Professor Rudy Rummel, it is now possible to demonstrate numerically the validity of the proposition that totalitarian regimes are the chief abusers of human rights:

> War is not the most deadly form of violence. Indeed, I have found that while about 37,000,000 people have been killed in battle by all foreign and domestic wars in our century, government democide [genocide and mass murder] have killed over 148,074,000 more. Plus, I am still counting. Over 85 percent of these people were killed by totalitarian governments.

So, the new paradigm for war and terrorism avoidance is a very simplistic and common sense model: If democracies make better neighbors, *a fortiori*, it is certainly in the best interests of the United States to do all it can to foster democratic values and human rights in the other nations and to thereby enlarge respect for the rule of law in international relations. In the words of Professor B. Russett, "[D] emocracies have almost never fought each other....By this reasoning, the more democracies there are in the world, the fewer potential adversaries we and other democracies will have and the wider the zone of peace."

All can understand the simplicity of Russett's argument. In fact, Professor Moore firmly believes this simple fact represents a "new and more accurate paradigm about war, peace, and democide." It replaces the old thinking of peace through appeasement and rubricates the only hope for reducing the threat of weapons of mass murder, terrorism, and human rights abuse. Appeasement leads to more aggression. This view is further amplified by a RAND study:

> The failure of regimes to provide for peaceful political change and the phenomenon of economies unable to keep pace with population growth and demands for more evenly distributed benefits can provide fertile ground for extremism and political violence affecting U.S. interests. For this reason, the United States has a stake in promoting political and economic reform as a means of

reducing the potential for terrorism, some of which, as in Latin America, the Middle East, and the Gulf, may be directed at us.

Unfortunately, the paradigm seems to be extremely difficult to propagate. In part, this is because democratic ideals are not spread through the use of force—of fire and sword—so that windows of opportunity for change generally only appear in the aftermath of the collapse of a totalitarian regime. This occurred in the Axis powers of Germany, Italy, and Japan following World War II and then again with the end of the Cold War in the former territories of the Soviet Union. In addition, the paradigm is difficult to advance because people in democracies are often lulled into complacency and apathy about the horrendous conditions of fellow humans on the planet. They forget the truth that democracies are far better systems of government than any other. To borrow a phrase from the British novelist Rebecca West: "The trouble with man is twofold; he cannot learn those truths that are too complicated and he forgets those truths that are too simple." The realization that democracies do not engage in terrorism or aggressive war is clearly a "simple truth" that must be reinforced at every turn.

If one accepts the paradigm as valid, three issues immediately arise. First, what precisely are the values associated with democracy? Second, are these values merely a Western ethnocentric assertion of power over other non-democratic nations or are they self-evident truths? Third, what is the best way to promote these values?

9.4 Defining Democratic Values and Democracy

In 1788, Massachusetts adopted a State Bill of Rights which proclaimed: "A frequent recurrence to fundamental principles is absolutely necessary to preserve the blessings of liberty and to maintain a free government." These fundamental principles generally refer to all of those basic rights associated with democratic forms of government and are best encapsulated in the Constitution's Bill of Rights approved by Congress in 1789 and ratified in 1791.

Before America stood up as a republic, early Western scholars such as John Locke, David Hume, Adam Smith, Baron de Montesquieu, and Jean-Jacques Rousseau wrote extensively on the subject of "civic humanism" or "natural rights" and the proper function of government in relation to the citizen. These scholars agreed with the premise that individuals came together to form national entities so that the individual could, within the framework of a government, better protect and advance his inherent rights to life, liberty, and property.

Contrary to the practice of the majority of the countries of their day, men like Rousseau claimed that Man "is born free" but "is everywhere in chains." These men pointed out that the government was formed to be the guardian of basic human freedoms, not the usurper. For instance, in his *Second Treatise of Government*, John Locke wrote: "The legislative or supreme authority cannot assume to itself a power to rule by extemporary, arbitrary decrees, but is bound to dispense justice, and to decide the rights of the subject by promulgated, standing laws, and known authorized judges."

The writings of these early scholars had a tremendous impact on the American rebels of 1776. Faced with the task of articulating a moral justification for their armed secession against the colonial rule of Great Britain, Thomas Jefferson and others were obliged to carefully translate Locke's natural rights into legal and enforceable rights. Apart from properly dealing with the continued evil of human servitude, which most assumed would die a natural death within a few decades, the American drafters were largely successful. In their Declaration of Independence to the British Crown, they declared that the individual, simply by virtue of his God-given being, possessed the "right to life, liberty, and the pursuit of happiness." The Declaration of Independence's powerful opening showed that the framers were not inventing out of whole cloth the ideas and ideals they embraced. The men who penned the Constitution and the Declaration of Independence were drawing on the wisdom of Biblical principles to bring together a proper balance between freedom and authority. Recognizing that freedom without authority is anarchy, and authority without freedom is tyranny, the Declaration of Independence proclaimed:

> We hold these truths to be self-evident, that all men are created equal, that they are endowed by their Creator with certain inalienable rights that among these are Life, Liberty, and the pursuit of Happiness. That to secure these rights, Governments are instituted among Men, deriving their just powers from the consent of the governed.

In two sentences, the Framers laid out a fantastic manifesto that recognized the right of men exercising their God-given rights through a democratic government formed to protect the fundamental freedoms of its citizens. For the Americans, these rights were rooted in Divine providence which made them inalienable and morally justified *ab initio*. As Benjamin Franklin remarked at the Constitutional Convention in 1787, "I have lived, Sir, a long time, and the longer I live, the more convincing proofs I see of this truth: that God governs the affairs of men."

With their freedom purchased through six long years of bloodshed on the battlefield, the colonial Americans produced one of the most phenomenal documents in the history of mankind—the Constitution of the United States of America. The Constitution established a republican government operating under concepts which forever united the terms freedom and democracy. In the minds of many, the terms are synonymous. Understandably, when one speaks of the desirability of promoting "democratic values," this does not necessarily imply the adoption of a direct democracy as the ideal form of government.

In point of fact, the United States of America was created as a representative democracy, i.e., a republic; it is not a true direct democracy in the fashion of the ancient Greek city-states. The founding fathers were extremely careful in their choice of government. They rejected the concept of a pure democracy where all citizens have an equal and direct voice in government and chose instead a representative democracy. The framers restricted the franchise of participants and established three separate independent branches of government, with checks and balances, to ensure that the authority of the central government was truly limited. *Webster's Third New International Dictionary* defines a representative democracy as "a form of government in which the supreme power is vested in the people and exercised by them indirectly through a system of representation and delegated authority in which the people choose their officials and representatives at periodically held free elections...."

Tragically, inherent in every democracy rest the seeds which will ultimately destroy it, for the real power rests not in the structure of government but in the character of the people that make up the nation. General "Light Horse" Harry Lee, the Revolutionary War cavalry hero, once observed that when virtue is absent from a people, the nation will collapse. In other words, the freedoms and blessings associated with capitalism and free enterprise cannot function without virtue. When the employer possesses virtue there is no need for workers to form unions because the boss will take better care of the wants and needs of the employees than any union ever could. In contrast, an employer without virtue will operate the company with selfish interests without regard to honesty and integrity. In turn, a worker with genuine virtue will work earnestly. Without virtue, a worker will produce little except slothfulness and deceit.

Virtue cannot be legislated, it must be taught in the home and reflected in the values of the society.

In short, virtue can be defined as "doing a right thing in a right way." Modern America, which once prided itself on individualism and the "Protestant work ethic," increasingly rejects its establishment principles and instead looks to a central government to provide for its needs from the cradle to the grave. In tracing the life expectancy of great democracies, it is interesting to note the words of historian Alexander Fraser Tytler (1748–1813), who wrote about the decline and fall of the Athenian Republic. Tytler concluded:

> A democracy cannot exist as a permanent form of government. It can only exist until the voters discover that they can vote themselves money from the public treasury. From that moment on, the majority always votes for the candidates promising the most benefits from the public treasury with a result that a democracy always collapses over loose fiscal policy always followed by dictatorship.

Considering that the United States of America is just shy of 250 years old, Mr. Tytler went on to develop a fascinating general trend in the rise and fall of the great nations. He wrote:

> The average age of the world's greatest civilizations has been 200 years. These nations have progressed through the following sequence:
>
> From bondage to spiritual faith;
> From spiritual faith to courage;
> From courage to liberty;
> From liberty to abundance;
> From abundance to selfishness;
> From selfishness to complacency;
> From complacency to apathy;
> From apathy to dependency;
> From dependency back to bondage.

If democratic principles do not always mesh with democracy as the best form of government, they certainly do equate to what Daniel Webster envisioned as "a state of society characterized by tolerance toward minorities, freedom of expression, and respect for the essential dignity and worth of the human individual with equal opportunity for each to develop freely to his fullest capacity in a cooperative community." It is certainly possible that a government that is honest, accountable, predictable, and efficient can conform to democratic principles and protect human rights. However, the modern era has demonstrated repeatedly that a representative democracy is best suited to produce democratic principles and is, therefore, the government of choice in reference to the paradigm for war avoidance.

Still, governmental authority in a State may be vested in one person, a small group, a large group, or the entire body. Measured in the light of human rights and democratic principles, none of these systems are necessarily per se worse than any other; it is just that representative democracies have institutional safeguards (such as checks and balances on power) that can guarantee fundamental freedoms over a longer term.

For instance, the Framers instituted three basic types of activities for the federal government. First, a system of checks and balances was established to ensure that the government fulfilled its obligation to protect the life, freedom, privacy, and property of law-abiding citizens. Second, laws were instituted to better regulate commercial and social disputes between individuals. And third, the government was asked to set up certain physical infrastructures to provide essential services that were beyond individual capabilities, such as providing for basic primary education, law enforcement, and a military establishment.

The factor that divides good government from bad government is in the degree to which the government allows the functioning of democratic principles under the framework of the law. Dictatorships have a pseudo "rule of law," but it is not based on principles of freedom. Accordingly, any so-called elections held in a totalitarian system can never be more than a cruel perversion of the concept. Clearly, a ruling system that provides its citizens with freedom of expression, peaceful assembly, a free market economy, and some degree of participation in government rests on democratic principles and a true rule of law. Thus, a monarchy, an aristocracy, or a representative democracy that rules for the common good of the citizen under democratic principles can each be positive manifestations of legitimate government. Other forms of government such as a tyranny or an oligarchy wield authority based solely on the self-interest of the ruling elite and refuse to embrace freedom.

In addressing the issue of writing democratic constitutions for the emerging democracies of Eastern Europe following the collapse of the Soviet Empire, Professor A. E. Dick Howard of the University of Virginia School of Law commented on this friction concerning what government is all about:

> The Bill of Rights of the United States Constitution declares what government may not do; it is what Justice Hugo Black once called a list of "thou shalt nots." The document reflects the view that the function of a bill of rights is to limit government's powers. Central and East European drafters have enlarged this meaning of "rights." A legacy of the twentieth-century notion of positive government, an age of entitlements, is bills of rights that declare affirmative rights. Such bills include, of course, the traditional negative rights, but they also spell out claims upon government, such as the right to an education, the right to a job, or the benefits of care in one's old age.

Forced equality through social engineering is the policy and propaganda of the totalitarian system. As Professor Howard discovered, many of the emerging democracies out of the former Soviet Union have still not shaken this old thinking, which has also infected large segments of the American society of the 21st Century. The true function of good government emphasizes freedom and self-determination which will always lead to varying degrees of social inequality. Faced with Lord Acton's often quoted truism that "power tends to corrupt, and absolute power corrupts absolutely," the government that adheres to principles of freedom and limited powers is much preferred. The siren song of "affirmative rights" for the people always leads to poverty and misery for the national entity.

But what if people want to choose a political system that denies fundamental freedoms? Coming out of the Nazi era, the post World War II German government was quick to address this question by enacting in their Basic Law a provision which holds that no citizen may use his freedom to destroy freedom. In other words, no political party that endorses non-democratic principles will be allowed to stand for office, they will be banned. This is a core principle of the *streitbare Demokratie* (disputative democracy), which contains mechanisms to protect the system of values that it has established. The *Bundestag* (federal parliament), the *Bundesrat* (federal council), and the federal government are entitled to file a motion to declare a political party as void. Accordingly, all Islamic political party movements that deny democratic principles would be banned. At Article 21:

(1) Political parties shall participate In the formation of the political will of the people. They may be freely established. Their internal organization must conform to democratic principles. They must publicly account for their assets and for the source and use of their funds.

(2) Parties that, by reason of their aims or the behavior of their adherents, seek to undermine or abolish the free democratic basic order or to endanger the existence of the Federal Republic of Germany shall be unconstitutional. The Federal Constitutional Court shall rule on the question of unconstitutionality.

Indeed, once a totalitarian party takes office, it will abolish all systems of freedom because it is the antithesis of freedom. A recent historical example of this strange paradox—where an extremist party manages to win at the ballot box—is found in the Algerian experience. When the first round of balloting in December 1991 went to the radical Taliban-styled Islamic Salvation Front (better known by its French acronym FIS), the Algerian military intervened to stop the extremists from taking power. Understanding that the FIS would not endorse principles of freedom if they took power, the Algerian Army banned the FIS and supported the secular State apparatus. Showing their true colors, the FIS then accelerated a murder and terror campaign (their tactic of choice was to slit the throat of anyone who did not agree with the Islamic movement) against the civilian population, resulting in the murder of nearly 200,000 people. Fortunately, the FIS's armed wing, the so-called Islamic Salvation Army, disbanded in January of 2000 and Algerians elected President Abdelaziz Bouteflika shortly thereafter. Although much remains to be done, President Boutelflika's Charter for Peace and National Reconciliation put the nation on the road to democratic reforms.

In the modern era, the terms democratic principles and fundamental freedoms have been joined by the concept of human rights. The report of the June 1993 World Conference on Human Rights, held in Vienna and attended by 171 States, defined the relationship between democracy, fundamental freedoms, and human rights as follows:

Democracy, development, and respect for human rights and fundamental freedoms are interdependent and mutually reinforcing. Democracy is based on the freely expressed will of the people to determine their own political, economic, social and cultural systems and their full participation in all aspects of their lives....The international community should support the strengthening and promoting of democracy, development and respect for human rights and fundamental freedoms in the entire world.

Finally, since some wrongly criticize the concept of democracy as a Western value, it may be more appropriate to speak to the world politic in terms of the normative concept of human rights. Human rights evoke a more inclusive standard, which can apply to all the peoples and nations of the world. As a practical matter, of course, there is no difference between democratic values and basic human rights.

9.5 Origins of Human Rights

When the Framers of the Constitution wrote about the Law of Nations, they were addressing those principles of international law that governed State-to-State contacts. At most, the individual was viewed only as an object in the process. As recently as sixty years ago, the leading treatise on international law reflected the absence of a legal recognition of the issue of international human rights. International law scholar Lassa Oppenheim wrote: "[A]part from obligations undertaken by treaty, a State is entitled to treat both its own nationals and stateless persons at discretion and that the manner in which it treats them is not a matter with which International Law, as a rule, concerns itself."

While general humanitarian concerns for individuals have always been around in the marketplace of world ideas, it has only been since the close of the Second World War that legal norms in the context of human rights have emerged. Before this period, humanitarian concerns such as eradicating the evil of slavery were handled to a large degree by each individual State. Nevertheless, as each of the Western powers eradicated the institution, the abolition of slavery gradually became a principle of customary international law. Thus, fueled by the formation of the United Nations in 1945, an entire system of human rights legal principles, some by treaty and some by custom, slowly emerged.

In the last half of the twentieth century, no concept has done more to advance positive change in the social and political spheres of human experience than human rights. In the quest for bettering the quality of human life, human rights have had a major impact in shaping world opinion and events. In this context, human rights have increasingly served as the basis for reaching consensus on defining the fundamental pillars upon which all "just" governments should be anchored. As the preamble to the Universal Declaration of Human Rights asserts, human rights serve "as a common standard of achievement for all peoples and all nations."

In the modern era, human rights have emerged as a significant moral and legal force in modern domestic and international relations. In its most comprehensive meaning, human rights encompass all those principles and concerns associated with ensuring respect for the inherent dignity of the individual human being. In this sense alone can individuals ever be called equal, since each human being, regardless of his abilities or handicaps, possesses the same right of respect for his person and property. The problem, of course, is in the extent to which individual governments are willing to define, recognize, and then enforce the inherent human rights each citizen possesses.

Because mankind is organized into national entities or States, human rights have their primary meaning as they relate to the relationship of the individual and the national entity. In contrast to the situation of only a few generations ago, when the sovereignty of the State was the fundamental principle upon which international law was based, the rapid development of international human rights norms and standards now requires the sovereignty of the State to be weighed and measured against what might be called the sovereignty of the individual.

Despite the phenomenal inroads that human rights have made in the world arena, the goal of universal acceptance and adherence has not been achieved; the path continues to be strewn with adversity. Although the term human rights rolls off the tongue with great ease, one of the most frustrating issues associated with the study of human rights is the fact that there is no standard definition of the term human rights. The legal definition of rights usually refers to claims recognized and enforced by law, but human rights can encompass a far broader category of issues, many not deemed to be legally binding in the context of either domestic or international law. Thus, without a clear definition, the range of matters human rights should encompass continues to be debated.

Juxtaposed to the strict definitional problem, another obstacle in reaching a universal consensus on defining human rights rests in the polarization of the term. Without question, the term human rights has numerous connotations, making it extremely popular over the entire political and social spectrum to describe, with equal vigor, almost any and every aspect of the human condition. Furthermore, because the term is freely used by groups with diametrically opposed agendas and ideologies—often without honest assessment or examination—human rights are often treated as a disposable tool to achieve a political end. The result is that the unwary or casual observer is left with a term that is saddled with wide-ranging ambiguities as to its meaning and goal.

For example, during the Cold War both the Soviet Union and the United States routinely accused one another of human rights abuses. The United States would accuse the Soviets of violating human rights, pointing to the systematic denial of all categories of human freedom related to person and property as a function of the totalitarian regime. In turn, the Soviets would vehemently charge the United States and other capitalist countries with "headline grabbing" human rights abuses (in order to divert attention from their own abuses and to further ongoing machinations to advance Communist ideology throughout the globe).

Of course, in the debate of which system of government commits the worst violations of human rights, one point is generally clear: totalitarian governments are hypocritical in their professed support for human rights; democracies are not. Although individual acts of human rights abuse can occur under any form of government, there is a vast difference between totalitarian regimes and democratic governments. Totalitarian regimes are guilty of institutional denials of human rights, routinely carried out as the *modus vivendi* of government.

In contrast, human rights violations in democracies are generally caused by individuals operating under their own authority and outside of normal institutional safeguards and procedures. Accordingly, democracies are far more likely to care about human rights and to investigate and punish those public officials guilty of human rights violations.

Another mark of the phenomenal degree of support for human rights in democracies is that human rights are accepted as vitally important considerations across the entire political spectrum. For instance, in democracies, all major political platforms, be they conservative or liberal, recognize and endorse the need for the promotion of the most fundamental categories of human rights, both in America and throughout the globe. Liberals and conservatives may disagree on the degree or method of promotion, but both advocate the pursuit of human rights as the primary vehicle for the advancement of peace and stability.

As a consequence of the support given to human rights by the democracies, the world community, by treaty and custom formed essentially since the close of World War II, has arrived at a general consensus on certain basic human rights which all mankind should enjoy. Because this basic category of international human rights is universally recognized, it is commonly referred to as "international human rights." In the realm of international law, international human rights can be generally defined as that body of universally recognized inalienable rights that every individual is entitled to and that every government must guarantee.

At least in the sphere of this consensus, international law no longer recognizes the unrestricted right of the State to deal with its citizens or aliens in any manner it so desires. International human rights law transcends international borders. The often-heard quip of England's King George when asked for help during France's reign of terror no longer applies: "If a country chooses to go mad within its own borders, it may do so."

Without question, the lynchpin of international human rights law advocates one of the most fundamental functions of the national entity—to protect the human rights of the individual. In this sense, respect for international human rights is the *sine qua non* of civilized society and failure of the State to afford such protection can lead to a wide range of sanctions—political, economic, and even judicial.

Apart from the desire to halt external aggression, the U.N. Charter was also designed to address fundamental issues related to international human rights. If the desire for curtailing aggressive war was the justification for restricting some aspects of the external exercise of a State's sovereignty, the drafters intended human rights to be the justification for examining a State's internal ability to generally treat its citizens in any manner it wished.

Although the references to human rights in the U.N. Charter are set out in extremely general terms, they nonetheless clearly set the tone for all future treaties and covenants related to human rights. For example, the preamble to the U.N. Charter states that the peoples of the United Nations have determined to "reaffirm faith in fundamental human rights, in the dignity and worth of the human person [and] in the equal rights of men and women...." This is followed by language in Article 1 (3) which, under the purpose of the U.N., calls for member nations to promote and encourage "respect for human rights and for fundamental freedoms for all without distinction as to race, sex, language, or religion...."

With the creation of the United Nations, work quickly began on a series of international agreements and instruments designed to accomplish the two major themes in the Charter—restricting war and promoting human rights. Many of the efforts resulted in widespread and immediate acceptance of various international agreements throughout the nations of the world, including the 1949 Geneva Conventions. While the Geneva Conventions do not deal with restricting warfare, *jus ad bellum*, they are deeply concerned with *jus in bello*.

It was at this time that human rights moved from a "vision in the minds of some men, of an ideal aspiration towards universal values of law," to the reality of a world that began to acknowledge the existence and validity of international human rights. Next to the U.N. Charter, the primary document that frames the basic principles, as well as the future aspirations, for an international legal corpus for human rights is the U.N. Universal Declaration of Human Rights. The Universal Declaration was passed unanimously (eight abstentions) by the General Assembly in 1948, just three years after the creation of the United Nations.

Unlike the U.N. Charter, the U.N. Universal Declaration of Human Rights is not yet regarded as legally binding among the nations of the world. The Universal Declaration is a declaration of the international body relating to moral and political issues of governments. Although it is not legally binding, the Universal Declaration has gained considerable authority as a legal guide to all member States and serves as a foundation for future expansion of international human rights law.

Another problem with the Universal Declaration is that it lacks machinery for enforcing any of the human rights that it lists. The Universal Declaration has, however, inspired two major covenants which contain more detailed assertions of fixed categories of human rights. Approved by the General Assembly in 1966, these are the International Covenant on Civil and Political Rights and the International Covenant on Economic, Social, and Cultural Rights. Both of these covenants continue to receive growing acceptance from many nations of the world community.

Obviously, the evolution of the international corpus for human rights law is still ongoing. As with all aspects of international law, international human rights law develops as States become bound by treaty or by custom. Even absent consent via treaty, nations can still be obligated. Again, when a norm or standard has reached widespread acceptance in the international community, it is said to have passed into the realm of customary international law. For example, in respect to the U.N. Charter, even those few nations who are not members of the United Nations are bound by the provisions of the U.N. Charter under the concept of customary international law.

9.6 The Corpus of Human Rights Law

What then is the current corpus of human rights and how much of it falls into the category of recognized international human rights law? Many scholars view human rights as chronologically evolving in "generations." For the purposes of this study, it is particularly helpful to divide human rights into three generations.

The first generation of human rights deals basically with the individual's right to be secure in the most sacred asset of all—his person. All nations are bound by treaty and custom to observe these basic protections which are clearly included as the most fundamental of international human rights. Specifically, a State violates international human rights law if, as a matter of State policy, it practices, encourages, or condones seven types of actions that have gained universal recognition. Codified in the Restatement (Third) of the Foreign Relations Law of the United States (1987), Section 702, Customary International Law of Human Rights, those actions consist of:

1. genocide;
2. slavery or slave trade;
3. the murder or causing the disappearance of individuals;
4. torture or other cruel, inhuman, or degrading treatment or punishment;
5. prolonged arbitrary detention;
6. systematic racial discrimination; and
7. a consistent pattern of gross violations of internationally recognized human rights.

Any nation that violates these first generation human rights is deemed to have committed a "gross violation of international human rights." No exceptions.

The second generation of human rights is related to political and civil claims. In short, the individual has the right to be free from the State in all civil and political endeavors. Second category rights are set forth in the International Covenant on Civil and Political Rights and include the broader civil and political freedoms of religion, movement, peaceful assembly, association, expression, privacy, family rights, fair and public trial, and participation in government—all sacred principles related directly to democratic principles of individual freedom. Unfortunately, while many countries have adopted these rights, nations who do not enter into international agreements to follow these rights are not obligated to do so. In other words, second generation rights are not yet customary international law.

Second generation human rights are fundamental to the complete development of the individual, for without the basic guarantees of freedom which these rights speak to, the full potential of the individual can never be realized. However, for those who mistakenly equate human rights with social equality, second generation rights are a paradox, as individuals are free to enjoy the consequences of their own decisions without government interference, good or bad. Furthermore, second generation human rights directly parallel the fundamental freedoms in democracies, concepts that are never offered under totalitarianism. A government committed to second generation human rights is tantamount to a democracy.

In contrast to the second generation of human rights, there is no great or growing international movement toward agreeing on the status of the third generation of human rights. Third generation rights are different from first and second generation rights because they move from restricting governmental behavior toward the individual, to mandating that the government perform numerous social and welfare actions for the individual. Third generation human rights include such issues as working conditions, social security, education, health care, resource development, food, the environment, humanitarian assistance, and peace.

While good government can certainly be measured by how closely it protects and provides for first and second generation human rights, it is not true that the promotion of the third category of human rights is beneficial to society as a whole, especially over the long term. Apart from very basic obligations for any government to provide for the general welfare, which all democracies pledge to do, good governments should shun panaceas washed in socialism. The obligation of the State is not to provide third generation human rights such as food, shelter, or employment to its citizens, but to protect the individual's freedom in the lawful pursuit of these things. Under this reasoning, the primary function of the State is to protect, not to engage in socialism and the redistribution of wealth.

9.7 Traditional Efforts of the United States to Promote Human Rights

If the United Nations, NGOs, and regional organizations have been less than effective in developing a serious methodology to promote the institutionalization of first and second generation human rights in new democracies, the United States government has only been slightly more effective. Recognizing that promoting human rights is in its best interest, as well as a responsibility to the world community, the United States relies on two means to achieve this end—foreign assistance funding and political pressure.

Political pressure is difficult to gauge in its success and varies according to each situation. In terms of politics, for example, the United States has signaled that it will not subordinate perceived security interests in Asia to the desire to promote human rights; the consequences for regional stability could be jeopardized if China is the recipient of an intensified human rights crusade. Under the Clinton, Bush, and Obama administrations, even linking China's trade benefits to its human rights record was viewed as counterproductive—China might become resentful and retaliate in ways that would be destabilizing for the region, such as not cooperating in the Security Council or making irresponsible arms sales. The Trump Administration took an opposite view and demanded fair trade deals with China while criticizing their human rights record and failure to warn the world of the COVID 19 pandemic that emanated from China.

The traditional mechanism for encouraging countries to develop acceptable human rights records rests with the policy of denying foreign assistance aid or security assistance to countries who are human rights abusers. Security assistance is generally defined as the complete body of statutory programs and authorities under which the United States provides defense articles, military training, and other defense-related services to foreign governments and international organizations for the purpose of enhancing American national policies and objectives. Without question, the security assistance program is a principal element of American foreign policy.

The main objective of security assistance is to enhance American strategic objectives, not only from a regional perspective, but also in key countries within the region. Thus, the basic elements of security assistance involve assisting allies and friendly nations in meeting security threats, securing route access over flight and base rights essential to rapid deployment of United States forces, promoting force commonalities, and improving or maintaining access to critical raw materials.

It is well known that there are also domestic benefits associated with the security assistance program. Not only does the production of defense items provide domestic employment, it generates capital investment and improves the nation's industrial defense mobilization base.

Although the Department of State is responsible for the operation of the security assistance program, it is the National Security Council (NSC) that establishes the overall strategic planning and goals of the program. From the military aspect of security assistance, the Defense Security Assistance Agency (DSAA) is the primary Department of Defense office.

Each United States military Unified Command (collectively they have responsibility for all major regions in the world where American forces are stationed) is required to develop a security assistance program for their region which will assist in achieving assigned strategic goals and missions. After developing a security assistance program, the Commander of each Unified (and Specified) Command (CINC) forwards his security assistance proposal to the Joint Chiefs of Staff (JCS) in Washington where they are evaluated and passed to the NSC for final incorporation into the overall United States strategic plan.

The subordinate component commands of Unified Commands are responsible for the actual implementation of security assistance programs within individual countries in the region. Furthermore, in the countries that are major recipients of security assistance, a Security Assistance Organization (SAO) operates on the ground as part of the Country Team to the American Ambassador in the country. The SAO includes all DOD elements located in the foreign country with assigned responsibilities for carrying out the various security assistance programs for that country. Because of their position, SAOs are afforded a great deal of deference by both the host nation and other Americans working in the host country.

Chief among the legislative authorities for security assistance is the Foreign Assistance Act (FAA) of 1961 (as amended). This act authorizes five basic types of programs as follows:

1. The Foreign Military Financing Program (FMFP). Under this program, defense articles are transferred to friendly nations either through grants, loans, or sales. Defense articles include such things as weapons, munitions, aircraft, vessels, and military equipment.
2. International military education and training (IMET). This program allows the United States military to provide training to foreign military students, primarily in the United States. A primary goal of IMET is to expose the foreign military students to the benefits of a free and democratic society based on the rule of law. Key in this process is the demonstration to the foreign soldiers of how a military is properly subordinated to civilian control. Not only are channels of communication opened between United States and foreign nationals, but it is hoped that the personal contacts made as a result of the training will encourage the promotion of democratic values and human rights in the future.
3. Antiterrorism assistance. A relatively new program, the antiterrorism program attempts to assist those democratic nations that are plagued by terrorist organizations.
4. Economic support fund. This program provides direct grant monies to the recipient nation in an effort to assist in economic recovery or development.
5. Peacekeeping operations. This provision authorizes assistance in the form of personnel and equipment to friendly countries and international organizations for peacekeeping operations.

The second major piece of security assistance legislation is the Arms Export Control Act (AECA). The AECA directly ties in with the applicable provisions of the FAA and provides for the sale of defense articles and services to other countries. The definition of what constitutes a defense article remains the same as under the FAA. A defense service includes any service, test, inspection, repair, training, publication, or other assistance, or defense information used for the purpose of making military sales.

A key element in the AECA defense service definition is "training." As defined in the act:

Training includes formal or informal instruction of foreign students in the United States or overseas by officers or employees of the United States, contract technicians, or contractors (including instruction at civilian institutions), or by correspondence courses, technical, educational, or information publications and media of all kinds, training aid, orientation, training exercise, and military advice to foreign military units and forces.

Congress exercises its authority in two ways: through the budget process and through the legislative process. Under the budget process, Congress does not simply allocate a fixed sum of money to the Department of State to allow them to operate the security assistance program through DSAA. Exercising their "power of the purse," Congress engages in micro-management by earmarking specific dollar amounts to specific countries.

From the earmarking of about half of the security assistance budget in the 1980s, Congress now earmarks about 90 percent of all security assistance monies. In addition, not content with earmarking monies to individual recipient States, Congress increasingly directs through functional accounts exactly how the earmarked money for a particular country will be spent. This Congressional practice has taken almost all of the flexibility away from the State Department and hence, the security assistance administrators.

The second manner in which Congress has inserted itself in the process rests in myriad legislative prohibitions on providing security assistance. Apart from numerous country-specific restrictions, a sampling of the general prohibitions reveals just how complex the administration of security assistance program has become:

1. The prohibition against American personnel performing defense services of a combatant nature. Set out at 21(c)(1) of the AECA, 22, "Personnel performing defense services sold under this act may not perform any duties of a combatant nature, including any duties related to training and advising that may engage United States personnel in combat activities outside the United States in connection with the performance of those defense services." Thus, if American military personnel find themselves in any situation where hostilities occur, or are imminent, they must cease training and withdraw from the area. This has occurred on many occasions in the past, particularly in situations where Army Special Forces are training host nation soldiers in unstable countries.

2. The prohibition against American forces training police forces, found at Section 660 of the FAA, provides that foreign assistance funds cannot be used to "provide training, advice, or financial support to police, prisons, or other law enforcement forces of a foreign government or for any program of internal intelligence or surveillance on behalf of a foreign government." This section has been amended to allow such training to longtime democracies with no standing armed forces and which do not violate human rights. Costa Rica, for example, has no military.

3. The Kennedy Amendment, at 502B of the FAA, requires that all federal assistance be cut off to any country that "engages in a consistent pattern of gross violations of internationally recognized human rights."

4. The Hickenlooper Amendment, at 620(e)(1) of the FAA, deals with halting aid to any nation that engages in the expropriation of American property.

5. The Symington-Glenn Amendments, at 669 and 670 of the FAA, deal with issues associated with the transfer of and receipt of nuclear materials. The intent is to keep nuclear arms from spreading to other countries.

6. The Brooke Amendment, at 620(q) of the FAA, mandates the complete termination of foreign assistance (to include United States military assistance) to any country more than twelve months in arrears on payment of debts accrued.

9.8 New Challenges and New Thinking

In terms of promoting peace and advancing human rights, the Middle East remains the most difficult area of the world for the United States to influence. A continuing pattern of violence and bloodshed accurately defines the character of the region, a pattern which was brought home to America with the heinous attacks by al-Qa'eda operatives on the United States, on September 11, 2001, and continues with terror attacks by Islamic radicals in the region abd beyond.

The policy of the United States toward the Middle East is still rooted primarily on maintaining stability in this oil-rich region, with human rights concerns often taking a back seat to financial concerns. Accordingly, the United States spends billions of dollars each year (in equal amounts) in military and economic assistance for the two major powers in the region—Israel and Egypt.

Unfortunately, Islamic radicalism that engages in hostilities against the United States and its allies still seek to fill a power vacuum left by the so-called Arab Spring. Islamic radicalism, which is diametrically opposed to most of the normative values of human rights is offered as the only alternative to the secular, yet non-democratic, Muslim and Arab leaders who are unwilling or unable to address the economic and social disparities of their people. The pivot for democratic advancement is certainly at stake in Iraq and Afghanistan. In reality, the policy of offering a more democratic form of government may be a "bridge too far" or a "bridge too soon."

9.9 Questions for Discussion

1. *Causes of aggression.* Dr. Stanton E. Samenow, Jr., INSIDE THE CRIMINAL MIND, 1984:

    > Criminals cause crime—not bad neighborhoods, inadequate parents, television, schools, drugs, or unemployment. Crime resides in the minds of human beings and is not caused by social conditions. Once we as a society recognize this simple fact, we shall take measures radically different from current ones. To be sure, we shall continue to remedy intolerable social conditions for this is worthwhile in and of itself. But we shall not expect criminals to change because of such efforts.

    Is Dr. Samenow's observation correct?

2. *Correct analysis but flawed execution?* Reflecting the fact that democracies do not engage in aggression and do a better job at promoting human rights concerns, democratization was a central core of the Bush Administration's policy for the Middle East. How can democratization be achieved when it appears that centrifugal forces of violence have now been unleashed in many parts of the Middle East? Will the Trump Administration's policy of "live and let live" in Iraq and Afghanistan achieve positive results?

3. *Was the War on Terror a battle of religions?* The 2006 National Security Strategy of the United States of America states:

    > While the War on Terror is a battle of ideas, it is not a battle of religions. The transnational terrorists confronting us today exploit the proud religion of Islam to serve a violent political vision: the establishment, by terrorism and subversion, of a totalitarian empire

that denies all political and religious freedom. These terrorists distort the idea of jihad into a call for murder against those they regard as apostates or unbelievers—including Christians, Jews, Hindus, other religious traditions, and all Muslims who disagree with them. Indeed, most of the terrorist attacks since September 11 have occurred in Muslim countries—most of the victims have been Muslims.

Is any one religion more likely to engage in terrorism than another? Although Biblical Christianity is distinguished from all other major world religions in that it rejects any system of human good deeds, morality, or ritual as the vehicle to achieve eternal relationship with God, Christians have engaged in terrorism. *See* Jeffrey F. Addicott, *The Misuse of Religion in the War on Terror*, 7 BARRY L. J. 109 (Fall 2006).

4. *What role does the concept of virtue play in the survivability of a democracy?* Tytler's observation about the rise and fall of nations seems to imply that democracies work only when a majority of the people are virtuous. R. E. Lee once observed that "when virtue is absent from the people, the nation will collapse." Define virtue. Explain how virtue is necessary for capitalism to function. Can socialism promote virtue?

Selected Bibliography

Defense Institute of Security Assistance Management. THE MANAGEMENT OF SECURITY ASSISTANCE, 12th ed. 1992.

Howard, A.E. Dick. CONSTITUTION MAKING IN EASTERN EUROPE, 1993.

Humphrey, John T. NO DISTANT MILLENNIUM: THE INTERNATIONAL LAW OF HUMAN RIGHTS, 1989.

Lesser, Ian O., et al. COUNTERING THE NEW TERRORISM, 1999.

Lillich, Richard B., and Frank C. Newman. INTERNATIONAL HUMAN RIGHTS, 1991.

O'Brien, William V. THE CONDUCT OF JUST AND LIMITED WAR, 1981.

Oppenheim, Lassa. INTERNATIONAL LAW: A TREATISE, 1955.

Simpkin, Richard. RACE TO THE SWIFT: THOUGHTS ON TWENTY-FIRST CENTURY WARFARE, 1985.

THE NATIONAL INTELLIGENCE STRATEGY OF THE UNITED STATES OF AMERICA, Aug. 2009. FIND UPDATED Version

Thieme, Robert B., Jr. THE INTEGRITY OF GOD. Houston, TX: R.B. Thieme, 1979.

Chapter 10

Leading the Way—
Pax Americana or the Rule of Law?

Let he who desires peace, prepare for war.

—Flavius Vegetius Renatus (first century A.D.)

Synopsis

The fact that the United States saved Western Europe and the free world in two World Wars by the use of its magnificent military establishment, coupled with its even greater industrial complex, does not imply that the end of the War on Terror will set the stage for a pax Americana. Much like President Roosevelt's attempt to color the participation of the United States in World War II with a far greater purpose than national self-interest, President Bush's concern for protecting the United States was also cognizant of promoting world stability. To his great credit, President Bush chose the rule of law as his rallying point and did not fall into the trap of embracing issues and matters that appealed to utopian ideals beyond the scope of the War on Terror. This error was made by his father, President George Herbert W. Bush, in his desire to advance an idea known as the *New World Order* in the context of the Gulf War. President Trump emphasized the need to use the U.S. military to fight and win clearly defined wars, but not to nation build. Biden is less dogmatic on the matter.

10.1 The United States Global Strategic View

Although the War on Terror caused a dramatic shift to homeland security as the primary mission of the United States military, the overall strategy since the end of the Cold War has been one of active engagement or deterrence through power projection. At least in theory, active engagement also has a positive aim of promoting democracy, regional stability, and economic prosperity. However, in the context of conducting "operations other than war," the orientation has shifted from containing the menace posed by an expansionist Soviet Union to responding to regional conflicts throughout the world.

Since regional conflicts may vary and are far less monolithic than the old Soviet threat, ad hoc coalitions have replaced formal alliances. This was seen in the 1991 Gulf War as well as in the ongoing

War on Terror. To support the active engagement theory, force generation has also changed from forward deployment to forward presence—no longer are large numbers of United States forces permanently stationed in foreign countries to ensure the peace. The Trump Administration has rejected keeping a large residual force in Iraq, Syria, or Afghanistan and replaced it with a new strategy which envisions a force projection of small contingents of American forces deployed on the foreign soil of other States, such as Yemen and the Philippines, to assist in blunting the impact of al-Qa'eda forces and other like-minded terrorist groups.

Another purpose of these small scale deployments of American fighters is to deter aggression simply by being present in the region. Ultimately, deterrence remains a key component of strategic policy in the post-War on Terror period, with the United States threatening the full scale use of force to punish aggression should the challenge arise.

Still, in the face of drastic military reductions in United States military forces since the 1990s, the elite ground forces available for these unique missions are being stretched to the breaking point. Demanding that the military do more with less causes many to express skepticism about maintaining the required effectiveness to fight and win a conflict with the ever elusive al-Qa'eda and the renegade States like Iran who seek access to weapons of mass murder.

One fact stands certain. The United States cannot take a strong leadership role in promoting democracy in liberated lands with an emasculated military. There is no historical basis to validate the proposition that a nation can successfully increase its influence in the world while simultaneously reducing its armed forces. If history has proven anything, it is that the machinations of aggressor nations bent on expansion are not stopped by negotiation or peace overtures. In dealing with aggressor nations, the avenues of unilateral military reduction, negotiation, or appeasement do not lead to the path of peace—all are false concepts washed in utopian nonsense. The shared revulsion against war and terrorism that all free people possess will have no good effect unless it is coupled with an enforcement mechanism rooted in the application of lawful violence or the threat of lawful violence.

10.2 American Leadership in National Security

Collective security has always required a dominant leader with a sufficient military establishment. Devoid of any military arm of its own, the United Nations could not deal with, for example, Saddam Hussein and his continued violations of international law. In the twentieth century, that has always meant the United States. This is true in every case in which international collective security has functioned. The lesson of the War on Terror is the same as that of the 1991 Gulf War and the Korean War: the United Nations does not have the capacity to guarantee the security of its members absent the direct participation of the United States.

In the real world, the question will be the same as it has always been. Will the people of the United States continue to possess the resolve to assist in the struggle to halt major acts of aggression in the future? As demonstrated in the War on Terror, it is probable that a majority of Americans will continue to possess such resolve, although there are clear signs that the pivot of patriots in the United States that truly understand these truths is rapidly shrinking. Apart from matters of self-interest, the United States of America does have a continuing responsibility to the world to enforce the rule of law. Judged by any positive standard, be it in the field of human rights, self-determination, economic opportunity, or privacy related to property and person, the United States still stands out as the pearl of all that is possible for any given nation to achieve. Furthermore, America, like great nations before it, has related all of these positive values to a strong heritage of law. The Framers of the nation established certain democratic values, and subsequent generations have generally exhibited the discipline and courage to maintain and expand those values. America is exceptional.

America's most fundamental asset does not reside in her military might or industrial complex. Those pillars merely provide support for the United States' most precious commodity—freedom as related to the rule of law. Although the United States military most certainly deterred the aggressiveness of the Soviet Empire from 1945 to 1991, it was the beacon of American freedom and capitalism that ultimately dispelled the darkness of communism. To the world, then, the United States offers a pattern of prosperity and freedom under the rule of law. This is the message that the United States must continue to send to the world.

The world is still a very dangerous place and, as never before, it is time for forward thinking in the long term as the nation prosecutes the War on Terror. Coming out of the Cold War, millions of people in Central Asia and Eastern Europe still have little frame of reference for a nation or, for that matter, a world that is ruled by law. Indeed, the governments of the Middle East lag far behind in fulfilling the requirements of first and second generation human rights.

Undeniably, the legitimate interest of the United States in halting international terrorism in the era of weapons of mass destruction has benefited the entire civilized world. For freedom loving peoples everywhere, the 2001 victory in Afghanistan and the successful conclusion of the Iraq War and destruction of ISIS ensured that the cost of maintaining freedom was paid by another generation of patriotic Americans. To a large degree, this sacrifice not only enforces the rule of law, but undoubtedly serves as a deterrent to other tyrants and terrorists. Unfortunately, memories of both tyrants and democracies are short and the struggle for freedom must be played out in each and every generation.

It is a fundamental principle that all free States have a common interest in maintaining peace. However, peace, like security, is a precious commodity rarely attained without great sacrifice. In addition, peace is far more than the absence of war; it is an elusive intangible which only takes on meaning when related to freedom. Although the goal of abolishing war, like eradicating crime, is certainly commendable, given the basic nature of man, neither goal is totally feasible. As long as there are demagogues like Sennacherib, Hitler, Stalin, Saddam Hussein, and Ahmadinejad, nation-states must have strong military establishments to protect themselves. Under this truism, the symbol of freedom for Americans is not a cracked Liberty Bell in Philadelphia, but the military uniform of its fighting men.

Accepting the premise that human beings are morally flawed creatures (Chapter 9), it stands to reason that the best that mankind can ever hope to achieve is to control aggression. Like criminals, aggressive nations and terrorists can only be deterred through the proper functioning of two principles: (1) the threat of lawful force; or (2) the application of lawful force. To the extent that the function of these two principles fail, wars will certainly continue to exist. Paradoxically, those groups who resist this truism, demonstrated by irrational demands for peace through the continued restriction of all categories of force, blissfully lay the groundwork for the next war.

The oft-heard saying, "violence never solves anything," is a favorite catch phrase for so-called "peace activists" and progressives. Of course, as is the case for many such glib expressions, it is a falsehood that does not stand up to reason or historical scrutiny. As illustrated by the Allied defeat of the Axis powers in World War II, only the application of lawful violence ultimately solved the problem of Axis aggression and murder. In short, the use of lawful violence in self-defense is a hard reality of life that must always remain as the number one legitimate option to secure the peace. While nonviolence expressed in the form of public demonstrations, boycotts, "sit-ins," etc., may be efficacious when confronting social injustice in certain organizations and governments that are based to some degree on democratic foundations, such activities seldom make any progress when used to confront committed totalitarian forces. Even Martin Luther King, an American champion of nonviolence, conceded that this tactic would be useless against tyrants.

> I felt that while war could never be a positive or absolute good, it could serve as a negative good in the sense of preventing the spread and growth of an evil force. War, as horrible as it is, might be preferable to surrender to a totalitarian system—Nazi, Fascist, or Communist.

Sadly, in the course of the human experience, it is sometimes the case that nothing except the employment of lawful violence will thwart the use of aggressive violence and the correct moral course is to employ lawful violence. Understanding this truth is fundamental to penetrating the state of mind of those who simply reject violence under any circumstances. Tragically, those most devoted to peace above all values seem ill prepared to recognize that the cost of not using lawful violence may only ensure a continuation of aggressive violence that often spirals out of control.

Peace activists who use religion (primarily their reading of "Christianity") to justify a rejection of force come in many varieties. Some try to mask their refusal to engage in violence with Bible verses taken out of context, while others simply make broad religious generalizations about the matter. For instance, William H. De Lancey, bishop of the Episcopal Diocese of New York, wrote a letter to President Abraham Lincoln in 1863 invoking religion to avoid participating in the American Civil War. He demanded that he and all other bishops and priests be exempted from the federal conscription laws. De Lancey wrote, "[I]t is contrary to their consciences as officers of Christ's kingdom to bear arms as soldiers and shed blood." Continuing with the letter, Bishop De Lancey reminded Lincoln that in the garden of Gethsemane on the occasion of his arrest, Christ told Peter in Matthew 26:52 that, "[t]hey that take the sword shall perish with the sword." Of course, in making his case, the bishop rejected the more sensible and Biblically correct view that this passage refers to the societal consequences of criminal behavior, i.e., criminals will be lawfully executed by the State for their crimes, and not a prohibition regarding the lawful use of force in combat activities.

If peace at any price, with compromise as the only means to achieve it, is the major concern of a national entity, then the destruction of that nation will be the inevitable consequence. Freedom, not peace, must always be the issue for free nations; when nations are no longer willing to pay the price of freedom, then they, too, will lose their freedom. As Woodrow Wilson so wisely reflected in May of 1917: "It is not an army that we must train for war; it is a nation."

Tragically, in every democratic nation rest the very seeds which will eventually destroy it, for the choice between freedom or peace must be made by each successive generation. With freedom, war is periodically inevitable. By reflexively choosing peace without maintaining the power to enforce the peace, war will come more often and with a greater probability of seeing the annihilation of the nation. Just as crime increases when society gets sentimental about the criminal and forgets about the victim, so too will the probability of war increase as the nation emphasizes peace instead of freedom.

When Spain was attacked by a series of coordinated terror bombings in March 2004, killing 200 commuters, the response to the al-Qa'eda-linked terrorists was to withdraw all Spanish military personnel from the then ongoing allied occupation of Iraq. This step signaled to the terrorists that terror attacks can produce a desired outcome. In quick step, the terrorists used additional terror threats and acts of terror to intimidate the Philippines, who withdrew their forces early from Iraq in response to a kidnapping and threat of beheading. On the other hand, threats to Italy and Australia to withdraw from Iraq were not successful even though in July of 2004, the Australians were warned that "we will shake the earth under your feet as we did in Indonesia [referring to the 2002 Bali bombing which killed over 200 people, mostly Australians on vacation], and lines of car bombs will not cease." Similarly, the Abu Jafs al-Masri Brigades' threat to "shake the earth" everywhere in Italy, unless the Italians withdrew their military from Iraq, did not cause the Italians to budge. The Italian and Australian leadership remembered the lesson of Munich—appeasement only encourages aggression.

Ultimately, the cost of achieving freedom can only be understood by those who have paid the price. Indeed, there is no permanent guarantee that the United States will continue to function as a national entity without a strong military-industrial complex coupled with the people who have the will to fight if necessary.

For this reason, it is dangerous rhetoric to blur the fundamental distinction between the need for the legitimate use of force and unlawful aggression. Despite disclaimers that the concept of "world peace" should not be related to restricting the use of force or promoting unilateral disarmament, the connotation is otherwise. No anti-war movement has ever been premised on patriotism or maintaining a strong and viable military, and no proponent of the use of lawful violence can ever hope to be immune from the wishful thinking of those who demand the dismantling of the very forces that sustain and protect the freedom of the nation—the military establishment.

On the other hand, the concept of the rule of law does not necessarily carry with it the connotation that man is capable of achieving the panacea of world peace. For the rule of law, it is enough if aggressive war can be controlled for a period of time. As international law expert Professor Bob Turner noted during the Gulf War of 1991: "At the root of United States policy in the Gulf War was the principle of upholding the Rule of Law. Article 2 (4) of the U.N. Charter outlaws armed international aggression, and the massive Iraqi invasion of Kuwait was a direct challenge to that principle."

In short, how does one react to those nations or groups who either contemplate the use of unlawful force or who actually engage in such unlawful force? In the modern world, the U.N. Charter is undeniably the foremost legal tool in dealing with and deterring aggression; it is an integral component of the rule of law. The classic McDougal and Feliciano, *Law and Minimum Public Order*, states:

> The most difficult problem which today confronts world public order is that of characterizing and preventing unlawful violence. The history is familiar how over the centuries—through *bellum justum*, the Covenant of the League of Nations, the Pact of Paris, the judgments at Nuremberg and Tokyo, and the U.N. Charter—the public order of the world community has at long last come to a prohibition of certain coercion as a method of international change and to a distinction between permissible and nonpermissible coercion.

Although history has proven time and again that the curtailment of aggression can only come through the threat of force, or the application of force, the authority for those responses must be firmly rooted in law. Despite this truism, the necessity for and legality of Article 51 is, nonetheless, constantly under attack by those groups who intentionally blur the difference between lawful and unlawful uses of force. In their search for the panacea of brotherhood, various peace groups refuse to acknowledge any distinction regarding the use of force. Left unchallenged, this attitude will only encourage aggression, not forestall it. For example, President Bush performed admirably in the task of articulating to the world the distinction between the unlawful use of force by an aggressor and the lawful use of force under the rule of law by civilized nations. In fact, those who advocate ending war by destroying the forests of bayonets (i.e., unilateral disarmament) hinder the validity of the rule of law to that extent.

Historically, the desire of numerous organizations to curtail or eliminate the use of force as a national option, regardless of the justification for the employment of that force, is always present in any debate on how to best answer aggression. While these voices are helpful if kept in proper perspective, appeasement is nothing new. The Biblical prophet Jeremiah heard the same voices almost 2,500 years ago as peace activists in the Southern Kingdom of Judah proposed how to deal with the aggression of Chaldean militarism. Jeremiah analyzed the peace at any cost advocates as follows: "They allege to solve the problems of my people, [they cry] 'Peace, peace' when there is no peace."

10.3 Peace, Freedom and Appeasement—Lessons from the Gulf War of 1991

The voices in the War on Terror who call for peace at any price say nothing new—the same voices occurred in the Gulf War of 1991, although far more loudly than in the War on Terror. Calling for peace in the Gulf War at any price, some paid little regard for even the most clearly worded rules and norms associated with the rule of law as it applies to the lawful use of force. This phenomenon extended all the way from the highest levels of the United Nations to, as to be expected, an assortment of politically active anti-war groups.

At the top echelon, this phenomenon was brought out rather dramatically on November 8, 1990, when none other than the Secretary General of the United Nations, Perez de Cuellar, opined that because no nation had taken military action against Iraq since the occupation of Kuwait in August 1990, "the passage of three months time had terminated the right of individual states to use force against Iraq under the 'collective self-defense' provisions of Article 51." Not only did de Cuellar's statement exhibit a gross misunderstanding of the U.N. Charter, it did nothing but encourage the continued aggression of the Iraqi military.

Certainly, de Cuellar knew that Article 51 did not create the right of self-defense, but that such a right was an inherent right which Article 51 simply acknowledged and reinforced. Furthermore, Iraq's aggression did not end on August 2, 1990, but was a continuing offense, since none of the Security Council resolutions demanding that Iraq leave Kuwait had succeeded in "maintaining international peace and security."

The policy implications of the Secretary General's position revealed its total absurdity; a rule that requires nations to respond immediately to an armed attack or else forfeit their rights to take defensive action effectively nullifies the principles embodied in Article 2(3) and 2(4) of the U.N. Charter. By making a mockery of this critical rule of law, de Cuellar sent two disastrous signals, one to Saddam Hussein and one to the community of nations. First, the Secretary General's total misreading of Article 51 only encouraged Iraq's continuing occupation of Kuwait and was completely counterproductive to the international movement to force Iraq out of Kuwait short of armed force. Second, the requirement that nations act immediately in self-defense is the antithesis of what the United Nation encourages, i.e., the peaceful settlement of disputes through diplomacy and every other peaceful channel for resolution of conflict. Finally, the longer the hesitation in the use of legitimate force (give peace a chance), the more probable that the same peace activists would view the coalition forces as the aggressor!

The more common variety of anti-war groups also hoped that the end of the Cold War would be the catalyst for their simplistic notions concerning the abolition of war. Advocating peace, but having no idea of what the concept must necessarily entail—the willingness to fight for peace—numerous anti-war activists demanded appeasement. Paradoxically, the loud demands for peace during the six month

Iraqi occupation of Kuwait probably ensured that the threat of force as a deterrence would most surely fail, leaving no alternative but the use of lawful violence.

As Saddam Hussein held firm in Kuwait with no signs of withdrawal, various religious groups also voiced dismay over those who contemplated the exercise of lawful armed force against Iraq under Article 51. For example, both the Vatican daily newspaper, *Losservatore Romano*, and the official publication of the Jesuit order, *La Civilta Cattolica*, spoke out against using force to expel Iraq from Kuwait. On November 17, 1990, *La Civilta Cattolica* wrote, "The [coming] war in the Gulf will be a moral shame and a political disaster."

In his traditional Christmas message, Pope John Paul II gave the following heartfelt warning to those who contemplated the use of force to expel Saddam Hussein: "May leaders be convinced that war is an adventure with no return. By reasoning, patience, and dialogue with respect for the inalienable rights of people and nations, it is possible to identify and travel the paths of understanding and peace." In the final analysis, the Pope's sincere desire for "[n]o more war, war never again" is a beautiful ideal but, unfortunately, can sometimes prove counterproductive in the maintenance of world peace. Often, such signals encourage aggression if no room is left for the use of lawful force to halt aggression *ab initio* or to challenge aggression once it has become entrenched. In fact, one commentator observed that of the thirty-eight times the Pope spoke out against the Gulf War, "[t]here was not an echo of a hint of a suggestion that the United States and its allies (including Italy) were in a battle against a tyrant who had just invaded and [sic] occupied and brutally destroyed a small neighbor...."

Some religious leaders, emotionally obsessed by the fact that large numbers of soldiers were going to be killed in war, irrationally concluded that all war in the modern era was immoral, regardless of the motivation. Fueled by reports that some Iraqi soldiers had been buried alive in their defensive positions by American tanks, a religious publicist, Guy Munger, concluded that "any discussion of whether Desert Storm was a just war seem[s] to border on the insane. Indeed, practical application of the theory may have ended with the crossbow." According to Munger, "modern war is always immoral." Of course, the argument is totally fallacious for two reasons. First, long before the crossbow, battle casualties could easily mount into the hundreds of thousands. For example, during the Second Punic War (219–202 B.C.), the Carthaginian forces under Hannibal killed in combat over 60,000 Roman soldiers in a single day. And second, Munger fails to understand the real world consequences associated with a refusal to defend oneself.

Claiming to be a spokesperson for morality and justice, the wife of Martin Luther King, Jr., Coretta King, also attempted to derail the United States-led military coalition to eject Saddam Hussein from Kuwait. She referred to the American actions as a "low [point] since the death of Dr. King." Speaking on January 11, 1991, Mrs. King called on a new anti-war movement to be launched on January 15, 1991, the date of the United Nations' deadline for Iraq to withdraw from Kuwait or face the use of force: "And so I am urging everyone who believes in Martin Luther King, Jr.'s dream of peace to use this holiday to launch a new anti-war movement that will not rest until a peaceful resolution of the conflict in the Persian Gulf is secured."

Failing to elaborate on how this peace movement could force a brutal dictator to relinquish his death grip on Kuwait, Mrs. King actually called the proposed American participation in the Gulf War "wrong and immoral." Like other peace activists who refuse to consider the application of force under any circumstances, Mrs. King's call for "peace-loving people everywhere to accelerate their efforts to stop it" did nothing except encourage the ruthlessness of the Iraqi occupation then occuring in Kuwait.

Similarly, the president of the Southern Christian Leadership Conference, Reverend Joseph Lowery, objected to the United States military action on moral grounds saying, "Let us call upon the nations to spend our resources on medical supplies, not military supplies; to make tractors, not tanks; to beat missiles into morsels of bread to feed the hungry; to build housing, not foxholes." Again, if history has demonstrated anything, it has revealed that utopian rhetoric about turning "swords into plowshares" is not helpful in deterring people and nations who exhibit aggressive tendencies.

Obviously, Man is always confronted with aggression; a world devoid of conflict is not something that is in the here and now. The attitude of any free people is to be well prepared for war so that the nation may either rattle the saber or, if necessary, employ the saber against forces of aggression. While some pacifists are keen to cherry pick statements in the Bible regarding the future millennium reign of Jesus Christ on the earth, those who wish to enter a new world before that escetalogical time in which "swords are turned into plowshares" need to recall the comments of Haynes Johnson of the *Washington Post*: "[this] is not the millennium; the new world order has not arrived." Unfortunately, the sincere but unrealistic belief that war can be curtailed by third-party dispute settlement processes or by massive disarming processes was not buried in the lessons of the Gulf War of 1991.

10.4 Peace, Freedom and Appeasement—Lessons from the War on Terror

While the murderous machinations of al-Qa'eda-styled militant Islam constantly invoke religious beliefs to justify the use of the most horrible forms of illegal violence, some voices in the West appropriate their own system of religious beliefs as a justification to advance platforms of pacifism in dealing with aggression. Many religious leaders in the West will align themselves with anti-war activists and then employ religion as the reason that they reject all forms of violence whatsoever, self-defense or otherwise. For these voices of appeasement, a misapplication of religious belief is used as a justification *not* to use lawful violence to curtail aggression. Paradoxically, as history has proven time and time again, appeasement—be it in the name of religion or not—cannot long curtail those intent on aggression. Such wishful thinking simply emboldens the aggressor and inevitably leads to an increase in the butcher's bill of human suffering. A sampling of remarks during the War on Terror is all that is necessary to address the theme of those who call for peace at any price, with little or no regard for the long standing norms and rules associated with the lawful use of force.

In her 2006 book, *The Mighty and the Almighty*, even the liberal-minded Madeleine Albright opposed the voices of appeasement that protested the pending military campaign against the Taliban regime in Afghanistan following the attacks of 9/11. Not only did she disagree with the official 2001 call by the World Council of Churches to not strike back against the terrorists, but she also questioned the soundness of prize winning author Alice Walker's naive admonishment that "the only punishment that works is love."

In November of 2002, as the United States and its coalition of the willing were gearing up to expand the War on Terror to Iraq, over 70 religious leaders in the United States and the United Kingdom issued a joint statement that condemned the contemplated use of what they termed "preemptive war" against the regime of Saddam Hussein. Recognizing that the Iraqi government had a duty to "stop its internal repression, to end its threats to peace, to abandon its efforts to develop weapons of mass destruction, and to respect the legitimate role of the United Nations in ensuring that it does so," the religious leaders nevertheless insisted that as "Christians" they were certain that the United States, Britain, and the international community could only employ the tools of "moral principles, political wisdom, and international law" to confront Saddam:

As Christians, we seek to be guided by the vision of a world in which nations do not attempt to resolve international problems by making war on other nations. It is a long held Christian principle that all governments and citizens are obliged to work for the avoidance of war.

In closing the statement, the group quoted the familiar Biblical passage "nation shall not lift up sword against nation," which, although very popular in anti-war circles, is grossly distorted from its proper scriptural context. The passage clearly deals with eschatological teachings about the future and not the current world we reside in. They wrote: "We reaffirm our religious hope for a world in which 'nation shall not lift up sword against nation.' We pray that our governments will be guided by moral principles, political wisdom, and legal standards, and will step back from their calls for war."

Similarly, in late 2002, the President of the United Methodist Council of Bishops wrote a pastoral letter to the United Methodist congregation, of which President Bush and Vice President Cheney are both members, stating that "war by the United States against a nation like Iraq goes against the very grain of *our understanding of the gospel*, our church's teachings, and our conscience [emphasis added]."

With the defeat of Saddam Hussein and the end of the international armed conflict with Iraq in May 2003, the Bush Administration was faced with an unexpected deadly level of sectarian violence fueled in part by a variety of criminal groups, al-Qa'eda terrorists, and Saddam loyalists. Nevertheless, the theme of religious-based anti-war activists remained the same. When Reverend Al Sharpton met anti-war activist Cindy Sheehan at an interfaith service on Sunday, August 28, 2005, outside of Crawford, Texas, he did so based on his "moral obligation" to oppose the war. In March of 2003, two well-known bishops and one church official were among 65 people arrested during an anti-war protest near the White House. United Methodist Bishop Joseph Sprague; Jim Winkler, the general secretary of the United Methodist Board of Church and Society; and Roman Catholic Bishop Thomas Gumbleton of Detroit were included among those arrested. Winkler said that his religious board had "stated that the war is wrong."

After receiving the 2002 Nobel Peace Prize in Oslo, Norway, former President Jimmy Carter concluded his December 10, 2002 remarks by asserting that God gives mankind the capacity for choice and that war is always an evil, even when necessary, and "never a good."

War may sometimes be a necessary evil. But no matter how necessary, it is always an evil, never a good. We will not learn to live together in peace by killing each other's children. The bond of our common humanity is stronger than the divisiveness of our fears and prejudices. God gives us the capacity for choice. We can choose to alleviate suffering. We can choose to work together for peace. We can make these changes—and we must.

While many leading religious leaders have issued statements condemning the use of force in both Iraq and in the Bush-era war in Afghanistan, the majority of Christians prior to the war in Iraq supported the use of force. For example, the 16 million-strong Southern Baptist Convention, the largest denomination in America (made up of Southern conservatives), sent a letter to President Bush "assuring him that the Iraqi threat satisfied the conditions of a 'just war.'" (Current opposition by the American public is not based on moral or religious grounds, but on a sense that the mission of bringing democratic reforms cannot be accomplished.) In addition, George Weigel, a biographer of Pope John Paul II as well as a leading Catholic commentator and Senior Fellow of the Ethics and Public Policy Center, also believed that the 2003 war against Iraq was justified.

In the case of Iraq, the crucial issue in the moral analysis is what we mean by an "aggression under way." When a vicious regime that has not hesitated to use chemical weapons against its own people and against a neighboring country, a regime that has no concept of the rule of law and that flagrantly violates its international obligations, works feverishly to obtain and deploy further weapons of mass destruction, I think a compelling moral case can be made that this is a matter of an "aggression under way." The nature of the regime, which is the crucial factor in the analysis, makes that plain. It surely makes no moral sense to say that the U.S. or the international community can only respond with armed force when an Iraqi missile carrying a weapon of mass destruction has been launched, or is being readied for launch. To be sure, there are serious questions of prudence to be addressed in thinking through the question of military action against the Iraqi regime. At the level of moral principle, however, it seems to me that there are, in fact, instances where it is not only right to "go first," but "going first" may even be morally obligatory. And I think this may well be one of those instances.

Weigel also criticized other "clerical opponents of war...[as giving] themselves over to a functional pacifism, a conviction that there are virtually no circumstances in which the proportionate and discriminate use of armed force can serve the goals of peace, order, justice and freedom." Indeed, some of the more extreme pacifists go so far as to blame the "Christian God" and President Bush as instigating an "American Inquisition" in the War on Terror. Curiously, when a liberal President, like Barack Obama, engages in combat activities to include the unprecedented use of drone attacks and the huge 2009-2010 deployment of U.S. soldiers in Afghanistan, the pacifists and leftists remain muted. There are no "Cindy Sheehans" or "World Council of Churchs" taking to the streets in massive outrage.

Still, for the committed pacifist, there simply should be no relationship between religion and warfare. Their interpretation of religion prohibits all forms of violence whatsoever. Further, they steadfastly oppose people who invoke God to justify violence in self-defense. While one can certainly agree with the utopian idea that war, crime, poverty, and a whole host of evils should not exist in the world, it is a fact that they do. When asked by his disciples what would be the signs that would signal His second coming to the world, Jesus Christ himself declared that wars would continue to be a part of the landscape until His return: "And you will be hearing of wars and rumors of wars; see that you are not frightened, for those things must take place, but that is not yet the end."

To some, pacifism is a fundamental aspect of being a "Christian." Liberals think that they are somehow reflecting the attitude and concepts of Jesus Christ by trying to abolish war. This is absurd because it is Biblically incorrect. To use the Bible to justify an uncompromising belief in pacifism requires one to distort, ignore, or otherwise explain away vast areas of scripture that speak approvingly of specific instances where violence is justified and necessary to protect various values and objects. Jesus of Nazareth himself engaged in physical violence (making a whip and striking the money changers in the Temple) during his three year ministry and would be considered by religious pacifists as quite "anti-Christian" in his dealings with the religious leaders and legalists of the day—calling them, among other things, "of your father the Devil" (Jn. 8:44a).

A fair understanding of the Bible does not support the human viewpoint expressed by the religious anti-war activist. In AD 425, Augustine, the Bishop of Hippo, strongly affirmed the idea that the Bible does not prohibit or condemn a Christian from engaging in combat on the battlefield. In a letter to a Roman Christian by the name of Boniface, Augustine told him to fight the invading tribes called the Vandals because "[w]ar is waged in order that peace may be obtained." As stated in Ecclesiastes and echoed throughout the Bible, in the affairs of mankind there is clearly "[a] time for war, and a time for peace." The hope is that when a soldier goes to war, he will be militarily prepared, per Psalms 144:1—"[God] teach my hands to war and my fingers to fight"—and that the national leadership will heed Proverbs 20:18, by choosing to "make war by wise guidance."

10.5 Stay with the Rule of Law

To a large degree, history is defined by the workings of spheres of power which are commonly categorized into eras. Within these eras, the trends of history are replete with great wars whose goal was to end all wars. While the natural tendency of mankind is to promote and to nourish the resulting periods of peace between wars, history gives no encouragement to the notion that war will be no more or that peace will be more than a mere handful of years. The collective memory of the world has traditionally proved to be very short. As Will and Ariel Durant wrote: "War is a constant of history. In the last 3,451 years of recorded history, only 268 have seen no war." Since the end of World War II there have been 70 major wars and 400 smaller conflicts. In fact, America has fought eleven major wars and over 180 smaller ones with over 1,000,000 Americans giving their lives.

With the liberation of Kuwait in 1991, President George H.W. Bush became the primary proponent of an ambiguous phrase which he called the "New World Order." President George H.W. Bush attempted to advance this phrase as an international rallying cry for the future of the world. The New World Order was to herald a new era in international affairs, an era of collective security sponsored and reinforced by the United Nations. Expectations for the fulfillment of this goal were understandably high and recalled the old Roman proverb, "For he who desires to become rich also wishes that desire to be soon accomplished." In reality, however, the natural desire to create some form of a New World Order quickly met with failure. Even more disturbing, the promotion of the term New World Order by President Bush served only to minimize or cast doubt on the viability of the rule of law. President George W. Bush was careful not to repeat this mistake as the War on Terror progressed. Catchy utopian phrases are counterproductive to the critical mission of promoting the rule of law and democratic behavior.

To the serious student of history, the concept of the New World Order is neither new in its origin, nor, as the concept might imply, universal in its interpretation; it has existed in many forms. From the *pax Romana* of ancient Rome to the *novus ordo seclorum* printed on the reverse side of the one-dollar bill, the concept of the New World Order has been used by public figures to represent a variety of agendas associated, of course, with a vision for how the world should be ruled.

In the past century, both the Germans under Adolf Hitler and the British under Winston Churchill used the concept to describe their respective notions about the world's future. Although both were seeking to rally public opinion to support a particular objective, they were diametrically opposed in their meaning and application of the concept. Hitler envisioned *Die neue Ordnung* (the New Order) as a world ruled by the master German race, while Churchill wielded it as a sword of international force against Nazi expansionism.

Addressing the League of Nations in 1936, Churchill warned of Hitler's continued pattern of aggression and announced that the "fateful moment [had] arrived for choice between the New Age and the Old." For Churchill, the new age for the world was squarely based on establishing a defensive alliance to defeat the Nazi's quest of conquering Europe and the world.

Adolf Hitler employed the concept in its most aggressive connotation and irrationally believed that he had a sacred mission to establish a New Order through terror, violence and warfare. The Axis powers set out the parameters of their New Order for the world by signing a joint agreement in Berlin, January

1942. Linking their New Order to economic prosperity, the Germans envisioned the world divided into four *Grossraumwirtschaften* (great economics), each led by an authoritarian leader under the ultimate control of Germany. Once the Axis forces had won World War II, "a conclave was to be held in Vienna to legalize Nazi Germany's hegemony within the New Order." Hitler's New Order would initially be made up of German-dominated Europe, Africa, and the Near East, but ultimately it would encompass the entire world.

In the end, Hitler's "New Order for the World" collapsed in a bloody inferno while "Churchill's New Age for the World" silently slipped into the bookshelves of history after it helped to inspire the formation of the United Nations. Although the concepts were similar, the meanings were not.

The New World Order witnessed its latest reincarnation during the Iraqi invasion of Kuwait in August of 1990. In an unprecedented use of the United Nations, President George H.W. Bush used the concept of the New World Order as the focal point for gathering world opinion against the Iraqi occupation of Kuwait. In an effort to consolidate support for the possible use of military force against Iraq, President Bush not only followed Churchill's example against Hitler, but simultaneously offered this old term to describe American foreign policy in the post-Cold War era.

Just a month after the invasion, President George H.W. Bush proclaimed that the New World Order "would be a world where the rule of law supplants the rule of the jungle. A world in which nations recognize the shared responsibility for freedom and justice. A world where the strong respect the rights of the weak." As the months passed and Iraq became more entrenched in Kuwait, the Bush Administration increased the usage of the concept. In a statement delivered on December 5, 1990, before the Senate Foreign Relations Committee, Secretary of State James Baker said, "Historically, we must stand with the people of Kuwait so that the annexation of Kuwait does not become the first reality that mars our vision of the new world order."

Without a doubt, America's vision of the New World Order was to be firmly rooted in the new-founded efficacy of the United Nations to function as the primary legal instrument for maintaining peace in the world, the assumption being that Gorbachev's Russia would no longer use its veto power to hinder the effectiveness of the Security Council. By the close of the Gulf War, the tenets of the New World Order were set: "Peaceful settlements of disputes, solidarity against aggression, reduced and controlled arsenals and just treatment of all peoples."

Unfortunately, from the viewpoint of epistemology, the concept of New World Order was not very successful for the administration of President George H.W. Bush. First, although the New World Order was undeniably catchy, the concept was not really a simple phrase to understand. In reality, the New World Order stood for a whole regime of policies, ranging all the way from universal human rights issues to the peaceful settlement of international disputes. Apart from a handful of scholars devoted to the study of those topics, the hope that a wider audience would understand the concept, without fully grasping the categories behind it, was the primary failure of its proponents.

Second, because President George H.W. Bush chose as his rallying cry a phrase that, throughout the past hundred years, had been used to stand for various propositions, he should have necessarily exerted an even greater amount of time and effort to achieve a minimum amount of association to his meaning. In other words, if a concept is to gain acceptance, the rate of forgetting must not exceed the rate of learning. This, too, was never accomplished, reflected in part by a remarkable lack of attention given to the phrase by the public media.

In his September 1991 address to the United Nations, President Bush specifically stressed the concept of the New World Order several times, even deliberately choosing the theme of the New World

Order to close out his final remarks to the world body. Seeking to establish a straightforward definition, the President dramatically spelled out the elements of the New World Order.

> [The] new world order [is] an order in which no nation must surrender one iota of its own sovereignty; an order characterized by the rule of law rather than the resort to force; the cooperative settlement of disputes, rather than anarchy and bloodshed; and an unstinting belief in human rights.

Unfortunately, this definition was not really the same given at the close of the Gulf War. Then it was "peaceful settlements of disputes, solidarity against aggression, reduced and controlled arsenals and just treatment of all people." In addition, despite a conscious effort by President Bush to fully sponsor the phrase, the domestic media concentrated on the President's condemnation of Iraqi interference with United Nations inspection teams and the ill-conceived "Zionism is racism" General Assembly resolution. Predictably, the news reports that followed Bush's speech failed to mention the New World Order even once. While one might criticize the news media for exhibiting a total failure to publicize the concept, judged by the standards of keeping it simple and promoting repetition, the blame also rested with the Bush administration.

As to simplicity, President George H.W. Bush erred by expanding his initial meaning of the New World Order, most associated with the enforcement of the international rule of law against the raw aggression of Iraq, to a definition which equated the New World Order to various categories of international principles, each requiring a sophisticated level of comprehension. By lumping other concepts ranging from nuclear disarmament to human rights with the concept of the New World Order, the vast majority of the public had no idea what the New World Order "really" entailed. At the time, Harvard's Joseph S. Nye, Jr., remarked, "No one really knows what it means."

Most of the world can quickly grasp the idea of halting an aggressor who has broken the law (e.g., Iraq broke the most critical provision of the rule of law, the prohibition of aggression, in its use of force against Kuwait). But, when one adds, for example, the concept of creating norms for international human rights to the concept of the New World Order, the audience is lost. A brief survey of the concept of humanitarian law reveals that it is, at best, an evolving idea that is not very well understood.

As to repetition, when the public was told that President George H.W. Bush was going to issue a major address to the nation on sweeping nuclear arms initiatives, many "New World Order watchers" anticipated that the concept would be woven throughout the speech. Set for September 27, 1991, the address would follow soon after the United Nations address, which provided President Bush with the perfect opportunity to promote the concept, but this time at the domestic level. Indeed, in President Bush's September 1990 address to the United Nations, he had already set the precedent and employed the concept of the New World Order to urge a worldwide ban on chemical weapons and to continue the efforts to stop the proliferation of nuclear and biological weapons. At that time, President Bush said, "It is in our hands to leave these dark machines [nuclear, chemical and biological weapons] behind, in the dark ages where they belong…to cap a historic movement toward a new world order, and a long era of peace."

When the 1991 address to the nation was made, President George H.W. Bush did not invoke the concept of the New World Order even once. President Bush concentrated on an entirely new concept called "the new age." Pointing out that not only had the Cold War ended, but the Soviet Union was undergoing drastic change, President Bush preferred to justify his proposals for disarmament as in keeping with the new age. Once again, the press exhibited no interest in reporting unfamiliar terminology; the new age was unmentioned.

In summation, after a full year-and-a-half of being in the marketplace of ideas, the New World Order was still unfamiliar to the American public. Consequently, the general domestic understanding of what the New World Order really meant remained inexorably clouded. Of course, if the American public could not understand the New World Order, it was certain the rest of the world was at an even greater disadvantage. This was especially true for emerging democracies. For example, having a vague frame of reference for the notion of a State ruled by law, the vast territories of the old Soviet Empire had only just begun to awaken from a seventy-year nightmare of the most vicious brutality. Although the republics had renounced the twisted and flawed premise upon which the Communist party had rested for seven decades, there was tremendous confusion. Indeed, even with the dawn of the twenty-first century, it will be some time before the former Communist States will be able to implement many of the components associated with democratic values. It is difficult enough for them to grasp the concept of being ruled by law and not by force.

Catchy phrases such as the New World Order have nothing positive to offer those who seek to foster, strengthen and advance the rule of law. If the United States is serious about promoting the rule of law as the basis for its War on Terror, then it must stand as the chief champion of the rule of law as the basis for the War on Terror. The challenge must be to abandon all such new age and new world phrases and to concentrate fully on the never ending business of promoting the rule of law in word as well as deed. In the never-ending struggle to move the credibility of the concept forward, the United States must exhibit a faithful sponsorship of the rule of law in every international forum available.

Many of the most fundamental values, particularly those dealing with the illegality of aggressive war, have been translated into well-rooted rules of law at the cost of untold blood and fortune. Hope remains that many more democratic values will be added to that book, and that the attendant sacrifices will not have been in vain. Although there is no need to speak of the United States as the world's policeman, there is a need for the United States to fully sponsor the rule of law, which remains the best hope to those nations that wish to exist in a sphere of freedom. As the United States fights the War on Terror, it must continuously place emphasis on the rule of law and avoid the use of any descriptive phrase that casts doubt on the supreme function of the rule of law.

10.6 America Must Stay the Course

Since the events of September 11, 2001, the world has entered into a period fraught with uncertainty and yet, strangely, there shines a renewed hope to enlarge the peace and advance human rights. The central hope rests in the great promise of a world more fully based on governments who adhere to human rights and democratic values.

More importantly, America's strongest weapon in the War on Terror did not rest with its military might or police functions. In the long run, America's strongest weapon was its uncompromising commitment to the freedoms and civil liberties embodied in the Constitution and reflected in the U.N. Charter. If we engage in tactics that violate the democratic principles that make up our rule of law, are we different from the terrorists at our gates? The United States of America can only ride the crests of the waves of history so long as it follows a rule of law rooted in human rights and democratic principles. America will drown in the sea of hypocrisy if it trades civil liberties for a mess of pottage. Terrorism consultant Brian Jenkins agrees that the best defense against the terrorists calls for a "continuing commitment to the basic values that … the nation stands for." The real genius of the United States is that it is a nation of immigrants that has managed to unite its disparate parts through common values of freedom and self-determination. These values are embodied in the Constitution and in the Declaration of Independence's expression of a people yearning to be free and to develop the talents given them by their Creator.

10.7 Questions for Discussion

1. *What is the proper role of nationalism in war?* See Edward Gibbons, THE HISTORY OF THE DECLINE AND FALL OF THE ROMAN EMPIRE, Vol. I, 85-86 (1914). Literally, the "peace of Rome," *Pax Romana* refers to the peace and prosperity in the known world, i.e., the Mediterranean, brought about by Roman rule from 27 BC to AD 180. Gibbon, widely recognized as the foremost modern scholar on the Roman Empire, places the high point of *pax Romana* at AD 96 to 180, the period of the Antoine Caesars:

   > If a man were called to fix the period in the history of the world during which the condition of the human race was most happy and prosperous, he would without hesitation, name that which elapsed from the death of Domitian [AD 96] to the accession of Commodus [AD 180]. The vast extent of the Roman Empire was governed by absolute power, under the guidance of virtue and wisdom. The armies were restrained by the firm but gentle hand of four successive emperors, whose characters and authority commanded in voluntary respect. The forms of the civil administration were carefully preserved by Nerva, Trajan, Hadrian, and the Antonines [Pius], who delighted in the image of liberty, and were pleased with considering themselves as the accountable ministers of the law.

2. Did President Trump believe in American exceptionalism? Critics painted President Obama as "apologizing" for American behavior in the past and not promoting the values and virtues of America. What is President Biden's position?

3. *Should foreign policy only be concerned with human rights?* *See* Madeleine Albright, THE MIGHTY AND THE ALMIGHTY (2006). In her chapter entitled, Good Intentions Gone Astray: Vietnam and the Shah, Albright talks about how the Carter policy of not sufficiently supporting the Shah of Iran in the late 1970s led to far greater human rights abuses under the mullahs:

   > Many rejoiced when the monarch was brought down, but from any objective standpoint, the practices of Iran's successor governments with regard to human rights have been far worse than the shah's. In the first few years alone, thousands of people were executed for political dissent and "moral crimes." The shah's secret police were replaced by religious "guardians of the faith," who were even more ruthless.

Selected Bibliography

Albright, Madeleine. THE MIGHTY AND THE ALMIGHTY, 2006.

Bonds, Russell S. *Pawn Takes Bishop*, CIVIL WAR TIMES, May 2006, at 53.

Carty, Anthony, and Gennady Danilenko. *Perestroika and International Law*, CURRENT ANGLO-SOVIET APPROACHES TO INTERNATIONAL LAW, 1, 1990.

Colombo, Furio. *Vatican: The Pope's War Record*, NEW REPUBLIC. Apr. 8, 1991, at 12. (The article compiled some of the Pope's statements about the use of force by the United States and its allies. On January 10, 1991: "This war is an adventure with no return." On January 16: "International law cannot be seen as a protection for hegemonic interests." On January 21: "The intoxication of war has prevailed over the courage of peace." On January 26: "This war is a threat to humanity." On February 4: "This war is a virus of death.")

Duke, Lynne. *Coretta Scott King Deplores Decision*, WASH. POST. Jan. 17, 1991, at A30 (quoting Rev. Joseph Lowery).

Elsner, Alan. *Christian Leaders Prominent in Anti-War Movement*, REUTERS, Feb. 8, 2003.

Gellman, Barton. *Reaction to Tactic They Invented Baffles 1st Division Members*, WASH. POST, Sept. 13, 1991, at A21.

Haberman, Clyde. *Pope, In Christmas Message, Warns on a Gulf War*, NEW YORK TIMES, 26. Dec. 1990, at A19 (quoting Pope John Paul II).

Interview by Zenit Daily Dispatch with George Weigel, a biographer of Pope John Paul II as well as a leading Catholic commentator, and Senior Fellow of the Ethics and Public Policy Center, Washington, D.C. Sept. 22, 2002. (discussing the Catholic moral teaching regarding what many claimed to be a pre-emptive strike in Iraq and the Catholic views of just war theory).

Johnson, Haynes. *Renewed Perils to Peace*, WASH. POST. Sept. 27, 1991, at A2.

King, Martin Luther, Jr. STRIDE TOWARD FREEDOM: THE MONTGOMERY STORY, 1958.

Munger, Guy. *Lessons From the Desert Death Plow*, NC CATHOLIC. Sept. 22, 1991, at 4.

Przetacznik, Frank. *The Catholic Concept of Peace as a Basic Collective Human Right*, 39 REVUE DE DROIT MILITAIRE ET DE DROIT DE LA GUERRE, 523, (1990).

Rich, Norman. HITLER'S WAR AIMS. 1973.

Schaff, Philip, ed. ST. AUGUSTINE, NICENE AND POST-NICENE FATHERS OF THE CHRISTIAN CHURCH, 1983.

Turner, Robert F. *The Gulf War—and Its Fallout*, FREEDOM REV, May–June 1991, at 17, 19.

Walker, Richard. *Martin Luther King's Widow Urges New Anti-War Movement*, REUTER LIBRARY REP, Jan. 11, 1991.

Chapter 11

Civil Litigation

In the face of this universal criminal liability it is hardly a stretch to ask how the civil justice system might more effectively also contribute to deterrence against such heinous acts [international terrorism].

—John Norton Moore

The area of civil litigation encompasses two major themes in the realm of terrorism. The first relates to cases brought by victims of terrorism against an "affected target" of terrorism under the sphere of tort law. The second relates to lawsuits directed against those individuals, groups, or States (or State agents) who commit or sponsor a terrorist attack. To be sure, the new and developing area of civil liability in either context is an open invitation for the courts to play a significant role in the realm of terrorism law.

11.1 Tort Liability Against Affected Targets

As in all cases of tort law, suits brought by individual victims against an affected target of terrorism, such as an owner of a building or an airline, must satisfy the common law elements of basic tort law: (1) the affected target owed a duty to the plaintiff; (2) the duty was breached; (3) there existed a causal relationship between the breach and the resulting injury; (4) and the plaintiff suffered an actual loss.

The new and developing area of civil liability in the context of civil actions brought by victims of terrorism against an affected target of terrorism, i.e., a particular business entity, under the sphere of tort law is extremely relevant to the issue of developing adequate business security—both in the physical world and cyberspace. Indeed, while no business can protect against every form of terrorist threat, courts will ultimately determine whether or not the affected business had developed appropriate and reasonable security methods and procedures. Accordingly, all business entities must take cognizance of at least four main themes.

- Understand the aims and objectives of the global terror threat posed by al-Qaeda-styled terror groups, sub-State terror groups, and "lone wolf" terrorists.

- Understand the specific threats to American business sectors that are deemed part of the nation's "critical infrastructure," i.e. energy, petro-chemical, electric utilities, communication, transportation, health, etc.
- Understand the varied legal issues associated with terrorism and criminal negligence claims against businesses that have suffered a terror attack or serious criminal act in cyberspace or the physical world.
- Develop a comprehensive review of how to develop appropriate security methods and procedures to mitigate potential legal liability to the business.

The most notable case related to these types of terrorism negligence claims is *In re September 11*. While most of the liability issues associated with the terror attacks of 9/11 were settled by a Special Master (using a seven billion dollar "pot" of money) established under the Air Transportation Safety and System Stabilization Act of 2001, *In re September 11* was a major tort liability case in which a handful of the victims who were injured, survivors of victims who were killed, and some who sustained property damage in the al-Qa'eda terror attacks on September 11, 2001, brought civil actions against airlines, airport security companies, owners and operators of buildings destroyed in the crash, and aircraft manufacturers. The 2003 U.S. District Court for the Southern District of New York, *In re September 11*, rendered some significant insight in its early rulings: (1) under New York law, the duty of airlines and airport security companies to secure aircraft against potential terrorists and weapons smuggled aboard extended to ground victims of crashes; (2) the crash of the planes hijacked by terrorists was within the class of foreseeable hazards resulting from negligently performed security screening by airlines; (3) federal statutes and regulations providing for protection of passengers and property on aircraft in the event of air piracy did not preempt plaintiff's negligence claim under New York law; (4) owners and operators of office buildings owed a duty under New York law to the building's occupants to create and implement adequate fire safety measures; (5) plaintiffs pleaded sufficient facts to alleged legal proximate cause against owners and operators; (6) plaintiff's allegations were sufficient to establish manufacturer's duty under Virginia and Pennsylvania law; and (7) the failure of manufacturers to design an impenetrable cockpit door was a proximate cause of the crashes.

In re SEPTEMBER 11
United States District Court for the Southern District of New York
280 F.Supp.2d 279 (Sep. 9th 2003)

OPINION BY: HELLERSTEIN, J.

The injured, and the representatives of the thousands who died from the terrorist-related aircraft crashes of September 11, 2001, are entitled to seek compensation. By act of Congress, they may seek compensation by filing claims with a Special Master established pursuant to the Air Transportation Safety and System Stabilization Act of 2001, Pub.L. No. 107-42, 115 Stat. 230 (2001) (codified at 49 U.S.C. § 40101) "the Act." Or they may seek compensation in the traditional manner, by alleging and proving their claims in lawsuits, with the aggregate of their damages capped at the limits of defendants' liability insurance. If they choose the former alternative, their claims will be paid through a Victim Compensation Fund from money appropriated by

Congress, within a relatively short period after filing. Claimants will not have to prove fault or show a duty to pay on the part of any defendant. The amount of their compensation, however, may be less than their possible recovery from lawsuits, for non-economic damages are limited to $250,000, economic damages are subject to formulas that are likely to be less generous than those often allowable in lawsuits, and punitive damages are unavailable. I have discussed, and upheld, certain portions of the Act and regulations related to the Fund in *Colaio v. Feinberg* , *262 F.Supp.2d 273 (S.D.N.Y. 2003)*, appeal filed, June 6, 2003. Approximately seventy of the injured and representatives of those who died, and ten entities which sustained property damage, have chosen to bring lawsuits against defendants whom they claim are legally responsible to compensate them: the airlines, the airport security companies, the airport operators, the airplane manufacturer, and the operators and owners of the World Trade Center. The motions before me challenge the legal sufficiency of these lawsuits, and ask me to dismiss the complaints because no duty to the plaintiffs existed and because the defendants could not reasonably have anticipated that terrorists would hijack several jumbo jet airplanes and crash them, killing passengers, crew, thousands on the ground, and themselves. I discuss in this opinion the legal duties owed by the air carriers, United and American Airlines, and other airlines and airport security companies affiliated with the air carriers to the plaintiffs who were killed and damaged on the ground in and around the Twin Towers and the Pentagon; by the Port Authority of New York and New Jersey "Port Authority" and World Trade Center Properties LLC "WTC Properties" to those killed and injured in and around the Twin Towers; and by the Boeing Company, the manufacturer of the "757" jets that were flown into the Pentagon and the field near Shanksville, Pennsylvania, to those killed and injured in the two crashes. I hold in this opinion that each of these defendants owed duties to the plaintiffs who sued them, and I reject as well defendants' alternative arguments for dismissal.

I. Background
A. Exclusive Jurisdiction and the Governing Law

The Air Transportation Safety and System Stabilization Act of 2001, Pub.L. No. 107-42, 115 Stat. 230 (2001) (codified at 49 U.S.C. § 40101) "the Act", passed in the weeks following the September 11 attacks, provides that those who bring suit "for damages arising out of the hijacking and subsequent crashes" must bring their suits in the United States District Court for the Southern District of New York. The Southern District has "original and exclusive jurisdiction" "over all actions brought for any claim (including any claim for loss of property, personal injury, or death) resulting from or relating to the terrorist-related aircraft crashes of September 11, 2001," with the exception of claims to recover collateral source obligations and claims against terrorists and their aiders, abettors and conspirators, Act § 408(c). The Act provides that the governing law shall be "derived from the law, including choice of law principles, of the State in which the crash occurred unless such law is inconsistent with or preempted by Federal law." Act § 408(b)(2). Thus, all cases, whether arising out of the crashes in New York, Virginia, or Pennsylvania, must be brought in the Southern District of New York, to be decided in accordance with the law of the state where the crash occurred.

B. The Complaints

Plaintiffs' individual pleadings have been consolidated into five master complaints, one for the victims of each crash and one for the property damage plaintiffs. Plaintiffs allege that the airlines, airport security companies, and airport operators negligently failed to fulfill their security responsibilities, and in consequence, the terrorists were able to hijack the airplanes and crash them into the World Trade Center, the Pentagon, and the field in Shanksville, Pennsylvania, killing passengers, crew, and thousands in the World Trade Center and the Pentagon and causing extensive property damage. The complaints allege that the owners and operators of the World Trade Center, World Trade Center Properties LLC and the Port Authority of New York and New Jersey, negligently designed, constructed, maintained, and operated the buildings, failing to provide adequate and effective evacuation routes and plans. Plaintiffs who died in the crashes of American flight 77 and United flight 93 also sue Boeing, the manufacturer of the two "757" airplanes, for strict tort liability, negligent product design, and breach of warranty.

…

iii. Scope of Duty to Ground Victims: the Issue of Foreseeability

Defendants argue that the ground victims lost their lives and suffered injuries from an event that was not reasonably foreseeable, for terrorists had not previously used a hijacked airplane as a suicidal weapon to destroy buildings and murder thousands. Defendants contend that because the events of September 11 were not within the reasonably foreseeable risks, any duty of care that they would owe to ground victims generally should not extend to the victims of September 11.

The scope of duty to a particular class of plaintiffs depends on the relationship to such plaintiffs, whether plaintiffs were within a zone of foreseeable harm, and whether the harm was within the class of reasonably foreseeable hazards that the duty exists to prevent. *Di Ponzio v. Riordan, 89 N.Y.2d 578, 657 N.Y.S.2d 377, 679 N.E.2d 616, 618 (1997)* (citations omitted). See also *Palsgraf v. Long Island R.R. Co., 248 N.Y. 339, 162 N.E. 99, 100-01 (1928)*.…

In order to be considered foreseeable, the precise manner in which the harm was inflicted need not be perfectly predicted. As *Di Ponzio v. Riordan* explained: "Where an individual breaches a legal duty and thereby causes an occurrence that is within the class of foreseeable hazards that the duty exists to prevent, the individual may be held liable, even though the harm may have been brought about in an unexpected way. On the other hand, no liability will result when the occurrence is not one that is normally associated with such hazards.…

…

Construing the factual allegations in the light most favorable to the plaintiffs, I conclude that the crash of the airplanes was within the class of foreseeable hazards resulting from negligently performed security screening. While it may be true that terrorists had not before deliberately flown airplanes into buildings, the airlines reasonably could foresee that crashes causing death and destruction on the ground was a hazard that would arise should hijackers take control of a plane. The intrusion by terrorists into the cockpit, coupled with the volatility of a hijacking situation, creates a foreseeable risk that hijacked airplanes might crash, jeopardizing innocent lives on the ground as well as in the airplane. While the crashes into the particular locations of the World Trade Center, Pentagon, and Shanksville field may not have been foreseen, the duty to screen passengers and items brought on board existed to prevent harms not only to passengers and crew, but also to the ground victims resulting from the crashes of hijacked planes, including the four planes hijacked on September 11.

…

B. World Trade Center Defendants' Motions to Dismiss

i. Background

The Port Authority of New York and New Jersey and WTC Properties LLC move to dismiss all claims brought against them as owners and operators of the World Trade Center for loss of life, personal injury, and damage to nearby property and businesses resulting from the collapse of the Twin Towers. The claims are alleged in two Master Complaints regarding Flights 11 and 175 in the consolidated litigation, and in numerous individual complaints. Plaintiffs allege that the WTC Defendants: 1) failed to design and construct the World Trade Center buildings according to safe engineering practices and to provide for safe escape routes and adequate sprinkler systems and fireproofing; 2) failed to inspect, discover, and repair unsafe and dangerous conditions, and to maintain fireproofing materials; 3) failed to develop adequate and safe evacuation and emergency management plans; 4) failed to apply, interpret and/or enforce applicable building and fire safety codes, regulations and practices; and 5) instructed Tower Two occupants to return to their offices and remain in the building even while the upper floors of Tower One were being consumed by uncontrolled fires following the airplane crash into Tower One. See Plaintiffs' Flight 11 Master Liability Complaint ¶ 85; Plaintiffs' Flight 175 Master Liability Complaint ¶ 82.

A number of other defendants whose interests are aligned with the Port Authority and World Trade Center Properties LLC—those who were named as defendants because they designed, constructed, operated, or maintained the World Trade Center buildings—were voluntarily dismissed earlier in the litigation.

The WTC Defendants argue that the complaints against them should be dismissed because they had no duty to anticipate and guard against deliberate and suicidal aircraft crashes into the Towers, and because any alleged negligence on their part was not a proximate cause of the plaintiffs' injuries. The Port Authority argues also that it is entitled to immunity because the complained-of conduct essentially consisted of governmental functions.

…

ii. Existence and Scope of Duty

The WTC Defendants contend that they owed no duty to "anticipate and guard against crimes unprecedented in human history." Plaintiffs argue that defendants owed a duty, not to foresee the crimes, but to have designed, constructed, repaired and maintained the World Trade Center structures to withstand the effects and spread of fire, to avoid building collapses caused by fire and, in designing and effectuating fire safety and evacuation procedures, to provide for the escape of more people.

The existence of a duty owed by the WTC Defendants to its lessees and business occupants has been clearly set out in New York law. "A landowner has a duty to exercise reasonable care under the circumstances in maintaining its property in a safe condition,"

…

iii. Proximate and Supervening Causation

The WTC Defendants argue that even if they are held to have owed a duty to the plaintiffs and even if a jury ultimately finds that they acted negligently, their negligence was not the proximate cause of plaintiffs' damages. This is because, they claim, the terrorist-related aircraft crashes into the Twin Towers were so extraordinary and unforeseeable as to constitute intervening and superceding causes, severing any link of causation to the WTC Defendants.

When an intervening act "is of such an extraordinary nature or so attenuates defendants' negligence from the ultimate injury that responsibility for the injury may not be reasonably attributed to the defendant," proximate cause is lacking. *Kush v. City of Buffalo, 59 N.Y.2d 26, 462 N.Y.S.2d 831, 449 N.E.2d 725, 729 (1983)*. Thus, "when such an intervening cause 'interrupts the natural sequence of events, turns aside their course, prevents the natural and probable result of the original act or omission, and produces a different result that could not have been reasonably anticipated,' it will prevent a recovery on account of the act or omission of the original wrongdoer." *Sheehan v. City of New York, 40 N.Y.2d 496, 387 N.Y.S.2d 92, 354 N.E.2d 832, 835-36 (1976)* (citations omitted). The "negligence complained of must have caused the occurrence of the accident from which the injuries flow." *Rivera v. City of New York, 11 N.Y.2d 856, 227 N.Y.S.2d 676, 182 N.E.2d 284, 285 (1962)*.

Generally, an intervening intentional or criminal act severs the liability of the original tort-feasor. *Kush, 462 N.Y.S.2d 831, 449 N.E.2d at 729*. But that "doctrine has no application when the intentional or criminal intervention of a third party or parties is reasonably foreseeable." *Id. In Bonsignore v. City of New York*, a New York City police officer shot and seriously wounded his wife. *683 F.2d 635 (2d Cir.1982)*. The wife sued the City, alleging that it was negligent in failing to identify officers who were unfit to carry guns and who would likely use them without proper restraint and in inappropriate circumstances, and in not recognizing that her husband was such an officer. The City defended on the ground of independent and supervening cause, arguing that the officer's intentional and criminal act severed any link of causation to its own alleged negligence. The Court of Appeals held in favor of the wife, ruling that since the officer's act was precisely that which the City should reasonably have foreseen, the police officer's intentional and criminal act was not an independent and supervening break between the City's negligence and the plaintiff's injury. See *id.* at 637-38.

At this early stage of the case and in the absence of a factual record, I find that plaintiffs have pleaded sufficient facts to allege legal proximate cause.

…

C. Boeing's Motions to Dismiss

Some of those who were injured and the successors of those who died in the Pentagon, in American Airlines flight 77 which crashed into the Pentagon, and in United Air Lines flight 93 which crashed into the Shanksville, Pennsylvania field, claim the right to recover against Boeing, the manufacturer of the two "757" jets flown by United and American. Plaintiffs allege that Boeing manufactured inadequate and defective cockpit doors, and thus made it possible for the hijackers to invade the cockpits and take over the aircraft. Boeing moves to dismiss the lawsuits.

I hold that plaintiffs have alleged legally sufficient claims for relief under the laws applicable to the claims, Virginia and Pennsylvania, respectively. I therefore deny the motion except for certain claims, as discussed below.

...

ii. Motion to Dismiss Claims Arising out of the Crash of American Airlines Flight 77

a. Background

Thus far, three individual complaints have been filed with respect to the flight 77 crash. They charge Boeing with strict tort liability and negligent design based on an unreasonably dangerous design of the cockpit doors. See *Edwards v. American Airlines, Inc.*, No. 02 Civ. 9234 (brought on behalf of a decedent who was a passenger on flight 77); *Powell v. Argenbright Security, Inc.*, *No. 02 Civ. 10160* (brought on behalf of a decedent who died while working at the Pentagon); *Gallop v. Argenbright Security, Inc., No. 03 Civ. 1016* (plaintiffs injured at the Pentagon site).

The Plaintiffs' First Amended Flight 77 Master Liability Complaint contains three counts applicable to Boeing. Count Six alleges strict tort liability for an unreasonably dangerous design of the cockpit doors. Count Seven alleges that Boeing breached its duty of care by failing to design the cockpit doors and accompanying locks in a manner that would prevent hijackers and/ or passengers from accessing the cockpit. Count Eight alleges that Boeing violated its express or implied warranty that the aircraft structure and frame, with respect to the cockpit doors, were fit for the purposes for which they were designed, intended and used.

...

Boeing argues that its design of the cockpit was not unreasonably dangerous in relation to reasonably foreseeable risks, and that the risk of death to passengers and ground victims caused by a terrorist hijacking was not reasonably foreseeable. The record at this point does not support Boeing's argument. There have been many efforts by terrorists to hijack airplanes, and too many have been successful. The practice of terrorists to blow themselves up in order to kill as many people as possible has also been prevalent. Although there have been no incidents before the ones of September 11, 2001 where terrorists combined both an airplane hijacking and a suicidal explosion, I am not able to say that the risk of crashes was not reasonably foreseeable to an airplane manufacturer. Plaintiffs have alleged that it was reasonably foreseeable that a failure to design a secure cockpit could contribute to a breaking and entering into, and a take-over of, a cockpit by hijackers or other unauthorized individuals, substantially increasing the risk of injury and death to people and damage to property. I hold that the allegation is sufficient to establish Boeing's duty.

Boeing also argues that the regulations of the Federal Aviation Administration ("FAA") relating to design of passenger airplanes did not require an impenetrable cockpit door, and thus its designs, which satisfied FAA requirements, could not be defective. However, the only support provided by Boeing for its argument is an after-the-fact FAA policy statement, issued to explain why the FAA, in 2002, was requiring airplane manufacturers to provide such doors even though the FAA previously had not done so.

Flight crew compartment doors on transport category airplanes have been designed principally to ensure privacy, so pilots could focus their entire attention to their normal and emergency flight duties. The doors have not been designed to provide an impenetrable barrier between the cabin and the flight crew compartment. Doors have not been required to meet any significant security threat, such as small arms fire or shrapnel, or the exercise of brute force to enter the flight crew compartment. *67 Fed.Reg. 12,820-12,824 (Mar. 19, 2002).*

Boeing has not proffered the parameters that existed when it manufactured its "757" jumbo-jet airplanes that United and American flew on September 11, 2001. Boeing also has not shown the extent to which FAA regulations determined how passenger airplanes were to be constructed. Although a FAA promulgation of standards for the design and manufacture of passenger aircraft may be entitled to weight in deciding whether Boeing was negligent, see, e.g., *Curtin v. Port Auth. of N.Y. and N.J., 183 F.Supp.2d 664, 671 (S.D.N.Y.2002)* (concluding that the standard of care with respect to aircraft evacuation procedures is a matter of federal, not state, law), statements by the FAA characterizing what its former regulations required does not dictate the totality of the duty owed by aircraft manufacturers. Boeing's argument is not sufficient to support its motion to dismiss the complaints against it.

d. Proximate Causation

Boeing next argues that its design of the cockpit doors on its "757" passenger aircraft, even if held to constitute an "unreasonably dangerous condition," was not the proximate cause of plaintiffs' injuries. Boeing argues that the criminal acts of the terrorists in hijacking the airplanes and using the airplanes as weapons of mass destruction constituted an "efficient intervening cause" which broke the "natural and continuous sequence" of events flowing from Boeing's allegedly inadequate design.

...

The record at this point does not support Boeing's argument that the invasion and take-over of the cockpit by the terrorists must, as a matter of law, be held to constitute an "efficient intervening act" that breaks the "natural and continuous sequence" flowing from Boeing's allegedly inadequate design. Plaintiffs allege that Boeing should have designed its cockpit door to prevent hijackers from invading the cockpit, that acts of terrorism, including hijackings of airplanes, were reasonably foreseeable, and that the lives of passengers, crew and ground victims would be imminently in danger from such hijackings. Virginia law does not require Boeing to have foreseen precisely how the injuries suffered on September 11, 2001 would be caused, as long as Boeing could reasonably have foreseen that "some injury" from its negligence "might probably result." See *Blondel v. Hays, 241 Va. 467, 403 S.E.2d 340, 344 (1991)* ("[A] reasonably prudent [person] ought under the circumstances to have foreseen that some injury might probably result from that negligence"). Given the critical nature of the cockpit area, and the inherent danger of crash when a plane is in flight, one cannot say that Boeing could not reasonably have foreseen the risk flowing from an inadequately constructed cockpit door.

...

Accordingly, I deny Boeing's motion to dismiss the complaints against it arising from the crash of flight 77 into the Pentagon.

iii. Motion to Dismiss Claims Arising out of the Crash of United Air Lines Flight 93

a. Background

The successors of the passengers who died in the crash of United Air Lines flight 93 in Shanksville have filed four lawsuits: *Burnett v. Argenbright, 02 Civ. 6168; Lyles v. Argenbright, 02 Civ. 7243; Cashman v. Argenbright, 02 Civ. 7608; and Driscoll v. Argenbright, 02 Civ. 7912.* Their allegations are encapsulated in Plaintiffs' Flight 93 Master Liability Complaint, which mirrors the Plaintiffs' First Amended Flight 77 Master Liability Complaint. The Flight 93 Master Complaint alleges claims against Boeing based on strict tort liability, for an unreasonably dangerous design of the cockpit doors (Count Five); negligence, for failure to design cockpit doors and accompanying locks in a manner that would prevent hijackers and/or passengers from accessing the cockpit (Count Six); and express or implied warranty, for creating a product that was unfit for the purposes for which it was designed, intended and used (Count Seven).

…

III. Conclusion

For the reasons stated, the motions to dismiss the complaints by the Aviation Defendants and the WTC Defendants are denied. The motion of Boeing to dismiss Counts Four and Six in the Flight 77 Master Complaint, Count Four in the Flight 93 Master Complaint, Count Three in *Edwards v. American Airlines, Inc., No. 02* Civ. 9234, Count Five in *Powell v. Argenbright Security, Inc., No. 02* Civ. 10160, and Count Five in *Gallop v. Argenbright Security, Inc., No. 03* Civ. 1016, is granted; the remainder of the motion is denied.

By this decision, substantially all preliminary matters have been resolved, with the exception of the Port Authority's motion to dismiss Mayore Estates LLC, 02 Civ. 7198(AKH). We are now ready to proceed with the discovery stages of the lawsuits. To this end, I will meet with all counsel for case management purposes on September 26, 2003, at 9:30 A.M., in Courtroom 14D, 500 Pearl Street, New York, N.Y. 10007. Liaison Counsel shall submit a proposed agenda by September 24, 2003.

SO ORDERED.

11.2 Suits Against State-Sponsors of Terrorism

For this reason, Congress expressly directed retroactive application to the Antiterrorism and Effective Death Penalty Act of 1996 (AEDPA), 8 U.S.C. § 1189, so that the law applied to any cause of action arising before or after the enactment of the AEDPA. In tandem with subsequent federal statutes dealing with terrorism civil lawsuits, this model ensures that terrorists and their supporters suffer significant financial punishment which functions both as a direct deterrence, and also as a disabling mechanism—the very core of the intent of punitive damages. Clearly, in the American justice system, the essence of punitive damages is to award the plaintiff(s) a significant money judgment in addition to actual damages against those defendants who acted with recklessness, intentional malice, or deceit. The wrongdoer is penalized by means of punitive damages in order to both deter future wrongdoing and to make a clear example to others. Nowhere is this context more applicable than in the sphere of curtailing international terrorism.

The second type of civil action associated with terrorism lawsuits are those claims brought against one of three categories of international terrorists and their sponsors: (1) purely non-State actors, individuals as well as groups; (2) States that sponsor terrorism, or their agents (Flatow Amendment); or (3) so-called non-FSIA (Foreign Sovereign Immunities Act) defendants, State actors committing acts of terrorism outside of their official capacity. Currently, under American jurisprudence, two main federal statutory frameworks exist: (1) the Flatow amendment to the Foreign Sovereign Immunities Act (FSIA), 28 U.S.C. §1605; and (2) the Antiterrorism Act (ATA), 18 U.S.C. §2333.

The so-called Flatow amendment provides that a foreign official of a designated State sponsor of terrorism, while acting within the scope of his office, can be civilly liable in an American court for violation of acts contained within the legislation. Further, as part of the 2008 Defense Authorization Act, Congress made it crystal clear that 1996 FSIA Amendments applied a statutory cause of action against the actual State that sponsored the terrorist act. Similarly, the ATA allows for private citizens to bring lawsuits for acts of international terrorism with the added deterrent goal of making it unprofitable for terrorists to solicit or maintain financial assets within the United States.

Added to the FSIA in 1996, the Flatow Amendment is codified at 28 U.S.C. § 1605A, creating an exception to foreign sovereign immunity in civil suits in which money damages are sought against a foreign State for personal injury or death that was caused by an act of "torture, extrajudicial killing, aircraft sabotage, hostage taking, or provision of material support or resources (as defined in section 2339A of Title 18) for such an act if such act or provision of material support is engaged in by an official, employee, or agent of such foreign state while acting within the scope of his or her office, employment, or agency..." or other terrorist acts. Although this exception applies only if the defendant foreign State was designated as a State sponsor of terrorism at the time the alleged acts occurred, the issue of punitive damages remains. Specifically, § 1605(A) (c) authorizes the full range of money damages which "may include economic damages, solatium, pain and suffering, and punitive damages." The Flatow Amendment provides that:

> [A]n official, employee, or agent of a foreign state designated as a state sponsor of terrorism... while acting within the scope of his or her office, employment, or agency shall be liable to a United States national or the national's legal representative for personal injury or death caused by acts of that official, employee, or agent for which the courts of the United States may maintain jurisdiction under for *money damages which may include economic damages, solatium, pain and suffering, and punitive damages* if the acts were among those described in [emphasis added].

In *Flatow v. Islamic Republic of Iran*, which dealt with a suicide bomber terror attack on a bus in the Gaza Strip in 1995, the federal court recognized that special compensatory and punitive damages were legitimate deterrence considerations since terrorism was directed not just at the immediate victims, but also at their family members and the society as a whole. Again, the goal of the terrorist is to "kill one and frighten ten thousand."

The malice associated with terrorist attacks transcends even that of premeditated murder. The intended audience of a terrorist attack is not limited to the families of those killed and wounded or even just Israelis, but in this case, the American public, for the purpose of affecting United States government support for Israel and the peace process. The terrorist's intent is to strike fear not only for one's own safety, but also for that of friends and family, and to manipulate that fear in order to achieve political objectives. Thus the character of the wrongful act itself increases the magnitude of the injury. It thus demands a corresponding increase in compensation for increased injury.

In the context of punitive damages, the matter of deterrence plays a central component since the goal of punitive damages is to create within the minds of those organizations and nations that sponsor terror and torture the realistic expectation of seizure and dissemination of assets in the form of large monetary damages against them. The court in *Flatow*, the foundational terror incident which directly prompted Congress to create a new statutory cause of action, set out the standard approach in regards to calculating punitive damages:

> Factors which may be considered in determining an appropriate amount of punitive damages may be grouped under a few broad headings, including: (1) the nature of the act itself, and the extent to which any civilized society would find that act repugnant; (2) the circumstances of its planning; (3) Defendants' economic status with regard to the ability of Defendants to pay; and (4) the basis upon which a Court might determine the amount of an award reasonably sufficient to deter like conduct in the future, both by the Defendants and others.

Expert testimony in *Flatow* also led to a standard calculation in awarding punitive damages three times the amount that the State which sponsors terrorism (in this case Iran) spends annually on terrorist activities. In *Flatow*, this multiplier produced a $300,000,000 punitive damages award. Again, under such a calculation punitive awards of this magnitude are designed for deterrence to: (1) deter State sponsors of terrorism, and (2) affect the ability of such nations to fund terrorist activities in the future.

The victim's family in *Flatow* was also allowed to recover compensatory damages for economic loss, pain and suffering, and solatium. The court calculated economic damages by adding the funeral bill of $4,470.00 with the loss of accretions to the estate in the amount of $1,508,750.00. The calculation for loss of accretions took into account inflation, rise in productivity, job advancement, and net earnings. Furthermore, the court awarded $1,000,000 for the three to five hours of pain and suffering the victim endured, after the terrorist attack, before she died.

The *Flatow* decision is also noted for its increased award of solatium damages which account for the additional suffering caused by the family members of a victim to a terrorist act. The court noted that "mental anguish, bereavement and grief resulting from the fact of decedent's death constitutes the preponderant element of a claim for solatium." The court then divided its solatium inquiry into determining: (1) the mental anguish suffered by the victim's family, and (2) the loss of decedent's society and comfort. Calculations for both of these damage types are fact intensive and not subject to exact models associated with economic loss.

Two main factors guided the analysis for both damage types: (1) the expected duration of the mental anguish; and (2) the nature of the relationship between the claimant and decedent. Since all acts of terrorism employ unlawful violence, the anguish of family members is prolonged well beyond what is experienced for a natural death. In turn, a more intimate family connection calls for greater levels of compensation for the victim's family member. Again, *Flatow* provides a superb standardized rubric for compensatory damages calculation.

Numerous factors enter into this analysis, including: strong emotional ties between the claimant and the decedent; decedent's position in the family birth order relative to the claimant; the relative maturity or immaturity of the claimants; whether decedent habitually provided advice and solace to claimants; whether the claimant shared interests and pursuits with decedent; as well as decedent's achievements and plans for the future which would have affected claimants.

Unlike the FSIA, the ATA does not specify what type of damages may be awarded. Neither does it clearly define the class of potential plaintiffs. Nevertheless, by allowing the "estate, survivors, or heirs" of a U.S. national killed by an act of terrorism to sue in federal district court and to recover treble damages and attorney's fees, it is certain that the intent of the law is to maximize the punishment of the wrongdoer so that it is *punitive* in nature. In American jurisprudence, the purpose of allowing for treble damages is always punitive in nature and designed to "punish past, and to deter future, unlawful conduct." The court used a treble damages formula in assessing damages against Iran. This approach is now standard.

Rooted in a common law tort framework, the ATA has no specific requirement that those recovering be citizens of the United States themselves (the statute provides no definition for "survivors" or "heirs"), nor does it specify the types of damages. Nevertheless, in the light of the legislative history and developing case law, the 2004 case of *Ungar v. Palestinian Authority*, sets the accepted methodology in determining these matters. Yaron Ungar and his wife were killed in a drive-by shooting by terrorists on June, 9, 1996, in Israel. Yaron's family brought suit under the ATA against multiple defendants including the Palestinian Authority. The district court found that Yaron's parents and siblings qualified to bring suit as "survivors" under the wording of 18 U.S.C. §2333(a), since Congress intended to use common law tort principles to extend civil liability to terrorist acts with the widest possible effect. The use of the term "survivors" evidences the intent that immediate family members, other than heirs, may seek compensation for the loss of a loved one. Indeed, allowing siblings and parents of those killed by terrorists to recover damages serves as an additional deterrence factor to terrorism.

In reference to the issue of damages, *Ungar* held that the primary purpose of the law was to empower the victims of terrorism to the fullest extent possible. Accordingly, *Ungar* allowed for the full range of damages set out under the FSIA. Ungar's two children (heirs), parents, and siblings were all awarded damages for loss of society and companionship. The children also recovered for loss of parental guidance and parental services which Ungar could no longer provide. "These services include such tasks as babysitting, feeding, bathing, doing the laundry, getting them ready for school, and similar assistance normally performed by a parent for a child." Economic damages will ordinarily include loss of earnings and funeral costs. Similar to *Flatow*, where the court considered inflation, rise in productivity, job advancement, and net earnings in its calculations of lost earnings, the Ungar family recovered lost earnings subject to Ungar's personal consumption.

Understanding that no rigid formula exists for computing damages associated with pain and suffering, the *Ungar* court heard expert testimony giving a step-by-step analysis of the drive-by shooting to accurately determine damages for pain and suffering. The Court considered in its calculation the fact that Ungar suffered painful bullet wounds in his arm and chest before being killed by a head shot while slumped in his car seat, as well as the mental pain Ungar experienced at seeing his wife's death shortly before his own. The court awarded $500,000 for the pain and suffering. In addition, Ungar's family received losses for mental anguish (solatium) which were calculated in a similar fashion to loss of society. Ungar's children, parents and three siblings received a total of $38,803,401 in compensatory damages for all the above mentioned losses.

In *Eisenfeld v. Islamic Republic of Iran*, a case involving a 1996 Iranian State-sponsored act of terrorism carried out by the terror organization HAMAS where a bus was bombed in Jerusalem, the court cited the *Flatow* punitive damages approach and awarded the two plaintiff decedents' estate a single award of $300,000,000 ($150,000,000 each). In *Boim v. Quranic Literacy Institute and Hold Land Foundation for Relief and Development*, the parents of a U.S. citizen murdered in a terror attack in Israel by the terrorist group HAMAS sued several individuals and organizations for the loss of their son. They were awarded damages using the treble damages formula. As seen in *Boim*, bringing civil litigation against a non-State actor can involve individuals as well as groups. While many plaintiffs win by default, the defendants in *Boim* offered a spirited defense touching a number of important statutory and Constitutional issues.

Despite the development of the current American terrorism jurisprudence, all is not well. The inability of victims to recover damages once they are awarded judgment in court stands as a major distorter of justice and deterrence. In some instances, Iran, the most notorious State-sponsor of terrorism, has removed or hidden assets from the reaches of American law. In other instances, the executive branch of the U.S. government has served to block recovery of assets under the notion that the Executive needs the flexibility to conduct foreign affairs. This occurred in both the Bush and Obama Administrations where they successfully blocked recovery initially granted by the D.C. federal district court to American POWs tortured during the 1991 Gulf War.

In *Acree v. Republic of Iraq*, the U.S. District Court for the District of Columbia not only reiterated the validity of punitive damages as a deterrence tool, it saw fit to award compensatory and punitive damages totaling over $959,000,000. In *Acree*, 17 American prisoners of war (POWs) during the 1991 Gulf War and their immediate family members sued the Republic of Iraq, its president, and its intelligence service, seeking compensatory and punitive damages for injuries suffered as a result of torture inflicted on the POWs while in Iraqi captivity between January and March 1991. In 2003, the District Court granted default judgment for the plaintiff POWs. In their complaint, "the POW plaintiffs described brutal and inhumane acts of physical and psychological torture suffered during their captivity, including severe beatings, starvation, mock executions, dark and unsanitary living conditions, and other violent and shocking acts."

The POW plaintiffs alleged that the acts of torture set forth in their complaint constituted "traditional torts of assault, battery and intentional infliction of emotional distress," and requested full compensatory and punitive damages for each of the 17 POW plaintiffs and their family members. On July 7, 2003, the court entered final judgment in favor of the plaintiffs. Based on extensive findings of fact regarding the specific injuries suffered by each plaintiff, the federal district court awarded compensatory and punitive damages to all of the POW plaintiffs and their family members totaling just under $1 billion. Unfortunately, the Bush Administration blocked payment and the Supreme Court upheld the Executive prerogative. A similar outcome occurred in the Obama Administration when the issue was revisited.

11.3 Proposed International Civil Legal Model

University of Virginia School of Law international law expert, Professor John Norton Moore strongly advocates that all nations adopt a strong legal model for civil lawsuits that incorporates significant punitive damages: "It is strongly in our interest to have every nation on earth copy the 1996 FSIA amendments." Nevertheless, Moore recognizes that punitive damages are not palatable to most civil law nations and pose a significant hurdle to developing a consensus that would truly hold renegade nations accountable for acts of terrorism committed by them or their agents. Adopting an American-styled deterrence model that not only provides for citizens to be compensated for acts of terror, but also brings with it the hammer of punitive damages is simply unrealistic. If real progress is to be made toward creating a global legal framework which can act to effectively suppress the scourge of international terrorism the concept of punitive damages must be framed within the parameters of compensatory damages.

In short, even if punitive damages have to be discarded in any attempt to develop a workable model for other democracies to honor judgments rendered by fellow democracies in terror cases, American precedents in setting damage awards under compensatory concepts would still produce meaningful and effective remedies. Since legal cases involving acts of terror have parallels in common law wrongful death and injury lawsuits, a brief overview of American judgments in these areas reveals that there is still significant *punch* in the compensatory arena. A reasonable pragmatic approach in dealing with compensatory damage awards would still act as a deterrent to States that support terrorism. Although the compensatory judgments are certainly not large *vis-à-vis* punitive damages, a flood of lawsuits wait hungrily at the door for satisfaction and would certainly make up for the discrepancy in short order.

Despite the perception that American courts grant exorbitant awards in wrongful death cases, the amount of compensatory damages in most instances is both practical and reasonable. Even in what can be considered high-profile cases, the awards granted reflect a judicious approach in terms of just compensation for the wrongs inflicted. Four examples illustrate. First, a 2004 civil lawsuit from a Texas State court in *Harris v. Harris* (2007) dealt with a wrongful death claim where a wife killed her husband (she suspected him of having sex with another woman) by intentionally hitting him with her car and then running the vehicle over his body multiple times. The parents of the victim sued the woman for wrongful death and received $1,858,750 each for pecuniary losses, loss of companionship, and mental anguish.

Second, in perhaps the most infamous wrongful death suit in the history of the United States, the verdict against O.J. Simpson, though totaling $33.5 million, awarded compensatory damages equaling only $8.5 million. A jury found that defendant Orenthal James (O.J.) Simpson committed these homicides willfully and wrongfully, with oppression and malice.

Third, in the case of the surviving family members of American sailors killed in the 2000 al-Qa'eda terror attack on the U.S.S. Cole, in Yemen, a Virginia federal judge granted an award just under $8 million. This civil action lawsuit claimed wrongful death, intentional infliction of emotional distress, and violations under the Foreign Sovereign Immunities Act and the Death on the High Seas Act against the Republic of Sudan. The family members claimed that the Republic of Sudan was liable for damages from the attack of the U.S.S. Cole in the Port of Aden, Yemen, because it provided material support and assistance to al- Qa'eda, the terrorist organization behind the attack. The compensatory award was split between 33 family members, with the amounts ranging from $117,418 to $471,327 each.

The final example returns to the most often cited American case dealing with compensatory damages: *Flatow v. Islamic Republic of Iran*, which dealt with a suicide bomber terror attack on a bus in the Gaza Strip in 1995. *Flatow* and a line of cases following *Flatow* set out valuable considerations associated with the long standing concept of compensatory damages in common law tort which are designed to compensate not just the immediate family of the victims, but also their family members. The *Flatow* court found that the vicious nature of terrorism inflicts a unique harm which is reflected in the resulting compensatory damages.

The next step in the process of developing civil litigation as a viable tool to fight terror is to propose for adoption a United Nations protocol that will allow State Parties to honor damage awards in terrorism civil litigation suits rendered by other State Parties. In his 2010 book, *Legal Issues in the Struggle Against Terror*, John Norton Moore offers such a draft protocol. Disregarding the punitive damages set out in American legislation, Moore provides the following at proposed Article 11:

> States Parties to this Protocol undertake to honor in their national legal systems judgments rendered by other States Parties under actions established consistent with this Protocol provided:
>> A judge of the honoring State Party reviews the foreign judgment and determines that the judgment was fair and consistent with due process of law;
>> *No State Party is required to honor damage awards, such as those for punitive damages, which are inconsistent with its own national law*; and
>> No attachment or execution shall be permitted against facilities protected by diplomatic or counselor immunity, military assets, or assets held by national central banks [emphasis added].

11.4 Conclusion

Fighting terrorism requires the use of all available legal tools, and the application of the power of the civil justice system represents a vastly underutilized potential of great impact. Understanding that international tort law has been around for centuries, it is imperative that the democracies of the international community take direct steps to capitalize on this essential legal tool as a weapon against terrorist States. Totalitarian regimes like Iran and North Korea are guilty of supporting terrorism and have too long been able to conceal huge financial assets within the borders and reach of many of the world's democratic States.

Apart from the fact that the attachment of assets in the United States to satisfy multi-million dollar verdicts against terror States like Iran are blocked by the Executive Branch in the interest of national security or other provisions of law, the need for an American-style civil action framework at the international level is much needed. Chief among the arguments against adopting an American-style civil action framework is the concern over punitive damages. Since punitive damages are generally not available in civil law systems and are very controversial in international practice, a proposed international protocol must limit damages to compensatory only. As discussed above, the use of compensatory damages would still deliver a significant blow to States that sponsor terrorism, particularly if the full range of compensation is provided.

A new United Nations convention on civil causes of action against States that sponsor terrorists would have as its key component an obligation on State parties to enact legislation to permit civil suits and honor the judgments issued by other States. Not only would the civil litigation serve as a permanent record of the terror act established by a competent court—an official record of condemnation—the damages awarded would serve as a deterrence to the machinations of the State that sponsored the terrorism.

At the end of the day, civil lawsuits are also intended to bring public shame within the international community to those nations who sponsor acts of terror. Since terrorist acts have long been criminalized in every democratically based legal system as well as in numerous United Nations sponsored conventions, it is essential that all democracies take the next step and develop a legal framework where the terror judgments of other democracies are given reciprocity.

11.5 Questions for Discussion

1. *Litigation as a deterrence to State-sponsored terrorism.* Some have argued that allowing civil actions against States who sponsor international terrorism is an important deterrence tool. Wendy Bay Lewis, *Civil Litigants as Citizen Diplomats*, VOIR DIRE, Spring 2003:

   > Litigation is an important weapon for several reasons. First, it opens a judicial front in the war against terrorism which supplements military, political, and economic sanctions. Second, as the result of globalization, there is an intricate network of individuals, groups, corporations, and nation-states which facilitate terrorism and make military and political measures less than adequate. Third, given the supremacy of the rule of law in a democracy, judicial outcomes eventually put pressure on the other two branches of government to be more accountable to the voters. For example, when the Pan Am plaintiffs' lawsuit initially faltered because Libya had immunity as a sovereign nation, Congress amended antiterrorism statutes to preclude immunity pleas by state sponsors of terrorism.

   On the other hand, has Congress opened the door for other nations to sue the United States for "terrorism"?

2. *What impact has the concept of civil liability against affected targets had on the development of new anti-terrorism technology?*

3. *Costs and Benefits.* Because enforcing a monetary judgment is often impossible, what would be the other benefits to the plaintiff of going through the process of a civil action?

Selected Bibliography

Moore, John Norton (ed). CIVIL LITIGATION AGAINST TERRORISM, 2004.

Murphy, John F. PUNISHING INTERNATIONAL TERRORISTS: THE LEGAL FRAMEWORK FOR POLICY INITIATIVES, 1985.

Strachman, David and James Steck. CIVIL TERRORISM LAW, 2008.

Appendix A

Selected Provisions of the Charter of the United Nations

June 26, 1945, 59 Stat. 1031, T.S. 993, 3 Bevans 1153, entered into force Oct. 24, 1945.

PREAMBLE

WE THE PEOPLES OF THE UNITED NATIONS DETERMINED

- to save succeeding generations from the scourge of war, which twice in our lifetime has brought untold sorrow to mankind, and
- to reaffirm faith in fundamental human rights, in the dignity and worth of the human person, in the equal rights of men and women and of nations large and small, and
- to establish conditions under which justice and respect for the obligations arising from treaties and other sources of international law can be maintained, and
- to promote social progress and better standards of life in larger freedom,

AND FOR THESE ENDS

- to practice tolerance and live together in peace with one another as good neighbors, and
- to unite our strength to maintain international peace and security, and
- to ensure by the acceptance of principles and the institution of methods, that armed force shall not be used, save in the common interest, and
- to employ international machinery for the promotion of the economic and social advancement of all peoples,

HAVE RESOLVED TO COMBINE OUR EFFORTS TO ACCOMPLISH THESE AIMS

Accordingly, our respective Governments, through representatives assembled in the city of San Francisco, who have exhibited their full powers found to be in good and due form, have agreed to the present Charter of the United Nations and do hereby establish an international organization to be known as the United Nations.

CHAPTER I
PURPOSES AND PRINCIPLES

Article 1

The Purposes of the United Nations are:

1. To maintain international peace and security, and to that end: to take effective collective measures for the prevention and removal of threats to the peace, and for the suppression of acts of aggression or other breaches of the peace, and to bring about by peaceful means, and in conformity with the principles of justice and international law, adjustment or settlement of international disputes or situations which might lead to a breach of the peace;

2. To develop friendly relations among nations based on respect for the principle of equal rights and self-determination of peoples, and to take other appropriate measures to strengthen universal peace;

3. To achieve international cooperation in solving international problems of an economic, social, cultural, or humanitarian character, and in promoting and encouraging respect for human rights and for fundamental freedoms for all without distinction as to race, sex, language, or religion; and

4. To be a center for harmonizing the actions of nations in the attainment of these common ends.

Article 2

The Organization and its Members, in pursuit of the Purposes stated in Article 1, shall act in accordance with the following Principles.

1. The Organization is based on the principle of the sovereign equality of all its Members.

2. All Members, in order to ensure to all of them the rights and benefits resulting from membership, shall fulfill in good faith the obligations assumed by them in accordance with the present Charter.

3. All Members shall settle their international disputes by peaceful means in such a manner that international peace and security, and justice, are not endangered.

4. All Members shall refrain in their international relations from the threat or use of force against the territorial integrity or political independence of any state, or in any other manner inconsistent with the Purposes of the United Nations.

5. All Members shall give the United Nations every assistance in any action it takes in accordance with the present Charter, and shall refrain from giving assistance to any state against which the United Nations is taking preventive or enforcement action.

6. The Organization shall ensure that states which are not Members of the United Nations act in accordance with these Principles so far as may be necessary for the maintenance of international peace and security.

7. Nothing contained in the present Charter shall authorize the United Nations to intervene in matters which are essentially within the domestic jurisdiction of any state or shall require the Members to submit such matters to settlement under the present Charter; but this principle shall not prejudice the application of enforcement measures under Chapter VII.

CHAPTER II
MEMBERSHIP

Article 3

The original Members of the United Nations shall be the states which, having participated in the United Nations Conference on International Organization at San Francisco, or having previously signed the Declaration by United Nations of January 1, 1942, sign the present Charter and ratify it in accordance with Article 110.

Article 4

1. Membership in the United Nations is open to all other peace-loving states which accept the obligations contained in the present Charter and, in the judgment of the Organization, are able and willing to carry out these obligations.
2. The admission of any such state to membership in the United Nations will be effected by a decision of the General Assembly upon the recommendation of the Security Council.

Article 5

A member of the United Nations against which preventive or enforcement action has been taken by the Security Council may be suspended from the exercise of the rights and privileges of membership by the General Assembly upon the recommendation of the Security Council. The exercise of these rights and privileges may be restored by the Security Council.

Article 6

A Member of the United Nations which has persistently violated the Principles contained in the present Charter may be expelled from the Organization by the General Assembly upon the recommendation of the Security Council.

CHAPTER III
ORGANS

Article 7

1. There are established as the principal organs of the United Nations: a General Assembly, a Security Council, an Economic and Social Council, a Trusteeship Council, an International Court of Justice, and a Secretariat.
2. Such subsidiary organs as may be found necessary may be established in accordance with the present Charter.

...

CHAPTER IV
THE GENERAL ASSEMBLY

Composition

Article 9

1. The General Assembly shall consist of all the Members of the United Nations.
2. Each member shall have not more than five representatives in the General Assembly.

Functions and Powers

Article 10

The General Assembly may discuss any questions or any matters within the scope of the present Charter or relating to the powers and functions of any organs provided for in the present Charter, and, except as provided in Article 12, may make recommendations to the Members of the United Nations or to the Security Council or to both on any such questions or matters.

...

Article 12

1. While the Security Council is exercising in respect of any dispute or situation the functions assigned to it in the present Charter, the General Assembly shall not make any recommendation with regard to that dispute or situation unless the Security Council so requests.
2. The Secretary-General, with the consent of the Security Council, shall notify the General Assembly at each session of any matters relative to the maintenance of international peace and security which are being dealt with by the Security Council and shall similarly notify the General Assembly, or the Members of the United Nations if the General Assembly is not in session, immediately the Security Council ceases to deal with such matters.

...

Voting

Article 18

1. Each member of the General Assembly shall have one vote.
2. Decisions of the General Assembly on important questions shall be made by a two-thirds majority of the members present and voting. These questions shall include: recommendations with respect to the maintenance of international peace and security, the election of the non-permanent members of the Security Council, the election of the members of the Economic and Social Council, the election of members of the Trusteeship Council in accordance with paragraph 1(c) of Article 86, the admission of new Members to the

United Nations, the suspension of the rights and privileges of membership, the expulsion of Members, questions relating to the operation of the trusteeship system, and budgetary questions.

3. Decisions on other questions, Composition including the determination of additional categories of questions to be decided by a two-thirds majority, shall be made by a majority of the members present and voting.

...

CHAPTER V
THE SECURITY COUNCIL

Article 23

1. The Security Council shall consist of fifteen Members of the United Nations. The Republic of China, France, Russia, the United Kingdom of Great Britain and Northern Ireland, and the United States of America shall be permanent members of the Security Council. The General Assembly shall elect ten other Members of the United Nations to be non-permanent members of the Security Council, due regard being specially paid, in the first instance to the contribution of Members of the United Nations to the maintenance of international peace and security and to the other purposes of the Organization, and also to equitable geographical distribution.

2. The non-permanent members of the Security Council shall be elected for a term of two years. In the first election of the non-permanent members after the increase of the membership of the Security Council from eleven to fifteen, two of the four additional members shall be chosen for a term of one year. A retiring member shall not be eligible for immediate re-election.

3. Each member of the Security Council shall have one representative.

Functions and Powers

Article 24

1. In order to ensure prompt and effective action by the United Nations, its Members confer on the Security Council primary responsibility for the maintenance of international peace and security, and agree that in carrying out its duties under this responsibility the Security Council acts on their behalf.

2. In discharging these duties the Security Council shall act in accordance with the Purposes and Principles of the United Nations. The specific powers granted to the Security Council for the discharge of these duties are laid down in Chapters VI, VII, VIII, and XII.

3. The Security Council shall submit annual and, when necessary, special reports to the General Assembly for its consideration.

Article 25

The Members of the United Nations agree to accept and carry out the decisions of the Security Council in accordance with the present Charter.

Article 26

In order to promote the establishment and maintenance of international peace and security with the least diversion for armaments of the world's human and economic resources, the Security Council shall be responsible for formulating, with the assistance of the Military Staff Committee referred to in Article 47, plans to be submitted to the Members of the United Nations for the establishment of a system for the regulation of armaments.

Voting

Article 27

1. Each member of the Security Council shall have one vote.
2. Decisions of the Security Council on procedural matters shall be made by an affirmative vote of nine members.
3. Decisions of the Security Council on all other matters shall be made by an affirmative vote of nine members including the concurring votes of the permanent members; provided that, in decisions under Chapter VI, and under paragraph 3 of Article 52, a party to a dispute shall abstain from voting.

....

CHAPTER VII
ACTION WITH RESPECT TO THREATS TO THE PEACE, BREACHES OF THE PEACE, AND ACTS OF AGGRESSION

Article 39

The Security Council shall determine the existence of any threat to the peace, breach of the peace, or act of aggression and shall make recommendations, or decide what measures shall be taken in accordance with Articles 41 and 42, to maintain or restore international peace and security.

Article 40

In order to prevent an aggravation of the situation, the Security Council may, before making the recommendations or deciding upon the measures provided for in Article 39, call upon the parties concerned to comply with such provisional measures as it deems necessary or desirable. Such provisional measures shall be without prejudice to the rights, claims, or position of the parties concerned. The Security Council shall duly take account of failure to comply with such provisional measures.

Article 41

The Security Council may decide what measures not involving the use of armed force are to be employed to give effect to its decisions, and it may call upon the Members of the United Nations to apply such measures. These may include complete or partial interruption of economic relations and of rail, sea, air, postal, telegraphic, radio, and other means of communication, and the severance of diplomatic relations.

Article 42

Should the Security Council consider that measures provided for in Article 41 would be inadequate or have proved to be inadequate, it may take such action by air, sea, or land forces as may be necessary to maintain or restore international peace and security. Such action may include demonstrations, blockade, and other operations by air, sea, or land forces of Members of the United Nations.

Article 43

1. All Members of the United Nations, in order to contribute to the maintenance of international peace and security, undertake to make available to the Security Council, on its call and in accordance with a special agreement or agreements, armed forces, assistance, and facilities, including rights of passage, necessary for the purpose of maintaining international peace and security.
2. Such agreement or agreements shall govern the numbers and types of forces, their degree of readiness and general location, and the nature of the facilities and assistance to be provided.
3. The agreement or agreements shall be negotiated as soon as possible on the initiative of the Security Council. They shall be concluded between the Security Council and Members or between the Security Council and groups of Members and shall be subject to ratification by the signatory states in accordance with their respective constitutional processes.

Article 44

When the Security Council has decided to use force it shall, before calling upon a Member not represented on it to provide armed forces in fulfillment of the obligations assumed under Article 43, invite that Member, if the Member so desires, to participate in the decisions of the Security Council concerning the employment of contingents of that Member's armed forces.

Article 45

In order to enable the United Nations to take urgent military measures Members shall hold immediately available national air-force contingents for combined international enforcement action. The strength and degree of readiness of these contingents and plans for their combined action shall be determined, within the limits laid down in the special agreement or agreements referred to in Article 43, by the Security Council with the assistance of the Military Staff Committee.

...

Article 51

Nothing in the present Charter shall impair the inherent right of individual or collective self-defense if an armed attack occurs against a Member of the United Nations, until the Security Council has taken measures necessary to maintain international peace and security. Measures taken by Members in the exercise of this right of self-defense shall be immediately reported to the Security Council and shall not in any way affect the authority and responsibility of the Security Council under the present Charter to take at any time such action as it deems necessary in order to maintain or restore international peace and security.

...

IN FAITH WHEREOF the representatives of the Governments of the United Nations have signed the present Charter.
DONE at the city of San Francisco the twenty-sixth day of June, one thousand nine hundred and forty-five.

Appendix B

War Powers Resolution

Public Law 93-148, 93rd Congress, H. J. Res. 542, November 7, 1973

Joint Resolution

Concerning the war powers of Congress and the President.

Resolved by the Senate and the House of Representatives of the United States of America in Congress assembled,

...

PURPOSE AND POLICY

SEC. 2.

(a) It is the purpose of this joint resolution to fulfill the intent of the framers of the Constitution of the United States and insure [sic] that the collective judgement of both the Congress and the President will apply to the introduction of United States Armed Forces into hostilities, or into situations where imminent involvement in hostilities is clearly indicated by the circumstances, and to the continued use of such forces in hostilities or in such situations.

(b) Under article I, section 8, of the Constitution, it is specifically provided that the Congress shall have the power to make all laws necessary and proper for carrying into execution, not only its own powers but also all other powers vested by the Constitution in the Government of the United States, or in any department or officer thereof.

(c) The constitutional powers of the President as Commander-in-Chief to introduce United States Armed Forces into hostilities, or into situations where imminent involvement in hostilities is clearly indicated by the circumstances, are exercised only pursuant to (1) a declaration of war, (2) specific statutory authorization, or (3) a national emergency created by attack upon the United States, its territories or possessions, or its armed forces.

CONSULTATION

SEC. 3.

The President in every possible instance shall consult with Congress before introducing

United States Armed Forces into hostilities or into situation where imminent involvement in hostilities is clearly indicated by the circumstances, and after every such introduction shall consult regularly with the Congress until United States Armed Forces are no longer engaged in hostilities or have been removed from such situations.

REPORTING

SEC. 4.

(a) In the absence of a declaration of war, in any case in which United States Armed Forces are introduced—

  (1) into hostilities or into situations where imminent involvement in hostilities is clearly indicated by the circumstances;

  (2) into the territory, airspace or waters of a foreign nation, while equipped for combat, except for deployments which relate solely to supply, replacement, repair, or training of such forces; or

  (3) in numbers which substantially enlarge United States Armed Forces equipped for combat already located in a foreign nation; the President shall submit within 48 hours to the Speaker of the House of Representatives and to the President pro tempore of the Senate a report, in writing, setting forth—

    (A) the circumstances necessitating the introduction of United States Armed Forces;

    (B) the constitutional and legislative authority under which such introduction took place; and

    (C) the estimated scope and duration of the hostilities or involvement.

(b) The President shall provide such other information as the Congress may request in the fulfillment of its constitutional responsibilities with respect to committing the Nation to war and to the use of United States Armed Forces abroad

(c) Whenever United States Armed Forces are introduced into hostilities or into any situation described in sub section (a) of this section, the President shall, so long as such armed forces continue to be engaged in such hostilities or situation, report to the Congress periodically on the status of such hostilities or situation as well as on the scope and duration of such hostilities or situation, but in no event shall he report to the Congress less often than once every six months.

CONGRESSIONAL ACTION

SEC. 5.

(a) Each report submitted pursuant to section 4(a)(1) shall be transmitted to the Speaker of the House of Representatives and to the President pro tempore of the Senate on the same calendar day. Each report so transmitted shall be referred to the Committee on Foreign Affairs of the House of Representatives and to the Committee on Foreign Relations of the Senate for appropriate action. If, when the report is transmitted, the Congress has adjourned sine die or has adjourned for any period in excess of three calendar days, the Speaker of the House of Representatives and the President pro tempore of the Senate, if they deem it advisable (or if petitioned by at least 30 percent of the membership of their respective Houses) shall jointly request the President to convene Congress in order that it may consider the report and take appropriate action pursuant to this section.

(b) Within sixty calendar days after a report is submitted or is required to be submitted pursuant to section 4(a)(1), whichever is earlier, the President shall terminate any use of United States Armed Forces with respect to which such report was submitted (or required to be submitted), unless the Congress

    (1) has declared war or has enacted a specific authorization for such use of United States Armed Forces,

    (2) has extended by law such sixty-day period, or

    (3) is physically unable to meet as a result of an armed attack upon the United States. Such sixty-day period shall be extended for not more than an additional thirty days if the President determines and certifies to the Congress in writing that unavoidable military necessity respecting the safety of United States Armed Forces requires the continued use of such armed forces in the course of bringing about a prompt removal of such forces.

(c) Notwithstanding subsection (b), at any time that United States Armed Forces are engaged in hostilities outside the territory of the United States, its possessions and territories without a declaration of war or specific statutory authorization, such forces shall be removed by the President if the Congress so directs by concurrent resolution.

CONGRESSIONAL PRIORITY PROCEDURES FOR JOINT RESOLUTION OR BILL

SEC. 6.

(a) Any joint resolution or bill introduced pursuant to section 5(b) at least thirty calendar days before the expiration of the sixty-day period specified in such section shall be referred to the Committee on Foreign Affairs of the House of Representatives or the Committee on Foreign Relations of the Senate, as the case may be, and such committee shall report one such joint resolution or bill, together with its recommendations, not later than twenty-four calendar days before the expiration of the sixty-day period specified in such section, unless such House shall otherwise determine by the yeas and nays.

(b) Any joint resolution or bill so reported shall become the pending business of the House in question (in the case of the Senate the time for debate shall be equally divided between the proponents and the opponents), and shall be voted on within three calendar days thereafter, unless such House shall otherwise determine by yeas and nays.

(c) Such a joint resolution or bill passed by one House shall be referred to the committee of the other House named in subsection (a) and shall be reported out not later than fourteen calendar days before the expiration of the sixty-day period specified in section 5(b). The joint resolution or bill so reported shall become the pending business of the House in question and shall be voted on within three calendar days after it has been reported, unless such House shall otherwise determine by yeas and nays.

(d) In the case of any disagreement between the two Houses of Congress with respect to a joint resolution or bill passed by both Houses, conferees shall be promptly appointed and the committee of conference shall make and file a report with respect to such resolution or bill not later than four calendar days before the expiration of the sixty-day period specified in section 5(b). In the event the conferees are unable to agree within 48 hours, they shall report back to their respective Houses in disagreement. Notwithstanding any rule in either House concerning the printing of conference reports in the Record or concerning any delay in the consideration of such reports, such report shall be acted on by both Houses not later than the expiration of such sixty-day period.

CONGRESSIONAL PRIORITY PROCEDURES FOR CONCURRENT RESOLUTION

SEC. 7.

(a) Any concurrent resolution introduced pursuant to section 5(b) at least thirty calendar days before the expiration of the sixty-day period specified in such section shall be referred to the Committee on Foreign Affairs of the House of Representatives or the Committee on Foreign Relations of the Senate, as the case may be, and one such concurrent resolution shall be reported out by such committee together with its recommendations within fifteen calendar days, unless such House shall otherwise determine by the yeas and nays.

(b) Any concurrent resolution so reported shall become the pending business of the House in question (in the case of the Senate the time for debate shall be equally divided between the proponents and the opponents), and shall be voted on within three calendar days thereafter, unless such House shall otherwise determine by yeas and nays.

(c) Such a concurrent resolution passed by one House shall be referred to the committee of the other House named in subsection (a) and shall be reported out by such committee together with its recommendations within fifteen calendar days and shall thereupon become the pending business of such House and shall be voted on within three calendar days after it has been reported, unless such House shall otherwise determine by yeas and nays.

(d) In the case of any disagreement between the two Houses of Congress with respect to a concurrent resolution passed by both Houses, conferees shall be promptly appointed and the committee of conference shall make and file a report with respect to such concurrent resolution within six calendar days after the legislation is referred to the committee of conference. Notwithstanding any rule in either House concerning the printing of conference reports in the Record or concerning any delay in the consideration of such reports, such report shall be acted on by both Houses not later than six calendar days after the conference report is filed. In the event the conferees are unable to agree within 48 hours, they shall report back to their respective Houses in disagreement.

INTERPRETATION OF JOINT RESOLUTION

SEC. 8.

(a) Authority to introduce United States Armed Forces into hostilities or into situations wherein involvement in hostilities is clearly indicated by the circumstances shall not be inferred—

(1) from any provision of law (whether or not in effect before the date of the enactment of this joint resolution), including any provision contained in any appropriation Act, unless such provision specifically authorizes the introduction of United States Armed

Forces into hostilities or into such situations and stating that it is intended to constitute specific statutory authorization within the meaning of this joint resolution; or

(2) from any treaty heretofore or hereafter ratified unless such treaty is implemented by legislation specifically authorizing the introduction of United States Armed Forces into hostilities or into such situations and stating that it is intended to constitute specific statutory authorization within the meaning of this joint resolution.

(b) Nothing in this joint resolution shall be construed to require any further specific statutory authorization to permit members of United States Armed Forces to participate jointly with members of the armed forces of one or more foreign countries in the headquarters operations of high-level military commands which were established prior to the date of enactment of this joint resolution and pursuant to the United Nations Charter or any treaty ratified by the United States prior to such date.

(c) For purposes of this joint resolution, the term "introduction of United States Armed Forces" includes the assignment of member of such armed forces to command, coordinate, participate in the movement of, or accompany the regular or irregular military forces of any foreign country or government when such military forces are engaged, or there exists an imminent threat that such forces will become engaged, in hostilities.

(d) Nothing in this joint resolution—

(1) is intended to alter the constitutional authority of the Congress or of the President, or the provision of existing treaties; or

(2) shall be construed as granting any authority to the President with respect to the introduction of United States Armed Forces into hostilities or into situations wherein involvement in hostilities is clearly indicated by the circumstances which authority he would not have had in the absence of this joint resolution.

SEPARABILITY CLAUSE

SEC. 9.

If any provision of this joint resolution or the application thereof to any person or circumstance is held invalid, the remainder of the joint resolution and the application of such provision to any other person or circumstance shall not be affected thereby.

EFFECTIVE DATE

SEC. 10.

This joint resolution shall take effect on the date of its enactment.

Appendix C

The United States Constitution (Selected Provisions)

We the People of the United States, in Order to form a more perfect Union, establish Justice, insure domestic Tranquility, provide for the common defence, promote the general Welfare, and secure the Blessings of Liberty to ourselves and our Posterity, do ordain and establish this Constitution for the United States of America.

Article I

Section 1

All legislative Powers herein granted shall be vested in a Congress of the United States, which shall consist of a Senate and House of Representatives.

…

Section 8

Clause 1: The Congress shall have Power To lay and collect Taxes, Duties, Imposts and Excises, to pay the Debts and provide for the common Defence and general Welfare of the United States; but all Duties, Imposts and Excises shall be uniform throughout the United States;

Clause 2: To borrow Money on the credit of the United States;

Clause 3: To regulate Commerce with foreign Nations, and among the several States, and with the Indian Tribes;

Clause 4: To establish an uniform Rule of Naturalization, and uniform Laws on the subject of Bankruptcies throughout the United States;

Clause 5: To coin Money, regulate the Value thereof, and of foreign Coin, and fix the Standard of Weights and Measures;

Clause 6: To provide for the Punishment of counterfeiting the Securities and current Coin of the United States;

Clause 7: To establish Post Offices and post Roads;

Clause 8: To promote the Progress of Science and useful Arts, by securing for limited Times to Authors and Inventors the exclusive Right to their respective Writings and Discoveries;

Clause 9: To constitute Tribunals inferior to the supreme Court;

Clause 10: To define and punish Piracies and Felonies committed on the high Seas, and Offences against the Law of Nations;

Clause 11: To declare War, grant Letters of Marque and Reprisal, and make Rules concerning Captures on Land and Water;

Clause 12: To raise and support Armies, but no Appropriation of Money to that Use shall be for a longer Term than two Years;

Clause 13: To provide and maintain a Navy;

Clause 14: To make Rules for the Government and Regulation of the land and naval Forces;

Clause 15: To provide for calling forth the Militia to execute the Laws of the Union, suppress Insurrections and repel Invasions;

Clause 16: To provide for organizing, arming, and disciplining, the Militia, and for governing such Part of them as may be employed in the Service of the United States, reserving to the States respectively, the Appointment of the Officers, and the Authority of training the Militia according to the discipline prescribed by Congress;

Clause 17: To exercise exclusive Legislation in all Cases whatsoever, over such District (not exceeding ten Miles square) as may, by Cession of particular States, and the Acceptance of Congress, become the Seat of the Government of the United States, and to exercise like Authority over all Places purchased by the Consent of the Legislature of the State in which the Same shall be, for the Erection of Forts, Magazines, Arsenals, Dock-Yards, and other needful Buildings;—And

Clause 18: To make all Laws which shall be necessary and proper for carrying into Execution the foregoing Powers, and all other Powers vested by this Constitution in the Government of the United States, or in any Department or Officer thereof.

...

Article II

Section 1

Clause 1: The executive Power shall be vested in a President of the United States of America. He shall hold his Office during the Term of four Years, and, together with the Vice President, chosen for the same Term, be elected, as follows

...

Section 2

Clause 1: The President shall be Commander in Chief of the Army and Navy of the United States, and of the Militia of the several States, when called into the actual Service of the United States; he may require the Opinion, in writing, of the principal Officer in each of the executive Departments, upon any Subject relating to the Duties of their respective Offices, and he shall have Power to grant Reprieves and Pardons for Offences against the United States, except in Cases of Impeachment.

Clause 2: He shall have Power, by and with the Advice and Consent of the Senate, to make Treaties, provided two thirds of the Senators present concur; and he shall nominate, and by and with the Advice and Consent of the Senate, shall appoint Ambassadors, other public Ministers and Consuls, Judges of the supreme Court, and all other Officers of the United States, whose Appointments are not herein otherwise provided for, and which shall be established by Law: but the Congress may by Law vest the Appointment of such inferior Officers, as they think proper, in the President alone, in the Courts of Law, or in the Heads of Departments.

...

GO. WASHINGTON—President and deputy from Virginia

[Signed also by the deputies of twelve States.]

Appendix D

Universal Declaration of Human Rights

PREAMBLE

Whereas recognition of the inherent dignity and of the equal and inalienable rights of all members of the human family is the foundation of freedom, justice and peace in the world,

Whereas disregard and contempt for human rights have resulted in barbarous acts which have outraged the conscience of mankind, and the advent of a world in which human beings shall enjoy freedom of speech and belief and freedom from fear and want has been proclaimed as the highest aspiration of the common people,

Whereas it is essential, if man is not to be compelled to have recourse, as a last resort, to rebellion against tyranny and oppression, that human rights should be protected by the rule of law,

Whereas it is essential to promote the development of friendly relations between nations,

Whereas the peoples of the United Nations have in the Charter reaffirmed their faith in fundamental human rights, in the dignity and worth of the human person and in the equal rights of men and women and have determined to promote social progress and better standards of life in larger freedom,

Whereas Member States have pledged themselves to achieve, in cooperation with the United Nations, the promotion of universal respect for and observance of human rights and fundamental freedoms,

Whereas a common understanding of these rights and freedoms is of the greatest importance for the full realization of this pledge,

Now, therefore,

The General Assembly,

Proclaims this Universal Declaration of Human Rights as a common standard of achievement for all peoples and all nations, to the end that every individual and every organ of society, keeping this Declaration constantly in mind, shall strive by teaching and education to promote respect for these rights and freedoms and by progressive measures, national and international, to secure their universal and effective recognition and observance, both among the peoples of Member States themselves and among the peoples of territories under their jurisdiction.

Article 1

All human beings are born free and equal in dignity and rights. They are endowed with reason and conscience and should act towards one another in a spirit of brotherhood.

Article 2

Everyone is entitled to all the rights and freedoms set forth in this Declaration, without distinction of any kind, such as race, colour, sex, language, religion, political or other opinion, national or social origin, property, birth or other status.
Furthermore, no distinction shall be made on the basis of the political, jurisdictional or international status of the country or territory to which a person belongs, whether it be independent, trust, non-self-governing or under any other limitation of sovereignty.

Article 3

Everyone has the right to life, liberty and security of person.

Article 4

No one shall be held in slavery or servitude; slavery and the slave trade shall be prohibited in all their forms.

Article 5

No one shall be subjected to torture or to cruel, inhuman or degrading treatment or punishment.

Article 6

Everyone has the right to recognition everywhere as a person before the law.

Article 7

All are equal before the law and are entitled without any discrimination to equal protection of the law. All are entitled to equal protection against any discrimination in violation of this Declaration and against any incitement to such discrimination.

Article 8

Everyone has the right to an effective remedy by the competent national tribunals for acts violating the fundamental rights granted him by the constitution or by law.

Article 9

No one shall be subjected to arbitrary arrest, detention or exile.

Article 10

Everyone is entitled in full equality to a fair and public hearing by an independent and impartial tribunal, in the determination of his rights and obligations and of any criminal charge against him.

Article 11

1. Everyone charged with a penal offence has the right to be presumed innocent until proved guilty according to law in a public trial at which he has had all the guarantees necessary for his defence.
2. No one shall be held guilty of any penal offence on account of any act or omission which did not constitute a penal offence, under national or international law, at the time when it was committed. Nor shall a heavier penalty be imposed than the one that was applicable at the time the penal offence was committed.

Article 12

No one shall be subjected to arbitrary interference with his privacy, family, home or correspondence, nor to attacks upon his honour and reputation. Everyone has the right to the protection of the law against such interference or attacks.

Article 13

1. Everyone has the right to freedom of movement and residence within the borders of each State.
2. Everyone has the right to leave any country, including his own, and to return to his country.

Article 14

1. Everyone has the right to seek and to enjoy in other countries asylum from persecution.
2. This right may not be invoked in the case of prosecutions genuinely arising from non-political crimes or from acts contrary to the purposes and principles of the United Nations.

Article 15

1. Everyone has the right to a nationality.
2. No one shall be arbitrarily deprived of his nationality nor denied the right to change his nationality.

Article 16

1. Men and women of full age, without any limitation due to race, nationality or religion, have the right to marry and to found a family. They are entitled to equal rights as to marriage, during marriage and at its dissolution.

2. Marriage shall be entered into only with the free and full consent of the intending spouses.

3. The family is the natural and fundamental group unit of society and is entitled to protection by society and the State.

Article 17

1. Everyone has the right to own property alone as well as in association with others.

2. No one shall be arbitrarily deprived of his property.

Article 18

Everyone has the right to freedom of thought, conscience and religion; this right includes freedom to change his religion or belief, and freedom, either alone or in community with others and in public or private, to manifest his religion or belief in teaching, practice, worship and observance.

Article 19

Everyone has the right to freedom of opinion and expression; this right includes freedom to hold opinions without interference and to seek, receive and impart information and ideas through any media and regardless of frontiers.

Article 20

1. Everyone has the right to freedom of peaceful assembly and association.

2. No one may be compelled to belong to an association.

Article 21

1. Everyone has the right to take part in the government of his country, directly or through freely chosen representatives.

2. Everyone has the right to equal access to public service in his country.

3. The will of the people shall be the basis of the authority of government; this will shall be expressed in periodic and genuine elections which shall be by universal and equal suffrage and shall be held by secret vote or by equivalent free voting procedures.

Article 22

Everyone, as a member of society, has the right to social security and is entitled to realization, through national effort and international co-operation and in accordance with the organization and resources of each State, of the economic, social and cultural rights indispensable for his dignity and the free development of his personality.

Article 23

1. Everyone has the right to work, to free choice of employment, to just and favourable conditions of work and to protection against unemployment.

2. Everyone, without any discrimination, has the right to equal pay for equal work.

3. Everyone who works has the right to just and favourable remuneration ensuring for himself and his family an existence worthy of human dignity, and supplemented, if necessary, by other means of social protection.

4. Everyone has the right to form and to join trade unions for the protection of his interests.

Article 24

Everyone has the right to rest and leisure, including reasonable limitation of working hours and periodic holidays with pay.

Article 25

1. Everyone has the right to a standard of living adequate for the health and well-being of himself and of his family, including food, clothing, housing and medical care and necessary social services, and the right to security in the event of unemployment, sickness, disability, widowhood, old age or other lack of livelihood in circumstances beyond his control.

2. Motherhood and childhood are entitled to special care and assistance. All children, whether born in or out of wedlock, shall enjoy the same social protection.

Article 26

1. Everyone has the right to education. Education shall be free, at least in the elementary and fundamental stages. Elementary education shall be compulsory. Technical and professional education shall be made generally available and higher education shall be equally accessible to all on the basis of merit.

2. Education shall be directed to the full development of the human personality and to the strengthening of respect for human rights and fundamental freedoms. It shall promote understanding, tolerance and friendship among all nations, racial or religious groups, and shall further the activities of the United Nations for the maintenance of peace.

3. Parents have a prior right to choose the kind of education that shall be given to their children.

Article 27

1. Everyone has the right freely to participate in the cultural life of the community, to enjoy the arts and to share in scientific advancement and its benefits.

2. Everyone has the right to the protection of the moral and material interests resulting from any scientific, literary or artistic production of which he is the author.

Article 28

Everyone is entitled to a social and international order in which the rights and freedoms set forth in this Declaration can be fully realized.

Article 29

1. Everyone has duties to the community in which alone the free and full development of his personality is possible.

2. In the exercise of his rights and freedoms, everyone shall be subject only to such limitations as are determined by law solely for the purpose of securing due recognition and respect for the rights and freedoms of others and of meeting the just requirements of morality, public order and the general welfare in a democratic society.

3. These rights and freedoms may in no case be exercised contrary to the purposes and principles of the United Nations.

Article 30

Nothing in this Declaration may be interpreted as implying for any State, group or person any right to engage in any activity or to perform any act aimed at the destruction of any of the rights and freedoms set forth herein.

Appendix E

International Covenant on Civil and Political Rights

Adopted and opened for signature, ratification and accession by General Assembly resolution 2200A (XXI) of 16 December 1966. Entry into force 23 March 1976, in accordance with Article 49.

PREAMBLE

Considering that, in accordance with the principles proclaimed in the Charter of the United Nations, recognition of the inherent dignity and of the equal and inalienable rights of all members of the human family is the foundation of freedom, justice and peace in the world,

Recognizing that these rights derive from the inherent dignity of the human person,

Recognizing that, in accordance with the Universal Declaration of Human Rights, the ideal of free human beings enjoying civil and political freedom and freedom from fear and want can only be achieved if conditions are created whereby everyone may enjoy his civil and political rights, as well as his economic, social and cultural rights,

Considering the obligation of States under the Charter of the United Nations to promote universal respect for, and observance of, human rights and freedoms,

Realizing that the individual, having duties to other individuals and to the community to which he belongs, is under a responsibility to strive for the promotion and observance of the rights recognized in the present Covenant,

Agree upon the following articles:

Part I

Article 1

1. All peoples have the right of self-determination. By virtue of that right they freely determine their political status and freely pursue their economic, social and cultural development.

2. All peoples may, for their own ends, freely dispose of their natural wealth and resources without prejudice to any obligations arising out of international economic co-operation, based upon the principle of mutual benefit, and international law. In no case may a people be deprived of its own means of subsistence.

3. The States Parties to the present Covenant, including those having responsibility for the administration of Non-Self-Governing and Trust Territories, shall promote the realization of the right of self-determination, and shall respect that right, in conformity with the provisions of the Charter of the United Nations.

Part II

Article 2

1. Each State Party to the present Covenant undertakes to respect and to ensure to all individuals within its territory and subject to its jurisdiction the rights recognized in the present Covenant, without distinction of any kind, such as race, colour, sex, language, religion, political or other opinion, national or social origin, property, birth or other status.

2. Where not already provided for by existing legislative or other measures, each State Party to the present Covenant undertakes to take the necessary steps, in accordance with its constitutional processes and with the provisions of the present Covenant, to adopt such laws or other measures as may be necessary to give effect to the rights recognized in the present Covenant.

3. Each State Party to the present Covenant undertakes:

    (a) To ensure that any person whose rights or freedoms as herein recognized are violated shall have an effective remedy, notwithstanding that the violation has been committed by persons acting in an official capacity;

    (b) To ensure that any person claiming such a remedy shall have his right thereto determined by competent judicial, administrative or legislative authorities, or by any other competent authority provided for by the legal system of the State, and to develop the possibilities of judicial remedy;

    (c) To ensure that the competent authorities shall enforce such remedies when granted.

Article 3

The States Parties to the present Covenant undertake to ensure the equal right of men and women to the enjoyment of all civil and political rights set forth in the present Covenant.

Article 4

1. In time of public emergency which threatens the life of the nation and the existence of which is officially proclaimed, the States Parties to the present Covenant may take measures derogating from their obligations under the present Covenant to the extent strictly required by the exigencies of the situation, provided that such measures are not inconsistent with their other obligations under international law and do not involve discrimination solely on the ground of race, colour, sex, language, religion or social origin.

2. No derogation from articles 6, 7, 8 (paragraphs I and 2), 11, 15, 16 and 18 may be made under this provision.

3. Any State Party to the present Covenant availing itself of the right of derogation shall immediately inform the other States Parties to the present Covenant, through the intermediary of the Secretary-General of the United Nations, of the provisions from which it has derogated and of the reasons by which it was actuated. A further communication shall be made, through the same intermediary, on the date on which it terminates such derogation.

Article 5

1. Nothing in the present Covenant may be interpreted as implying for any State, group or person any right to engage in any activity or perform any act aimed at the destruction of any of the rights and freedoms recognized herein or at their limitation to a greater extent than is provided for in the present Covenant.

2. There shall be no restriction upon or derogation from any of the fundamental human rights recognized or existing in any State Party to the present Covenant pursuant to law, conventions, regulations or custom on the pretext that the present Covenant does not recognize such rights or that it recognizes them to a lesser extent.

Part III

Article 6

1. Every human being has the inherent right to life. This right shall be protected by law. No one shall be arbitrarily deprived of his life.

2. In countries which have not abolished the death penalty, sentence of death may be imposed only for the most serious crimes in accordance with the law in force at the time of the commission of the crime and not contrary to the provisions of the present Covenant and to the Convention on the Prevention and Punishment of the Crime of Genocide. This penalty can only be carried out pursuant to a final judgement rendered by a competent court.

3. When deprivation of life constitutes the crime of genocide, it is understood that nothing in this article shall authorize any State Party to the present Covenant to derogate in any way from any obligation assumed under the provisions of the Convention on the Prevention and Punishment of the Crime of Genocide.

4. Anyone sentenced to death shall have the right to seek pardon or commutation of the sentence. Amnesty, pardon or commutation of the sentence of death may be granted in all cases.

5. Sentence of death shall not be imposed for crimes committed by persons below eighteen years of age and shall not be carried out on pregnant women.

6. Nothing in this article shall be invoked to delay or to prevent the abolition of capital punishment by any State Party to the present Covenant.

Article 7

No one shall be subjected to torture or to cruel, inhuman or degrading treatment or punishment. In particular, no one shall be subjected without his free consent to medical or scientific experimentation.

Article 8

1. No one shall be held in slavery; slavery and the slave-trade in all their forms shall be prohibited.

2. No one shall be held in servitude.

3. (a) No one shall be required to perform forced or compulsory labour;

   (b) Paragraph 3(a) shall not be held to preclude, in countries where imprisonment with hard labour may be imposed as a punishment for a crime, the performance of hard labour in pursuance of a sentence to such punishment by a competent court;

   (c) For the purpose of this paragraph the term "forced or compulsory labour" shall not include:

      (i) Any work or service, not referred to in subparagraph (b), normally required of a person who is under detention in consequence of a lawful order of a court, or of a person during conditional release from such detention;

      (ii) Any service of a military character and, in countries where conscientious objection is recognized, any national service required by law of conscientious objectors;

      (iii) Any service exacted in cases of emergency or calamity threatening the life or well-being of the community;

      (iv) Any work or service which forms part of normal civil obligations.

Article 9

1. Everyone has the right to liberty and security of person. No one shall be subjected to arbitrary arrest or detention. No one shall be deprived of his liberty except on such grounds and in accordance with such procedure as are established by law.

2. Anyone who is arrested shall be informed, at the time of arrest, of the reasons for his arrest and shall be promptly informed of any charges against him.

3. Anyone arrested or detained on a criminal charge shall be brought promptly before a judge or other officer authorized by law to exercise judicial power and shall be entitled to trial within a reasonable time or to release. It shall not be the general rule that persons awaiting trial shall be detained in custody, but release may be subject to guarantees to appear for trial, at any other stage of the judicial proceedings, and, should occasion arise, for execution of the judgement.

4. Anyone who is deprived of his liberty by arrest or detention shall be entitled to take proceedings before a court, in order that court may decide without delay on the lawfulness of his detention and order his release if the detention is not lawful.

5. Anyone who has been the victim of unlawful arrest or detention shall have an enforceable right to compensation.

Article 10

1. All persons deprived of their liberty shall be treated with humanity and with respect for the inherent dignity of the human person.

2. (a) Accused persons shall, save in exceptional circumstances, be segregated from convicted persons and shall be subject to separate treatment appropriate to their status as unconvicted persons;

(b) Accused juvenile persons shall be separated from adults and brought as speedily as possible for adjudication.

3. The penitentiary system shall comprise treatment of prisoners the essential aim of which shall be their reformation and social rehabilitation. Juvenile offenders shall be segregated from adults and be accorded treatment appropriate to their age and legal status.

Article 11

No one shall be imprisoned merely on the ground of inability to fulfil a contractual obligation.

Article 12

1. Everyone lawfully within the territory of a State shall, within that territory, have the right to liberty of movement and freedom to choose his residence.

2. Everyone shall be free to leave any country, including his own.

3. The above-mentioned rights shall not be subject to any restrictions except those which are provided by law, are necessary to protect national security, public order (ordre public), public health or morals or the rights and freedoms of others, and are consistent with the other rights recognized in the present Covenant.

4. No one shall be arbitrarily deprived of the right to enter his own country.

Article 13

An alien lawfully in the territory of a State Party to the present Covenant may be expelled therefrom only in pursuance of a decision reached in accordance with law and shall, except where compelling reasons of national security otherwise require, be allowed to submit the reasons against his expulsion and to have his case reviewed by, and be represented for the purpose before, the competent authority or a person or persons especially designated by the competent authority.

Article 14

1. All persons shall be equal before the courts and tribunals. In the determination of any criminal charge against him, or of his rights and obligations in a suit at law, everyone shall be entitled to a fair and public hearing by a competent, independent and impartial tribunal established by law. The press and the public may be excluded from all or part of a trial for reasons of morals, public order (ordre public) or national security in a democratic society, or when the interest of the private lives of the parties so requires, or to the extent strictly necessary in the opinion of the court in special circumstances where publicity would prejudice the interests of justice; but any judgement rendered in a criminal case or in a suit at law shall be made public except where the interest of juvenile persons otherwise requires or the proceedings concern matrimonial disputes or the guardianship of children.

2. Everyone charged with a criminal offence shall have the right to be presumed innocent until proved guilty according to law.

3. In the determination of any criminal charge against him, everyone shall be entitled to the following minimum guarantees, in full equality:

    (a) To be informed promptly and in detail in a language which he understands of the nature and cause of the charge against him;

    (b) To have adequate time and facilities for the preparation of his defence and to communicate with counsel of his own choosing;

    (c) To be tried without undue delay;

    (d) To be tried in his presence, and to defend himself in person or through legal assistance of his own choosing; to be informed, if he does not have legal assistance, of this right; and to have legal assistance assigned to him, in any case where the interests of justice so require, and without payment by him in any such case if he does not have sufficient means to pay for it;

    (e) To examine, or have examined, the witnesses against him and to obtain the attendance and examination of witnesses on his behalf under the same conditions as witnesses against him;

    (f) To have the free assistance of an interpreter if he cannot understand or speak the language used in court;

    (g) Not to be compelled to testify against himself or to confess guilt.

4. In the case of juvenile persons, the procedure shall be such as will take account of their age and the desirability of promoting their rehabilitation.

5. Everyone convicted of a crime shall have the right to his conviction and sentence being reviewed by a higher tribunal according to law.

6. When a person has by a final decision been convicted of a criminal offence and when subsequently his conviction has been reversed or he has been pardoned on the ground that a new or newly discovered fact shows conclusively that there has been a miscarriage of justice, the person who has suffered punishment as a result of such conviction shall be compensated according to law, unless it is proved that the non-disclosure of the unknown fact in time is wholly or partly attributable to him.

7. No one shall be liable to be tried or punished again for an offence for which he has already been finally convicted or acquitted in accordance with the law and penal procedure of each country.

Article 15

1. No one shall be held guilty of any criminal offence on account of any act or omission which did not constitute a criminal offence, under national or international law, at the time when it was committed. Nor shall a heavier penalty be imposed than the one that was applicable at the time when the criminal offence was committed. If, subsequent to the commission of the offence, provision is made by law for the imposition of the lighter penalty, the offender shall benefit thereby.

2. Nothing in this article shall prejudice the trial and punishment of any person for any act or omission which, at the time when it was committed, was criminal according to the general principles of law recognized by the community of nations.

Article 16

Everyone shall have the right to recognition everywhere as a person before the law.

Article 17

1. No one shall be subjected to arbitrary or unlawful interference with his privacy, family, home or correspondence, nor to unlawful attacks on his honour and reputation.

2. Everyone has the right to the protection of the law against such interference or attacks.

Article 18

1. Everyone shall have the right to freedom of thought, conscience and religion. This right shall include freedom to have or to adopt a religion or belief of his choice, and freedom, either individually or in community with others and in public or private, to manifest his religion or belief in worship, observance, practice and teaching.

2. No one shall be subject to coercion which would impair his freedom to have or to adopt a religion or belief of his choice.

3. Freedom to manifest one's religion or beliefs may be subject only to such limitations as are prescribed by law and are necessary to protect public safety, order, health, or morals or the fundamental rights and freedoms of others.

4. The States Parties to the present Covenant undertake to have respect for the liberty of parents and, when applicable, legal guardians to ensure the religious and moral education of their children in conformity with their own convictions.

Article 19

1. Everyone shall have the right to hold opinions without interference.

2. Everyone shall have the right to freedom of expression; this right shall include freedom to seek, receive and impart information and ideas of all kinds, regardless of frontiers, either orally, in writing or in print, in the form of art, or through any other media of his choice.

3. The exercise of the rights provided for in paragraph 2 of this article carries with it special duties and responsibilities. It may therefore be subject to certain restrictions, but these shall only be such as are provided by law and are necessary:

    (a) For respect of the rights or reputations of others;

    (b) For the protection of national security or of public order (ordre public), or of public health or morals.

Article 20

1. Any propaganda for war shall be prohibited by law.

2. Any advocacy of national, racial or religious hatred that constitutes incitement to discrimination, hostility or violence shall be prohibited by law.

Article 21

The right of peaceful assembly shall be recognized. No restrictions may be placed on the exercise of this right other than those imposed in conformity with the law and which are necessary in a democratic society in the interests of national security or public safety, public order (ordre public), the protection of public health or morals or the protection of the rights and freedoms of others.

Article 22

1. Everyone shall have the right to freedom of association with others, including the right to form and join trade unions for the protection of his interests.

2. No restrictions may be placed on the exercise of this right other than those which are prescribed by law and which are necessary in a democratic society in the interests of national security or public safety, public order (ordre public), the protection of public health or morals or the protection of the rights and freedoms of others....

Article 23

1. The family is the natural and fundamental group unit of society and is entitled to protection by society and the State.
2. The right of men and women of marriageable age to marry and to found a family shall be recognized.
3. No marriage shall be entered into without the free and full consent of the intending spouses.
4. States Parties to the present Covenant shall take appropriate steps to ensure equality of rights and responsibilities of spouses as to marriage, during marriage and at its dissolution. In the case of dissolution, provision shall be made for the necessary protection of any children.

Article 24

1. Every child shall have, without any discrimination as to race, colour, sex, language, religion, national or social origin, property or birth, the right to such measures of protection as are required by his status as a minor, on the part of his family, society and the State.
2. Every child shall be registered immediately after birth and shall have a name.
3. Every child has the right to acquire a nationality.

Article 25

Every citizen shall have the right and the opportunity, without any of the distinctions mentioned in article 2 and without unreasonable restrictions:
(a) To take part in the conduct of public affairs, directly or through freely chosen representatives;
(b) To vote and to be elected at genuine periodic elections which shall be by universal and equal suffrage and shall be held by secret ballot, guaranteeing the free expression of the will of the electors;
(c) To have access, on general terms of equality, to public service in his country.

Article 26

All persons are equal before the law and are entitled without any discrimination to the equal protection of the law. In this respect, the law shall prohibit any discrimination and guarantee to all persons equal and effective protection against discrimination on any ground such as race, colour, sex, language, religion, political or other opinion, national or social origin, property, birth or other status.

Article 27

In those States in which ethnic, religious or linguistic minorities exist, persons belonging to such minorities shall not be denied the right, in community with the other members of their group, to enjoy their own culture, to profess and practice their own religion, or to use their own language.

About the Author

Jeffrey F. Addicott is a Distinguished Professor of Law and the Director of the Warrior Defense Project at St. Mary's University School of Law (www.stmarytx.edu/ctl), San Antonio, Texas, where he teaches a variety of courses to include National Security Law and Terrorism Law. An active duty Army officer in the Judge Advocate General's Corps for twenty years (he retired in 2000 at the rank of Lieutenant Colonel), Professor Addicott spent a quarter of his career as the senior legal advisor to the United States Army's Special Forces. An internationally recognized authority in terrorism law, Professor Addicott not only lectures and participates in professional and academic organizations both in the United States and overseas, he is a frequent contributor to national and international media outlets.

Foreign presentations include numerous professional lectures at universities and government institutions in India, China, Sultanate of Oman, Colombia, Peru, Ukraine, Germany, France, Austria, Canada, Thailand, Japan, Honduras, Haiti, Egypt, Kuwait, Panama, Guatemala, Albania, Okinawa, Cuba, South Korea, England, Mexico, Sweden, Ireland, Scotland, Greece, Israel, Russia, and Uruguay. Presentations in the United States include over 900 appearances at universities, public and private State and Federal institutions, as well as more than 5,000 appearances on radio, print, and television broadcasts to include the Wall Street Journal, New York Times, Washington Post, Miami Herald, Dallas Star-Tribune, San Antonio Express-News, Los Angeles Times, Chicago Tribune, Washington Times, Washington Examiner, FOX NEWS Channel, MSNBC, CNN, ABC, PBS, NBC, CBS, NPR, BBC, One America News, Voice of Russia, and al-Jazeera.

Professor Addicott is a prolific author, publishing over one hundred books, articles, and monographs on a variety of legal topics. Among his many contributions to the field, Professor Addicott pioneered the teaching of law of war and human rights courses to the militaries of numerous nascent democracies in Eastern Europe and Latin America. For these efforts he was awarded the Legion of Merit, named the "Army Judge Advocate of the Year" and honored as a co-recipient of the American Bar Association's Hodson Award.

Dr. Addicott served as the Associate Dean for Administration and Finance at St. Mary's University School of Law (2006-2007). He is also the 2007 recipient of St. Mary's University Alumni Association's "St. Mary's University School of Law Distinguished Faculty Award." Lieutenant Colonel Addicott (U.S. Army, Ret.) served in senior legal positions in Germany, Korea, Panama, and throughout the United States. Professor Addicott holds a Doctor of Juridical Science (SJD) and Master of Laws (LLM) from the University of Virginia School of Law. He also received a Master of Laws (LLM) from the Judge Advocate General's School, a Juris Doctor (JD) from the University of Alabama School of Law and a Bachelor of Arts with "Honors in Government" (BA) from the University of Maryland.

Index